SYMBOLIC
IMMORTALITY

Smithsonian Series in Ethnographic Inquiry

William L. Merrill and Ivan Karp, Series Editors

Ethnography as fieldwork, analysis, and literary form is the distinguishing feature of modern anthropology. Guided by the assumption that anthropological theory and ethnography are inextricably linked, this series is devoted to exploring the ethonographic enterprise.

ADVISORY BOARD

SYMBOLIC
IMMORTALITY

THE TLINGIT POTLATCH OF THE NINETEENTH CENTURY

SERGEI KAN

Smithsonian Institution Press
Washington and London

Designer, Linda McKnight.

Editor and Electronic Publication Specialist,
Craig Reynolds.

The Smithsonian Press produced this volume using
Ventura Publisher, MS-DOS Version 2.0. The editor
generated galleys and page proofs with an in-house
laser printer, and the Press sent the Ventura files to a
typesetting firm for high-quality final output.

Library of Congress
Cataloging-in-Publication Data

Symbolic immortality: the Tlingit potlatch
of the nineteenth century / Sergei Kan.

        p.   cm. — (Smithsonian series
in ethnographic inquiry)
     Bibliography: p.
     Includes index.
     ISBN 0-87474-686-8 (cloth) ; 1-56098-309-4 (paper)
     1. Tlingit Indians—Mortuary customs. 2. Potlatch.
3. Indians of North America—Northwest Coast of
North America—Mortuary customs.
I. Title. II. Series.
E99.T6k34 1989
393'.08997—dc19   88-38200

   6   5   4   3
99 98 97 96 95

To Alla with love and gratitude

You . . . handed me my life, as from a book shelf, blowing off the dust.

Boris Pasternak, *From Superstition*

(translated by Richard Dauenhauer)

Contents

ACKNOWLEDGEMENTS

This study has been an important part of my life for the last ten years, and hence the list of people and institutions I would like to thank is quite long. My initial interest in Native North America developed during my undergraduate years at Boston University, where I had the privilege of studying with Dennis Tedlock and the late Eva Hunt. As a graduate student in anthropology at the University of Chicago, I developed a theoretical agenda and narrowed my areal interests to southeastern Alaska, under the guidance of several scholars, particularly Nancy Munn, George W. Stocking, Jr., Jean Comaroff, and John Comaroff. Their comments on my doctoral thesis helped transform it into the present study. As the chairman of my dissertation committee and a good friend, Raymond D. Fogelson deserves special credit for being so generous with his time and sharing his ideas and books from his library.

My doctoral dissertation, which I have drastically revised and expanded while working on this book, was based on thirteen months of ethnographic and historical research conducted among the Tlingit of Alaska in 1979 and 1980 and subsequent research in several libraries and archives. Since the completion of the thesis in 1982, I have returned to southeastern Alaska for two brief visits in 1984 and two more in 1987 and have corresponded regularly with several friends/key informants. Additional historical research was also conducted between 1982 and 1987.

The focus of my field work has been on the Northern Tlingit, with much of the time spent in Sitka. Several months were also spent in Angoon, and brief periods in Juneau and Kake. In Sitka I was also able to work with informants from several major Tlingit communities to the north and the south.

Of all the Tlingit friends and teachers who have shared their knowledge and opened their homes to me, a special word of thanks must be given to Mark Jacobs, Jr. An extremely knowledgeable native historian and a wonderful human being, he has taught me a great deal about his people. Mark's letters have been the lifeline that continues to link me to the Tlingit community, wherever I happen to be at the moment.

Another special person most instrumental in helping me overcome the status of an outsider is, unfortunately, no longer with us. Charlotte Young, a woman with a big heart, who adopted me into her Kook Hít Taan lineage of the Kaagwaantaan clan, left this world in 1982. Her extended family, however, will always remain my own. Among its members I would like to give special thanks to Thomas Young, Sr., my dear brother-in-law (ax káani) and Freda Lang, my niece. Other Tlingit friends who have made a difference in my life and research include Mary Marks, Monte Littlefield, Esther Littlefield, John Littlefield, Andrew Hope, III, Ethel McKinnen, Harold Jacobs, Adelaide Jacobs, Patrick Paul, Naja Williams, Herb Bradley, Jimmy and Lydia George, George Jim, Sr., Matthew and Bessy Fred, Mary Willis, Emma Demmert, Frank Mercer, Nellie Lord, Annie Dick, Matilda Lyons, and Nora Dauenhauer. Many of the elders who taught me so much in 1979-1980 have passed away since then, a loss I mourn together with their families and friends. Among them are Charlie Joseph, Sr., George Davis, Moses Rose, Helen Howard, Henry Benson, Pete Nielsen, A. P. Johnson, and Emma Thomas. My association with three native organizations, the Alaska Native Brotherhood and Sisterhood, Sitka Community Association, and the Sitka Native Education Program, has also been crucial in my work.

In Alaska I have also enjoyed the friendship and received the help of numerous other individuals, including Charles and Edith Bovee and Evelyn Bonner of Sheldon Jackson College, Peter Corey of Sheldon Jackson Museum, Isabel Miller and Marilyn Knapp of the Sitka Historical Society, Robert Carlson of Mt. Edgecumbe Hospital, the staffs of the Alaska State Historical Library and the Sitka National Historical Park, Richard Dauenhauer, Joe Ashby, Peter and Marilyn Rosi, Frank and Ruth Roth, Lynn Chassin-Kelly and Jeff Kelly, Ernest Manewal and Mary-Therese Thompson, Eugene and Nancy Ervine, and Betty Hulbert.

Special words of gratitude must be given to those clergymen of the Orthodox Church in America who allowed me to examine parish archives and attend church services and other functions without being a member. Among these kind persons are His Grace the Right Reverend Gregory, Bishop of Sitka and All Alaska, Fr. Eugene Bourdukofsky of St. Michael's Cathedral in Sitka and his wife Matushka Maria, Archimandrite Innocent of St. Nicholas Russian Orthodox Church in Juneau, and Fr. Michael Williams and his wife Matushka Emily.

I also thank all those scholars who have read the various drafts and portions of this manuscript and offered valuable suggestions. They are Margaret Blackman, Robin Ridington, Wally Olson, Margaret Seguin, Catherine McClellan, John Adams, Robert McKinley, Vern Carroll, Richard Ford, Roy Rappaport, and Ivan Karp. For reading the entire manuscript and making numerous insightful comments, Peter Metcalf and William Merrill deserve my special appreciation. This manuscript would not have made it into a book without Rachael Cohen, who applied her word processing genius to it, and the assistance of the editors of the Smithsonian Institution Press, particularly Daniel Goodwin and Craig Reynolds.

The various stages of my research were supported by grants from the National Endowment for the Humanities, the Jacobs Research Funds, and the Wenner-Gren Foundation for Anthropological Research. At the University of Michigan, I received financial help from the Center for Russian and East European Studies, the Faculty Fund, and the Horace H. Rackham School of Graduate Studies.

Last but not least, I must offer gratitude to all the members of my family who have given me moral and material support over these years. No words, however, are adequate to thank my wife Alla Kan whose love, faith, and good humor have kept me going even when things were tough. To her this book is dedicated.

Fig. 1: Northwest Coast Culture Area in the Nineteenth Century. Map courtesy of Wayne Suttles.

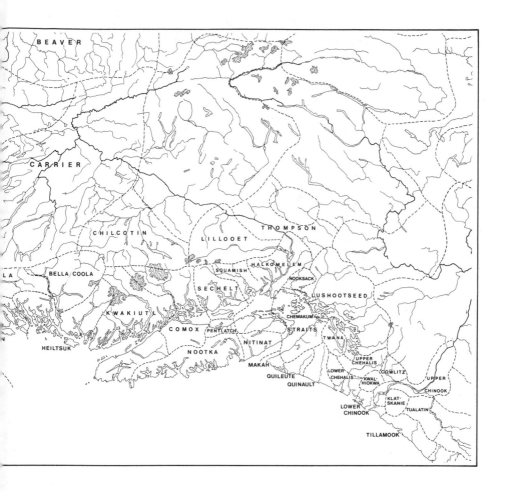

Table 1: Tlingit Alphabet. It is easier to teach spelling by presenting letters as an alphabet rather than a chart. In particular, *w* is treated as just another letter.

a	ch	j	s	ts'
aa	ch'	k	s'	w
e	d	k'	sh	x
ei	dl	k̲	t	x'
i	dz	k̲'	t'	x̲
ee	g	l	tl	x̲'
u	g̲	l'	tl'	y
oo	h	n	ts	

Source: Dauenhauer, N., and Dauenhauer, R. 1976:222.

Table 2: Tlingit Technical Sound Chart

		Front of Mouth						Back of Mouth		
		dental	lateral	alveolar	alveo-palatal	velar	velar-rounded	uvular	uvular-rounded	glottal
stops	Plain	d	dl	dz	j	g	gw	g̲	g̲w	
	Aspirated	t	tl	ts	ch	k	kw	k̲	k̲w	
	Glottalized (pinched)	t'	tl'	ts'	ch'	k'	k'w	k̲'	k̲'w	
fricatives	Aspirated		l	s	sh	x	xw	x̲	x̲w	h
	Glottalized		l'	s'		x'	x'w	x̲'	x̲'w	
sonants	Nasal	n								
	Semivowels					y	w			

	lateral	alveolar	alveo-palatal	velar
Vowels short	a	i	e	u
long	aa	ee	ei	oo
Tones high	'			
low				

unmarked, formerly '

Source: Dauenhauer, N., and Dauenhauer, R. 1976:222.

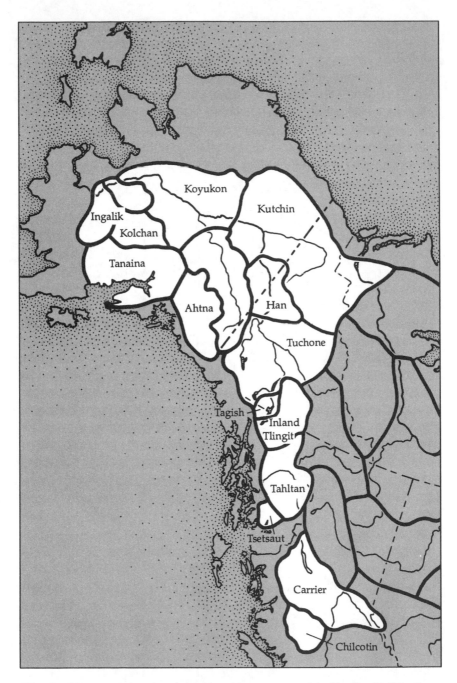

Fig. 2: Western Subarctic Athapaskans. Map courtesy of the Handbook of North American Indians. Vol. 6, Subarctic.

INTRODUCTION

The Past in the Present

In early August of 1979, when I nervously got off the plane in Sitka, Alaska, I had no idea that the focus of my ethnographic research and the subject of my dissertation would be the nineteenth century Tlingit mortuary rites. Of course, I knew about the centrality of the ancestors and the mortuary complex in the Tlingit culture of the past from the published works I had read in preparation for fieldwork. During a previous brief visit to southeastern Alaska, I had even heard that the memorial potlatch, the final ritual of the mortuary cycle, was still in existence.

Although fascinated by this information, I was reluctant to focus on this topic. A number of anthropologists had warned me about the Northwest Coast Indians' mistrust of, if not hostility toward, anthropologists, particularly those trying to obtain information on the non-Christian beliefs and practices, especially the potlatch. I also heard stories about several fledgling ethnographers who had been forced to leave local native communities after trying too hard to be allowed to participate in traditional ceremonies (e.g., Hyman quoted in Glazer 1972:88–93).

And so I proposed a dissertation that would explore the role of Christianity (particularly Russian Orthodoxy) in the historical transfor-

1

mation of Tlingit culture, from the nineteenth century to the present. This seemed to be a safer topic which could be studied through both archival research and participant observation, since the church is a domain of Tlingit life that is open to any sympathetic non-native.[1] Participation in church services turned out to be an excellent opportunity to make contact and gradually develop rapport with many Tlingit. A great deal of data on this subject was collected and has been utilized in several of my publications (Kan 1985, 1987; Kamenskii 1985), as well as a monograph on Tlingit ethnohistory currently being written.

I must explain why I redirected my major efforts from my proposed topic to the mortuary complex of the nineteenth century. On that gray rainy day when my life and research in southeastern Alaska began, the Tlingit community was paying its last respects to one of its leaders, a man who headed a major local matrilineage and was also active in civic and religious institutions of his people. I went to his funeral, which began with a heavily attended memorial service in the Orthodox cathedral, followed by a procession to the cemetery and a luncheon held in the Alaska Native Brotherhood hall. There, for the first time, I heard Tlingit ritual oratory and caught a first glimpse of the persistence of indigenous concepts and social relations. As I got to know the deceased's family and gradually began sharing its sorrow, I was allowed to attend his subsequent memorial rites. In the months following the funeral, aspects of traditional pre-Christian culture became more obvious and culminated in the memorial potlatch, conducted in large part according to the basic rules established long before the Tlingit converted to Christianity and became significantly affected by Western culture.

Other deaths afflicting the native community later that year initiated new cycles of mortuary rituals, and once again I was called upon to pay my respects. Conversations with Tlingit friends and acquaintances inevitably turned to death and the relationship between the living and the dead. By then ethnographic research had already become intertwined with close personal relationships with a number of people, including several chief mourners. Formal interviews were rarely conducted, with conversation ranging freely over such diverse topics as Tlingit history and contemporary politics, Christianity, and what some Tlingit call "old customs." For at least some of the survivors, these discussions seemed to have a therapeutic function, while they helped me understand how distinct the Tlingit view of death had remained, despite a long history of European contact and colonization. Rapport established through empathy, friendship, and exchange of services and knowledge opened new windows on traditional beliefs and practices—some untouched by Christianity and Western culture and others syncretized with them—that were still vital, especially in the life of the older people.[2]

It became clear that the mortuary/ancestral complex was the most conservative aspect of Tlingit culture, serving as one of the main links between the past and the present.[3] It was the major context in which matrilineality, dualism, and (modified) hierarchy—the basic principles of the indigenous sociocultural order—were still operating. Beliefs in reincarnation, communication with the dead through dreams, and the survivors' duty to honor their dead matrikin through respectable funerals and memorial rites still shaped the relationship between the living and their ancestors. Pedigree and forms of symbolic property inherited from the ancestors in the matriline (e.g., names, regalia, myths, and songs) remained important elements of the total social identity of the more conservative people, while relative rank and status of matrilineal groups and at least some of their individual members was still negotiated and crystallized in the memorial potlatch. In fact, after years of shielding indigenous ceremonialism from missionaries, government officials, and other critics, the Tlingit were becoming less defensive about it, with even the more Americanized among them renewing their participation in potlatches. With many of the younger people beginning to take pride in their heritage, ancestral songs and dances were once again being taught, this time under the auspices of Indian Education programs. Worried that their own death would bring about a significant decline in ritual expertise, traditionalist elders at the time were doing their best to revive some previously neglected elements of the potlatch, so as to conduct it as much as possible according to the way their own elders had taught them around the turn of the century.

At the same time, many aspects of Tlingit life and experience were now determined by cultural values and social relations established in the post-contact era, and much of Tlingit destiny was now shaped by social, political, and economic forces outside their society. Thus, while traditional subsistence activities and sharing of food persisted, a large portion of the income was now derived from participation in the market economy where economic action was more individualized. The nuclear family and the extended household, both based on bilateral ties rather than the matrilineage, were now the principal units of residence, production, and consumption. Participation in the various institutions of the non-native society was now essential for Tlingit survival and membership in an array of political, religious, and civic organizations crucial for the constitution of the social self.

With the past remaining alive in the present, comprehending contemporary Tlingit experience seemed impossible without a good grasp of the nineteenth century culture and society.[4] That era directly preceded the beginning of fundamental changes in the Tlingit way of life, which occurred in the 1880s–1900s, and is fairly well documented in the existing ethnographic literature. In addition, glimpses of that period could still be obtained from some of the elders. Understanding the mortuary complex was particularly important, because it was in that context, and especially in the potlatch, that much of the negotiation and the maintenance and enhancement of rank, power, and prestige of individuals and social groups seemed to have taken place in the past. More broadly, death for the Tlingit, as de Laguna (1972:531) puts it, "was the supreme event, providing the major occasions and themes for cultural elaboration and emphasis." This topic also seemed more urgent than any other, because of the impending passing of the elderly traditionalists whose knowledge was largely unmatched by the next generation.[5]

Despite the centrality of ceremonialism in the Northwest Coast anthropological agenda in general, and the Tlingit one in particular, a lot of work remained to be done. Some new data could still be obtained from the native people themselves, while previously collected information could on occasion be verified and modified with their assistance. The ethnographic record pertaining to the nineteenth century could also be expanded and corrected by incorporating information from the published and unpublished works by Russian observers, underutilized by American anthropologists who could not read Russian (e.g., Khlebnikov [1817–1832] 1976; Veniaminov [1840] 1984; Markov 1849; Tikhmenev [1861–1863] 1978; Golovin [1863] 1983; Donskoi 1893; Kamenskii [1906] 1985; Alaska Church Collection). A few gems of information could also be still located in turn-of-the-century Russian and American periodicals, United Stated Government publications, and archival documents, as well as observations by European and American visitors and residents of southeastern Alaska (e.g., Teichmann [1925] 1963; Cracroft [1870] 1981; Willard 1884; Wilbur n.d.). Memories of and comments on traditional practices and beliefs recorded by the Tlingit themselves provided another, badly needed perspective on the nineteenth century culture (Wells n.d.; Billman 1964; Shotridge n.d.; 1917; 1920; 1922; 1928; Peck 1975; Johnson n.d.).

My own field work proved indispensable not only because of some valuable "memory ethnography" it generated. Participation in a ritual gives one an appreciation of its complexity, its meaning to the participants, and its emotional dimension, difficult to obtain from reading about it. In my case, by taking part in potlatches and other traditional rituals, first as a guest and then as an adopted member of one of the Sitka clans, I was able to record songs and oratory, rarely incorporated into the previous analyses of Tlingit ceremonialism. More importantly, I observed the politics of the potlatch, including its preparation and backstage activities and negotiations, and recorded comments about the ritual procedure and the sponsors' conduct made by the participants themselves, during and after the ceremony. Such data is largely missing from previous ethnographic works, many of which are based on interviews with informants about the potlatch rather than on participant observation.

Taking part in a variety of native activities, formal and informal, as well as conversing with a large number of persons of all ages gave me a sense of the Tlingit social practice and the emotional tone of their life (ethos), the latter being more elusive but nonetheless essential for understanding their nineteenth century culture. Even though I was almost one hundred years away from the era that interested me, by cross-checking my own observations against the data previously collected, I was able to expand the existing knowledge about the Tlingit culture of the past century. My experience challenges a view expressed by some Northwest Coast scholars (e.g., Goldman 1975:24; Ringel 1979; Walens 1981:20) that the ethnographic records of this region's indigenous peoples have been, as far as possible, completed.

Northwest Coast Ethnology

Despite all I have said so far, the main goal of this work is not to add new data but to systematize and analyze the existing material and to offer new and more nuanced and theoretically oriented interpretations of the nineteenth century Tlingit culture, with a particular focus on the mortuary/ancestral complex.

In fact, the work of my predecessors, American anthropologists of mainly the Boasian tradition, remains the chief source of the data I use here. Without the research of such scholars as Swanton (1908; 1909), Emmons (1920–1945), Olson (1933–1954; 1967), McClellan (1954; 1975) and, most of all, de Laguna (1960; 1972), this project would not have been possible. Based primarily on the information collected from the late nineteenth century until the early 1950s from mostly elderly informants reminiscing about the past, these works exhibit the strengths as well as some of the weaknesses of the approach, exemplified by Boas' own ethnography of the neighboring Kwakiutl. The value of these ethnographies comes primarily from their attempt to paint a comprehensive picture of Tlingit culture from the native point of view and their special concern with mythology, religion, and other aspects of the ideational dimension of native experience. They suffer, however, from a lack of integration, with data presented under such traditional headings of a "classic monograph," as economy, kinship, religion, and so forth.[6]

While most of these works acknowledge the centrality of the mortuary complex in Tlingit culture, they make only a limited effort to explore why this was the case or how exactly the sociopolitical organization was reproduced or constituted in the context of the mortuary rites.[7] Some of my predecessors who, unlike most of the Boasians, were not satisfied with limiting their presentation to the native view of the Tlingit potlatch as a memorial ritual, tried to offer their own assessment of this complex phenomenon. Unfortunately, their comments emphasized only its sociopolitical side, i.e., prestige-aggrandizement, thus reiterating the popular functionalist view of Northwest Coast ceremonialism (Oberg 1973:127–128; Olson 1967:111; compare Barnett 1938; Garfield 1939; Codere 1950; Drucker and Heizer 1967).[8]

More recent work on Tlingit ceremonialism by Rosman and Rubel (1971) exemplifies another tradition in Northwest Coast ethnology—a reanalysis of the Boasians' corpus without the benefit of fieldwork. In this case, the model applied is that of structuralism and the focus is exclusively on the relationship between the potlatch and the social structure. While offering some useful insights on this subject, this work suffers from its reliance on too limited a body of ethnography (which leads to misinterpretation of the data) and from its attempt to reduce a complex and multifaceted phenomenon to a simple scheme.[9]

Elsewhere in Northwest Coast research, in spite of the Boasian legacy, more work has been done by scholars concerned with general analytic issues and comparison. The potlatch and other systems of ritualized exchange of material and symbolic capital have been the center of attention, with functionalist, marxist, cultural materialist, psychoanalytic, structuralist and, more recently, symbolic and interpretive approaches applied to them.[10] A number of interesting insights have been generated, particularly in those studies where the theory does not overshadow the ethnography and where the texture of the native experience has been preserved (e.g., Adams 1973; Goldman 1975; Seguin 1985).

Nevertheless, Mauss' (1967) insightful characterization of the potlatch as a "total social phenomenon," that is, simultaneously "mythological," "religious," "social," "economic," "jural," and so forth, remains an often quoted but rarely substantiated proposition. Analyses that separate "religion" from "politics" and then concentrate on one or the other violate the spirit of Northwest Coast cultures, in which the two were not distinct domains but different aspects of the same process.

Even more rare in Northwest Coast ethnology are works that examine the individual and collective management of meaning in the process of competition for valued social and economic resources. With the exception of two recent works on the Haida, an article by Stearns (1984), and a doctoral dissertation by Boelscher (1985), Northwest Coast studies continue to treat the social and symbolic orders as given and determined rather than as created by actors in social practice.

In the process of reconstructing and analyzing those aspects of Tlingit culture and society that pertained to the mortuary/ancestral complex, I found that I had to understand Tlingit ethnopsychology and its manifestations in social practice. The focus on the person is essential for several reasons. Firstly, without it one can hardly make sense of the transformations the deceased underwent in the mortuary rites. Secondly, ethnopsychology provides an advantageous and novel angle for examining the Tlingit sociopolitical organization and social action. With the exception of de Laguna's (1954) seminal paper on the subject, from which I use valuable data, supplementing and modifying it with the material obtained from my own informants and various earlier sources, studies of Northwest Coast social organization and ceremonialism focus on the group and neglect the person, even though many of them contain interesting ethnopsychological material. As a result, the relationship between individual and society in this region is poorly understood, and Mauss' (1938) limited view of the Northwest Coast native as a personage rather than a true person, i.e., an actor incarnating his or her ancestors and playing the same social and ceremonial roles as they did, is still held by some authors. Thirdly, by focusing on the delineation of the aristocrat as the ideal social person, I gain a much better understanding of the cultural foundation of rank and the dominant role of the aristocracy in the mortuary/ancestral complex.

By overcoming the compartmentalization of sociocultural reality, prominent in Northwest Coast ethnology, this study provides the first comprehensive analysis of the Tlingit mortuary complex and, through it, of the major aspects of the nineteenth century Tlingit culture.

Culture Through Its Key Ritual System

Interpretation of cultures through their rituals is a well established form of anthropological endeavor. Exemplified by such early classics as Bateson's *Naven* (1936) and Richards' *Chisungu* (1956), it became firmly established in the 1960s and 1970s, through the efforts of Geertz, V. Turner, and other scholars practicing what has often been labelled "symbolic anthropology." The hallmark of this approach has been the insistence on ritual's ability to interarticulate, through its symbols, "ultimate existential concerns, immediate personal and affective concerns, and ongoing structural problems and conflicts" (Ortner 1978:98). Taking symbols to be dynamic entities that are multivocal and ambiguous, patterned by events and informed by passions of human interaction, practitioners of symbolic analysis engage in a detailed examination of the semantic mechanisms by which symbols and meanings are interrelated and moved towards the conclusion and resolution of the rite.

In this study, I have found symbolic analysis to be essential for exploring Tlingit cosmology, eschatology, and ethnopsychology, as well as the rich meanings of the mortuary rituals themselves, including the treatment of the deceased, the taboos imposed upon the mourners, and the various forms of exchange between the hosts (mourners) and the guests.[11] Unlike most of my predecessors who focused mainly on the exchange of material goods in Northwest Coast ceremonials, I subject oratory, singing, dancing, and other performative genres to the same scrutiny, treating them as codes for communication between the ritual participants.

Whether one likes it or not, however, the use of such data, much of it recorded during the potlatches I attended, is seriously limited by a fundamental Tlingit cultural principle of treating verbal genres (and other prerogatives) as the inalienable property of matrilineal groups. Hence verbatim reproduction of speeches, ancestral myths, and songs without permission of the lineage or clan owning it is an insult to its members. Since such permission could not possibly be obtained from all of the people I have recorded over the years and because I believe that Tlingit texts should be published by native linguists and historians who are better qualified for that than I am and whose kinship ties with the owners allow them to do so (see Dauenhauer and Dauenhauer 1981; 1987), I use only brief quotations to illustrate my argument and provide data for structural and symbolic analysis. I either rely on published texts (for example, Swanton 1908; de Laguna 1972; Dauenhauer and Dauenhauer 1981) or try to paraphrase the ones that I myself have recorded.

Mortuary Ritual in a Ranked Society

Among the various criticisms of symbolic anthropology, there is one that is particularly valid and serious. It questions the assumption that all rituals necessarily display cultural depth and argues that at least some of them "brim with platitudes" (R. Rosaldo 1984). It also points out that preoccupation with ritual leads to the neglect of the informal practices of everyday life, which might be of much greater cultural significance. While agreeing with this, I justify my focus on the ritual with the following argument. To begin with, for the nineteenth century Tlingit, we have a lot more data on ceremonial than everyday life, and we can only very cautiously use observations on the latter by the twentieth century ethnographers, since so much of the lived-in world of this people has changed in the last one hundred years. More importantly, in this case, we are dealing not with *a* ritual but with *the* central ceremonial system of the entire sociocultural order, which reached into almost every domain of Tlingit life. In fact, as I argue throughout this work, this ranked society was, to a large extent, *constituted* in the context of the mortuary rites, and especially the memorial potlatch (compare Bloch 1982). In these rites, an attempt was made to reach an agreement on the current distribution of power and prestige among the participating individuals and groups, by arranging all of them in a hierarchy. Hence understanding the workings of these rites is indispensable for getting at the essential features of the nineteenth century Tlingit culture and society, and particularly the political process.[12]

This emphasis on hierarchy and the dominant role played by the aristocracy in the ceremonial context raises an important analytic question of the relationship between ritual and the wider sociocultural order in which it is embedded. It indicates that rituals, in a given society, rarely reflect, engage, and affect the entire spectrum of cultural values and social relations. Instead they emphasize some of them and downplay or mask others. Exploring the causes of a greater focus on hierarchical relationships and values in the Tlingit mortuary ritual than in daily life is a key issue addressed in this study.

Despite the prevalence of hierarchy and competition, Tlingit mortuary rites were also characterized by a strong emphasis on equality, unity, and cooperation between matrikin as well as balanced reciprocity between members of the two moieties, one acting as hosts and the other as guests. Once again, we see a contrast between everyday life where conflicts and disagreements between matrilineal relatives were common and ritual in which they tried to achieve maximum cooperation and present a unified front to members of the opposite moiety. At the same time, the intermoiety relations themselves, which tended to be fragile and sensitive, were presented as harmonious and dominated by balanced reciprocity. In this study, I examine whether these contradictory principles of hierarchy and equality, and competition and cooperation were reconciled in the ritual domain and, if so, how this reconciliation was accomplished and how effective it was.

The focus on hierarchy and equality makes the findings of this work directly relevant for understanding both "ranked" and "egalitarian" societies, as well as numerous intermediate cases. My study demonstrates that hierarchical tendencies and inequality are rarely absent from egalitarian societies, just as egalitarian values and relationships persist in the hierarchical ones.[13] To explore this issue, I compare the Tlingit sociopolitical organization and mortuary complex with those of the western Subarctic Athapaskans. Since the Tlingit are currently believed to have originated from an antecedent Proto-

Athapaskan culture of hunters and gatherers located in the interior, egalitarian tendencies in their culture and society might represent an earlier ideological substratum which impeded the transformation of a ranked society into a class one.

By now it should have become clear that I am interested in combining symbolic analysis of ritual with a systematic sociology. In other words, my concern is with exploring which particular aspects of the Tlingit sociopolitical system were interarticulated with the ancestral/mortuary complex. Of course, an analysis of a sociocultural order that no longer exists has its inherent limitations. As I have already stated, information on social practice is especially difficult to come by. Much of the available data contains few references to real life conflicts or individual strategies. Biographical data on individual actors and information on specific events and political dramas are also in short supply, preventing me from analyzing in depth a complex interaction between "custom and the exigencies of historical situation, mediated by human activity" (Stromberg 1986:9). Nevertheless, I try to make the best use of the few pieces of information on these topics available from previous accounts and those that my own informants shared with me. I must point out, however, that traditionalist Tlingit are reluctant to discuss conflicts and especially feuds and wars, since mentioning old troubles has a potential for rekindling them. Respecting this view, I bring up such episodes only after suppressing the identity of the individuals and kin groups engaged in conflict, unless my information comes from published sources.

For these reasons, my account presents a somewhat idealized version of the mortuary complex, in which regional and village variation is minimized. There is a certain bias here, however, towards the northern Tlingit, since much of my data comes from Sitka, Yakutat, Angoon, and Klukwaan. The picture of the rituals I paint is pieced together from numerous accounts and, hence, represents an ideal type. My focus is on the structure of the mortuary rites and their invariant characteristics. Some of the more idiosyncratic features of specific funerals and potlatches are, however, mentioned whenever this information is relevant to the analysis.

Because of their prominence in Tlingit life and their spectacular nature, nineteenth century mortuary rites of aristocrats are much better documented than those of commoners. Unfortunate as this bias is, it does not constitute a major problem for my analysis, since aristocratic death rites were the cultural ideal and the context in which the more intense negotiation of rank and status occurred. A male bias in much of the available data on mortuary rites is also unfortunate but cannot be corrected by contemporary ethnography, since the ritual role of women has clearly increased in this century. Again, however, it does not represent a major obstacle for this study, since heads of matrilineal groups whose mortuary rites I analyze were usually men and because rank rather than gender was the main criterion for social differentiation (compare de Laguna 1972:532).

Another common criticism of symbolic anthropology is "its underdeveloped sense of the politics of culture" (Ortner 1984:132). In other words, until fairly recently, most symbolic analyses of ritual, myth, and other ideational phenomena lacked an interest in the use of culture as an ideology legitimating the existing authority and justifying relations of asymmetry, inequality, and domination, by presenting them as natural, eternal, and unchangeable (compare Keesing 1982).

This work overcomes this limitation by treating the double role of the Tlingit ancestral/mortuary complex as both religious and political phenomenon as a major subject. However, unlike the marxists and some of the recent practice-oriented anthropologists (e.g., Bourdieu), I see religious beliefs and rituals as more than a form of false consciousness or a symbolic resource pragmatically manipulated by actors (especially those with power). In my view, the political use of the dead was interarticulated with their veneration as the beloved ancestors, inspiring strong emotions in the participants and motivating them for actions that sometimes complemented and sometimes conflicted with the prestige-oriented ones.

Thus, among the nineteenth century Tlingit, the ancestors were the source of hereditary prerogatives which defined the destiny and social identity of every free person and his or her matrilineal group. Beliefs about the dead, including the need to show them respect by sponsoring memorial rites in which they were given offerings were fundamental to the Tlingit culture. At the same time, because the aristocracy controlled and supervised the access to the tangible and intangible prerogatives of their clans and played the leading role in the mortuary rites, the ancestral/mortuary complex served as the basis of its dominant role in society. In addition, the ancestors and the culturally sanctified attitudes and feelings towards them were used by all of the ritual participants as a form of rhetoric to portray their more aggressive and prestige-oriented actions and words as manifestations of grief and "love and respect" for the dead.

Potlatch as Double Obsequies and the Anthropology of Death

While all rituals tend to generate and utilize emotions and emotionally colored religious beliefs, mortuary rituals are much more likely to do so. This idea, I believe, must be central to any analysis of death-related cultural phenomena. Much of the anthropological work on the subject, however, has had a different agenda.

Most of the studies of mortuary ritual, beginning with Goody's (1962) classic work on death, property, and the ancestors among the LoDagaa, acknowledge their debt to Hertz's ([1907] 1960) essay "Contribution to the Study of the Collective Representation of Death." On the basis of case studies mainly from the Malayo-Polynesian-speaking peoples, Hertz developed a model of primary and secondary disposal of the remains of the dead in which the process of the corpse's decay, the mourning regulations imposed on the bereaved and the transformation of the spirit of the deceased parallel each other. Once the corpse has fully deteriorated or has been destroyed by human means and the double obsequies carried out, mourning comes to an end and the spirit of the deceased is firmly established in its new existence.

Hertz's insights, which clearly applied to cultures far beyond the region he studied, have stimulated sociological investigations of the relationship between the deceased and the survivors (Goody 1962; Douglas 1969; Bloch 1971) as well as analyses of the symbolism of the corpse, of the mourners' observances, and their relationship to the deceased's material and noncorporeal attributes (Huntington and Metcalf 1979; Metcalf 1982; Danforth 1982; Bloch and Parry 1982). As Huntington and Metcalf (1979:62) point out, the analytic power of Hertz's model is its essentially structuralist logic which examines the interrelationship between the transformations of the deceased and the mourners. Hertz's other important contribution is his demonstration of the various forms which the secondary treatment of the deceased could take (from natural decay to cremation) and of the double obsequies' ability to increase "the room for manoeuvre in those aspect of funerary rites which are concerned with renewing, reorganizing and relegitimizing relations between the living" (Humphreys 1981:268).

Of course there is no reason to expect that in all societies the correspondence outlined by Hertz's will be as neat as in his model. The latter should not be a straitjacket but simply a guide for analysis, pointing at those aspects of the mortuary complex (e.g., the symbolism of the corpse) that require particular attention. In my own analysis, I have found Hertz's ideas, as well as Van Gennep's ([1909] 1960) model of the rites of passage, to be such a guide.[14]

Inspired by reading Hertz at an early stage in my research, I began to see the Tlingit potlatch as a secondary treatment of the deceased (Kan 1986). The idea seemed quite obvious, yet previous analyses of this rite paid little attention to its mortuary dimension, treating it as being of minor importance, compared to its economic and sociopolitical functions (e.g., Oberg 1973; Rosman and Rubel 1971; Tollefson 1976). The Tlingit themselves, however, emphasized the potlatch's mortuary/commemorative nature, referring to it as "finishing the (dead) body." The memorial potlatch marked the final stage in the transformation of the various attributes of the deceased and involved the repackaging of the cremated remains and the construction of a new container for them, the distribution of the decedent's various noncorporeal entities and ancestral prerogatives among the descendants, the lifting of mourning taboos, and so forth. Even those potlatches that were not part of a sequence of mortuary rites for a particular person had to be justified as the occasion for honoring the deceased and repairing or rebuilding the grave structure.

Treating the potlatch as double obsequies allows me to make sense of a number of practices that seem to be at odds with the ritual's more mundane prestige-oriented function (e.g., proscriptions against performing the potlatch during daytime; supernatural sanctions against withholding even a tiny portion of the wealth set aside for distribution; and similar taboos). More importantly, the incorporation of the dead, believed to be the recipients of the spiritual essence of all of the food and gifts distributed to members of the opposite moiety, into the analysis of the Tlingit potlatch greatly expands and clarifies the picture of this complex ritual and forces us to deal with the interrelationship of its religious and political dimensions. This, in turn, calls for a modification of our existing theories of exchange in those prestate societies—from incipiently ranked to highly stratified—where the dead are seen as participating in cycles of reciprocity and where they are among the valuable cultural resources that have to be reproduced in the mortuary rites. This idea was first proposed by Mauss himself, who was fascinated with Northwest Coast potlatches and included them in his essay *The Gift* ([1925] 1967). More recently, it was elaborated in Weiner's (1976) study of the Trobriand mortuary exchange. It has not, however, been prominent in Northwest Coast ethnology, despite the fact that, as I demonstrate, the dead played a much greater role in the ceremonial life of this culture area than has previously been assumed (compare Wike 1952).[15]

As I have already pointed out, my interests in this work are not limited to exploring the Tlingit culture and society from the inside. Part of my agenda is cross-cultural comparison, aimed at establishing how a particular type of sociopolitical order tends to generate, through the logic of its workings, a certain type of cultural perception of death and the ancestors, and a certain kind of mortuary complex. I am particularly interested in establishing the nature of societies whose mortuary rites include double obsequies and play the central role in reproducing the sociocultural order. Hence I attempt to correlate this type of mortuary rites with such key aspects of culture and society as ranking, moiety dualism, unilineal descent, gaining of prestige through the distribution of wealth, cult of ancestors, and so forth. Although the primary region within which such comparisons are made is the western Subarctic and the Northwest Coast, important similarities established here with societies of the Malayo-Polynesian area suggest that my findings have cross-cultural relevance and raise interesting questions for future studies in comparative ethnology (compare, Rosman and Rubel 1981; 1983).

In the process of reconstructing and analyzing the Tlingit mortuary complex, I develop a model of a comprehensive mortuary analysis, which goes beyond either the disposal of the dead or the politics of the mortuary ritual. Death forces human beings to confront the central questions of their existence—the relationship between the temporary and the permanent in social life, between the individual and the group, between the past and the present (compare Humphreys 1981). As Berger (1969) points out, the socially constructed world we inhabit is our shield against the terror of death. Witnessing the death of others—especially significant others—and anticipating our own death, we are forced to question the ad hoc cognitive and normative operating procedures of our normal social life. Death presents society with a formidable problem not only because it is an obvious threat to the continuity of human relations, but because it threatens the basic assumptions of order on which society rests. To maintain the reality of this socially constructed world in the face of death, mankind often relies on religion or other powerful ideological systems that promise what Lifton (1983) calls a sense of "symbolic immortality"—a continuous symbolic relationship between our finite individual lives and what has gone before us and what will come after.

An anthropological analysis of the mortuary complex must incorporate this crucial dimension and relate it to whatever social, political or economic functions a particular mortuary ritual might have. In fact, this interrelationship between the otherworldly and the more mundane concerns is the hallmark of the mortuary ritual and should be the cornerstone of mortuary analysis (compare Keesing 1982).

Emotion in the Mortuary Ritual

As a ritual that deals with the loss of significant others, the funeral is more likely to evoke and utilize such emotions as love, grief, anger, and fear. Emotions are powerful motivating forces for the mourners' conduct; yet emotions have not been systematically incorporated into anthropological interpretations of the mortuary ritual.[16] Without looking at emotions, we limit our understanding of the meaning that death-related rituals have for their participants (compare R. Rosaldo 1984). Thus a recent review article on the subject complains that the existing works give the impression of "coolness and remoteness" (Palgi and Abramovitch 1984:385).

This tendency to relegate emotions to the sidelines of ethnography and anthropological theory reflects a common view that emotions occupy the more natural and biological provinces of human experience, and hence are inaccessible to the methods of cultural analysis (compare Lutz and White 1986). In the last decade a dissatisfaction with this view has developed among anthropologists, including those traditionally indifferent or even hostile to "psychological anthropology."

The notion that ethnographic works that ignore emotions distort the lives of the people being described and remove potential key variables from their explanations has been eloquently expressed by Schieffelin (1976) in a study of the ceremonial life of the Kaluli of New Guinea. While acknowledging the centrality of reciprocity in the culture of the Kaluli and other New Guinea peoples, Schieffelin criticizes anthropological works on this geographic area for ignoring the emotional dimension of human experience and treating reciprocity only under the rubric of politics, economics, social structure, and exchange systems. In his own analysis of the Gisaro ceremony, the most salient cultural practice of the Kaluli, Schieffelin demonstrates that the people he describes do not come to understand their lives by explicating them in a rationalized system of ideas. Instead, "they play out and resolve the issues of their lives in a passionate and dramatic ceremonial performance that shakes the participants profoundly and calls upon their deepest emotional resources" (Schieffelin 1976:211). This sort of criticism is particularly valid when addressed to the anthropological work on death (see R. Rosaldo 1984).

The reasons for the avoidance of emotion in mortuary analysis are fairly obvious. Because of our own cultural bias, i.e., the privatization of death in contemporary western societies, anthropologists tend to be reluctant to intrude in people's lives at a time of anguish. While accounts of mortuary rituals are numerous, in-depth interviewing of mourners and other methods aimed at grasping the funeral's emotional dimension are rare. Northwest Coast ethnography is no exception.[17]

Here the legacy of Hertz is more of an obstacle than an inspiration. In his view, which has become standard in anthropology, "we can neither assume the universality of particular modes of feeling nor [assume] that similar signs of emotion correspond to the same underlying sentiments in different cultures" (Huntington and Metcalf 1979:24). Hertz's insight about the ritual orchestration of the expression of emotion is an important warning for those applying simplistic psychological interpretations to another culture's way of death. And yet it should not deter us from trying to establish how the participants' emotions are stimulated, utilized, and dealt with in the mortuary ritual.

From Durkheim, Hertz, and Radcliffe-Brown we have also inherited the notion that expressions of emotion in the mortuary ritual are orchestrated and determined by such sociocultural factors as the age, gender, and status of the deceased, the nature of kinship ties between him and the mourners, and so forth. The validity of this view does not negate the fact that ritualized behavior, while often independent of actual felt emotion, strives to produce emotional feeling for ritual participants and tries to link these emotions to the prevailing ritual form. In fact, it is critical for the overall aims of a ritual performance, that it establishes some connection, realized and understood by participants, between the conventionalized display of emotion in performance and the real, internal, and privately felt emotional and mental condition of the actors involved (Kapferer 1979a).

Because of this difficulty in getting inside the individual's emotional world, even sensitive ethnographers fail to differentiate spontaneous and sincere expressions of grief and other emotions from a simple going through the motions. Weiner, for example, admits her inability "to ascertain how much of the enormous public outbursts of sorrow in the Trobriand funeral is histrionics and how much is actual grief" (1976:69). At the same time, despite these standard precautions in evaluating emotions in another culture, ethnographers frequently insert personal observations on the intensity and sincerity of the mourners' emotion, based on common sense psychology and empathy. Thus Metcalf (1982:43) states that the period immediately following death was undoubtedly "intensely emotionally involving" for the Berawan (compare Danforth 1982).

Some ethnographers make a reasonable point that an odd tension often exists between the requirement to express grief and the unlocking of real emotion that occurs because of the obligatory collective display of grief. Neither the native participant nor the anthropologist, who often identifies and grieves with the mourners, can easily sort out within himself or herself whether the emotion is caused by the participation in the ritual or whether it is there in the first place (Metcalf 1982:43). Other scholars try to avoid this entire issue by pointing out that in the society they studied, no distinction is made between genuine individual feelings and artificial institutionalized expressions of emotion, so common in western cultures (Bloch 1982:214). Even if that is the case among the Merina whom Bloch describes, what about other cultures, including the Tlingit, where such an opposition does exist?

Anthropological analysis, in my view, must incorporate powerful emotions generated by death and stimulated by and displayed in the mortuary ritual, because they make its consequences more significant, long-lasting, and meaningful for the participants. Thus, for example, in the Tlingit potlatch, reciprocal relations with one's affines were often strengthened not simply because gifts and ritual services were exchanged, or even because they benefited the dead, but because at least some of the guests empathized with the hosts' sorrow.

In addition, as a link between cultural values and individual behavior, emotions motivate action. A chief who has exhausted all of his own resources and has even borrowed wealth from his affines in order to sponsor an impressive memorial potlatch may not be motivated exclusively by the desire to increase his own status and surpass that of his rivals, as the standard anthropological interpretation of this ritual tells us. Other motives, such as deep sorrow caused by the death of his beloved maternal uncle or guilt resulting from feeling that he has not shown him enough respect in the past, may just as well be behind his special generosity. In many cases, various political, religious, and emotional motives may be intertwined, so that neither the mourner nor the ethnographer can sort them out.

Finally, by serving as a resolution of norm and motivation, emotions reinforce important social values. Thus if a particular feeling itself is defined as the proper reaction of a "good person", and if the behaviors consequent upon it are socially valuable, an emotional disposition toward socially correct action is created. "Good" people tend to have socially approved feelings which the individual expresses by selecting from a range of socially valuable behaviors (Gerber 1985).

The approach I am advocating begins by looking at emotions as culturally constituted systems, suggesting to individuals what they should feel and how they should behave, and what they might expect from others (compare H. Geertz 1959; Myers 1979; M. Rosaldo 1984; Levy 1984; Schieffelin 1985; Lutz 1985). This view does not deny that emotions arise from a universal biological substrate.[18] However, it treats them as an organized, verbally expressed set of feeling concepts which are more readily available to the ethnographer than unarticulated inner psychological states (Gerber 1984:122).[19] These are the concepts that Geertz calls "experience-near" and which LeVine refers to as "compromise formations," that is, institutionalized forms of adaptation between personality and sociocultural systems (Myers 1979:344–345).

In the context of mortuary analysis, this approach is particularly useful when the ritual (or other forms of social action) can no longer be observed, as is the case with the present study, or when the mourners and other participants in the funeral cannot be interviewed or have psychological tests administered to them.[20] Thus, I begin with the Tlingit theory of grief and mourning, data on which are available for the nineteenth century. This theory recognized the power of emotion and its relatively uncontrollable nature, and allowed some freedom for expressing it. However, idiosyncratic manifestations of grief were discouraged as dangerous to the mourner and the deceased, as well as their matrikin, and were seen as much less appropriate than the wailing, lamenting, singing, and other more ritualized forms of mourning.

How can one tell if the nineteenth century mourners were able to live up to this model of grief and mourning and what was their actual emotional experience? I believe these are important questions and that mortuary analysis' next step is to move from the culturally constituted "feeling concepts" to actual felt emotions or "sensations" (Karp 1977). To accomplish this in a study of the past is not an easy task. Accounts by non-native observers, one of my major sources, are useful but biased and incomplete. Comments on the subject by the Tlingit themselves, recorded by ethnographers, are more valuable but even more scarce. Judging by my own observations, the Tlingit do discuss and evaluate the mourners' behavior, once the funeral is over. Within and without the context of the memorial potlatch, they are even more prone to make private, off the cuff comments about the mourners' alleged feelings and their ritual expression. It is always enlightening to compare the mourners' own view of their feelings and experience with that of their kin, affines, and other participants in the ritual.[21] Of course this type of data obtained in the modern era, when formalized mourning has seriously diminished and a lot more tolerance is shown for idiosyncratic expressions of grief, could be applied to the nineteenth century mortuary rites only with great caution.

Even more rare, in a study of mortuary rituals of the past, is the data on informal grieving and comforting offered to the mourners outside the ritual context. Even though there is virtually no information on this subject for the nineteenth century Tlingit, today it is an important aspect of the mourning process, with the deceased's kin receiving considerable emotional support outside the ritual domain. I suspect that this was also the case in the past, even though the ritualized mourning was seen as more appropriate and was valued higher. Any mortuary analysis that deals with a living culture must incorporate this dimension of mourning. Unfortunately, so far, there has been no attempt to do so, with anthropologists continuing to collapse the ritual process and the process of mourning.[22]

A strategy that is feasible in any mortuary analysis is to examine the mourner's position within a field of social relations, in order to grasp his or her emotional experience (compare R. Rosaldo 1984). Thus, chief mourners would be more likely to actually experience the emotions that their ritual conduct is supposed to express. If such data were available for the Tlingit, it would have been interesting to construct biographical profiles of several matrilineal relatives of the deceased and to examine the relationship between their emotions and their ritual conduct.[23]

Of course, one has to be careful not to assume that those closer to the deceased would necessarily feel the emotions they express in the funeral stronger than those more distant. As R. Rosaldo (1984:187) points out, "A death can touch one deeply because of its resonance with other personal losses, rather than because of one's intimate ties with the deceased." As a matter of fact, in the Tlingit funeral and potlatch, mourning was structured in such a way and expressed through such ritual forms that it linked past and present losses and encouraged all of the deceased's matrikin, and even their opposites, to share grief.

The last question that a rounded mortuary analysis must consider is the effectiveness of mortuary rites in helping the mourners overcome their sorrow. Despite the limitations of the data, I address this issue to get a sense of the participants' experience, their expectations, and the degree of satisfaction that they derived from this elaborate and symbolically rich ritual system.

Cultural Background

The Tlingit culture portrayed in this study is that of the era between the late eighteenth century, when intensive maritime fur trade was established with the Europeans, and the late nineteenth century, when American colonization began to cause thoroughgoing changes in Tlingit economy, social organization, and world view. The bulk of the ethnographic data used here relates to the period 1830–80. By compressing this hundred-year-period into a synchronic dimension, one obviously simplifies the situation. The nineteenth century sociocultural system was far from static. The Tlingit never lived in an ecological or social vacuum and changes in their society undoubtedly occurred prior to contact as well. But these can be documented properly only when the quantity and the quality of the archaeological data increases significantly. As far as the nineteenth century is concerned, important technological and some socioeconomic changes were caused by the fur trade and other forms of interaction with the Europeans. Nevertheless, as far as we can tell from the rather limited existing data, these changes did not significantly affect the underlying structural principles of the social order, basic cultural values, or ethos, so that my synchronic approach is justified.[24]

In the nineteenth century, the Tlingit occupied some five hundred miles of the coastal zone of southeastern Alaska from the Canadian boundary to Yakutat Bay. According to native tradition, some Tlingit groups came into their present territories from the coast farther south, while others entered from the interior. While the archaeological record for their homeland is still rather limited, there is strong evidence indicating that prehistoric peoples occupied southeastern Alaska at least 10,000 years ago.[25] The intermediate period from ca. 8,000/7,500–4,500 BP currently constitutes a gap in the archaeological record of the region. From ca. 4,500 BP onwards a subsistence pattern resembling that of the post-contact period can be discerned, suggesting that the population of that era could have been ancestral to the Tlingit.

Estimates of the nineteenth century Tlingit population are far from accurate and range from 5,850 for the year 1835 to 8,597 in 1861, and 4,583 according to the census of 1890.[26] The Tlingit did not constitute a single "tribe" or political unit, "but rather a nationality, united through conscious possession of a common language and culture and by the name *lingít*, by which they call themselves" (de Laguna 1983:71). Their language is no longer considered to be part of a so-called Na-Dene genetic group, which in Sapir's view included Tlingit, Haida, and Subarctic Athapaskan languages. According to a more recent hypothesis (Krauss and Golla 1981:68), it might be a "hybrid" between Athapaskan-Eyak and an unrelated stock.

The climate of *lingít aaní*, "Tlingit country," is relatively mild, due to the warm Japanese Current. The rugged coast is fringed with numerous islands, and nearly everywhere mountains rise sharply from the water's edge, leaving only a narrow strip of open ground. Rainfall is heavy throughout the year, and particularly during the winter months. The land is covered with bushes, brushes, and moss. This dense forest and rugged terrain made land travel very difficult, but the water provided easy communication. The sea and the rivers were the chief sources of food for the Tlingit. Salmon and other species of fish were the chief staple. The beach offered shellfish, clams, and other edible invertebrates. Seal, sea lions, and other sea mammals were also numerous. Game—bear, deer, mountain goat—supplemented the diet.

Food was generally abundant, but obtaining it was not easy and involved both sexes. Men specialized in fishing and hunting, while women gathered berries and "beach food."[27] Very little food was gathered during winter months, when the weather was at its worst, and that time was spent in making artifacts, feasting, visiting, and storytelling. In the summer, at the height of subsistence activities, people moved to summer camps where they dwelled in rather flimsy plank structures. Wood was the main material used by men for construction of large winter houses and making of artifacts, including canoes, boxes, bowls, and so forth. Bark and roots were used by women to make clothing, baskets, and other household objects. A highly distinctive art style of the area was executed mainly in wood carving and painting, monopolized by men. Most of the artifacts were covered with stylized designs of crests representing the matrilineal group of the owner(s). Weaving of ceremonial ("Chilkat") blankets was done by women who followed crest designs painted by men on wooden boards (see Jonaitis 1986).

The eighteen to twenty local groups among the Tlingit were not political units but have often been called "tribes" for convenience.[28] The Tlingit themselves refer to them as -ḵwáan, "inhabitants of such-and-such a place," for example, Sheet'kaḵwáan, "inhabitants of Sitka." Ḵwáans were subdivided into villages consisting of a number of winter houses occupied by ten to twenty inhabitants, or even more. Neither "tribal" nor village solidarity were strong, because of the crosscutting kinship ties based on matrilineal descent.

The basic unit of Tlingit society was the exogamous, matrilineal descent group, the clan (naa).[29] It owned territory, which included rights to such natural resources as fishing streams, berrying and hunting grounds, beaches, firewood, and fresh water. Ownership often involved the clan's right to enjoy the first products of the season, frequently shared at a feast, and then, if resources were in abundance, to "open" the place to other groups. In fact, once the season was open any person could hunt, fish, or pick berries anywhere, as long as he or she appealed to a member of the owning clan. Such a request, which acknowledged the owners' rights, was always phrased in the idioms of consanguinity or affinity, and could not be refused. As de Laguna (1983:80) suggests, Tlingit country seems to have been aboriginally

> a land of plenty, with a relatively small population that did not press upon resources. This would permit both lavish hospitality and the existence of many unclaimed areas, as well as, perhaps, the lack of incentive to form organized political units to defend clan or tribal territories.

In addition to material, each clan owned symbolic property, including crests, ancestral myths, songs, dances, hereditary names/titles, and other prerogatives. Each clan traced its origins to a particular locality, but many of the clans were divided between several villages and even tribes. Such localized clan segments or "sub-clans" were rather independent of each other and were the true property-holding and political units. The total number of clans for the period under review is difficult to establish. While de Laguna suggests some 60 to 70, this number fluctuated constantly, as independent clans developed out of some sub-clans, while other clans died out.

Each clan or sub-clan was usually subdivided into several matrilineages identified with a house and hence called "houses" by the Tlingit. The house was the smallest unit of society, possessing its own head, its own territories within or subordinate to larger plots owned by the clan as a whole, its own crests in addition to, or as variants of, the crests of its clan, its own set of personal names and ceremonial prerogatives, and its own history.

Because of virilocal postmarital residence, the women and children living in the house tended not to belong to the matrilineage that owned it. Avunculocal residence for at least some of the boys after the age of eight to ten ensured the continuity of the house ownership and the sacred lore belonging to the matrilineage. Residents of the house were the basic unit of production and consumption, although individual subsistence activities were also pursued. Ideally, providing for the entire house had priority over supplying one's nuclear family with food. Subsistence activities as well as trade, warfare, and redistribution of surplus food and wealth in the potlatch were supervised by the male heads of matrilineal groups, who also acted as guardians and trustees of their material and symbolic property, and as ritual experts.

The entire Tlingit nation was also divided into two matrilineal exogamous moieties, Ravens and Eagles (Wolves, in some localities).[30] They had no chiefs and owned no property, but played a key role in social life, as regulators of marriage and exchange of ritual services at life crises, death being the most important one. Marriage with real or classificatory bilateral cross-cousins linked houses and clans of the two moieties. Ideally, the two houses in the opposite moieties were continually linked in marriage, so that one was expected to marry into his or her father's house. However, affinal ties with several clans were often established to create politically advantageous friendly unions with several groups in different villages or even tribes. As de Laguna (1952:9) points out, "The father-child link and the affinal link were considered as equivalent or as symbolically the same, even in cases where they are not actually identical, and they furnish the basic pattern upon which all inter-moiety relationships are built." She also clearly identified the most fundamental principle of the Tlingit social order, describing it as follows: "The web of paternal and affinal bonds creates the fabric of Tlingit society, and *all* social intercourse is consciously conceived as between relatives of different categories, just as if they were members of an extended conjugal family" (de Laguna 1983:74).

Tlingit society was ranked but there were no formal grades, so that ranking was inexact and subject to dispute and re-evaluation. "It was ultimately tested in the publicity of the potlatch, an occasion on which the chief of the host clan reaffirmed his claims to inherited titles or other prerogatives, assumed new ones and bestowed names-titles on junior members of his clan" (de Laguna 1983:75). The high-ranking members of the matrilineal groups and their immediate matrikin constituted the aristocracy; their status was based on a combination of ascription and achievement, i.e., defined by birth, inherited and acquired wealth, personal accomplishments, and character. Age added to their prestige. The "commoners" were simply the aristocrats' junior matrikin. On the bottom of this rather fluid social hierarchy was a small group of illegitimate children, outcasts abandoned by their kin, and the so-called "dried-fish slaves" who depended on the charity of others. True slaves, captured or bought from other coastal nations further south, and occasionally from other Tlingit tribes, were outside the Tlingit society, not being granted full personhood. Houses within the clan and clans within the moiety, the local tribe, and between moieties were also ranked, but on no exact scale. High-ranking clans were large in numbers, rich, successful in war and trade, and especially in recent potlatches.

Extensive trade in food and luxury items between the Tlingit and the various coastal and interior native groups was carried out in the pre- and post-contact period. Trade routes into the interior were owned by matrilineal groups which vigorously protected this prerogative. Warfare was waged against other Tlingit tribes as well as foreign coastal groups to the north and especially to the south, and was aimed at capturing slaves and booty, although in the native mind, avenging insult or injury was the main cause of hostilities. An emphasis on lineage and clan solidarity and on defending the reputation of one's matrilineal group at any cost resulted in frequent feuding and fighting, although attempts were often made to settle the dispute by exchanging property and performing a special peace ritual.

Shamans were in charge of communication with superhuman powers and spirits, healing, foretelling the future, identifying witches, and protecting warriors on a raid. Lay persons could also acquire superhuman power and good fortune through various observances aimed at achieving physical and moral purity.

A strong emphasis on proper public conduct and etiquette made daily social intercourse highly formalized. Nevertheless, informal visiting, sharing of food, and exchange of gifts and services within the village were common and gave ample opportunity for relaxation, joking, and other ways of having a good time.

In concluding this ethnographic sketch, I must point out how some of the incompatible norms and values as well as the contradictory organizing principles of the sociocultural order configured the lived-in world of the nineteenth century Tlingit and its endemic modes of conflict. One of the major contradictions was between the principles of hierarchy and equality. Hierarchy resulted in an unequal distribution of status and power within the matrilineal group, which often clashed with the ideology of the unity and solidarity of matrikin. Predicated upon this contradiction was jealousy and the resulting conflicts common between the closest matrikin. The main problem here was that such conflicts, unless they were very minor and could be settled informally, could not be resolved in any culturally sanctioned way, except by expelling the disputants from the group, which meant social death. The latter practice was the last resort; more often intralineage and intraclan conflicts smoldered for long periods of time without resolution. No wonder that witchcraft accusations were often leveled against the victim's close matrikin.

Another strategy in dealing with conflicts within the matrilineal group was to blame members of the opposite moiety. Intermoiety disputes were common, with an emphasis on upholding the dignity of the kinship group encouraging demands of restitution for even minor injuries caused by outsiders. If an exchange of gifts and mutual feasting could not resolve the problem, the disputants resorted to violence which could last for a long time, until a formalized peace ceremony was decided upon. The law of maintaining a strict balance in intermoiety relations was so fundamental that equalizing the losses on each side was a prerequisite for peace. The combined status of those slain on the one side had to equal that of the other, which meant that, prior to establishing peace, the victors often had to sacrifice their own kin or at least pay heavy indemnity. Using Levy's (1984) terminology, one could say that intramoiety conflict was "hypocognized," while intermoiety conflict was "hypercognized."

At the same time, consanguineal and affinal relations supplemented or balanced each other out, with the former being often more tense and constrained by the senior matrikin's control over the juniors, in contrast to the latter that tended to be more relaxed. In other words, despite the cultural ideology, lineage, clan, and moiety mates had a lot more sources of conflict than affines, from jealousy over each other's spouses to disputed crests.

Related to the above-mentioned contradiction was a tension between the values of cooperation and conformity of the individual to the group, on the one hand, and personal autonomy and ambitiousness, on the other. This conflict may be phrased as ascription imposing limitations on achievement, i.e., not allowing the individual to rise too far above the rank of his or her parents. While the value of "love" between matrikin discouraged aggressive self-aggrandizement and egotism, an emphasis on hierarchy stimulated it. Ideally, the person's success, manifested in increased status and rank, benefited his or her matrilineal group, raising its own position vis-à-vis other groups in both moieties. But the danger of an upwardly mobile individual neglecting his or her kinship obligations, acting selfishly, or identifying more strongly with high-ranking persons in other clans was real.

These and some other conflicts, contradictions, and oppositions were played out and manipulated in the ceremonial system, and particularly the mortuary complex, where an attempt was made to reconcile them. Funerals and potlatches presented a rather sharp contrast with daily life, allowing for the largest concentration of persons, dispersed during the summer or living in other communities, providing a context for a stronger and more open—though mostly ritualized—expression of emotion, and giving the participants an opportunity to subtly air their grievances and disagreements and achieve some consensus through oratorical metaphors, gift-giving and other forms of symbolic action.

Nineteenth-Century History

First contacted by the Russians in 1741, the Tlingit became deeply involved in the maritime fur trade with visiting Europeans, trading sea otter pelts for firearms, iron tools, tobacco and various luxury items, including beads, glassware, blankets, and fancy clothing. In an attempt to control this trade, the Russian-American Company established two forts/trading posts, one in Yakutat in 1795 and another in Sitka in 1799. Resenting encroachment on their land, and other Russian abuses, the Tlingit destroyed the latter in 1801 and the former in 1805. No further

Russian settlement in Yakutat was ever established (de Laguna 1972), but Sitka was recaptured in 1804 and a new fort built there, called *Novo-Arkhangel'sk* (New Archangel), remained the capital of Russian America until 1867 (see Lisianskii 1814; Khlebnikov 1976; Tikhmenev 1978). Another fort was established by the Russians among the Stikine Tlingit in the south in 1834, but in 1839 the area in which it was located was leased to the Hudson's Bay Company which established its own Fort Stikine at the mouth of the Stikine River. That enterprise was not particularly successful and lasted only until 1848 (see Klein 1987).

The Tlingit tolerated European forts as long as they did not interfere in their own trade with and middleman role vis-à-vis the interior Athapaskan tribes. They welcomed European trade items and traded energetically and shrewdly, heavily depleting the sea otter population by the 1830s. They fiercely defended their political independence, however, responding quickly to any insult or injury from the whites. Documenting the more specific changes in Tlingit culture and society brought about by the maritime fur trade would require more archival research than has been done so far; from the existing published data it appears that, with the exception of material culture, changes were relatively insignificant (Kan 1985; 1987). In other words, the basic cultural values, underlying principles of the sociocultural order, and major forms of social action were reproduced rather than transformed. As Wike (1951:102) put it, "Northwest Coast society rushed out to meet the sea otter trade, to use it, and to shape it to the society's own ends."

The indigenous tradition of intertribal trade and barter, and the accumulation and distribution of wealth minimized the novelty of commerce with Europeans and reduced its effects on Tlingit society (compare, Wike 1951:103). Thus, sea otter hunting did not significantly promote individualization of production, since it had to be carried out collectively. Neither was the hierarchical social structure significantly affected. Lineage and clan heads and other aristocrats controlled much of the trade, bringing more furs than commoners and acting as representatives of and spokesmen for their matrikin. In fact, the Europeans themselves strengthened the aristocrats' power and status by courting them with gifts and referring to them as "chiefs."[31] The scale of warfare increased as well, with the Tlingit coveting trade items and slaves owned by other native groups, and competing over trade routes. Again, the aristocracy retained its leadership position by controlling much of this activity.

Despite its control, however, some new wealth did trickle down to the commoners, who were able to trade some pelts on their own. These nouveaux riches must have tried to increase their participation in potlatching or even sponsor potlatches of their own. Some scholars (e.g., Stanley 1958:66) believe that this new development increased the pressures upon high-ranking persons to consolidate their positions of privilege and increased their concern with crests, names, and other diagnostics of status. Depopulation caused by several disastrous epidemics must have also caused some changes in the social hierarchy, with some high-ranking titles becoming vacant and available for persons of lower rank. The frequency and scale of potlatching undoubtedly increased in the nineteenth century, with more wealth being distributed and more people attending. Hudson's Bay and some other types of blankets, a standard measure of wealth, replaced animal skins. Little evidence exists, however, that the Tlingit potlatch became significantly more competitive or lost its "religious" characteristics, as has been suggested for the Kwakiutl and some of the other Northwest Coast groups (Codere 1950; 1961; Piddocke 1965; Wike 1952).

I should point out that the Tlingit culture was by its very nature a conservative one, due, to a large extent, to the central role played by ancestral prerogatives and values in the life of the living. The Russians' failure to eliminate or at least minimize slavery and warfare, and a very limited success of their missionary efforts, prior to the sale of Alaska to the United States in 1867, attest to this conservatism.

With the Tlingit loss of independence and self-determination, resulting from American colonization, their culture and society began to undergo much more significant changes. But even that was a gradual process, which did not gain momentum until the last two decades of the nineteenth century.[32]

Outline of the Book

Much of this book follows the sequence of mortuary rites, from the moment of death to the memorial potlatch. Chapter I presents a synopsis of this cycle, set in motion by the death of a house head. Part I is devoted to the reconstruction and symbolic/sociological analysis of those aspects of Tlingit culture and society that pertain directly to the mortuary/ancestral complex. Chapter II examines the explicit cultural ideas about the model of the human being as well as its underlying structural principles. Chapter III focuses on how the person was fully socialized by imprinting on the outside layer of the body and incorporating into its "inside" the various attributes of the individual's matrilineal group. The central cultural concept of *shagóon*, the origin and destiny of the matrilineal group established by the ancestors, is also examined. Chapter IV looks at the aristocrat as the "cultural/moral person" par excellence and shows how ethnopsychology broadens the picture and helps clarify the much-debated issue of Tlingit and Northwest Coast ranking.

Part II analyzes the funeral, beginning with Chapter V which reconstructs Tlingit eschatology and attitudes towards death, explaining the location of the dead in the universe and the treatment of the corpse. Chapter VI analyzes the funeral, focusing on the symbolic transformation of the deceased, the mourners, and the opposite moiety—actors in the ritual drama. Chapter VII looks at the political aspects of this same ritual, particularly the competition over status and prestige among the mourners and the use of the "rhetoric of grief" to legitimize and mask it.

The memorial potlatch is the subject of Part III, with the analysis again divided between the ritual's "religious" (death-related, commemorative, emotional) and "political" dimensions, discussed in Chapters VIII and IX, respectively. Part IV is devoted to issues of general analytic interest. Chapter X presents a "controlled comparison" of the Tlingit and the western Subarctic Athapaskan mortuary complexes (see fig. 1), with two goals in mind. On the one hand, it helps bring out the essential features of Tlingit culture and thus expand the basis of my interpretation of the main causes of the mortuary complex's centrality in it. On the other hand, it enables me to move from a specific case to a general issue of correlation between elaborate mortuary rites (including double obsequies) and particular types of ideological and sociopolitical systems. A brief comparison of Tlingit mortuary rites with those of their coastal neighbors to the south (see fig. 2) provides additional material for constructing a model of the mortuary complex in egalitarian and ranked societies.

The Conclusion sums up the study's major findings, finalizing the discussion of the nature of the mortuary/ancestral complex and the reasons for its centrality in the nineteenth century Tlingit sociocultural order. While doing that, it also examines the implications of this work for the anthropology of death, outlining a more comprehensive model of mortuary analysis, which combines attention to the political, religious, and often neglected but essential emotional dimensions of death-related rituals.

chapter one

OUTLINE OF THE MORTUARY RITES

The Funeral

Let us imagine ourselves entering a Tlingit winter house whose head has just been pronounced dead.[1] We see several members of the opposite moiety washing the body, combing the hair, painting the face with the deceased's crest symbols, and wrapping the corpse in several blankets. The dead person is being placed in the back of the house in a sitting or reclining position: knees drawn up to the body and bound, hands placed on the knees. He is wearing a wooden headdress representing one of his crests. One Chilkat blanket, also depicting crests, is thrown over the lower limbs, and another covers the body up to the chin. The deceased is equipped with warm mittens and moccasins as well as a spear or a knife (see fig. 3). All around him, his personal possessions (weapons, tools, and fishing gear) and treasures (furs, blankets, and copper shields) are displayed, along with the furs and blankets donated by his immediate matrikin. He is also surrounded with crest-bearing objects owned by his lineage and clan. A number of slaves, belonging to the deceased himself or donated by his close matrikin, are also stationed near the body.[2]

The community learns the sad news from the sound of a box drum beaten by the close male affines of the deceased and from the announcement they make by calling loudly from the porch of his house.

Fig. 3. Chief Shakes of Wrangell displayed in state, with a shakee.át *on his head, a Chilkat blanket over the lower part of his body, and crest headdresses and other regalia around him. An 1885–1887 sketch by A. P. Niblack. Niblack 1890, p. XVIII, fig. 353.*

Regular activities are temporarily suspended, since each resident of the village is expected to visit the house of mourning. The rank and status of the deceased determines whether it is his lineage, his clan, or the local segment of his entire moiety that is being affected by his demise. The length of the wake is also correlated with his position in the social hierarchy. Four is the standard number of days between death and cremation, but those of the highest rank lie in state for eight. The dead person's house/lineage is most strongly affected; its members suspend all of their mundane activities for the duration of the wake and observe various taboos. The mourners begin the wake by fasting and then eat only very little, abstain from sexual relations, idle talk, and unnecessary movement. Their faces are painted black and their hair is cut or singed. They wear old garments tied around their waists.

Lineage mates of the deceased remain near the body for the entire wake, while his more distant matrikin periodically visit his house to wail and sing a set of special "crying songs." These periods of ritualized collective mourning are followed by the more quiet and personalized expressions of sorrow by the chief mourners, who speak to the deceased, sing laments, keen, and sob. The female mourners sit in front of the corpse and perform most of the keening and wailing, while the men stand in the front of the house, striking the floor with special staffs in time with the singing (see fig. 4).

The mourners' female affines assist with the wailing, while the male ones prepare the funeral pyre behind the house. Several young men from the opposite moiety guard the body from witches during the entire wake. The dead person's spouse joins the mourners, with the widow's mourning observances being more elaborate than those of either the widower or the deceased's lineage mates (see figs. 5, 6).

Every night of the wake, the mourners hold a small feast for their affines, the focus of which is the smoking of tobacco. The hosts also burn some tobacco and invoke the name of the deceased lying in state and those of other dead members of their lineage. The mourners sing their own crying songs as well as those lent to them by their fathers and paternal grandfathers participating in the ceremony. The guests help with the singing, one of them acting as the drummer. Sometimes there is also a modest feast in which the guests are served the favorite food of the deceased, who is believed to share their meal, just as he is supposed to partake of the tobacco they smoke. The leading guests eulogize the deceased and comfort the mourners with words of condolence (Swanton 1909:372–373; Shotridge 1917:105–109; Olson 1967:59).

On the morning after the last night of the wake, the male affines of the deceased carry the body out of the house, in a woven cedar bark mat or blanket, to be cremated on the pyre prepared behind the house. The body is never taken out through the door; instead, an opening is made in the rear wall or, occasionally, the smokehole is used. Ashes from the fireplace and a dog are thrown out after the corpse.

The funeral pyre, located in the cemetery belonging to the clan of the deceased, is a box-like receptacle made of logs piled up in a crisscross fashion. It is about four feet wide and six to eight feet long and is filled with kindling and fine wood which has already been covered with seal or eulachen grease and lit. The corpse is placed inside this crib and then covered with several animal skins and blankets, including a ceremonial one. Some of the deceased's personal possessions are also placed on the pyre. Members of both moieties take part in cremation. Male matrikin of the departed stand a short distance away from the pyre, still dressed in their mourning attire. Under the direction of a song leader, they perform another set of the mourning

Fig. 4. "Funeral of a Tlingit Chief." A drawing made in Sitka by I. G. Voznesenskii in 1844. Blomkvist 1951:290.

songs owned by their clan. While singing, the men strike a box drum or wooden boards with their staffs. The female mourners, sitting some distance away, with their backs to the fire, help with the singing. They are assisted by the women of the opposite moiety. Several brothers-in-law of the deceased tend the fire and periodically add some of his personal possessions to it. At this time, a slave destined to join the deceased in the afterworld is killed and his body placed on the pyre. As his master's corpse is being consumed, the matrikin and the spouse of the deceased blacken their faces with charcoal from the fire, while their wailing and sobbing comes to a climax. A few hours later, after the fire has consumed the body, the mourners depart, while their female affines collect the charred bones and ashes, wrap them in furs or blankets, place them in a decorated bentwood box and deposit it inside a grave house belonging to the lineage of the deceased.[3]

The mourners cleanse themselves in the sea, replace their mourning attire with festive garments, and begin preparing for the first in a series of memorial feasts to be held between cremation and the memorial potlatch. The number and the scale of these feasts are determined by the rank and status of the deceased and of his matrikin as well as by their wealth. The first post-cremation feast bears the same

Fig. 5. An early 1900s photograph of a Sitka aristocrat's funeral with the widow seated in front of the coffin. Photo by E. W. Merrill. Alaska Historical Library.

name as and resembles the "smoking feast" that is held while the body lies in state, except that more food is served and some small gifts are distributed to the guests, tokens of the much larger ones to be given to them in the potlatch.

In 1888 Emmons participated in such a feast held in the village of Hoonah in memory of a shaman, whose body had been disposed of the day before. The hosts were the Kaagwaantaan clan, and the guests belonged to the widow's clan, the T'akdeintaan. In his unpublished manuscript, Emmons (1920–1945, Ch. XI:34–37) vividly describes the ceremony:

> The body of the house was cleared and the floor swept with eagle wings. The fire was built of yellow cedar logs. . . . It was lighted about 6 p.m., as the guests commenced to arrive. As they entered, they were shown to their places by the two head men of the [deceased's] wife's clan, those of the highest rank being seated on the floor space back of the fire, facing the door, the principal chief of the Tuck-dane-tan [T'akdeintaan] occupied the center, the men in front and the women in the rear. The shaman's family [lineage] and clan occupied the front right hand corner and were crowded in front about the doorway. No word of

welcome was spoken to the guests. They simply took their seats, indicated to them by the ushers.

When all had assembled, the bunches of the long black leaf tobacco *gunge* [*gánch*] were handed to the ushers by members of the dead shaman's family. The donor's name was called when it was handed to the brother of the dead, who, in turn, handed it to an old man by his side, who cut it up for smoking. After all the tobacco had been received four or more strands were put in the fire at each corner and burned as an offering to the spirit of the dead, who was believed to receive it for use as it was given. The box of old pipes, carved in animal figures claimed as family [lineage] and clan crests [of the deceased] . . . was brought out, the pipes filled and lighted and handed to the most honored guests commencing with the women who smoked only a little while and then handed them to their men. Most of the guests provided their own pipes which were already filled or tobacco given to them.

For some time they smoked in silence, some having their pipes refilled. Then a Tuck-dane-tan [T'akdeintaan] standing by the fire, broke off pieces of tobacco and throwing them into the fire called out "a gift to ...", giving the names of those long since dead the most honored to the family, he having been prompted by the brother of the dead shaman. The remainder of the tobacco was distributed by the ushers to the guests, the amounts received being proportional to the social standing of the recipient.

When the distribution was finished the chief of the guests made a speech in short sentences of thanks mentioning the name of practically every male member among the hosts, even to boys of 8 and 10. As each name was mentioned, he was answered, "ah." The older brother of the deceased replied, after which the assemblage broke up. The next evening the family of the shaman feasted [his] wife's family. One year afterward a feast for the dead was given at which time those who performed the various services for the dead and built the grave house were potlatched in payment for their work.

The Cemetery

The first European descriptions of Tlingit mortuary structures date back to the last two decades of the eighteenth century (see Niblack 1890:327–329, 351–356; Keithahn 1963; de Laguna 1972:539–542). Although this information is rather sketchy, the nature of the basic types of containers for human remains can be established. All of the sources indicate that cremation was the predominant mode of disposal of the dead.[4] The charred bones and ashes were deposited inside large boxes placed on top of one, two or, most often, four posts, whose height varied from six to fifteen feet. The front of the box was often decorated with a painted or carved representation of a crest of the deceased's

Fig. 6. An 1899 Chilkat funeral. Photo by F. B. Bourn. Alaska Historical Library.

matrilineal group. Some structures consisted of two boxes placed at different heights, one of which contained the cremated remains of the body and the other the skull.[5]

The best descriptions of the late eighteenth century Tlingit graves come from Malaspina, the leader of a Spanish expedition that contacted the Tlingit in the Yakutat area, and Suria, a member of that expedition, who also made drawings of several mortuary structures (see de Laguna 1972:540–542, 976–978; *To the Totem Shore* 1986: 176–189; see fig. 7). In addition to two box-like structures supported by four posts, which were observed in other parts of southeastern Alaska, the Spaniards saw a large bear-like wooden figure on a post, which held a box under its claws, containing a bowl-shaped basket, a wolf skin, and a piece of board, and probably some human remains as well. Another unusual structure they described was a grave monument containing the ashes of the father of one of the local chiefs and consisting of two boxes. The upper one had a carved face of a bear on its front and was supported with posts on each side, carved to represent killer whale fins and decorated with hair. The lower box rested on the ground and was surmounted with a crest hat, with a tall pile of cylinders rising from its top.

Fig. 7. Grave monuments of the family of the current chief of Port Mulgrave (Yakutat area), 1791. Aquatint by Suria. Museo Naval, Madrid. De Laguna 1972:977.

It appears that such spectacular grave structures contained the remains of the aristocracy, while those of ordinary people rested in boxes elevated on posts. It also seems that these early graves were already arranged in accordance with the clan affiliation of the deceased. Some of the graves, most likely those of the aristocracy, were decorated with animal skins (Krause 1956:31) and contained objects of indigenous and European origin.

In the middle of the nineteenth century, two major types of mortuary structures existed: grave house and mortuary pole. The former was the box on four posts, described earlier, which had been lowered closer to the ground. By the end of the century, this most common container for human remains was lowered even further, with many grave houses standing on the ground. Its front was often covered with planks on which a crest was represented by carving or painting. Sometimes a wooden figure of a crest animal surmounted this structure (Emmons 1920–1945, ch. XI:38–39; Niblack 1890: plate LXV; see fig. 8). The mortuary pole was usually a plain post with a single figure of a crest animal on the top. The box with the remains was placed in the back of the crest animal. Finally, some of the poles contained no human remains but were erected to commemorate the death of a high-ranking person.[6]

The mortuary and memorial poles were reserved for the aristocracy. The former stood either in the cemetery or near the deceased's house, while the latter was always located near or in front of it. It appears that the mortuary poles contained the remains of one or, at most, two or three persons. Grave house of high-ranking persons usually contained the remains of no more than a few deceased. However, ordinary grave houses often contained up to a dozen boxes with bones and ashes. Aristocratic grave houses were similar in design to those of the commoners but were larger and more elaborately decorated. All of these structures were labelled by a single term _ḵaa daakeidí_, "a person's cover" or "a person's box."

Immediately following cremation, the bones and ashes were usually placed in a temporary container, probably a grave house. A year or more later, they were redeposited into a new box which was placed inside a new or rebuilt grave house or a mortuary pole. This act was described as "finishing the body" and, like all the other funerary services, was performed by the mourners' opposites. It was immediately followed by a memorial potlatch.

The Memorial Potlatch

The scale of the memorial potlatch varied, depending on the rank, status, and wealth of the deceased and of his matrikin. Low-ranking lineages and houses honored their dead kin by giving a small feast, whereas the potlatch in memory of a clan head involved the entire village, plus many out-of-town guests. The point is that any death, with the exception of that of a slave, required the participation of the affinal/paternal kin of the deceased who performed the funerary services and had to be publicly thanked, feasted, and remunerated. Some matrilineal groups that could not afford a big potlatch and were embarrassed to give a small one joined their matrikin of higher rank, when the latter memorialized their own dead relatives.

Not to give a memorial feast meant to show a lack of respect to the deceased as well as the mourners' opposites. Until the latter had been "paid off" (as the modern Tlingit say when they use English), the cycle of mortuary feasts was incomplete, with the deceased and his matrikin remaining in a state of limbo. The remains were said to be "un-

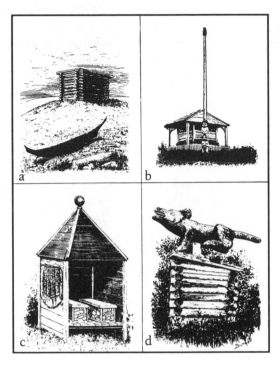

Fig. 8. Tlingit graves
sketched and photographed
by A. P. Niblack in 1885–
1887: a) shaman's grave;
b) grave probably of Chief
Shustocks, near Wrangell;
c) northern grave house,
Sitka; d) chief's grave, Wrangell. Niblack 1890, pl. LXV,
figs. 346–349.

finished," while the survivors, and especially the deceased's successor, continued observing some of the mourning taboos and appeared in public in their mourning attire. Besides involving the installation of the remains in their final resting place, the potlatch marked and celebrated the final dissolution of the various other attributes constituting the complete social persona of the deceased and their distribution to several locations. Thus, at that time, the ghost was expected to settle forever in the cemetery, while the spirit was believed to find a permanent home in the distant, immaterial "village of the dead." Another one of his noncorporeal entities, the reincarnated spirit, was expected to return to the living by being reborn through a baby delivered by a close female matrilineal relative of the deceased, prior to the potlatch. The dead person's names and regalia were ritually bestowed upon his matrikin, while his position in the social order, his title, wealth, and spouse were publicly given to his successor.

As I have mentioned earlier, the rank and status of the deceased and of his matrikin determined the type of funerary structure erected as his final resting place, with the mortuary pole being a more respectful way to honor him and calling for a more elaborate potlatch. The largest one of all was given when a lineage head was immortalized by the rebuilding of his house. A memorial potlatch for a person of low rank might be limited to a feast; whereas the one given for an aristocrat always involved a distribution of gifts.

In the discussion of the potlatch, a distinction must be made between its invariant core and its other elements. As McClellan (1954:78) points out in her excellent summary of this ritual, "the potlatch itself varies considerably in its combinations and sequences of events, depending on the locality, the whims and fortunes of the hosts, and the purpose of a particular event." Every potlatch, however, involved the feasting and payment by members of one moiety to those of another, which honored the dead and allowed the living to display their clan regalia, recite their origin myths, and perform their ancestral songs and dances, and thus to maintain or raise their rank and status. While a summary of this core of the memorial potlatch follows, some of its additional elements are mentioned and analyzed in subsequent chapters.

A memorial potlatch given in honor of a house head was usually sponsored by that group, with the assistance of other local lineages of his clan. Although the deceased's heir and successor, who was also the chief mourner, carried a significant part of the financial burden, he could not sponsor the potlatch without the help of his lineage and clan relatives. The accumulation of everything needed for the ceremony could take from one to several years. Potlatches took place in the late fall and winter, after the completion of most of the subsistence activities. The guests were recruited from the local as well as the high-ranking out-of-town affinal/paternal kin of the hosts. If the latter had not been able to assist the mourners during the funeral, they were now asked to participate in "finishing the body." The presence of some out-of-town guests was a prerequisite for a major potlatch.

In addition to preparations and rehearsing of songs and dances, the chief hosts fasted, abstained from sex, and engaged in various magical activities aimed at ensuring their success in the potlatch. The out-of-town guests were informed about the ceremony long in advance. The invitation was delivered by several brothers-in-law of the deceased, called *naa káani*, "in-laws of the clan." The guests too rehearsed their songs and dances, and used magic aimed at bringing them success in their performance as well as generous gifts.

When they arrived in the vicinity of the hosts' village, the guests did not immediately land but spent the night nearby. The next day, their arrival took place, which involved a spectacular ceremony. Here is how one American observer described what he saw at Ft. Wrangell in 1896:

> [on the shore] there were probably fifty yards of canvas raised as a shield behind which the main preparation went on. In a short time the strangers appeared. There were seven large canoes lashed side by side. . . . In the bow of each stood a chief dressed richly. . . . Each chief held a beautiful silk flag, not letting it wave, but holding the flag down to the staff.
>
> They came on slowly and when near the shore, stopped and all chanted one of their weird songs. At its conclusion the curtain on shore dropped. There was the figure of a huge whale, made of black muslin stretched over a frame, with fins and tail flopping. Around this were several natives with large head dresses, representing porpoise, seal and lizards [?]. These all kept moving in a stooping posture around the whale. Behind these were about three hundred men and women dressed like the visitors in the canoes. They set up a chant. Those in the canoes answered. This was kept up until four songs were sung by each [side]. In the meantime hands full of light feathers were thrown among them.
>
> When the singing ceased, a boy fancifully dressed having in his hand a big bow and arrow led by two chiefs approached the shore. He drew the bow and pointed the arrow twice at the canoes, the crowd keeping silent. The third time he held it pointed toward the canoes then lowered the point and shot into the water. Then a shout went up that could be heard for miles, the canoes pulled to land and the feasting began. (Anonymous quoted in Sheets 1909)

In addition to this mock battle between the host and the guest parties, their leaders engaged in a bellicose verbal exchange, using obscure metaphors which alluded to the history of their respective lineages and clans and could be fully understood only by the aristocracy. At the conclusion of this ceremony, the chief host would often go into the water to greet his guests and order his junior male matrikin to show them great respect by carrying them ashore along with their canoes. The out-of-town guests stayed in the house of the chief host and in other houses of his clan for the duration of the potlatch.

Usually the potlatch proper did not start until after the four days of feasting and entertainment. The hosts provided the food, while the local and the out-of-town guests sang and danced, competing against each other. Large amounts of foods were served and selected guests engaged in eating contests. They performed costumed shows and entertaining songs belonging to their non-Tlingit neighbors.

Unlike these preliminary ceremonies, the potlatch proper, which could last one or two days and nights, was dominated by the hosts. The latter put on their ancestral regalia and wore them until the ritual was over. The chief host delivered a speech formally welcoming the guests and explaining the reasons for the ceremony. Then he and all of the other hosts publicly mourned their recently departed relative for the last time. After four crying songs, the most ancient and sacred, were performed by the mourners, they wailed and cried, and then uttered four prolonged "u" sounds, which meant that they were expelling sadness from their bodies. At that time some of the chief guests would rise and deliver speeches of condolence, answered by the hosts' words of gratitude. The guests might also perform some of their clan dances to comfort the bereaved.

Following that, the mood of the hosts changed to a more joyful one and they began feasting the guests. The spiritual essence of all of the food given to the guests was believed to be consumed by the hosts' own departed matrikin as well as the clan ancestors of the guests. In addition, some food was thrown into the fire and the names of the hosts' ancestors were invoked. After the meal, the hosts donned the ceremonial attire representing their crests, including the wooden head-dresses, the most sacred of all. They performed eight special songs and dances describing their crests and then began bringing the gifts for distribution. In the pre-contact period, these included furs, tanned skins, a few slaves, and large shields (tináa) made of copper. In the second half of the nineteenth century, these indigenous objects were supplemented and gradually replaced by blankets, bolts of calico and other types of cloth, and money. Each host, even a small child, made a contribution and expressed his or her feelings of sorrow for the dead person and love for the affines, singing a clan song or delivering a speech. The songs of sorrow reminded the hosts of their own departed matrikin and brought tears to their eyes. Once again, the guests would try to comfort the mourners by singing, dancing, or delivering speeches. The hosts also explained how they were related to the particular guests and thanked those of them who had helped them most in times of sorrow. At that time, another eight sacred potlatch songs were performed by the hosts.

Before the distribution of wealth, the chief host and other members of his clan, most of them juniors, were given new names. The chief host, who for the first time wore his predecessor's ceremonial garments, was thus officially installed in his new position. If a new house was being dedicated, this was the time to recite its history and to announce its name (usually the same as that of the previous structure that stood in its place). Junior members of the host moiety could also be tattooed and/or have their ears pierced at that time. The distribution of gifts was carried out by the hosts' brothers-in-law *(naa káani)*. The name of each recipient and the nature and the size of each gift was announced, along with the name of a specific matrilineal ancestor of the donor(s), who was the recipient of the spiritual essence of each gift. Some of the property donated by the hosts was thrown into the fire, so as to send it directly to their deceased matrikin. Copper shields and slaves could be killed as well, the former by sinking and the latter by breaking their necks. The leading guests, members of the aristocracy, and those closely tied to the chief hosts through marriage received much larger gifts than lower-ranking guests. The shields and slaves were reserved exclusively for those of high rank.

In addition to singing the serious clan songs describing their ancestral crests and their mythical history, the hosts performed the more lively love songs, addressed to their guests. Such songs required a response from the guests who sang a few of their own love songs. Another popular genre, performed mainly by the hosts, consisted of the songs and dances imitating the spirits, once owned by the shamans of the singers' clan.

The guests thanked the hosts for their generosity with their speeches, songs, and dances, performed in the house of the chief host as well as other houses of his clan. The guests continued to be feasted by the hosts and might also give a small return potlatch, as an expression of gratitude. In it, the emphasis was on songs, dances, and feasting rather than gift-giving. Finally, the guests departed, loaded with presents and food.[7]

part one

THE PERSON AND THE SOCIAL ORDER

chapter two

THE OUTSIDE AND THE INSIDE
The Tlingit View of the Human Being

Beginning with the pioneering work of Van Gennep (1960), Hertz (1973), and Mauss (1973), anthropological research has demonstrated that the relationship between the human body and the collectivity is a "crucial dimension of consciousness in all societies" (Comaroff 1985:6; compare Douglas 1966; 1973; V. Turner 1967; Needham 1973; Blacking 1977; T. Turner 1980). The body mediates all human action in the social world and is, thus, an excellent raw material which society can use to transform humans as biological creatures into social beings. Because the body is so much a part of the natural, that is, the unreflective dimension of human existence, cultural categories and values that have taken root in it acquire the appearance of transcendental truths. This, in turn, allows the body, as a cultural system, to be used as a powerful ideology that can serve to justify gender or rank inequality, to legitimize authority, and so forth.[1]

Material Components of the Person

While the Tlingit had no simple term for the body as a whole, they did refer to its outer layers as (ḵaa) daadleeyí, "flesh/meat around (the person)" (compare de Laguna 1972:758).[2] This suggests a notion of a container or a cover for some other components of the person. De Laguna (1972:758) mentions another term, *ax̱ daa*, "my outer side," which she compares to *aas daayí*, "bark" or "tree's cover."[3] In addition, informants often described the human body as the house of the spirit. It was also believed that in the mythical era, animals could easily shed their skin or fur as an outer garment and reveal their anthropomorphic self.

Beneath the surface of the skin ([k̲aa] *ch'áatwu*) and the flesh were the bones (sing. [*kaa*] *s'aag̲í*), which figured prominently in the Tlingit model of the person. Animal and fish bones had to be treated with respect in order to ensure their rebirth.[4] Thus, salmon were believed to be a race of supernatural beings who dwelt in a great house under the sea, where they went about in human form. At a certain time of the year, these salmon-people returned to the stream of their birth, dressed in garments of salmon-fish, that is, assuming the form of fish to sacrifice themselves. Once dead, the spirit of each fish returned to the house beneath the sea. If its bones had been returned to the water, the creature resumed its human form with no discomfort, and could repeat the trip next season. If some bones had been thrown away on land, when resurrected the salmon-person might lack an arm or a leg, would become angry, and would refuse to run again in the stream in which he had been so poorly treated (Peratrovich 1959:119).[5]

Similarly, following the cremation of a human body, *all* of the remaining bones and ashes had to be gathered and placed in a mortuary container. It appears that the bones of the deceased were perceived as containing some essential element of his personhood. This belief explains why wrapping the bones in furs or blankets was said to "keep them warm." If a person died away from home, the body was cremated on the spot, but all of the bones and ashes were brought back and deposited among the remains of his matrilineal relatives.[6]

The notion that the bones constituted the major material component as well as the blueprint of the body is also supported by the frequent use of the skeletal or "x-ray" image in Tlingit art. The bones underneath the skin are depicted on many representations of crests as well as on shamanistic paraphernalia. Instead of showing the entire skeleton, the Tlingit artist would often select certain bones, usually the backbone, which connects many bones in the body (compare Jonaitis 1986:130).

In addition to the backbone, there were eight special ("long") bones, considered to be the most important ones. They symbolized the living human being as a whole and served as the explanation of the sacredness of *eight*, the most common ritual number (Veniaminov 1984:424; Olson 1933–1954, notebook 6:71; de Laguna 1972:761; Mc-Clellan 1975:386–387; Kan 1979–1987). This number figured prominently in all of the Tlingit rites of passage as well as the practices aimed at obtaining good fortune and superhuman power. Thus, for example, the death of a high-ranking person called, ideally, for eight memorial rituals; the ultimate goal of an ambitious aristocrat was to sponsor eight potlatches in his lifetime.

These eight bones, sometimes referred to as joints, were counted from the top of the body to the bottom, in the clockwise direction, believed to be the direction of the sun and, consequently, of life, health, and rebirth (see below). They included the right forearm, right upper arm, left upper arm, left forearm, left thigh, left lower leg, right lower leg, and right thigh (de Laguna 1972:761). I suggest that these particular bones were chosen because the limbs constitute the extreme points of the body's extension into space. These points were symbolically marked, just as the eight corners (i.e., the places where the main beams forming the frame of the structure joined each other) of a newly-constructed winter house were marked, in a clockwise direction, with the blood of slaves or with fish oil during the rite of the dedication (Kan 1979–1987; Olson 1967:62).[7] Because the human body stood at the center of the Tlingit universe and the body's wholeness was symbolized by the eight bones, they were a perfect model for proper ritual conduct.[8]

A gradual hardening of the bones in a growing body, in contrast to the flesh which always remained soft, served as an indicator of the person's maturity: only the one whose bones had become solid was considered mature. This meant that one could no longer feel any soft cartilage at the joints, a condition which a male should reach by the time he is about twenty-five years old, according to McClellan (1975:329), who reported the existence of this belief among the Southern Tuchone, an Athapaskan group neighboring on the Tlingit. This close association of the bones with life, rebirth, and ritual potency explains their frequent use by shamans, witches, and ordinary human beings who sought and manipulated superhuman power (Emmons 1920–1945, ch. IX:13).[9]

Nonmaterial Components of the Person

In the Tlingit view of the person, a key distinction was made between the more idiosyncratic elements existing only as part of a living person and those immortal ones that were passed on through the matriline. An important attribute of a live human (and nonhuman) being was the breath, *daséikw* or *x'aséikw*, from *di-saa*, "to breathe." This term was also used to refer to the person's life (-force) and was comparable to the word "spirit" in some usages (Jeff Leer, personal communication, 1985; compare Veniaminov 1846:50). When a feather laid upon the lips of a moribund person ceased to move it meant death (de Laguna 1972:761). This explains why the jaws of the deceased were often kept artificially open and why the door of the house was supposed to be open when the dying person took his last breath (de Laguna 1972:761; compare Emmons quoted in Jonaitis 1978:66). Linguistic evidence suggests that breathing was also associated with the human ability to speak, give names to human beings and other living creatures, and call upon them.[10]

Another spiritual entity which existed primarily within a live body was the (*kaa*) *toowú*, (person's) "mind," "soul," "inner being," "feelings," or "inside." It was related to *tu*, a theme prefix indicating the inside of a closed container (Story and Naish 1973:350; de Laguna 1972:763). References to (*kaa*) *toowú*, this internal source and locus of thoughts and emotions, appear in such common expressions as *ax tuwáa sigoo*, "I want," *wáa sá ituwatee?* "how are you?," literally, "how do you feel?" *ax toowú yanéekw*, "I am sad," literally, "my mind/feelings are in pain," *a daa yoo tukataan*, "let me think it over," and *du toowú wulitseen*, "he/she became brave," literally, "his/her mind became strong" (Naish and Story 1973:226).

At death, the person's *toowú* left the body and presumably disappeared forever, since it is not mentioned in the descriptions of the land of the dead.[11] It appears that it could not exist without the body, its container. However, like other noncorporeal components of the person, the *kaa toowú* could be personified, for example, as a chickadee or a spider spinning its web close to one's head, seen as the loving thoughts of a friend, including those of a deceased one, which were believed to linger near the corpse and could even appear some time after the funeral.[12]

Unlike the breath and the mind/soul, several other nonmaterial entities were immortal and continued their existence in other locations, including the bodies of other people. One of them, (_ḵaa_) _yakgwahéiyagu_, denoted the spirit of a living or a dead human being (McClellan 1975:333–335; Kan 1979–1987). According to Swanton (1908:460) and de Laguna (1972:765–766), this entity continued to exist after the body died, visiting the living in dreams and reincarnating in a matrilineal descendant of the deceased.[13] The etymology of this word is difficult to establish, although de Laguna (1972:765) suspects that it meant approximately "a person's entity that is able to return" (analogous to the French word _revenant_). The capture of this entity by an evil spirit caused illness or death. It could also leave the body during sleep, coma, or a shamanistic seance, visiting other persons and entering their dreams. Thus a shaman could help his patient identify the person bewitching him by putting the witch's _yakgwahéiyagu_ into the patient's dream (de Laguna 1972:759). Death was perceived as being analogous to sleep, except that the spirit of the deceased failed to reenter the body. This idea is evident in the expression "sleep lives face to face with death" and the belief that a person who slept or yawned too much was bringing himself closer to death (de Laguna 1972:759).

Another frequently mentioned noncorporeal entity was the (_ḵaa_) _yahaayí_, which referred to the human spirit after death, shadow, reflection of the face, and, more recently, picture and photograph.[14] According to Leer (personal communication, 1985), it is based on a verb stem (-_ha_) referring to occult motion. As de Laguna (1972:766) explains,

> the basic idea is thus that of "image," or visible likeness or simulacrum, and is especially appropriate in describing a child as being or having "the image of her grandmother" when the child is the woman's reincarnation. A similar concept of simulacrum is involved in the explanation given to me that the fisherman catches and eats the same fish over again, provided that he burns their bones and so enables them to live and return in the next year's run. "When you get that fish, it is not the real fish. It's just the picture of it--_tsha_ [?] _yahaayí_."[15]

(_Ḵaa_) _yahaayí_ was also used as a metaphor denoting a resemblance between the ego and a member of a social category other than his own. Thus an aristocrat who violated the rules of appropriate behavior was called a "_yahaayí_ of a bastard."[16]

Following death, the *(ḵaa) yakgwahéiyagu* became the ghost that dwelled in the cemetery behind the village as well as the spirit that travelled to the village of the dead located far in the interior (Veniaminov 1984:398; Kamenskii 1985:71–73; Swanton 1908:460; de Laguna 1972:765). It remained in that distant abode forever, dwelling in the noncorporeal house of the lineage of the deceased together with his other matrilineal ancestors. The *(ḵaa) yahaayí*, however, stayed there only until it was able to return to the world of the living to be reincarnated in one of the deceased's close matrilineal relatives.

The same term, *s'igeekáawu*, was used for the ghost which dwelled in the nearby "village of the dead" (i.e., the cemetery) as well as the spirit located in the distant one. Both of the villages were called *s'igeekáawu aaní* (from *aan*, "village"). However, the interior one was sometimes also referred to as *ḵaa yahaayí aaní* (Swanton 1909:92; see Chapter V).

De Laguna's (1972:765–766) older informants in the 1940s–50s and some of my own in 1979–84 still used the terms *ḵaa yakgwahéiyagu* and *ḵaa yahaayí* occasionally but were somewhat uncertain about the difference between them. Nevertheless, they still distinguished between one entity that left the body at death and remained forever in the land of the dead (or the Christian Heaven) and another one that eventually returned and was reincarnated. Their views were not unlike those of their late nineteenth-century ancestors, summarized by Emmons (1920–1945, ch. VI:27) as follows:

> The Tlingit recognize three entities in man: *the material body; the spirit,* a vital central force through which the body functions during life and which, leaving the body, causes death; and *the soul,* a spiritual element that has no mechanical connection with the body and is eternal, dwelling in the spirit land or returning from time to time to live in different bodies. [Italics mine]

The data presented here allows me to distinguish among the deceased's ghost, spirit, and reincarnated spirit.

Keeping the Body Dry, Hard, and Heavy

The fear of pollution, and the consequent preoccupation with purity were central to the Tlingit view of the human body. Throughout their entire life, the Tlingit subjected themselves to periodic fasting, sexual abstinence, bathing in the cold sea, drinking salt water, scraping of the body with a special stone, and similar practices as an integral part of their rituals. With some modifications, these activities were involved in all Tlingit rites of passage (e.g., female puberty confinement, mourning, and in other crucial transitions) as well as in the preparation for hunting, warfare, potlatch, and other important and/or dangerous undertakings.

These practices aimed at self-purification were not unique to the Tlingit but were observed by most of the Northwest Coast Indians, Athapaskans, and other Native North Americans (Hultkrantz 1979). Drucker (1950:288), who also noted the importance of the ritual self-purification on the Northwest Coast, emphasized the practice of scraping away a good deal of epidermis in order to cleanse the body of human odors obnoxious to game as well as the supernatural powers who conferred good fortune on man.

This interpretation might apply to some of the area cultures but does not account for all of the aspects of self-purification among the Tlingit. An examination of the terms used to describe the goals of this activity suggests that in addition to removing the body scents, the Tlingit ritualist was trying to make the body drier, harder and heavier. This idea was emphasized by the use of various stones as scratchers, amulets, plates, and representations of wealth, longevity, and other attributes desired by the ritualist.[17] For example, the clothes of the Inland Tlingit pubescent female were weighed down with large stones in order to anchor her and prevent her from dying at a young age (McClellan 1975:387–388). Among the Coastal Tlingit, the rock for rubbing the mouth of the girl undergoing the puberty ritual was supposed to "make the lips lazy and the tongue heavy, so she would not cause trouble with her mouth" (i.e., cause by her gossip conflicts leading to feuding and warfare; de Laguna 1972:521). De Laguna's informants were quite explicit about the meaning of using the rocks, calling them "good, because they are heavy and cannot be moved" (de Laguna 1972:521).

To avoid wetness and make the body drier, the ritualist could only eat dried fish and dried meat. This designation of dry things and states as ritually potent and positive, in opposition to wet ones, is not surprising, given the damp, rainy environment of the Pacific Northwest. Throughout the entire Tlingit ceremonial system, we find an identification of dryness with the security of the human habitat and wetness with the danger of the sea and the forest (see Chapter V). A perfect example of this was the first in a series of rituals for the dedication of a newly built house, called "the drying of the house" (Olson 1967:62). Its name suggests a transformation of the wet wood from the forest into the dry timber brought into the human domain to construct the winter house, the ultimate cultural space. Similarly, the main methods of preserving food and preventing it from rotting were drying and smoking. In other words, the bodies of animals and fish were transformed into human food by means of the man-made fire.

The stone was a perfect symbol of dryness, hardness, and weightiness as well as longevity. It was the hardest, the most stationary, and the longest-lasting object in the Tlingit universe. No wonder that the matrilineal groups indicated their ownership of certain bodies of water and beaches by leaving their marks on large rocks (Emmons 1908). According to one of Swanton's informants, "Years ago people passing these rocks prayed to them, stuffed pieces of their clothing into the crevices, and asked the rock for long life" (1909:106). Unusually shaped rocks were often explained as human beings from the myth time turned, for one reason or another, into stone.[18] A certain mythological character famous for his strength was called *Eech*, "Rock" (Swanton 1909:193). In some ritual contexts, rocks represented people or were associated with human life. For instance, an Inland Tlingit pubescent girl, while in seclusion, had several stones placed around her. She referred to these stones as her children and wished these children to be "like stones and never die" (McClellan 1975:388).

Rocks (and other heavy objects) were also used to symbolize wealth. During the initiation quest of a prospective shaman, his helpers "pile up such things as stones to represent the property the shaman will accumulate. It is said that one shaman piled up snow and as a result was poor, for snow melts away" (Olson 1967:111). When a shaman was not satisfied with the amount of goods paid for his services, he asked for something "heavier" (McClellan 1975:539). In fact, this suggests that he was demanding more valuable gifts, since the same verb *ya-daal* was used to refer to heavy (usually inanimate) things, as well as precious, important, or highly esteemed objects, persons, and abstract phenomena, e.g., *'yadáli saa áwe i jeewú*, "you have an important (valuable, aristocratic) name." The same root *daal* with a different extensor *li* formed a stative verb "to be heavy" (usually in reference a live creature) and a transitive verb "to esteem someone equal to or better than another," e.g., _ḵaa yáanáx i kooxlidáal_, "I rate you higher than others, I think you are above everyone," literally, "I make you heavier than anyone" (Naish and Story 1973:81, 107–108, 113–114, 286–287).

These examples indicate that, throughout their entire lives and particularly during the rites of passage and the periods of preparation for dangerous and important activities, the Tlingit strove towards decreasing the polluting wetness of their bodies and increasing their dryness, hardness, and weight, the conditions symbolized by the stone and described as _té yáx kudaal_, "stonelike heavy" (compare de Laguna 1972:521). The goal of the Tlingit ritual self-purification was to acquire _laxeitl_, "good fortune, blessing." Whether it came only from super-human creatures and spirits, as Drucker suggests in the passage quoted above, or also from showing respect to the impersonal sacred order of the world by keeping one's body pure, as some of the Tlingit data suggest, it brought success to one's undertakings, good health, long life, and wealth (see Chapter V). On the other hand, the lack of purity and the presence of pollution in one's body resulted in _jinaháa_, "bad luck" or _ligaas_, the latter term referring to impure substances, unclean or ritually prohibited foods, violation of taboos, and other unlucky phenomena (Kan 1979–1987; de Laguna 1972:527–528).

Thus, the opposition between wet and dry was homologous to that between impure and pure, bad luck and good luck and, ultimately, between death and life. The last opposition was dramatically ex-pressed in one of the myths describing the birth of Raven, the Tlingit Creator-Transformer, as well as the myth describing his creation of man. According to the versions recorded by Veniaminov (1984:388), Swanton (1909:80–81) and several others, Raven's wicked maternal uncle kept destroying his sister's children, until she was advised to swallow a smooth stone from the bottom of the sea exposed at low tide. According to Swanton's informant (1909:80–81), the baby Raven she then gave birth to was called _Eechshaak'w_, "the name of a hard rock" and _Táḵl-éesh_, Hammer-father. Being made of stone, Raven was very strong and would not age or die, so that his uncle failed to destroy him (de Laguna 1972:845; 856). The original human population of the world, destroyed by the Flood, was transformed by Raven into rocks that cover the present surface of the earth. After the Flood, he created a new race out of leaves, which made them mortal. According to another version of the same myth, recorded by Swanton (1909:81),

> Raven tried to make them out of a rock and a leaf at the same time, but the rock was slow while the leaf was very quick. Therefore human beings came from the leaf. . . . That is why there is death in the world. If man had come from the rock there would be no death. Years ago people used to say when they were getting old, "We are unfortunate in not having been made from a rock. Being made from a leaf, we must die."

This version is a particularly interesting commentary on the fate of mankind. It suggests that being too much like stone was against human nature. The price to be paid for immortality was the lack of movement or, one might say, the absence of sociality. On the other hand, the ability to move was linked to mortality. This idea was reinforced by an emphasis on movement in the young age and its gradual decrease, as the person aged. Thus, while the old people spent much of their time sitting, including their favorite pastime of sitting on *rocks* for hours, observing (possibly meditating upon) the world around them, the young ones were supposed to "sit ready to get up all the time" and were discouraged from sitting on rocks, since that was supposed to make them slow as hunters (de Laguna 1972:513).[19]

The Inside Controlling the Outside

In addition to ensuring longevity and good fortune, the manipulation of the body and the marking of its surface (the outside, in my terminology) was aimed at keeping it under the control of society, represented by the person's own moral consciousness (i.e., mind/soul or what I refer to as the inside).

Most of the eyewitness accounts of the nineteenth-century Tlingit social life (e.g., Veniaminov 1984:431–434; Krause 1956: passim), as well as those based on memory ethnography (e.g., Olson 1956; de Laguna 1972:467–468), mention a great emphasis put on proper public conduct, self-restraint, and dignity, as well as an extraordinary sensitivity to ridicule and public embarrassment. This was, certainly, a "shame" culture, where the individual's conduct was carefully scrutinized and even minor *faux pas* could threaten his or her status and rank.[20]

The society's effort to control the individual began immediately after his or her birth, when the newborn's paternal aunt examined the body to see if it had a perfect form and straight limbs (Kan 1979– 1987).[21] Seriously deformed infants, especially of aristocratic background, were often killed.[22] The baby's carrier or pouch, made from a large basket cut in half, had a thin board down its middle "to keep the body of the baby straight and prevent it from being disfigured" (de Laguna 1965:6). Over the entire carrier was a skin cover that laced down the front, within which the baby was rigidly confined, leaving only the head free. As de Laguna's informant explained, "it keeps them straight so they don't get broken bones. The body don't get out of shape, and there is also something to keep their ears flat to their head . . . some sort of cap" (de Laguna 1965:6). The baby's body, as well as the umbilical cord, were subjected to a number of magical exercises to insure its health and future proficiency in such gender-related skills as hunting for men and basket-making for women (de Laguna 1972:504– 507; Drucker 1950:206; Kan 1979–1987).

The child's instruction also began early, even prior to birth itself. Thus I was told that a pregnant woman spoke to the fetus, instructing it in the proper ways to behave (Kan 1979–1987).[23] In addition to imposing its mold upon the infant's body, immediately after its arrival in this world, the society began restricting its behavior, the very minute the baby opened its mouth for the first time and began to cry. At that point, its breath was caught in a bag and carried to a well-trodden path so that it would be stepped upon. This process was supposed to prevent the child from crying too much (Swanton 1908:429). The child's lips were regularly rubbed with a special stone, until it was grown, to ensure that it became a quiet and peaceable person, who would "hold his hand over his mouth" (Olson 1956:681). As the child grew older, its body was manipulated further, to strengthen it and impose the appropriate markers of gender and rank on it, while the child's instruction in the norms and rules of society also intensified.[24]

In fact, the ritual treatment and marking of the growing body, the process of physical training, and education through verbal instruction, were interrelated and aimed at a single goal of producing a person who looked, behaved, spoke, and thought like a true Tlingit. This socialization of the child was based on the native theory of the relationship between the person's spiritual and material components. One postulate of this theory was that by strengthening his body the person was also strengthening his mind/soul. Thus, the practice of making boys bathe in icy cold water and whipping them with branches as they came out was aimed not only at turning them into strong hunters and warriors but making them physically pure as well as brave and patient. This is why the same term *latseen*, "strength," was used to describe both physical strength and moral fortitude, acquired through the above mentioned exercises, as well as the good fortune and future success they were supposed to bring.[25] One might also say that the goal of Tlingit education was to bring the child's physical and noncorporeal components into mutual harmony.

However, the emphasis on constantly monitoring and restraining one's actions, words and even facial expression, especially in public, suggests that the body was seen as being in need of control. Even a brief look at the Tlingit view of the characteristics of proper behavior and ideal personality is sufficient to confirm this (see also Chapter IV). A model person was even-tempered and mild-mannered, not greedy with food, careful of his or her words, always conscious of etiquette, respectful towards superiors and not condescending towards inferiors. Because of strong preoccupation with physical perfection, persons with serious bodily defects and handicaps could not aspire to high rank and status in Tlingit society.[26] Expression of emotion also had to be controlled and restrained, and this restraint greatly impressed many European observers (Krause 1956:109–110). Although there were a number of contexts in which strong anger or joy could be expressed, they were sharply separated from those situations where extreme self-control was required.[27]

The Tlingit used several methods of transforming the "natural" skin into the "social" one (T. Turner 1980), including perforation, incision, painting, and others. In addition, clothing was used as another layer of the body's surface and was believed to be closely associated with it. Of the unclothed areas of the body, the head and the face were the most important ones. The face was the main surface upon which the emotions as well as the social identity of the person were depicted.[28] Thus, damage to the face was seen as the most embarrassing. According to Emmons (1920–1945, ch. IX:14), "the Tlingit had a horror of personal disfigurement. In their hand to hand duels they delivered their blows only upon the body . . . . They never struck each other in the face." If a man of high status injured his face by falling down, especially in public, he was supposed to remain indoors until the marks had healed, and then give a small feast to his own clan to compensate it for the shame brought to it by this disfigurement (Oberg 1934:150). In addition, he and his clan gave a feast to those members of the opposite moiety who had witnessed the accident. As a matter of fact, any embarrassing event in the person's own life or in the life of his predecessors was referred to as a "(black) mark on his face" (de Laguna 1972:468). As one of my informants stated, "We, the old [i.e., traditionalist] Tlingit people, have a very thin skin on our face: the shame makes it red easily . . . but the young ones have no shame at all" (Kan 1979–1987). On the other hand, an individual's honorable action was said to "have lifted the faces of his kinsmen" (Kan 1979–1987).

Red and black colors, and a combination of both, were used to denote various emotional states, for example, black signified anger and sorrow, while red was used to paint the faces of the peace ritual's participants.[29] Sometimes the face was painted to hide the person's identity or emotional state, as, for example, when a warrior, who was suddenly surprised, would grab a piece of charcoal from the fire and rub it over his face to disguise his personality and hide any expression of fear (Emmons 1916:16). The perforation of the children's ears, nose, and lower lip seems to have been aimed at socializing the orifices of the head, which mediated between the inside and the outside of the body. The type of decoration (feather, copper ring, and others) worn in these orifices depended on the person's rank (see Chapter IV).

Women had an additional incision on their face, for wearing the labret. Sources disagree on whether the initial cut in the lower lip was made during the girl's infancy or the puberty confinement (Krause 1956:96–100). In any case, the first regular labret was the sign of her maturity and marriageability.[30] This decoration was the mark of womanhood par excellence. Europeans described Tlingit women being as much embarrassed about appearing without the labret as Western women would have been if caught naked.[31] The size of the labret increased as the woman grew older, marking the stages of her life's career. Aristocratic women wore labrets that were larger and made of more expensive materials, such as copper and abalone (Knapp and Childe 1896:63–64). Slaves were not allowed to wear them at all. Several native interpretations of the purpose of the labret, besides being a mark of womanhood (Jones 1914:68), have been reported. The most common one was that it prevented the woman from talking too much and made her speak slowly and quietly (Knapp and Childe 1896:79). According to Harrington's notes, based on the information obtained from a male informant, "A high-born Tlingit woman talked very little. The high-born Tlingit people had had experience of women talking too much and thereby causing gossip, dissensions, and wars, and that was why they made the women wear plugs" (quoted in de Laguna 1972:444). De Laguna and I heard similar folk interpretations and rationalizations of this custom. This explanation suggests a notion that societal control over the woman's body had to be especially strong (see Chapter VI).

However, the rule of controlling and weighing one's words was also applied to both genders, especially the high-born. The Tlingit believed in the power of the spoken word, which could be used for good or bad purposes. A careless comment could easily precipitate a fight or a feud, especially when addressed to members of the opposite moiety. When embarrassed, the Tlingit covered their mouths. Yawning was discouraged because that was how the dead communicated with one another—for them a yawn was a loud sound. Useful knowledge as well as evil secrets were transmitted from the mouths of animals to those of shaman and witches.[32]

Another surface of the head that was subjected to rigid cultural ordering was the scalp. The fundamental distinction between slaves and free persons was marked by the short hair of the former and the long hair of the latter. Women's hair was especially long; it was periodically trimmed but never cut. Long, thick hair was one of the main attributes of femininity, while its raven black color represented youth, so that special magic was used to prevent it from turning grey in older age.[33]

Men tied their own hair in a special knot before going into battle, and held on to a slain enemy's hair when scalping him. In fact, Emmons (1920–1945, Shukoff's Account:1–2) was told that the reason men wore long hair was to make it easier for them to scalp their slain enemies or to cut their heads off.[34] The shaman never cut his hair but wore it tangled into knots and balls. His hair was believed to be the seat of his life and power and cutting it was supposed to kill him.

A further association between hair and human life inhered in the notion that each person's life was like a line or a long hair. Violation of taboos, especially by initiates and other persons in liminal states, could cut his or her own line as well as those of his or her kin (Kan 1979–1987; compare McClellan 1975:335–336; compare Chapter VI). This special concern with grooming the hair and its association with the person's life itself was undoubtedly inspired by several of its qualities.

As Comaroff put it, "Human hair, in its protrusion from the body in space, its quality of both life and lifelessness, and its capacity for styling, is well suited to signify the extension of the persona in the social world; it lends itself to constriction through socialization" (1985:110; compare Leach 1958; T. Turner 1980; Obeyesekere 1981).

Aside from the head, special attention was paid to the hands, which remained unclothed and, among the aristocracy, were tattooed with the person's clan crest (see Chapters III and IV). The rest of the body was covered with clothing consisting of natural substances (skins, roots, wood) transformed through human labor into a social skin which both protected and concealed the natural one. Close association existed between the person's self and his or her clothing. In this respect, the latter was analogous to various bodily effluvia and such substances as hair and fingernails, which were periodically separated from the body. To harm his or her victim, the witch had to obtain these substances, clothing, or some of the victim's leftover food and then bring these into physical contact with the remains of the dead in the cemetery.[35]

Conclusion

In the Tlingit phenomenology of the person, the corporeal entities were sharply contrasted with the noncorporeal ones. The former, associated with the idiosyncratic individual, included the skin, the flesh, and the bones. The first two were perceived as wet, soft, and light and hence more susceptible to pollution. Throughout the person's life, various ritual observances were used to increase the dryness, hardness, and weight of the skin and the flesh. These outside layers and surfaces of the body were also seen as requiring societal control, in order to prevent unrestrained or shameful behavior. Hence, throughout the entire life cycle, the body was manipulated and modified to fit the model of a proper social person.

A very appropriate indigenous image that conjures this model of the body is a tightly closed container, a wooden box, so prominent in Tlingit life. I have already mentioned the homology between the body and the house, and would only add that boxes, houses, and human bodies were all containers of such valuables as property, knowledge, and human inhabitants. A container's contents could be released only very carefully and under special circumstances. Thus, certain treasured possessions of the house as well as its crests, hidden in boxes, could only be brought into the open in the course of the potlatch, just as certain words were only appropriate in that same ritual context.[36]

The homology between the body and the wooden containers that were so common in the Tlingit life is further supported by the use of the terms for body parts to refer to the parts of the house, particularly the door, which was the mouth of the house (x'awool, "doorway," from x'e, "mouth"). Similar to the human mouth, which had to be kept closed or covered most of the time, the door was quite small, so that one had to bend to go through it. Just as the bones—especially the "eight long ones"—and the spiritual components survived the person, the beams and posts forming the frame of the house survived the rest of the structure and were often incorporated into a new one, which retained the name and the inhabitants of the old one.[37]

Low-ranking individuals, outcasts, slaves, and especially persons who were not Tlingit, whose bodies did not conform to this model and who did not control and restrict whatever emerged from their inside into the public domain, were seen as incomplete persons, not fully human, lacking the refinement of a true lingít, the term denoting both "Tlingit" and "person."[38]

Despite the importance of the skin, and especially the face, as the surface upon which the social identity of the person (gender, age, rank) was depicted, it ultimately succumbed to the wet process of decomposition. The only weapon against it was cremation. In a way, the skin was only a mask, a temporary incarnation of the permanent noncorporeal components of the inside of the body. As Walens (1981:61) aptly puts it in his discussion of the Kwakiutl model of the human body,

> Beneath the skin is the human himself, his soul, his heart, his emotions and intellect, and all those parts of him that define him as an individual and a human being. . . . The skin is a medium that defines the individual by giving surface character to the individual and by limiting his behavior; but it is also a medium that conceals the true self beneath it.

chapter three

SHAGÓON AND THE SOCIAL PERSON
The Cultural Ideal

So far my discussion of the Tlingit view of the person has been focused on those attributes and characteristics that distinguished a human being from a nonhuman one, a Tlingit from a non-Tlingit, a free person from a slave. However, without the immortal ancestral heritage passed down primarily, though not exclusively, through the maternal line, the Tlingit individual lacked the most important dimension of his or her *social* identity.

Despite the importance of moieties for the ordering of the Tlingit social universe, the real unit of society was the exogamous, matrilineal clan, *naa*. Clans were believed to have originated after the Great Flood that marked the beginning of the present era in the history of mankind. It was during the Flood that future clans were believed to have separated from each other and migrated from the interior "back to the coast." In the course of that migration, they acquired the most important and sacred attributes of their collective identity, such as crests and their material representations, names of houses and persons, subsistence areas, myths, songs, and similar prerogatives. It was in the clan that political and legal authority was vested and personal loyalty centered (compare de Laguna 1983:71–72).[1]

The unity and solidarity of clan relatives were emphasized by the obligatory sharing of property and food that characterized their relationships. Mutual help among lineage mates was supposed to be particularly strong, yet it was also incumbent upon everyone belonging to the same clan to house and feed any of its members who should visit them, no matter how great the distance between their respective communities might be (Swanton 1908:427).[2] No immediate return was expected from matrikin, although a person who only received and gave nothing back was not respected. The relationship between consanguines was juxtaposed to that between affines, where balanced, rather than generalized, reciprocity characterized the exchange of gifts and services. Theoretically an individual was entitled to borrow any personal possession from his or her clanmate without payment. Assistance from clan relatives in subsistence activities, warfare, and other pursuits was not asked for but expected, and a person who refused to offer it was marked as a marginal member or even a nonmember of his or her matrilineal group. One of the key terms used to characterize intramoiety relationships was "love" (_kusax̱án_). The most commonly used idiom describing this sentiment was the mother's care for and nourishment of her child. Sharing of food was one of the main media of intraclan interaction, and matrikin were expected to "feed each other all of their lives" (Kan 1979–1987).

Close identification of clan relatives with each other was strengthened and dramatized every time one of them was insulted or injured, not to mention killed by a member of another clan. The victim's entire _naa_ was considered to be hurt and was responsible for avenging the wrong and wiping the shame "off its face." If a person injured a member of another clan, his or her own matrilineal group was held responsible and had to offer indemnity. When a clan was in a state of war, all of its male members were supposed to participate and show great bravery. The most honorable way to die was to do so on the battlefield and especially to volunteer to be killed in place of another, often senior, member of one's own clan, in a ceremonial slaying aimed at balancing the number of deaths on each of the warring sides, such balance being a prerequisite for restoring peace between the sides. To conceal the identity of one's clan, when overpowered by an enemy, was a terrible disgrace, even if it was done to save one's life (Olson 1967:70).[3] On the other hand, a person's accomplishments reflected favorably on his or her entire matrilineal group. Thus, every Tlingit was responsible for maintaining the well-being and reputation of his or her _naa_.

In light of this great emphasis on the solidarity of clan relatives, whose selves were seen as being extremely close to each other, it is not surprising that hurting and especially killing a fellow clansman was a terrible crime. Unlike conflicts between members of the opposite moieties, intraclan violence and serious disputes could not be resolved by an exchange of gifts or the peace ceremony. Minor insults and injuries were supposed to be ignored or forgotten, while those guilty of seriously injuring or murdering a clan relative were banished from the group or killed by its members. Both solutions involved the criminal's death: social, in the first case, and physical, in the second. Similarly, incestuous relations between clan members were punished by exile or death of both of the individuals involved.

This unity of clan relatives, especially members of the same house/lineage, was based on and manifested in several types of entities that together constituted a complete social persona. Since they figured so prominently in the funeral, we must discuss them in some detail. In many native ethnopsychologies (e.g., Kirkpatrick and White 1985), the maternal and paternal relatives of an individual contribute different elements that together constitute the total social person. This also seems to have been the case with the nineteenth-century Tlingit theory of the person. Unfortunately, much of it has been replaced by Western/Christian notions and can no longer be recovered.[4] Nevertheless, it is possible to outline the main features of this theory, using the data collected by de Laguna (1954; 1972) and others, as well as some additional information of my own.

The flesh and the skin were seen as a contribution of the child's maternal and paternal relatives, since its physical characteristics were expected to resemble those of its mother, father, and other kin from both moieties.[5] The maternal kin's contribution to the construction of the total social person had to be greater, since it was mentioned more often. Thus, for example, birthmarks and other marks on a child's skin were seen as the signs of the reincarnation of a certain of its clan relatives, and reincarnation was not supposed to occur across the moiety line. At the same time, a typical statement addressed to a person whose father belonged to the speaker's clan was a reference to a resemblance between his or her face and those of his or her classificatory fathers (Olson 1967:15–16).[6] There are also some indications that the bones were believed to be formed from the substance contributed by the mother (and possibly other matrikin). For example, the

Inland Tlingit said that the aristocratic status "followed the woman's backbone" (McClellan 1975:495).

The spiritual entities constituting the human being were seen as acquired primarily from his or her matrikin, since, after death, one spiritual entity dwelled in the distant village of the dead (in the non-corporeal house occupied by the lineage kin of the deceased) and another entity reincarnated in one of the deceased's close matrilineal descendants. However, the person's *yahaayí*, manifested primarily in the face, could be inherited from the paternal kin as well (de Laguna 1972:780–781). Behavioral characteristics could be inherited from one's maternal as well as paternal kin. Entire clans, as well as their classificatory children, were believed to possess such qualities as, for example, bravery.

An illegitimate child or one whose parents belonged to the same moiety was called *tléil du shagóon yan wuní*, a euphemism literally meaning "his ancestry is not settled," freely translated as, "he has no father to look ahead [and back] to," and explained in the following way, "it [the child] is not finished, like a carving" (McClellan 1975:381).[7] In fact, fatherless children were seen as incomplete persons, and this perception explains the practice of killing them at birth, especially if the parents were of aristocratic background. Such a child was called *tatóok yadí*, "cave/hole child," which suggests a comparison to an animal, born in a cave or a pit, without the assistance of other persons, especially its father's sister, a key participant in most Tlingit deliveries.

Despite the importance of the paternal side, the most essential attributes of the individual's social persona were shared with his or her clan relatives. Together they constituted the clan's *shagóon*, best translated as its "origin/destiny," established in the past by its matrilineal ancestors and continuing to order its members' lives, generation after generation (Kan 1979–1987; compare de Laguna 1972:813–814). Without discussing the *shagóon*'s key components and markers, particularly those forming part of the individual's social persona, we can neither interpret the meaning of the Tlingit mortuary rites nor comprehend the essential principles and characteristics of their entire sociocultural order.

Shagóon, which might be called the root concept in Tlingit culture, is a very complex notion. In its primary sense, it signified an individual's or a matrilineal group's ancestors, heritage, origin, and destiny. As one of de Laguna's (1972:813) informants explained, "*Shagóon* could be future, could be past. . . . In the future—that's what's going to happen, like who is going to be born through us, and where we are going to move, and what's going to happen." I was told by one elderly friend that *shagóon* meant "my ancestors before me who know what is going to happen [to me and my matrikin]" (Kan 1979–1987). The clan's totemic animal(s) as well as the crest(s) representing it were also called *shagóon*.[8] This term could be used with the possessive pronoun of the first person singular (*ax shagóon*), but more often that of the first person plural was used (*haa shagóon*).

In addition, because the ancestral past and the clan's destiny were imbued with sacredness, *shagóon* was also used to refer to an impersonal and abstract supreme being, which seems to have been an indigenous concept, as well as the personified creator in the guise of the Raven (Holmberg 1856:343). Thus, when facing a terrible danger, a Tlingit would pray to the *ax shagóon* or the *haa shagóon*, pleading for help. It appears that this was an address to the supreme being, although it is possible that the ancestors themselves were appealed to. If that was the case, these were not individual ancestors but a depersonalized collectivity of benign ancestral spirits (see Chapter V).[9] The idea of *shagóon's* connection with individual and collective good fortune is further supported by its antonym, *jinaháa*, translated as both "bad luck" and "unknown future" (Davis 1976:92; Kan 1979–1987).

The most important symbols of the matrilineal group, as well as its most jealously guarded possessions, were its crests. While all of the clans constituting a single moiety were entitled to the use of its crest (either raven or eagle/wolf), an individual person identified more strongly with the crests of his or her clan and house/lineage. As Emmons (1907:347) aptly put it, "The totem [crest] is . . . the birthright, as real as life itself. The personal guardian spirit may in extreme cases be destroyed or driven away . . . but no act can ever change the relationship of the Tlingit to his clan." Crests were named entities or objects, usually referring to animals, which were owned by matrilineal groups who were privileged to represent them on totem poles, house fronts, ceremonial headdresses and robes, and certain other objects of material culture. As Halpin (1984a:17–18) puts it in her discussion of Tsimshian culture, crests "were a legacy from myth time, acquired by the ancestors, and held in perpetuity by their [matri]lineal descendants."[10]

Most clans had one or several major crests and a number of secondary ones. The former were believed to have been acquired during the above-mentioned migration of clan ancestors' from the interior to the coast. The acquisition of each of the clan's crests was described and depicted in the myths, songs, and dances owned by it. As a rule this act involved an encounter between the clan's ancestors and an animal or other creature, which became the clan's crest. Although there was no taboo on killing one's crest animal, a certain affinity and resemblance between members of a matrilineal group and their crest animal was believed to exist. Thus, for example, members of the clan that claimed the brown bear as its crest were said to be brave. If members of a clan saw its crest animal being slain or mistreated by a person from another clan (and especially another moiety), they were expected to demand retribution.[11] Many of the clan's distinctions and prerogatives, including names, songs, houses, ceremonial calls, and so forth, were felt to be associated with its totemic crests. De Laguna (1972:451) suggests that "one might almost say that the members of the sib [clan] are the human embodiments of the totemic entities." The sacredness of the crest was indicated by its reverential treatment by its owners. When a certain object bearing the crest, for example, a canoe, began to show signs of deterioration, it had to be burned and mourned as a human being, rather than simply discarded (Kan 1979–1987). Its name was always transferred to a new object representing the same crest. Thus, the crest remained immortal, surviving its temporary representations, just as man's spiritual components survived the body.

Crests claimed by a clan were depicted on the surface of its members' bodies. They were tattooed on their hands, painted on their faces, and represented on the jewelry they wore. The bond between the person and his clan crest and the influence of the latter on the person's destiny were indicated by the above-mentioned practice of rubbing the child's mouth with a special stone depicting its clan crest. Some clans even owned certain facial expressions or scowls representing their crest animal.[12] In contrast to everyday clothing, the ceremonial garments always depicted clan crests. Thus, it was during potlatches and other rites involving the presence of the opposite moiety that a Tlingit achieved the most complete identification with his or her matrilineal ancestors and their totemic crest(s).

Unlike the crests, which the individual shared with other members of his matrilineal group, his names were his more intimate possessions, linking him with specific ancestors rather than the undifferentiated *shagóon* of his clan.[13] All of his names came from a large stock owned by his clan or, more often, his house. Each individual was given a number of names, from the birth names (or "real names," as de Laguna [1972:781] calls them) and the pet names given to the child by its mother, to the ceremonial ones bestowed in the potlatch, which were more like honorary titles.

The birth names were more closely linked to the individual's idiosyncratic persona, since they were usually taken from a certain ancestor whose spirit was believed to be reincarnated in him. Frequently an elderly person himself announced the identity of the woman, through whom he or she wished to come back to life. If the identity of the spirit was in doubt, a name of a close matrilineal ancestor (often a grandparent) was given and the act of naming itself, in effect, achieved reincarnation. As one of de Laguna's (1972:787) informants put it "the dead spirit knows it and the child knows it too. Then she knows who she is, whose spirit she belongs too." The spirit of the deceased whose name had been given was supposed to hear it announced and enter the child's body (de Laguna 1972:787). A child was often given more than one birth name and in that case not all of them were believed to represent a reincarnated spirit.[14]

The ceremonial titles, sometimes referred to as "big names," could only be given in a ritual context, in the presence of the opposite moiety, and had to be accompanied by a distribution of gifts among them. The memorial potlatch was the only context in which this was done and it was primarily in the potlatch that the big names were used. These names did not imply reincarnation, although the fact that the recipient was often a direct matrilineal descendant of and a member of the same house as the name's previous owner often led to the view that the former resembled the latter, in one way or another.[15]

Since each matrilineal group owned a limited stock of names and recycled them every two or three generations, we could say that the names themselves, especially the birth names and potlatch titles, rather than the people temporarily carrying them, were its true members. As long as there were persons to give the names to, the matrilineal group was alive and, if there were not enough people to carry them, members of related houses and clans were adopted and given the names.[16]

The idea that the names were primary and their holders secondary is supported by the fact that each ranked title carried a certain prestige and social value (Olson 1967:48). These could be lost through their holders' inability to participate in potlatches and meet other social obligation expected of them, but it took more than one generation to lower a high ranking name's status and value. According to Olson (1933–1954, notebook 9:65), a person repaying a debt usually paid more than the original amount "for the honor of his name." If a debt was passed on for more than one generation, a larger amount was usually paid. The was not considered interest but a question of the name's honor.

The names were much more than labels: they resembled such "man-made" attributes of the individual's social persona as ceremonial garments and crest objects. Thus, Olson (1933–1945, notebook 5:52) was told that "those to be reincarnated go to a place no one knows where and when they are to come back *they carry (as a bundle) under their arm that same name* which is therefore given to them" (italics mine). Emmons (1920–1945, ch. VI:22) reported that "the name was considered as almost part of the person, like hair or body secretions."[17] The name was said to be given "to the face of" its recipient (Johnson 1979:6) and was described as having weight.[18]

The link between an individual's personhood and his or her name was also indicated by the practice of renaming a person, especially a child, who was afflicted by a severe illness, as if to start his life anew by giving him a different identity. Occasionally two persons had the same name. In most cases, they resided in different communities and rarely came in contact with each other. However, if it happened, de Laguna found they treated each other very affectionately and addressed each other as *ax x'ai*, probably meaning "my darling," or *ax saayí*, "my name" (de Laguna 1972:781; 783). Individuals carrying the same name were treated as if they were the same person, so that the kin terms that might apply to one man and his family were used for his namesake and the latter's family as well (de Laguna 1972:476).[19] The Tlingit were very anxious to see their names perpetuated and would sometimes relinquish and bestow them on their junior matrikin, to make sure they "would not die" (Kan 1979–1987). If an elderly person was angry at his matrikin, he might announce that he was never coming back. At his death the survivors' sorrow was particularly great, because his name was "dying forever" (Olson 1933–1954, notebook 9:4).

The names themselves often referred to the holder's crest. For example, a name might be an allusion to a certain characteristic of the crest animal. The name "Rough Skin" was owned by the Frog Clan and referred to the skin of this animal.[20] Thus the names reinforced the bond between the individual and the *shagóon* of his or her matrilineal group.[21]

In addition to being imprinted upon the body of its members, the *shagóon* of a lineage or clan was passed down to them in the form of ancestral myths, songs and dances, many of them depicting and describing the ancestors' exploits and crests. By learning about the history of one's matrilineal group through these media, a Tlingit internalized the essential attributes of his group's identity and became a truly mature person.[22]

The Social Reality

The ideology of matrilineal solidarity was powerful and pervasive, yet it was frequently contradicted at the level of social action and practice. As I have stated earlier, intralineage conflicts were common, with the closest matrikin often being the most bitter enemies. Unequal distribution of power, authority, prestige, and wealth among lineage mates was at the root of much of the jealousy that pitted a person (especially male) against his older sibling of the same sex, or nephews against their maternal uncles. If the disputants were two males vying for leadership in their house, each supported by his immediate kin, their conflict often led to fission, with the junior male establishing his own "daughter house" as an independent unit. This process was endemic to the matrilineage, since the house could accommodate only so many persons, before it became overcrowded. Yet because of a heavy emphasis on lineage solidarity, this fission was often seen as unfortunate and blamed on some in-married members of the opposite moiety. Thus, for example, a conflict between two male lineage mates would be attributed to a sexual liaison one of them allegedly tried to establish with the wife of the other.[23] More tragic than fission were witchcraft accusations which often tore the lineage apart.

Just as bitter were disputes between lineages of the same clan. These, however, centered more often on shared crests and other attributes of the common *shagóon*, rather than on interpersonal conflicts. Thus, for example, when a daughter house tried to establish itself as a fully independent unit by laying claims on the original crest of its "mother house," the latter was likely to reject them. The former had to either invent a new crest, whose value would remain rather low for at least some time, or use a modification of the original one. For example, if the killer whale was claimed by the mother house, its new offshoot might begin to claim the killer whale's dorsal fin. If the two houses managed to maintain friendly relations, they would be seen as closely related and would cooperate in warfare, potlatching, and other activities. However, the more powerful of the two, which was usually, but not necessarily, the mother one, might downplay that tie by referring to the members of the other one as the "people of the house next door," or denigrate their status by making allusions to slaves and low caste persons among their ancestors.

Finally, the most bitter conflicts occurred between two clans of the same moiety. Their causes were similar to the intraclan ones, but here warfare was a common solution. Theoretically, clans of the same moiety were not supposed to fight and in some areas could not even perform the peace ritual, but accounts of warfare reveal that intramoiety violence was equally if not more common than intermoiety violence (see Olson 1967; de Laguna 1972). Thus, two powerful clans could share the same major crest, due to independent invention or common ancestry, yet might refuse to see each other as closely related. As long as they lived far away from each other, the disagreement might simmer, without erupting. If, however, they began residing in the same community, as happened in the post-contact era, with the consolidation of native groups in areas of European and American presence, confrontation was inevitable. Sometime, a solution could be reached through negotiation and potlatching, with the more powerful clan usually enforcing its will on the weaker one (see Chapters VII and IX), but often such conflicts remained unresolved.[24] Of course, their ties and kinship sentiments were not expected to be as strong as those between lineage and clan mates.

Related to this contradiction between the cultural ideal and the reality of social life, was a discrepancy between the *shagóon*'s denial of time and the individuality of the human being, on the one hand, and the actual life of persons and their matrilineal groups, on the other. Thus, ideally, the clan had a limited supply of names and other ancestral prerogatives, perpetually recycled in every generation. In this cyclical model, the living were the incarnations of their dead matrikin, whose life they were said to be imitating. This concept left little room for individuality and made a person's idiosyncratic biography and accomplishments relatively insignificant.

In real life, crests, names, and other attributes of *shagóon* were constantly added to the stock of sacred possessions of the matrilineal clan and lineage. These could be invented, transferred from other groups as gifts, or captured from them through force or as compensation for damages (compare de Laguna 1952:4–5). Despite the fact that the clan's older prerogatives were valued higher than its more recent ones, exotic objects were often adopted as new crests, just as exotic trade items were sought as treasures.[25] Some prerogatives, such as names, might even be abandoned, if their last bearer had seriously disgraced his matrilineal group.[26] The hierarchy of titles within a lineage or clan was also far from immutable. Through personal success in accumulating wealth, potlatching, and other activities, an individual could increase the value of his or her name, value which remained attached to the name in the next generation. Of course, the name's position in the hierarchy could also be lowered.[27]

Despite the emphasis on pedigree and ascription, individual and collective achievement were also important in Tlingit social life. A person was expected to do his best to increase his personal status and prestige and, through that, the status and prestige of his matrilineal group. Theoretically, individual effort was supposed to be coordinated and harmonized with the collective one, but such coordination was not always the case. Hence, despite the centrality of matrilineal solidarity and conformity, individual effort and personal autonomy were important, and a person's life was not a carbon copy of that of his or her deceased namesake.

chapter four

THE ARISTOCRAT AS
THE IDEAL PERSON

In spite of the centrality of the ideology of matrilineal unity and solidarity, members of the same lineage or clan did not have equal knowledge of and access to their group's *shagóon*. The ethos of love between matrikin, united by their reverence for the ancestors and the ancestral crests, as well as the bonds of sharing, mutual care, and collective responsibility, coexisted with inequality, hierarchy, and the subordination of juniors to seniors, women to men (in certain contexts), and especially commoners to aristocrats. While I can discuss the relationship between the young and the old only very briefly, and must postpone the analysis of the position and image of the woman until Chapter VI, the role of the aristocracy in social life and the conceptual/symbolic foundation of its status and power will be examined in some detail.

Although much has been written about hierarchical relationships in Northwest Coast societies, they have not been examined from the point of view of ethnopsychology. By analyzing the Tlingit theory of the person as an ideology legitimizing ranking and inequality, I offer a more nuanced and rounded interpretation of the nature of hierarchy in that society which combines indigenous and exogenous criteria. This discussion sheds new light on the much-debated issue of rank versus class in Northwest Coast societies, while also building a foundation for my analysis of the mortuary rites of the aristocracy.

The Old and the Young, the Seniors and the Juniors

Old people were treated with great respect. Their judgments were deferred to, even if they were senile or ignorant (Kan 1979–1987; de Laguna 1972:465). The oldest member of a matrilineal group was called *kaa shukaadekáa,* literally, "the first one;" also glossed as "the wisest person," "the head person," "the advisor." This could be either a man or a woman whose age linked him or her with the group's *shagóon.* Structurally and symbolically the clan's oldest member was already on the way to becoming an ancestor and hence occupied an intermediate position between the living and the dead matrikin. Because of that, the funeral of a *kaa shukaadekáa* rivaled that of a high-ranking aristocrat in its elaborateness. Senior members of a clan were idealized by their younger matrikin, just as "the ancestors of past generations were held up as models of conduct to be emulated by the living" (de Laguna 1972:465). Even the head of the matrilineal group had to listen to the elders and defer to their judgment. On the other hand, doubt was often cast upon the accuracy of a statement simply because the person who made it was young (de Laguna 1972:465). The respectful way to treat elderly persons was to offer them the tastiest food, never to argue with or interrupt them, not to look them straight in the face, and not to pass them in the street (de Laguna 1972:529–530; 476–477; Kan 1979–1987). The proper way to address any elderly member of one's own, as well as the opposite moiety, was *ax léelk'w,* "my grandparent." The fact that this term does not indicate either the gender of the addressee or his or her moiety affiliation suggests that from the point of view of their special wisdom and authority, the elders constituted a single undifferentiated group.[1]

What gave the elders such power and prestige? The most obvious answer is their knowledge of their matrilineal group's *shagóon.* However, I believe that the indigenous view of their bodies and noncorporeal components was also the basis of their superiority. As I have demonstrated in Chapter II, man's struggle for the purity and heaviness of his body was a life-long endeavor. I suggest that an older person's body was perceived as heavier and more pure. Those who had passed the age of sexual activity had an additional advantage vis-à-vis their younger kin: their bones were drier and heavier. Finally, because of their greater wisdom and experience, their spiritual attributes (the inside) had greater control over their behavior and the body itself (the outside). The elders were seen as being wiser because they had more thoroughly internalized the rules of social conduct than their younger kin, who were expected to possess less self-control.

In my opinion, these ideas explained and legitimized the superiority of the old over the young. They also justified the submission of the younger sibling to the authority of the older one[2] and the man's power over his sisters' children.[3] Seniority was one of two idioms of authority, aristocratic status being the other one. In fact, the two were interrelated, since heads of matrilineal groups and other aristocrats were perceived, as and often were, the senior kin.

Northwest Coast Sociopolitical Systems: Class Versus Rank

The debate about the nature of stratification on the Northwest Coast began as early as the 1930s and is still going on. Its main issue has been whether Northwest Coast societies had classes or ranks. The basis and the nature of the aristocracy's authority and power, the degree of social mobility, and the negotiability of status differences between the aristocrats and commoners have also been central to this discussion (compare Adams 1981). Despite some important differences between them, most of the existing arguments can be reduced to two major positions. On the one hand, such scholars as Drucker (1939; 1963:124–131; 1965:47–49), Codere ([1957] 1967), Fried (1967:109–184), Murdock (1936), Halpin (1973), Seguin (1985), Boelscher (1985), and several others insist that Northwest Coast societies were rank-based. Thus Drucker (1939) spoke of an "unbroken series of graduated statuses," rather than "classes," while Codere (1967:150) argued that Kwakiutl commoners could not be considered a class, since they had no "continuous or special function" and no "identity, continuity, or homogeneity as a group, and no distinguishing culture or subculture." On the other hand, Ray (1955), Garfield (1939), Ruyle (1973), Kobrinsky (1975), Adams (1973), and Blackman (1982) indicate that classes did exist, some of them adding that the upper class exploited the lower one. Tlingit ethnographers also disagree on this. While Shotridge (1913), Oberg (1973), and Tollefson (1976) used the term "class" and insisted on a relatively sharp distinction between the upper and the lower class, Olson (1967) and de Laguna (1972; 1983) spoke of graded ranks rather than classes.

A major problem with this debate has been a disagreement among its participants about the exact meaning of the term class. In addition, until fairly recently many of them did not systematically consider whether social stratification was an objective or a subjective reality for the native people themselves. Even those few studies that did examine the indigenous view of rank, such as Suttles' ([1958] 1967) classic paper on "private knowledge, morality, and social class" among the Coast Salish and Goldman's insightful (1975) analysis of Kwakiutl religion, failed to pay equal attention to the symbolism and the sociology of stratification. My own objective is to overcome the one-sidedness of these works by looking at rank from the perspective of an outsider as well as from that of the Tlingit themselves, and by examining it as a total social phenomenon, paying attention to its religious, political, and other dimensions and their interrelationship.

Ranking in Tlingit Society: The Ethnographic Evidence

To make sense of the nature of Tlingit social stratification, one must begin by evaluating the earliest descriptions of that society, made in the first half of the nineteenth century, before it was seriously affected by contact with the Europeans and especially the Americans. Despite their biases, a number of early Russian observers made insightful comments on the subject. Thus Langsdorff, who visited several Tlingit communities in the early 1800s, saw chiefship and high rank being based on achievement rather than ascription. In his words,

> age, superiority of natural understanding, or temporal wealth . . . or the great numbers of persons of which a family consists—these seem to be the requisites for obtaining respect and distinction among the Tlingit. The proper designation of a chief among them seems to be the head of a numerous family; he exercises unlimited power over all the branches and members of it, they are his subjects. . . . (1814, vol. 2:129–130; italics mine)

Lisianskii, who visited Sitka during the same period, agreed with this view, when he said that, despite the inheritance of property "from uncle to nephew," the position of leadership usually went to the "strongest man and the one who had more relatives." However, in contrast to Langsdorff, he thought that the chiefs' authority over their subjects was rather limited ([1812] 1947:216).

Khlebnikov, who, between 1817 and 1832, compiled fairly detailed notes about the Tlingit, agreed with Lisianskii that

> The chiefs in each clan are acknowledged as elders, but *have no authority over anyone.* They cannot assign anyone to a particular job or service. A chief might be accompanied on a long-distance expedition or assisted in some work only as a gesture of good will. *The status of chiefs is hereditary.* . . . The status of a Tlingit is established according to the number of relatives; but his wealth consists of slaves. (1985:86; translation and italics mine)[4]

Finally, Veniaminov, a Russian missionary who observed the Tlingit in the 1830s, noted that despite the importance of wealth in determining status, the impoverished descendants of the nobility retained their rank for several generations (1984:424).

Comments like these suggest that the leadership position and aristocratic status in Tlingit society were based on a combination of ascription and achievement, with the headman's pedigree and wealth, as well as the size of the kinship group under his authority, being the key factors determining his rank and status. It also appears that his control over his kin was rather limited.

Krause, a German naturalist who spent an entire winter in the early 1880s in a northern Tlingit village and visited several others further south, reiterated the views of his Russian predecessors and emphasized the crucial role played by aristocrats in ceremonial life. In his words,

> The power of the [clan] chief is very limited and the direction which it takes depends on the personality of the individual. Only in cooperative undertakings and in council is he a leader; in everything else every family head is entirely free to do anything which is not counter to custom and which does not infringe on the rights of others. . . . Also the so-called aristocracy does not possess any particular privileges except the high esteem in which they are held by their tribesmen. At feasts they are given places of honor and the richest presents are given to them. For the death or injury of an important person greater compensation is demanded than for a person of lesser rank; two or more lives being payment for one chief. (1956:77–84)

Differing perceptions of the relative significance of heredity and wealth as determining factors in establishing individual and collective rank and status continued in the late nineteenth and the early twentieth centuries. Thus, Jones, a Presbyterian missionary who labored among the Tlingit in the 1900s, wrote that,

there are four strata of Thlinget [sic] society, the high, medium, low and the
slaves. . . . They all mingle in the community, the low and the high visiting and
talking with one another. But in marriage, at feasts, in public councils, and in
the settlement of wrongs and injuries, class distinctions are always asserted.
(1914:59)

Even in Jones' time, wealth could not override hereditary status. Thus,
for example, when one low-ranking man gave a substantial
bridewealth for a woman of high rank, her family refused to accept it
(1914:59). Writing at the turn of the century, Emmons stated that "the
position and blood of a high caste family is respected even if it becomes poor" (n.d.: notebook 7).

Much of the data on the traditional system of social stratification
obtained by the anthropologists in the twentieth century comes from
memory ethnography. Nevertheless, some fundamental indigenous
ideas about rank and status have persisted (particularly among the
older and the more conservative people) and the manifestation of these
ideas in social action could still be observed (see Olson 1967; de
Laguna 1972; Kan 1979–1987).

Most of the ethnographers agree that the criteria for defining a
person's aristocratic status were fairly clear. They included the high
rank and wealth of his parents (especially the mother), the number and
the scale of the potlatches sponsored by them in his honor, his marriage to a person of equal or higher rank, and his accomplishments in
those activities that generated wealth and enabled him to give his own
potlatch(es) or actively participate in those given by his matrikin (compare Olson 1967:47–48). De Laguna (1972:461–462; 1983:74–75) sum-
marizes these criteria succinctly as birth, age, wealth (inherited and
acquired), personal accomplishments, and character.

The existing data also indicate the absence of classes or castes
sharply separated from each other. Instead, there was a series of
graduated statuses, with each free person having his or her own particular status in it, from high to low. Ranking was not absolute, instead,
each person's status was evaluated relative to that of another. The
same was true of matrilineal groups. As de Laguna (1972:461–462)
points out,

When comparisons were made, they seem to have been largely in terms of
specific individuals, as between a chief and a man in his sib [clan] who could
not aspire to his position, or between a man in one sib and a person in another
who was of equal rank and so could be exchanged for him in a peace
ceremony.[5]

Thus, while aristocracy was a well defined cultural category, a person's membership in it and the relative ranking of individuals and kinship groups was open to dispute, negotiation, and re-evaluation. It was ultimately tested and temporarily frozen in the course of the potlatch. This fluidity of rank was particularly true of the persons located between those on the very top of the hierarchy, whose aristocratic status was absolutely clear, and those on the very bottom, whose commoner status was undeniable. Completely outside this social order were the slaves—the only group that could be characterized as a separate class.

Just as the occupants of the house were ranked, so were the houses within the clan. The head of the leading house in the clan was its chief or "big man" (lingít tlein). The heads of the other houses and the clan elders formed his council. There was no village or tribal chief, although the head of the most prestigious clan in the community had more influence and prestige than his peers in other clans. Clans were also graded within the moiety, within the local tribe, and between moieties and tribes, but on no exact scale. Some houses and clans were described as low-ranking, while others were seen as very high, because of their wealth, their numbers, their many crests, their past victories in war, and the lavishness of their recent potlatches (compare de Laguna 1983:74–75).

On the basis of the information obtained by ethnographers in this century, the following preliminary conclusions about the Tlingit system of social stratification can be made. Heads of matrilineal groups and their immediate matrikin, who were the most likely candidates for the aristocracy, did not form a separate class but were seen as the senior relatives of their lineage and clan mates of lower rank. In fact, a major problem, pointed out by most ethnographers, has been defining the commoners as a group and obtaining information about them (e.g., Olson 1967:47–48; see below).[6]

The heads of the matrilineal groups acted as the custodians of their collective corporeal and noncorporeal possessions. Thus they did not own the subsistence areas belonging to their lineages and clans but supervised their use by their matrikin. As informants often put it, the chief "took care of the land," that is, allotted the hunting grounds within his territory to his various male matrikin (Kan 1979–1987; compare de Laguna 1972:361). He was also responsible for deciding when the hunting and fishing seasons would open and made sure that each man obtained about the same amount of animals and fish. There are even some indications that in certain communities, the chiefs redistributed the surplus food they accumulated to the poor members of the group. They also granted permission to nonmembers to obtain food in the areas owned by their kinship group, once the latter had obtained enough provisions. The chiefs did some fishing and hunting themselves but also received part of their kinsmen's catch. Even though there was no legal obligation to share with the chief, the hunters felt morally obliged to do so (de Laguna 1972:379–380).

In addition to serving as the trustees of their matrikin's subsistence areas, lineage heads, along with their immediate kin, supervised trade with other Tlingit as well as with foreign tribes (compare Tyjberg 1977) and acted as war leaders. Few important decisions were made unilaterally by the heads of the matrilineal groups; instead, they consulted the council of elders and aristocrats that existed on the level of the house as well as the clan (compare Emmons 1920–1945, ch. IX:12; Tollefson 1976:100; Kan 1979–1987). All of the activities supervised by the chiefs resulted in the accumulation of the surplus food, furs, and exotic trade items in the hands of the aristocracy. Their duty was to use that wealth to sponsor feasts for their own matrikin, and potlatches that involved the participation of the opposite moiety.

Prestige Structures

If the Tlingit aristocracy was neither a caste nor a class, what was it? I propose to look at it as Weber's (1958) "status group" or Sahlins' (1968) "status level." A good summary of Weber's views on this subject is provided by Giddens:

> The status situation of an individual refers to the evaluations which others make of him or his social position, thus attributing to him some form of (positive or negative) social prestige or esteem. A status group is a number of individuals who share the same status situation. Status groups, unlike classes, are almost always conscious of their common position.
>
> Status groups normally manifest their distinctiveness through following a particular life-style, and through placing restrictions upon the manner in which others may interact with them. (1971:166–167, quoted in Ortner and Whitehead 1981:14)[7]

I also suggest that the Tlingit sociopolitical organization could be characterized as a "prestige structure" (or "prestige system"), a concept introduced by Ortner and Whitehead (1981:13), following Weber. In their model, prestige—or "social honor" or "social value"—assumes somewhat different qualities and falls in different quantities on different persons and groups within a society. The "prestige structure," then, includes "the sets of prestige positions or levels that result from a particular line of social evaluation, the mechanisms by which individuals and groups arrive at given levels or positions, and the overall conditions of reproduction of the system of statuses" (Ortner and Whitehead 1981:13).

The usefulness of this concept is demonstrated by Ortner's (1981) own analysis of gender and sexuality in Polynesia, a "culture area" which shares with the Tlingit and other Northwest Coast societies an emphasis on ranking and the hierarchy of statuses (compare Goldman 1970; 1975). In fact, the structure and functioning of the Polynesian rank system, as summarized by Ortner, are rather similar to those of the Tlingit.[8] To begin with, as she points out,

> rank in Polynesia operates through the kinship system. The primary units of social, economic, and political organization are (internally stratified) descent groups, at the apex of which stand the "chiefs" who collectively constitute the "aristocracy" of the society. Such descent groups are sometimes ranked in relation to one another. . . . Ranking is continuous from top to bottom, the principles of seniority of descent producing a gradation of superiority and inferiority that encompasses all members of the group. In addition, a categorical distinction is made between "aristocracy" and one or more nonaristocratic status groups. The terminological distinction is clear enough, but there is no clear separation between the low-ranking "aristocrats" and the high-ranking "commoners." (1981:362)

As with the Tlingit, Polynesian commoners were hard to identify, since all members of a tribe were connected with well-born families. Nevertheless, Ortner argues, there seems to have been a definite rule which stated that within the descent group, "the aristocracy" consisted of the senior line—the chief, his senior son, *his* senior son, and so on. Thus, from a perspective external to any given descent group, the aristocracy of the society as a whole consisted of all the senior lines of all the descent groups.

Tendencies toward the consolidation of the aristocracy into a society-wide self-conscious group were present with respect to marriage as well as in visiting and feasting patterns. Nevertheless, says

Ortner, the fact that in most Polynesian societies the aristocrats were the commoners' senior kin placed constraints on class formation, as well as on class conflict. The aristocracy shared at least as many interests with their own commoner kin as with other members of their status group. The chief was more a representative of his kinship group within the aristocratic circle, than a member of an exclusive class with interests divergent from those of the class of commoners.

Ortner (1981:362) also suggests that Polynesian politics, economics, and religion are all best understood with reference to the descent group organization and tendencies towards ranking. Thus she sees power and authority as being

> fairly directly ordered by the nesting structure of the ranked units within the descent group. Chiefs have both more power and wider power; lesser aristocrats (such as heads of junior lineages) have less power, and over smaller units; and so down to household heads. Power is a direct function of status position. It is not primarily a function of wealth per se (though chiefs are generally a little richer than everyone else); and it is not, except in the most complex, "stratified" societies, a direct function of control over economic production.

Similar to the chief's political authority, his role in the economy was a function of his kinship seniority. In the absence of force-sanctioned surplus extraction mechanisms, his capacity to draw resources to himself depended upon normal mechanisms of kinship prestations and exchanges. Although chiefs had a certain regulatory role in production and were the ultimate titular owners of all the land, they, as well as the aristocracy in general, did not have actual control over the distribution of the means of production (primarily land), or over the actual execution of production. However, within the distribution system the chief was focal. Surplus food and other types of wealth were given to him by his kinsmen, and he in turn redistributed most of it through the structure of the kin group. Redistribution was one of the most important duties and privileges of chiefship in Polynesia; it demonstrated the chief's power in terms of his ability to command resources from a wide group, as well as his leadership qualities, in the sense that his wide distributions appeared as generosity, and as concern for the welfare of his entire kin group (Ortner 1981:364).

Finally, the aristocrats' access to supernatural power and the degree of their personal sacredness followed the same lines as their political power and authority and their special role in the economy. Ortner insists on the centrality of religious beliefs in the structure and functioning of societies organized by the principles of rank and hierarchy. As she and Whitehead point out,

> prestige structures are always supported by, indeed they appear as direct expressions of, definite beliefs and symbolic associations that make sensible and compelling the ordering of human relations into patterns of deference and condescension, respect and disregard, and in many cases command and obedience. These beliefs and symbolic associations may be looked at as a legitimating ideology. A system of social value differentiation, founded on whatever material base, is fragile and incomplete without such an ideology. (1981:14)

Many of the key features of Polynesian hierarchical societies outlined here also characterized Northwest Coast societies, although they were probably less developed among the Tlingit than among the Coast Tsimshian or the Nootka. While the nature of the economy and the political system in Northwest Coast societies has been described and analyzed in several anthropological works, the relationship between them and the ideational system has not been sufficiently explored.[9]

Beliefs about the special qualities of the aristocrats' social persona which served to legitimize their superior position in the Tlingit social hierarchy, were an important part of the latter system. Ethnopsychological ideas served as the yardstick by which an individual's rank and status were measured. My symbolic analysis of the native view of the person not only sheds new light on the question of Tlingit (and Northwest Coast) rank but also serves as the foundation for the main goal of this work, the interpretation of the Tlingit mortuary rites in general, and those of the aristocracy in particular.

Aristocratic Status and Power in Light of Ethnopsychology

The importance of both ascription and achievement in the Tlingit view of the aristocracy, suggested earlier, is well illustrated by the treatment of an aristocrat's body, beginning at birth. The significance of ascription should not be underestimated. Only a child of a wealthy aristocratic couple had a good chance to rise high in the social hierarchy. Until such a child reached maturity, its parents had to mark every major stage of its life with a feast and a distribution of gifts among the child's affinal/paternal kin. These life cycle rites involved marking the child's body with the signs of aristocratic status and bringing it into physical contact with wealth.[10] Sometimes such rites as the piercing of the child's ears, nose septum, and lip (for the girl), tattooing of its hands, and naming were performed as part of a memorial potlatch. Quite often, however, separate feasts were held, which cost the parents even more.

The key role in these mini-potlatches in honor of children was played by the child's father, who distributed gifts to members of his own moiety, who were often his siblings and other close matrikin. This seems to contradict the fundamental principle of the exchange of gifts and services between members of the opposite moieties. Veniaminov (1984:424), the first to report this type of ritual, understood its uniqueness very well, when he pointed out that it was performed on rare occasions and by very few wealthy men, because unlike the memorial potlatch, the expenses incurred when giving a feast for one's children could never be recouped.[11] According to him, only the persons with pierced ears were considered aristocrats, and even those of their descendants whose own ears were not pierced (because their families did not have the means to sponsor the ear-piercing ceremony) were respected. Each perforation required a separate feast, and only the very wealthy could sponsor eight of them, so that their children had eight holes in their ears (Veniaminov 1984:424).[12] Olson (1967:69) agrees with this information, indicating that

> only a very high born and very rich man may give such feasts. And the right to do so is hereditary. His own lineage in his clan must have done so in the past. The songs the host sings are those sung by the first man in the ancestry who gave such a feast. This one and all others who gave these feasts are named. Thus he publicly validates his right to give the feast. . . . A man who attempts such a festival without the inherited rights is sure to be greeted with smirks and silence.

This seems to indicate the aristocracy's efforts to make its status strictly hereditary and prevent others from joining their social group. However, occasionally a man without such a hereditary right gave an ear-piercing rite for his children. As long as he did not claim the hereditary right to do so he was not ridiculed. (Olson 1967:69)

Aristocrats used every opportunity to reiterate and raise their children's and through them, their own status and rank. Thus, a high-ranking father or maternal uncle of a newborn infant could transform a relatively low-key naming ceremony into a small feast with the distribution of food and gifts to members of the moiety opposite to that of the infant. While an ordinary child's first name was not a valuable ceremonial title, an aristocratic child could receive one very early in its life. The giving of such a title to a small child was an indication that he was expected to sponsor large-scale potlatches himself when he grew up (Veniaminov 1984:416).

The Pure and Heavy Body

The marking and decoration of the bodies of aristocratic children could be seen as an imposition of society's control on the natural (i.e., uncontrolled) body. In addition to being more controlled, the bodies of aristocrats were made heavier by being brought into physical contact with wealth (i.e., heavy objects). Thus, the climax of a potlatch that took place in Sitka in 1877 was the naming of the chief host's grandchildren. In the course of it, the children's foreheads were rubbed with a special copper shield (*tinaa,*) a valuable piece of property, owned only by the aristocracy, which was later dropped into the sea (see Chapter IX). According to a participant who later described this ceremony, "this was a sign of great respect and high honor" (Wells quoted in Billman 1964:63). Similarly, among the Inland Tlingit, a man could begin making his daughter an aristocrat immediately after she was born or at the feast held immediately after the completion of her puberty confinement. In either case, she was placed on top of the gifts about to be distributed among her paternal/affinal kin (McClellan 1975:495).

The same role was played by the special clothing worn by the aristocracy. It not only decorated their bodies but made them heavier by placing a layer of valuable objects on them. Among the Yakutat Tlingit, this clothing was made of sea otter and marten skin. As one of de Laguna's informants put it, "Mink was the cheapest skin. Royalties used marten. A cape of royalty would never fit a common person. No matter how you put it on, no matter how it was thrown on you, if you were common, it wouldn't fit. If it fits, no matter how you look, you are royalty" (1972:464). This statement also suggests that the aristocrats' clothing was intimately connected with their bodies, which were heavier than those of the commoners, and that valuable (heavy) clothing could be associated only with an aristocrat's body. The decorations worn by the aristocracy, such as nose-rings, earrings, bracelets, and others, were also heavier than those used by commoners, since they were made of more valuable materials such as copper, shark's teeth, and abalone shells rather than bone or stone.[13]

Unlike the commoners, who donned their finery only on special occasions, the nobility wore valuable clothing all the time. According to Holmberg ([1854] 1985:13), the rich painted their faces daily, while the poor did so only when the color began to fade. Similarly, while the

commoners wore the designs of their crests, in the form of face painting, only during the potlatch, the aristocrats' hands were permanently
marked with tattoos depicting them.[14]

Despite the importance of the parents' contribution to a person's
rank and status, a Tlingit could not claim aristocratic status without
maintaining the purity and weight of the outside as well as the inside
of his or her body. The body's special purity was achieved by the
lengthening of the periods of ritual seclusion and abstinence as well as
by increasing the amount of physical training an aristocratic youngster
underwent. For example, an aristocratic female's puberty confinement
lasted much longer, so as to make her skin whiter. For that purpose all
of her body was covered with soft skins of the underground squirrel
pasted to it with pine pitch (Shotridge 1929:146). Aristocrats washed
their body and scraped it with special rocks more often than commoners. As a result, it became "pure" "crystal clear," "whiter than
snow," "like the sun," and "with no stains in it." A person whose body
and spirit were "clean" or "pure" was called a *l ulitoogu ḵáa* (de Laguna
1972:463; 467; 529; Kan 1979–1987).[15]

The link between this state of physical and spiritual purity, and
success in various undertakings, from potlatching to the acquisition of
wealth, may be illustrated with the following examples. Thus, I think
that the use of the steambath (indoor or outdoor) as a kind of a men's
house, where the head of the house and his male kin purified themselves, told stories, sang songs, and discussed important issues, was not
accidental (Krause 1956:113–114; de Laguna 1972:305–306). While
many, if not all, Tlingit men and women observed the rules of physical
purity to ensure success in various undertakings, the aristocrats were
expected to be more involved in these activities. Their greater wealth
served as the indication of their greater purity. The amulets and other
magical substances owned by the aristocrats were considered more
potent than those of ordinary persons. Thus all of the people of high
rank owned a special "wealth box" containing

> miscellaneous odds and ends which were never shown to another [person],
> indeed their whereabouts was always kept a secret. Any curious article out of
> the common was appropriated to this use. . . . These articles were used to rub
> over the body after a bath, and were supposed to bring good fortune to the
> possessor. (Emmons, Field Museum, Collection Notes, notebook 2, catalogue #
> 78466)[16]

The fact that this box was passed down from a man to his sister's son
indicates the importance of the combination of ascription and achieve-

ment. It was not enough to inherit a "wealth box"—one had to follow all of the rules that were required to make it a source of wealth. If a person did not use it properly, the charms disappeared from inside and he became poorer than before (Swanton 1908:448).

Since the bodies of the aristocrats were more pure than those of the common people, they required more intensive purification, if they happened to become polluted. Thus, for example, a woman of high rank who had been captured and kept as a slave by another clan and later redeemed by her matrikin, had to undergo a special rite of purification to restore her original status and rank. A female slave took her to the river, bathed her, burned her clothes and dressed her in new garments. Back in the house three valuable copper shields, supplied by her maternal uncle, were rubbed over her body. This was supposed to scrape off and wash off the slavery by means of a heavy object of great value (Olson 1967:54).

Another suggestive term, *dook*, "solid" or "closed," was used to describe the aristocrats' imperviousness to witchcraft. Of such a physically and morally pure person one would say, "the surface of his mind is impenetrable" (*toowú daakdzidóok* [?]). De Laguna's (1972:735) informant, speaking in English, rephrased it as "just solid like rock; nothing can get into them." He meant that a witch would see this quality and would not bother him. Nor could one persuade a solid person to go wrong. As de Laguna explained (1972:735), this solid feeling is like physical strength (*latseen*)[17] and is achieved through the same hardening exercises, icy baths, and similar activities.[18] Since a person susceptible to being bewitched was considered morally inferior, the notion that the bodies of aristocrats were solid and closed reinforced their image as persons morally superior to the rest of the population.

Finally, the aristocrats were frequently referred to as heavy (*yadaal*); the same word was the root of the terms denoting important and highly esteemed people and things (compare Chapter II). This suggests that, like the bones of the body, the aristocracy formed the more solid and permanent part of the population. The association between the aristocracy and the (solid) bones is made clear by the term *li-s'aak*, which was used to describe both a *bony* fish and an *ambitious* person (Story and Naish 1973:18; 33).

A clear indicator of the greater purity and solidity of the aristocrat's body was the custom of preserving the skull or the scalp of a high-ranking person or a brave warrior slain in battle, reported by a number of lay observers and ethnographers (Wilbur n.d.:279; Swanton

1908:58; Olson 1967:80; de Laguna 19772:540–541).[19] Emmons' (1920–1945, Shukoff's Account:2) informant, Shukoff, gave the following description of this practice:

> In those days, if any relative or friend died during war or by natural death, his friend or relative would take [the] scalp off and preserve it, and wrap [the] scalp in valuable fur robes, [such] as marten or fox . . . and then put them in [a] wooden [bentwood] box . . . called *lákt*. These scalps could only be seen during big festivities and then they [the mourners] would give away and tear many blankets, and women would mourn.

Another account refers specifically to the scalp of a dead chief, which was wrapped in the best blankets owned by the deceased and deposited in a decorated box. It was removed only on the occasion of an important festival by the nearest living matrilineal relative of the deceased. "On such occasion the relative takes from the box these relics of the dear departed, and discourses upon his many virtues, while the surrounding friends are expected to lament . . . as their grief is revivified" (Chase 1893:52). Finally, one of de Laguna's (1972:584) informants explained that the scalp was thought of by the matrikin of the deceased as "just like human being." As I have indicated earlier, the head was seen as the major part of the body and often treated as its metonym in art and ritual. The scalp and/or the skull retained some of the spiritual essence of the deceased (Keithahn 1954; de Laguna 1960:156). The head of an aristocrat was the most important and pure part of his body and could be kept by the living, despite a general fear of pollution emanating from the corpse.[20]

Aristocrat—"Person of the Village"

Let us now turn to the terms that denote aristocrats, to see if they expressed some of the same associations that I have already outlined. The most common ones were: *aan ḵáawu*, literally, "person of the village;" *aan lingídi*, "person of the village;" and *aanyádi*, sing., "child of the village," *aanyátx'i*, pl.—the only term for the aristocracy which was used in plural. The presence of the word for "village" in all of these terms is notable. It becomes even more telling if we contrast it with the terms for the person on the very bottom of society, an outcast or a bastard, which are *nichkaḵáawu*, "person of the beach" or "person of the rocks," and *nichkayádi*, "child of the beach" or "child of the rocks." The beach was a marginal area between the land and the sea, the place for depositing refuse and discarding the bodies of dead slaves; "food from the beach," i.e., marine invertebrates collected by women, had lower status than the fish and game obtained by men and was considered polluting for initiates and other persons in a state of ritual liminality. Thus, these terms denoted the aristocrats as persons linked to the center of sociality and of the universe, and those of low caste as the people associated with a marginal domain of the universe.

This contrast could also be interpreted as an opposition between center and periphery. It was further reiterated by the fact that the original settlers of a community, considered its owners, occupied the central area in the row of houses and were flanked by the houses of the subsequent arrivals. The poorest houses were established away from the sources of fresh water and the salmon streams, and their inhabitants were referred to as "people between villages"(Olson 1967:47). Within the house itself, the chief (*hít s'aatí*, "master of the house") and his wife occupied the center of the rear part and were flanked by his immediate junior male matrikin.

This rear portion of the house was referred to as its "head" and was, in fact, its most sacred area, separated from the rest of the house by a wooden screen representing the crest of the lineage inhabiting it. It was behind this screen that the *hít s'aatí* dwelled and the sacred ancestral regalia of the lineage were kept. The "head" of the house was opposed to its front, which was occupied by the persons of low rank and the slaves, referred to collectively as "dwellers by the door." No wonder that the head of the lineage or any leader (including a military one) was called *ḵaa sháade háni*, "the person standing at the head," and the head of a clan, *naa sháade háni*, "clan head person." This series of oppositions between the social categories located at the two extremes of the entire hierarchy can be summarized as follows:

aristocracy: persons of low rank/outcasts/slaves
village: beach
center: periphery
back: front
human habitat: wilderness/animal habitat

Aristocrats and Shagóon

These notions about the aristocrat as the ideal moral/social person help explain his role as the guardian and trustee of his matrilineal group's sacred possessions. On the one hand, since only a person whose body was pure could handle and wear the sacred regalia (*at.óow*) of his matrilineal group, an *aanyádi* was the logical person for

that. On the other hand, aristocratic youngsters received special training in the sacred oral tradition of their lineage and clan. Only they
were expected to know the complete (i.e., correct) versions of the
origin myths of their matrilineal group and have the command of the
esoteric potlatch rhetoric (referred to as "heavy words").[21] To increase
their knowledge further, the young men of the highest rank were sent
to stay with their matrikin in other localities, so that they could learn
the oral traditions of other houses and clans. This enabled them to
respond properly to the esoteric rhetoric addressed to them by members of other matrilineal groups, used in potlatches and peace negotiations (see Chapters VIII and IX).

The ultimate control over the matrilineal group's *shagóon* was
vested in its head. Hence it was he, the *hít s'aatí*, who dwelled in the
rear of the house, where its regalia were stored. He bestowed the
names/titles on his matrikin and gave them permission to use the
group's regalia, while he wore the most valuable representations of
crests himself. Theoretically every member of a matrilineal group had
the right to wear any of its crests, with the exception of the most
valuable ones. It was the duty of the head of the group to give his
matrikin an opportunity to do so, in return for their contributions to
the potlatch that he sponsored. However, in reality, only the chief
himself and his closest matrikin made much use of the privilege to
wear the *at.óow* of their house or clan (de Laguna 1972:458). Some of
the lesser crest objects seem to have been owned by the *aanyátx'i* and
passed down from a man to his heir. The distinction between collective
and individual rights was somewhat blurred. Thus, while the chief
was not supposed to sell or give away as presents his house or clan
crest objects, there are indications that this was sometimes done (Olson
1967:37).[22]

Similarly, because of their knowledge of the esoteric rules surrounding hunting and fishing, the heads of houses and lineages were
seen as the natural trustees of their groups' subsistence areas. As we
have seen earlier, the chief could not force his matrikin to provide him
with food and furs, but as his juniors they were expected to show him
respect by sharing their catch with him. He, in turn, was expected to
share with them his special knowledge of the land and its inhabitants,
as well as his hunting magic believed to be superior to that of other
men whose bodies were supposed to be less pure.[23]

The chief's leading role in trading activities also depended on his
command of the esoteric information, since trading was heavily ritual-

ized (see Gunther 1972; compare also Tyjberg 1977). Finally, his role as the head of a war party was also linked to his knowledge of the sacred (as well as the superior bravery expected of him).[24] As a result of its role in trade and warfare, the aristocracy accumulated more wealth, including exotic objects and slaves, both of which served as the most valuable potlatch gifts and were exchanged exclusively between persons of high rank (see Chapter IX).

The aristocrats' near monopoly on their matrilineal group's sacred traditions and their role as the guardians of the sacred objects representing their lineage and clan crests determined their leading role in potlatches and other ceremonies. In those contexts, aristocrats raised their own rank and status as well as those of their entire matrikin. Despite occasional violations of the fundamental principle of mutual help between the leaders of a matrilineal group and the rest of its members, it appears that the latter strongly identified with the former. The prestige of the head of a house or clan became their entire group's collective prestige. The chiefs and the aanyátx'i could not afford to neglect their matrikin. The ordinary members of a matrilineal group could always refuse to help their leader in a potlatch or a war raid he was organizing, thus ruining his chances of maintaining or raising his status. The dissatisfied commoners could also join a junior relative of the chief who resented his authority and tried to establish an offshoot house of his own (see below). Thus, the nobles and the commoners existed in a symbiotic relationship, in which the former exchanged their ritual expertise and esoteric knowledge for the latter's labor and active assistance in potlatches and other ceremonies.

My analysis clearly demonstrates that it is incorrect to refer to the aanyátx'i as a class. Despite the strong ties between and identification of the high-ranking persons of different matrilineal groups, their primary bonds were still with their own lineage and house relatives. While one could argue that the beliefs about the physical and moral superiority of the aristocracy was an ideology that legitimized their dominance over the rest of the population, it appears that the commoners subscribed to the same set of values and did not perceive themselves as a separate group with separate interests. In fact, the dividing line between the aristocrats and the commoners was not very clear and there was never a definite agreement, even within a matrilineal group itself, who was an aanyádi and who was not. The existing data show no evidence of an ideology that would have challenged the aristocracy's dominant role. If the commoners ever expressed dissatisfaction with their own subordinate position, it was phrased in terms of their desire to be reborn as *aanyátx'i* (Veniaminov 1984:399).

Morality, Rank, Respect, and the Identity of the Commoners

In addition to proper pedigree and marriage ties, inherited and personally accumulated wealth, and physical and spiritual purity, an *aanyádi* had to live up to a high standard of morality and etiquette. The personal qualities expected of him were contrasted sharply with the moral characteristics attributed to persons of the lowest rank.

Just as an improper act committed by an aristocrat required a distribution of gifts to "wash off the shame," his or her virtues could be celebrated and extolled by having a feast. Thus, one high-ranking man in Yakutat gave a potlatch in which he honored his sister's daughter for having never quarreled and gave large sums of money to the four members of the opposite moiety who had robed her for the occasion. In addition a slave was freed in her honor (de Laguna 1972:637).

The *aanyátx'i* represented the ideal of morality and proper conduct, and were supposed to be emulated by the rest of the people. They were expected to be wise, generous, decorous in their conduct, mild-tempered, and modest.[25] They were not supposed to be condescending to those below them in rank and had to ignore minor breaches of etiquette on the part of others. A high-ranking person did not have to brag about his status and pedigree; everybody recognized him by his conduct and could establish his status simply from his name and house/clan membership. To brag about oneself was to remind others of their lower status. Olson reports that a certain high-ranking man was publicly reprimanded by the elders for the habit of saying, "*Aanyátx'i kudzitee ka tsu nichkakáax'u*," "'there are aristocrats and there are people of low rank.'" In fact, a high-ranking person, speaking in public, would often belittle his status by calling himself "poor" (Olson 1967:48).[26]

The idea of respect seems to be the key to the entire concept of aristocratic status. This term *kaa yáa* + *a-ya-ya-nei* has been frequently used in discussions of human interaction, especially in the public and ritual contexts.[27] English-speaking Tlingit continue to use it to describe proper, decorous treatment of others, which calls for respectful behavior in return. Such behavior included ritual avoidance between certain categories of relatives, generous gift-giving, and other types of formalized action vis-à-vis others. In addition, a person of rank had to have great self-respect, which implied the conduct that corresponded to his rank and status (compare de Laguna 1972:509; Kan 1979–1987).

This notion was undoubtedly present in other Northwest Coast cultures, where similar conduct and morality were expected of the high-born. Thus, all of the modern scholars of Haida culture have commented on the centrality of the idea of respect, as well as self-respect (Blackman 1982:141; Stearns 1984; Boelscher 1985:133–152).[28]

Of course, not all of the *aanyátx'i* conformed to this ideal, so that references to chiefs and their kin who were arrogant and greedy and looked down on their junior kin are not uncommon. Some aristocrats used their position and power to get rid of rivals and, as Oberg (1934:146) put it, were "able to decide legal issues to their advantage at the expense of their less important kinsmen." The main problem for aristocrats was to maintain their special status and prerogatives, while remaining the benevolent senior kin of the lower ranking members of their matrilineal groups.

Because of the lack of data on the daily life of the nineteenth century Tlingit, it is difficult to determine how much of a discrepancy there was between the prescribed and the actual behavior of aristocrats vis-à-vis their matrikin of lower rank. We do know, however, that despite violations of this code of conduct and the aristocracy's attempts to limit upward mobility of those below them, public opinion strongly censured those *aanyátx'i* who were disrespectful towards commoners.

In addition to some contradictions between the aristocratic morality and the actual behavior of *aanyátx'i*, there was some discrepancy between the various qualities attributed to them and the forms of conduct expected of them. For example, some sources indicate that they were hard-working and skilled in all of the occupations of their gender.[29] On the other hand, equally common are references to the chiefs, and especially their children, not doing any work (Krause 1956:109; Oberg 1973:81).[30] As Swanton's informant, chief Katishan, commented about some wealthy protagonists of the story he was telling, "As they were now very proud and had plenty of people to work for them, the husband and wife spent much time sitting on the roof of their house looking about" (1909:112). I believe that the emphasis on hard work, on the one hand, and the reliance on the work of others, on the other, are two sides of the same coin. As an ideal person, the aristocrat had to excel in all of the skills and activities expected of his gender and age group. However, as an expert on ritual and other esoteric subjects, he spent less time performing mundane tasks. Finally, to be able not to work was a clear expression of wealth and the ability to control the labor of others, i.e., junior matrikin and slaves.

Aristocrats had to be very careful about their conduct, since any transgression threatened to lower their status and rank. The most ominous threat was that of being called a *nichkakáawu yahaayí*, "an image/reflection/spirit of an outcast" (Olson 1967:48). Aristocratic status could always be lost as a result of improper marriage, the practice of witchcraft, cowardice in battle, and the inability to sponsor a potlatch. An aristocrat and a *nichkakáawu* defined each other, each one possessing the characteristics that the other lacked. The *nichkakáawu* was seen as greedy, lazy, improvident, cowardly, and immodest. The size of this group is unclear but does not appear to have been large. Its members included illegitimate children, persons who had committed serious crimes, and those who could not or did not want to obtain their own food.[31] In fact, such persons were closer to slaves and were called "dried fish slaves," because they sold themselves to their matrikin for some food, to keep from starving (de Laguna 1972:469). Unlike the majority of the slaves, who were captured enemies, dried fish slaves could redeem themselves through hard work. Nevertheless, they served as highly visible examples of reprehensibility for the rest of the people and especially the high-born. While slavery is discussed in some detail in several subsequent chapters, here I should emphasize that the *nichkakáawu* and the slaves existed not only as a social category but as a moral imperative as well. Their existence was a constant reminder to those above them of the consequences of not showing respect to others and of having no self-respect.[32]

While a *nichkakawu's* place was on the margin of the Tlingit society, a slave was entirely outside it. Hence, the rules of proper conduct and morality did not apply to him at all. Thus, in the Tlingit view slaves could ignore the fundamental law of moiety exogamy (de Laguna 1972:470). Even their appearance (e.g., short hair) distinguished them sharply from the rest of the populace. In a way, slaves were not persons; whereas the outcasts and the bastards were incomplete persons.

While the identity of those on the very bottom of the social hierarchy was clearly defined, it is much more difficult to identify the commoners. Similar to other Northwest Coast languages, Tlingit lacks definite terms for this group (de Laguna 1972:462; compare Boelscher

1985:134–136). Those recorded by ethnographers do not seem to be labels for a clearly defined group but, instead, simple descriptions of certain qualities or predicaments of those who lacked aristocratic status and, in some contexts, could even be applied to the aristocrats themselves. For example, the term *eesháan yádi*, "poor child," is derived from the verb *li-.eeshaan* signifying being poor in spirit and ability as much as in possessions (Story and Naish 1973:155). However, *eeshaan* may also be used to express sympathy to an unfortunate person (Kan 1979-1987). Another term, *k'anashgidéi káa*, also signifies poverty, but, contrary to Olson (1967:47–48), it did not necessarily serve as the label for those located between the aristocracy and the free persons of the lowest rank. Thus, it could be used by the potlatch hosts as an expression of their modesty and respect for the guests. My own informants gave no labels for this group and simply stated that they were "not aristocrats" or "just people" (*lingít*; Kan 1979–1987).

Several factors account for the lack of definite and all-encompassing terms for commoners. Firstly, it was disrespectful to mention the lower status of one's addressee, especially if he were a matrilineal relative (compare Boelscher 1985:103). Euphemisms, such as "people of the house next door," were used to refer to clan relatives of lower rank than oneself. Secondly, as I have said earlier, many people who could not claim to be *aanyátx'i* still saw themselves as the latter's matrikin, and in fact, some of them did raise their status through hard work, military prowess, marriage to a person of higher rank, and active participation in potlatching. A possibility of entering the ranks of the aristocracy always existed, although it increased somewhat in the post-contact period, when commoners became able to accumulate wealth through their trade with the Europeans.

A brief look at the issue of the identity of commoners in other Northwest Coast societies helps clarify it for the Tlingit. In his discussion of rank and status among the Coast Salish, Suttles (1967) described the indigenous view of the social order as an "inverted pear," with the majority of the population being reckoned as "noble," and the minority as "low class people" ("class" being the term used by the English-speaking Salish themselves). The most important dimension of this high class/low class distinction, was its ideological function. Low class people were considered worthless and marginal, while the upper class was associated with morality and knowledge. As Suttles ([1958] 1967:175) suggested, this "myth of morality is the private property of the upper class."

A similar picture of Haida society has been painted by Murdock (1936:19) and more recently by Boelscher (1985:115), who argues that "Haida society, in its public self-image, emerges as exclusively composed of chiefs. . . . the category of commoners existed mainly as a moral imperative pointing out what happens if reciprocal obligation is declined and ritual observance neglected."[33]

All of the anthropologists who have studied the Coast Tsimshian, beginning with Boas (1916:497) and Garfield (1939:177), reported the existence of a significant distinction between the aristocrats and the commoners. More recently, Halpin (1973; 1984) and Seguin (1984; 1985) offered an interesting discussion of the Coast Tsimshian stratification, more conscious of the native view of status groups. Both scholars stress that those of the highest rank, the chiefs and their immediate matrikin, were called the "real" or the "ripe" people. Like their Tlingit counterparts, they were not supposed to marry persons of lower rank. The next group was constituted by "the other people," that is, named, ranked persons not of the chiefly class (Seguin 1985:6). Halpin (1973:106) calls them members of the "councilor category." The third category were the people without rank, called "unhealed" or "green." Similar to the Tlingit nichkayátx'i, they were, in Halpin's words, "less a status level than a moral condition" (1973:106). The size of this group is not known, but does not seem to have been large. The "unhealed" people were on the margins of the Tsimshian society, and membership in that group, unlike the first two, was not expressed in terms of descent. Slaves were entirely outside the Tsimshian society proper.

The system of stratification among the Nishka and the Gitksan, the interior relatives of the Coast Tsimshian, was more simple. Thus Adams (1973:37) speaks of only two "classes" among the latter, "chiefs" (or "real people") and "commoners" (or "ordinary people"), plus the class of slaves, who came from other tribes and had no formal rights to the local resources. Adams further subdivided the real people into "chiefs," "princes," and "nobles." The chiefs were heads of chiefly lineages who owned crest designs and contributed most to potlatches. Their sisters' sons and other close junior matrikin were the "princes." Those of their direct descendants who did not inherit their positions became "nobles."[34]

Despite the fact that, at least among the Coast Tsimshian, the chiefs had greater power and authority than their Tlingit counterparts, some mobility between them and the "councilors" was possible (Boas 1916:498). Contrary to Garfield's insistence on the "real people's" separate "class interests," the latter, like their Tlingit counterparts, depended on the support of their lower-ranking matrikin and, in her own words, exerted authority "mainly through the prestige of their position" rather than through formalized political power (1939:182).

Conclusion

In this chapter, I have undertaken what might appear as a rather lengthy detour into the subject of the nature of aristocratic status and power. By combining the outside observers' view of the Tlingit system of rank with my own analysis of the indigenous model of the aristocracy, I have demonstrated that their ideas about rank were based on the same principles and oppositions that underlay their cosmology and ethnopsychology. Thus, high and low rank were associated, respectively, with ritual purity and pollution, spatial dimensions (e.g., center/periphery), food, clothing, body decoration and other oppositions. In this model, the aristocrat represented the ideal person, a paragon of perfection, virtue, and morality, and was linked to the sacred; whereas those below him in rank were associated (to a greater or lesser degree) with the profane. Thus, Tlingit ethnosociology, based in large part on ethnopsychology, served as an ideology legitimizing the aristocracy's dominant role in social and, particularly, ceremonial life. It was both based on and expressed in the aristocracy's control over the tangible and intangible resources of their respective matrilineal groups. At the same time, beliefs about personhood, status, and power were shared by the entire society, with every individual aspiring to a higher position in the social hierarchy.

While this ethnopsychological approach has not been systematically applied to other Northwest Coast societies, several recent works do indicate the presence of strikingly similar symbolic forms of conceptualization of rank and status among the southern neighbors of the Tlingit. For example, Adams (1973:31–36) reports that his Gitksan informants contrasted the chiefs, described as people who were "good" and "clean" and "stayed put," with the commoners, who were said to be "dirty," "ignorant," and "always moving around." Because spirits of the dead liked to return to persons who were "clean" and "showed respect" by giving away wealth in feasts, there was considerable moral and practical pressure on the aristocrats to remain "pure," train knowledgeable and "clean" heirs, and continue potlatching (compare

Halpin 1973; Seguin 1984:115–118; 1985:44–61; Boelscher 1985:133–152; Goldman 1975; Walens 1981).[35]

My own analysis and the ethnopsychological data found in a number of Northwest Coast ethnographies further support my earlier proposition that the indigenous societies of this culture area were organized by principles similar to those of the hierarchical societies in other parts of the world, such as Polynesia (compare Goldman 1970; 1975:1; Ortner 1981:359). Hierarchical societies, as Dumont (1970) has argued, are characterized by the encompassing status of prestige criteria vis-à-vis other principles of social organization. This means that persons and categories of persons are ranked according to criteria of social and religious value (e.g., Indian "purity" or Polynesian "mana") that ideally transcend political and economic realities. Another key characteristic of hierarchical societies, in Dumont's model, is their "holism," i.e., the fact that the various social strata are seen not as independent units but as differentiated, functionally specialized precipitates of a prior whole and that relations between their members are organized in terms of mutual reciprocities and obligations (Ortner 1981:359).

Of course, there were significant differences between the Northwest Coast systems of rank and such hierarchical social systems as India or even Polynesia. The former were, by and large, less complex, with the status group of the aristocracy being open to individuals of lower rank. To draw a sharp distinction between the nobility and the commoners in Northwest Coast societies, as Goldman (1975) has done, is a mistake. Even among the more rigidly stratified societies of this region, the aristocracy did not constitute a separate caste, as Goldman suggests for the Kwakiutl in the following statement: "the main categories of the social community are counterparts of spiritual realms, each distinct and closed to the others, connected only by ritual relations that serve to sustain their separation" (Goldman 1975:55). Despite such important differences, there are clear grounds for comparison between the sociocultural order of the Tlingit and of other Northwest Coast peoples, on the one hand, and of hierarchical societies elsewhere in the world, on the other.

part two

THE FUNERAL

chapter five

COSMOLOGY, ESCHATOLOGY, AND THE NATURE OF DEATH

To begin the analysis of the funeral, we must establish the Tlingit view of death and of the transformations that the corporeal and the noncorporeal attributes of the deceased underwent in its aftermath. To explain the route followed by the deceased and his fate in the afterworld, we must also situate the village of the dead in the larger cosmos. Finally, to grasp the ethos of the funeral, we need to get a sense of the Tlingit attitudes towards death and their view of the relationship between the living and the dead.

The Onset of Death and the Deceased's Exit from the House

As I have suggested in Chapter II, death was perceived as a permanent separation of the body (which became a *ḵaa naawú*, "dead person") and its spiritual components (*x'aséikw*, "breath," *ḵaa toowú*, "soul/mind," *ḵaa yakgwahéiyagu*, "spirit," and others). It appears that the *ḵaa toowú* was the first one to depart. Unlike sleep or trance which involved its temporary separation from the body, death occurred when this essential spiritual entity did not come back at all. The first signs of the impending death were periods of prolonged unconsciousness and hallucinations experienced by a seriously ill person, which were interpreted as the _ḵaa toowú_'s straying further and further away from its body. Because the dying person often reported seeing the faces of his departed kin hovering over him, it was believed that during this time he was in direct communication with the spirits of the dead who were trying to assuage his fear by promising to guide and protect him on the journey to the other world and by describing the warm welcome awaiting him there (Kan 1979–1987; Emmons 1920–1945, ch. VI:14; Swanton 1908:462).[1] So afraid were the living of touching the corpse, that they often began to wash and dress the deceased at this very moment, without waiting for the cessation of breath[2]—the more tangible and certain sign of death.[3]

Occasionally a person believed to be dead came back to life and described his visit to the land of the dead. This temporary death (coma?) as well as the shaman's spiritual journey, believed to take place during trance, were the main sources of information about the afterworld (see below).

In addition to the polluting corpse, there was also one noncorporeal attribute of the deceased that his matrikin had to be protected from. This was the entity I have labelled the "ghost." The native term for it, _s'igeeḵáawu_, suggests its association with the physical remains, since, according to my informants, it is composed of the words _s'aagí_, "bone" and _ḵáa_, "person."[4] Along with the cremated remains, i.e., bones and ashes, _s'igeeḵáawu_ dwelled in the cemetery, called, appropriately, _s'igeeḵáawu aaní_, "village of the bones' people."

Until the body was taken outside to be cremated, the ghost dwelled inside the house and its presence was experienced by the living as a light tickle or itch, usually compared to the sensation of running water (Story and Naish 1973:228). The crackling of the fire was believed to be the voice of the ghost trying to communicate with the living. The notion that the ghost of the deceased lying in state poses a threat to the living is widespread and is explained by Hertz (1960:36–37) as resulting from the ghost's liminal state between life and death. However, the Tlingit explanation of its malevolence had its culture-specific logic, meaningful only within the larger ideology of unity and solidarity of the matrikin. Like many other peoples, the Tlingit feared the ghost because of its tendency to take a living person along to the land of the dead, but they attributed this not to an inherently evil nature but to its fear of being lonely. Hence, the most vulnerable of all those present during the wake were the close matrilineal relatives of the deceased, and particularly small children, who were the objects of special affection and whose weak persona was more closely tied to the domain of the dead than that of the adults (see below).[5]

Among at least some of the Tlingit groups (McClellan 1975:398; Kan 1979–1987), a stone was put in each of the corpse's hands to prevent the ghost from taking some other member of the matrilineal group along. Food and water were placed in the fire during the wake not only to provide nourishment for the ghost but also to attempt to appease it.

The desire to prevent the ghost from returning to disturb the living explains the taboo on using the door to take the corpse out of the house.[6] Unlike the pure breath that was let out through the door (de Laguna 1972:532), the corpse left the house through a hole in its back wall; occasionally, the smokehole was used.[7] A handful of ashes from the fireplace was thrown after the body to purify the house (see below). A live puppy or a dead dog was also thrown out, in an effort to deceive the ghost, who was expected to grab the animal instead of a human being (Swanton 1908:430). The use of the dog makes sense, in light of its liminal position in the native classification of living creatures.[8]

The departure of the deceased from this world also paralleled the newborn's first entrance into the house. Because of the fear of pollution emanating from the various substances associated with birth, the woman delivered her baby in a special hut constructed behind the house. Only after a period of several days, could the purified mother and her infant return to the house. At that time, all of its inhabitants left the dwelling, except for the father and/or the four persons selected to perform a special ritual of purification. According to Olson (1933–1954, notebook 9:76), the infant was laid on the doorstep, while the father threw a shovel of ashes out the door, so that some of it fell on the baby. In another description of this rite, the four selected persons (paternal kin of the child?) each threw four pinches of ashes, across the cradle (Drucker 1950:275). In both cases, the ashes were supposed to protect the baby from the pollution associated with birth and ensure its long life. It seems that the ashes were also purifying the house itself, as they did at the time of the corpse's departure (see below).

The two transitions appear to be similar, except that the stages of one were the reversal of the other. However, a more encompassing view that incorporates the entire human life cycle suggests that they were parts of the same eternal cycle of death and rebirth. Thus, the deceased left the house through the back to be cremated and then journeyed towards the interior to the village of the dead. After some time, he was reborn through a close matrilineal relative. The birth took place behind the house, an area associated with persons in polluting and liminal states and with the beginning and the end of life, i.e., the dead and the menstruating and parturient women. This interpretation is also suggested by the fetal posture of the corpse when placed on the pyre, which itself resembled a baby's crib. Because the sun was associated with life and rebirth, the fact that cremation took place at sunrise and that the deceased was oriented towards the east further illustrate the pervasiveness of the notion that life and death formed an unbroken, eternal cycle.[9]

In comparison to the corpse, however, the newborn was less dangerous and polluting and could enter the house through the door. This cyclical model of life is further conveyed by a belief, reported by Olson (1933–1954, notebook 10:28), that the old people died on the same day and month in which they were born, and a vaguely defined concept of an "old people's bay" (*shaan geeyí*). According to de Laguna (1972:530), it was apparently a figure of speech used to describe the onset of old age ("feeling the breeze from the old people's bay") and the circular journey taken by the human being throughout his or her life.[10] Senile old people were often compared to children (de Laguna 1972:530).

This parallelism between the rites of birth and death was well understood and elegantly expressed by Hertz (1960:80):

> As for birth, it accomplishes for the collective consciousness the same transformation as death but the other way around. The individual leaves the invisible and mysterious world that his soul has inhabited, and he enters the society of the living. The transition from one group to another, whether real or imaginary, always supposes a profound renewal of the individual which is marked by such customs as the acquisition of a new name, the changing of clothes or the way of life. This operation is considered to be full of risks because it involves a stirring to action of necessary but dangerous forces. The body of the new-born child is no less sacred than the corpse.

Tlingit concepts of the circularity of life and of an overlap between death and new life are best exemplified by the belief in reincarnation, a key element of Tlingit ethnopsychology and eschatology.

Reincarnation[11]

Theoretically, every Tlingit was believed to be a reincarnation of a member of the same lineage or, at least, the same clan.[12] An elderly or a dying person could announce through whom he or she wished to be reborn. The spirit of a deceased relative could also be induced to come back through a particular woman. The most common method of accomplishing this was to take fingernails, hair, and other substances from the corpse and to put them into the belt worn by the woman (Swanton 1908:429; Drucker 1950:291).[13] While the body was being cremated, the woman who wished to bring the spirit of the deceased back to life was led around the pyre eight times; she then sketched a path from it, about six to seven inches long, squatted at the end of it, and urinated (possibly imitating the posture of the woman during childbirth or opening the womb), while calling the spirit to return (de Laguna 1972:777–778). The latter would sometimes appear in her dream or she might hear his voice during waking life (Veniaminov 1984:399). Finally, the spirit's identity could also be established post factum, by naming the child or observing its behavior and listening to its comments that indicated an intimate knowledge of the life of a certain deceased matrilineal relative. The spirit was supposed to enter the woman's body at conception, making the fetus a quasi-person, which explains why when a pregnant woman died, the fetus was buried separately from her (Emmons 1920–1945, chapter VI:25).

Many children allegedly made references to their previous lives, saying "then ashes I was, not yet I was born" (de Laguna 1972:776). They also pointed out places they said they had visited and objects they had supposedly possessed in their previous life. They might also address an older relative by kinship terms that would have been appropriate between the person they spoke to and their matrilineal ancestor whose spirit they themselves possessed (Kan 1979–1987). As children grew older, parents began discouraging them from such behavior. It appears that they were worried that the child's mind (probably *toowú*) was still in its previous life or in the land of the dead. By the time of adolescence, children were expected to forget about their previous existence. Thus, maturity marked the end of a liminal period in a person's life, when his or her previous and current lives overlapped. High infant mortality might have contributed to this view of the vulnerability of small children, whose deaths were often seen as a sign of their wish to return to the land of the dead.[14]

The return to life of one of the spiritual attributes of the deceased was described most dramatically in the accounts allegedly given by persons who remembered the experience of leaving their old body at death and coming back through a new one. One such man, Askadut, believed to have had such an experience, allegedly left the most detailed account of this process, which was obtained from Yakutat informants (de Laguna 1972:767–769). Having died, Askadut could still see his own body being propped up in the back of his house, during the wake. He tried to reenter it but could not. He also attempted to speak to his kin but all they heard was the crackling of the fire. After cremation, he began an arduous journey to the land of the dead. It is not clear how he managed to leave it, after having spent some time there. On his way back, he followed a river for a while and then sat down at the foot of a tree near the riverbank. The tree began to drip, so he moved to another one, until finally he found a dry one, with a nice mossy place under it. Here he sat down, leaning against the trunk. He remained there for nine days and each day he heard the splash of the mud and sand falling into the water. Finally the bank caved in underneath him and he fell down into the water. The next thing he saw was his own sister holding him as her newborn infant.

As de Laguna (1972:767–769) points out, this account makes several references to childbirth, including a mossy area under a dry tree, which symbolized a matrilineal relative of the deceased through whom he was to be reborn (the wet tree represented the women of the opposite moiety who could not play that role),[15] the nine days representing the months of pregnancy, and the water into which Askadut finally fell representing the fluids expelled from the woman's body during delivery. Askadut's story and a number of similar accounts recorded by de Laguna (1972:772–776) and myself (Kan 1979–1987) demonstrate that, in the Tlingit view, no clear-cut separation between life and death existed.

Smoke, Ashes, and the Power of Fire

In light of the Tlingit life-long effort to minimize the pollution of the wet components of the person and the fear of the ultimate pollution emanating from the corpse (i.e., the outside layer of the person no longer controlled by its inside), cremation appears logical. The fire consumed the perishable flesh, reduced the material elements of the body to the permanent (dry, heavy, and hard) bones, and released the various spiritual components of the person. In addition, it freed the spiritual essence (inside) of the deceased's material possessions, which his spirit could now use in the other world. In Hertz's (1960:46) words, "to make an object or a living being pass from this world into the next, to free or create the soul, it must be destroyed. . . . As the visible object vanishes it is reconstructed in the beyond, transformed to a greater or lesser degree. The same belief applies to the body of the deceased." Cremation quickened the slow natural process of decomposition. Once again, Hertz's idea that temporary burial (and other forms of temporary exposure of the corpse) and cremation are both ways of separating the flesh from the bones, seems to apply perfectly well to the Tlingit case:

> This transformation is not . . . a mere physical disintegration; it changes the character of the corpse, turns it into a new body, and is, consequently, a necessary condition for the salvation of the soul. *This is precisely the meaning of cremation: far from destroying the body of the deceased, it recreates it and makes it capable of entering a new life; it thus achieves the same result as the temporary exposure, but in a much faster way.* The violent action of the fire spares the dead and the living the sorrows and dangers involved in the transformation of the corpse; or at least, it shortens that period considerably by accomplishing all at once the destruction of the flesh and the reduction of the body to immutable elements which in nature happen slowly and progressively. (Hertz 1960:46; italics mine)

Cremation also ensured that the deceased remained warm in the village of the dead. Although he was expected to be continually warmed and fed by his living matrikin who sent him clothing and food through the fire, this initial charge of heat was essential in determining the fate of the spirit in the afterworld. Only those who had been cremated found a place near the fire in the house of their lineage, in the village of the dead. Those unfortunate ones whose bodies had not been so treated led a miserable existence there: unable to stay close to the fireplace, they sat along the walls shivering.[16]

Although due to the natural properties of fire, cremation has some universal meanings, fire played a special role in Tlingit culture and daily life. In the words of a native ethnographer, it was "the most important item in the comfort of [Tlingit] life" (Shotridge 1929:137). In this land of perennial rain, it had positive connotations, like the sun itself, with which it was linguistically and symbolically connected. The same root *gaan* is found in the following verbs: *si-gaan*, "burn," *ka-ya-gaan*, "burn, cremate," *ka-di-gaan*, "shine, produce light by burning," and *a-di-gaan*, "shine," of the sun.

Located in the center of the Tlingit house, the fireplace was the focus of all of its residents' collective activities, the place where they periodically gathered to share the food cooked on it and to get warm.[17] Fire transformed the raw and wet substances from the outside into the cooked and dried food that sustained human life. By eliminating these substances' natural tendency to decay, it prolonged their life span, enabling man to engage in consuming, storing, and exchanging them, thus making social life possible.[18] A brightly shining fire was the sign of the house's prosperity (Shotridge 1929:146).[19] On the contrary, by putting out the fire in the house, its residents indicated their anger or sadness.[20]

The use of fire distinguished human life from the animals' existence in the wilderness. This idea was clearly expressed in one of the episodes of the cycle of creation myths, in which Raven brings light to human beings. Those who became frightened by it and ran into the woods or the water became animals and fish; whereas those who accepted it remained human. Located in the center of the house, which itself was the center of the human-occupied space, the fire was firmly associated with humanity and social life and was opposed to the peripheral domains of the rain-soaked forest and the sea.

Its ability to transform material objects into noncorporeal entities and to send them upwards in the form of smoke made the fire a perfect mediator between the living and the dead as well as between the bottom and the top. Situated below the smokehole, the fireplace was the house's link with the outside, and especially with the immaterial land of the dead.[21] In the house of the spirits the essences of the food, clothing, and other objects burned by the living descended through the smokehole upon the spirits sitting around the fireplace. Similarly, gifts to humans from superhuman beings came down from above through the smokehole; while a halibut hook thrown by a fisherman entered the underwater house of this fish through the smokehole (Swanton 1909:39). As the major intermediary between the two, the shaman had a special association with the fireplace, around which he conducted his seances, and the smokehole, through which his corpse was usually taken out of the house.[22] Finally, among the Inland Tlingit, animals who appeared in temporary human guise always made a point of staying on the opposite side of the fire from men, while a ghost who returned for his relative talked to him from across the fire (McClellan 1975:76).

These examples indicate that the fire not only linked different spatial/social domains but separated them as well.[23] This explains why ashes (i.e., burned wood) figured so prominently in the ritual practices aimed at keeping the dead away from the living. Thus, while the body lay in state, children were protected from the ghost by splitting the end of a small stick, filling it with charcoal, and placing it above their bed, with the split end pointing toward the spirit-land (Knapp and Childe 1896:159).[24] Among the Inland Tlingit, a pregnant woman, who had to protect the fetus from pollution emanating from the corpse, was allowed to attend cremation or visit the cemetery only after she had been sprinkled with ashes (McClellan 1975:378). One of my elderly informants explained that, if bothered by a ghost, one should mark the corners of the house with charcoal. She also reported that children could be prevented from dwelling upon their previous life too much by giving them charcoal from the fireplace to eat. "Once they have eaten the charcoal, they forget about the place they came from [i.e., the land of the dead]" (Kan 1979–1987; compare McClellan 1975:353).

At the same time, smoke, whose upward movement paralleled the spirit's journey to the village of the dead (see below), was one of the main media of communication between the worlds of the living and the dead. This might explain the prominent place of the smoking ritual in the cycle of mortuary rites. Although the existing accounts assign it to several different stages of the funeral, it appears that the most important one (s'eik̲ yis k̲u.éex', "smoking party," from s'eik̲, "smoke" and ya.eex', "invite to a feast") took place every night of the wake or at least the night before cremation. Additional smoking parties could also be held immediately after the disposal of the body (see Chapter I; compare de Laguna 1972:533–534; Emmons 1920–1945, ch. VI:17). In the course of that ceremony, members of the moiety opposite to that of the deceased, were offered tobacco by his matrikin, who then joined them in silent smoking. The use of special pipes, decorated with crest designs, emphasized the sacredness of this rite. All of the participating guests, including women and children, had to smoke (or at least chew) tobacco, to ensure that it would reach the hosts' departed matrikin. Some tobacco was also placed at the four corners of the fire for the spirit of the recently deceased person as well as his matrilineal ancestors, whose names were invoked. Tobacco was also smoked on other important occasions, such as in the initial stages of the building of a new house (Swanton 1909:342) and whenever visitors arrived from another village. In addition, it was offered to spirits whenever a person wished to placate them or ask for something.[25] I suggest that the significance of the tobacco smoking in the funeral rites was due to its special purity and, possibly, dryness, compared to any other substance consumed by man. Hence, it could be used by the mourners while they were still observing the mourning fast, and was a perfect substance to be shared between the living and the dead.[26]

The importance of the substances created by burning—charcoal, ashes, and smoke—in the Tlingit ceremonial life, and particularly in the interaction between the living and the dead may also be explained if we compare the transformations that wood and the human body underwent in the process of burning. The former became heat, light, smoke, charcoal, and ashes. The first three substances are noncorporeal and expanding, difficult to contain. From the Tlingit point of view, they might be seen as being the spiritual essence of the wood, in contrast to charcoal and ashes, which were its material remains. When a corpse was cremated, the impure flesh was destroyed, like the wet wood. The immortal spiritual attributes of the person were released and travelled upward, like smoke, to the realm of the dead. Finally, the bones and ashes remained as the purified material remains of the deceased and were preserved to be subsequently manipulated by the living, just as charcoal was. This interpretation is further supported by the notion, mentioned by my informants, that the Tlingit were made out of wood, rather than leaves, as was indicated earlier (Kan 1979–1987).

The Tlingit Universe and the Land of the Dead

To explain the location and the nature of the land of the dead, we must situate it in the larger universe.[27] Let us then begin by trying to retrace the journey undertaken by the spirit of the deceased following cremation.

The key feature of the Tlingit eschatology was the notion that there were two villages of the dead, both called "s'igeekáawu aaní,"—one being the cemetery located behind the village of the living where the bones were stored and the ghosts lived, and the other a distant noncorporeal village where the spirits dwelled. The ghost's location in the cemetery, in association with the cremated remains, was never explicitly stated but was indicated by the fact that witches visited the graves to interact with the dead (see below), while ordinary people stayed away from this domain of dangerous spiritual forces. Once the funeral was over, the ghost rarely visited and bothered the living, as long as the latter avoided disturbing the remains of the deceased and periodically sent him food and clothing. Hence it appears that, following cremation, the attention of the living turned to the spiritual entities of the deceased that dwelled in the distant and invisible s'igeekáawu aaní. The remains of the dead located in the cemetery became the focus of attention only during the periodic repairing or replacing of their deteriorated containers, which was the occasion for potlatching.

Having been released by cremation, the spirit began its journey to the distant s'igeekáawu aaní, following a trail which led from the cemetery, through the thick woods, and up the mountain slopes. "He went up into the woods" was a common euphemism for dying and the domain of the dead itself was often referred to as dagankú (from daak, "inland, from water to shore;" Kan 1979–1987).

The following descriptions of this journey and of the village of the dead itself come from the persons who had allegedly died and then came back to life after a few days, while their bodies were still lying in state. One of these accounts was recorded by Swanton (1908:461):

> In olden days a certain person died and thought it was so hard to walk up into the ghosts' country that he came back. Then he said to the people, "I haven't any moccasins. I haven't any gloves on. That is a very hard place to go through, for there are lots of devil clubs and others kinds of bushes in the way. You must also sing songs when anybody dies. It is the same as a road for him

and will lead him. There are wolves and bears along the way, which one has to protect himself against."

The second one was obtained by Krause (1956:191–192; compare Knapp and Childe 1896:158–159):

> Once there was a Tlingit . . . who wandered along the way to the land of ghosts [spirits] and came back to life and told his tribesmen what he experienced and saw. Right behind his house he found a wide and pretty path that led to the other side of the mountains where the ghosts [spirits] of the dead stay. First he came to a wide river on whose shores many souls gathered. These were the unfortunate ones who had no friends among the dead who could take them across in their canoes. If one has many friends they come on call and take one across and ask about news from the other world, how their friends are and whether they are coming soon. Our man was warned by the ghosts on this side of the river that if he once crossed he could not return and that he should return while he still could, before his corpse was cremated. Their waiting place is a terrible one and their life is miserable, with much suffering from hunger and thirst. . . . Even the fortunate ghosts who got to the other side did not lead an enviable life since they received only as much food and drink as was used by their friends on earth.

In the village of the dead, the spirit forgot about its previous life and death, found its lineage house, and joined its matrilineal kin (Emmons 1920–1945, ch. 6:28). The houses in s'igeekáawu aaní were arranged in exactly the same manner as in the village of the living and the cemetery—houses of the same clan were located together and the same name was used for the house of the living, the gravehouse of that lineage, and the invisible house of its deceased members (De Laguna 1972:542; Swanton 1908:461–463). The life of the spirits did not differ significantly from that of the living, except that they did not have to work but depended on their living matrikin for their survival.[28] The same distinctions between persons based on gender, status, and matrilineal origin operated in their society. Those of the dead who were periodically fed whenever their kin ate a meal and were also remembered in potlatches in which they were offered food, water, tobacco, clothing, and gifts, sat close to the fire in their houses, and led a relatively happy life; whereas the forgotten ones, forced to sit along the walls, suffered thirst and hunger and gradually sank into oblivion. The status of the deceased in s'igeekáawu aaní depended heavily on the feasts given in his honor by his living kin: those who were remembered enjoyed more respect from their fellow-spirits.[29] At some point, often one year after the person's death, one of his spiritual attributes left the village of the dead to become reincarnated in one of his matrilineal descendants. Another one presumably remained forever in the noncorporeal *s'igeekáawu aaní*.

The question of the "bilocality of the dead,"[30] i.e., the relationship between the two villages of the dead, one visible and near, the other invisible and distant, is puzzling not only to a Western observer but also troubled Louis Shotridge, the first native-born ethnographer of the Tlingit (1917:108). I suggest that the visible *s'igeekáawu aaní* served as a material representation (outside) of the invisible one (inside). Throughout Tlingit mythology, one often encounters another reality behind the visible, material world.[31] For example, in one myth, a stranger who first appears to the protagonist as a human being later turns out to be a bear, while his large house is really a den. Hence, a small gravehouse had a noncorporeal double in the spiritual realm, whose size was similar to that of the house in the village of the living. That is why small amounts of food burned by the living were said to grow in the *s'igeekáawu aaní* to satisfy the spirits' appetite (Shotridge 1917:108).

Thus, the cemetery served as a metonym for the distant village of the dead or as its miniature model, which the living manipulated to affect the condition of the spirit. They could, for example, "dress" the bones in new blankets to "keep the spirit warm" (Krause 1956:157). The cemetery also served as a visual representation of the attitude of the living to their departed matrilineal ancestors. Thus a gravehouse in a state of disrepair indicated neglect due to the poverty of the living. Such poverty prevented the living from asking their affines to fix the graves, since the living relatives had no wealth to give the affines. In one mythical account of a chief's journey to the distant *s'igeekáawu aaní*, the spirits that had died a long time ago and were forgotten by their descendants were called "Mossy-eyes;" whereas the ones called the "Dry-eyes" were fed and kept warm by their kin (Swanton 1908:462–463). These names invoke an image of a dilapidated old gravehouse covered with *wet* moss and a recently built or repaired *dry* one. Of course, gravehouses of aristocrats were more likely to remain in good condition, with freshly painted crests indicating the identity of their inhabitants.

The location of the domain of the dead on the mountain side, behind and above that of the living was not an accident. The interior, where the rivers flowing down to the coast began their course, was believed to have been the original home of the Tlingit, prior to their migration down to the sea shore. It was also the home where Raven retired to, having performed all of the acts of creation (Veniaminov 1984:387).[32] Thus the deceased retraced the mythical journey of his ancestors, travelling back in space as well as time. In addition, as we have seen, the interior was the direction of the rising sun and rebirth.

The immaterial *s'igeekáawu aaní* was located on the margin of the larger Tlingit universe, far away from the village of the living, the center of the cosmos. The village of the living occupied a narrow strip of the beach and some cleared ground between the water and the woods. The house always faced the water, showing its painted front to the visitors arriving from other communities. The space in front of the house was the public domain occupied by smokehouses, beached canoes, and similar items. Behind the house were storage facilities, menstrual and birth huts, and gravehouses. This was the more private space, kept hidden from members of other clans. Both the sea and the deep woods were considered dangerous areas, outside human control. At the same time, it was there that the male sought food, wealth, and magical power. He travelled on the water to reach other coastal peoples, who were both his enemies and sources of wealth. In the interior, where he felt less secure, the Tlingit encountered the Athapaskans, called *Gunanaa*, "The Strange People," who traded copper and furs for the products of the sea and, in the post-contact era, for European artifacts. The village was the core of the Tlingit universe, its inside, while the sea and the forest were its periphery, its outside. The house itself was strongly associated with the women who spend more time there than the men, raising children, preparing food and making household objects out of the raw substances brought in by men who hunted on the water and in the forest. Women's subsistence activities rarely took them far away from the house: they gathered berries in bushes behind the village and collected the "beach food" in front of it.[33] The safety of the house and the village was contrasted with the dangers of the forest and the ocean and figured prominently in Tlingit oratory and mythology (see Kan 1978).[34]

Despite the preeminence of marine hunting and fishing in Tlingit subsistence activities, the land was seen as a safer domain, associated with human life. The individual's life as a whole was symbolized by an old tree growing behind the village, which was the focus of many magical practices intended to prolong life. Thus, for example, the baby's moss diapers were carefully carried away from the water and the village and buried under an old tree or an old stump (i.e., the remains of a long-lived tree). Here, too, were buried the dishes and clothes used by an adolescent girl during her puberty confinement. The same tree was the focus of the ritual aimed at preventing the recurrence of drowning—the survivor's clothes were tied to it (de Laguna 1972:764–765; Kan 1979–1987).

Drowning was the most feared mode of death, since it made the recovery of the body and cremation unlikely. Unless the body was recovered and cremated, the spirit of the deceased could not be reincarnated and was lost forever. A victim of drowning was captured by a "land otter person" (kóoshdaa káa), who appeared to him in the guise of a close relative.[35] The unfortunate one was lured into the underwater house of the land otters and, after tasting their food and sleeping with their women, was transformed gradually into a kóoshdaa káa himself. To prevent this capture and transformation from happening, the kin of the deceased cast food into the water, hoping that it would reach the drowned person. The kóoshdaa káa was frightening because of its anthropomorphic qualities and the ability to appear as a human being. It was a marginal creature par excellence, inhabiting both land and water, playing and whistling like a human being and making fun of man by throwing rocks at him.[36] A person lost in the woods could also turn into a kóoshdaa káa, but the chances of finding him were greater. Cases of such recovery have been reported, with the victim described as acting like a wild animal (biting, eating raw food, and disregarding other human habits).[37] Another form of bad death, also associated with the sea, was that of an unconfessed witch: his or her body was consigned to the water, like that of a slave, who too was not considered a full person to be cremated.

While not being able to cremate the body of a victim of drowning created anxiety among his relatives, there were two categories of persons whose bodies were not cremated. They stood above or outside the world of the ordinary people. A brief look at these exceptions from the general rule provides additional support for my interpretation of cremation.

The Shaman and the Warrior—the Tlingit Supermen

Just as the shaman's life differed so markedly from that of others, so did his funeral and the disposal of his body. His face was not painted with the crest designs of his matrilineal group and his body was not placed in the back of the house for the duration of the wake. Instead, every night it was moved from one corner to the next, in the direction of the sun. The body was taken out of the house through the smokehole and was deposited in a grave house, which it entered from an opening in the roof (Knapp and Childe 1896:148). The shaman's grave was located in an isolated spot, away from the cemetery.

The shaman's body was not supposed to decay but to dry up, turning into a mummy. In fact, it was believed to be resistant to fire. Some of the shaman's paraphernalia were deposited with him in the gravehouse. Only a prospective shaman who wished to obtain the deceased's power would dare to visit the grave to spend the night lying in the gravehouse. Ritually unprepared lay persons were in danger of falling ill if they disturbed a dead shaman's peace. If they happened to see his grave, they left an offering of tobacco and food, praying for good fortune.

In light of the Tlingit notions of purity and pollution of the human body, discussed in Chapter II, this special treatment of the shaman's corpse could be interpreted as follows. The shaman's special purity was accomplished by his life-long observance of numerous rules and taboos, much stricter than those imposed upon the laity. This preserved the shaman's corpse from decay. In a way, the shaman did not die at all, since his outside (skin and flesh) remained linked to his inside (bones and immaterial attributes). Because the shaman was intact, offerings could be given to him directly rather than through the fire, and his grave remained a source of tremendous superhuman power. The movement of the shaman's body during the funeral emphasized the circular movement associated with his seances and the vertical axis (top/bottom; fireplace/smokehole), which contrasted sharply with the horizontal one (front/back; door/rear wall) reserved for the rest of the people.[38]

Another category of persons whose bodies did not require cremation was the brave warriors slain in battle. According to Swanton (1908: 429–431), a warrior "was too valiant to care to stay around the fire like weak people." Spirits of dead warriors went to special place, called keewakáawu,[39] which was a cold place in the sky, where they spent time engaged in games and military maneuvers. The living saw them in the form of the Northern Lights. They were believed to have plenty of food and to be served by the slaves killed at their funeral and by the enemies they had slain (Kamenskii 1985:71).[40] This special fate of the brave men who died in battle might be a consequence of their constant training designed to purify and toughen their bodies. It might have also been a special reward for those whose death was the most glorious one.

Despite this glorification of the warrior's death and afterlife, there was some ambiguity in the Tlingit view of his fate in *keewakáawu*. Thus, when the Northern Lights had a reddish color, it indicated that the dead warriors were happy to welcome another one into their midst (Swanton 1908:463; Jones 1914:163). Some accounts referred to it as a cold place, without lineage houses and other attributes of civilized life. This suggests that, while the warriors were glorified and perceived as physically stronger and, possibly, more pure than the rest of the people, they were placed outside the domain of the ordinary dead, where they could only engage in war-related activities (see Chapter IX for further discussion of warfare).

Finally, according to some sources (e.g., Swanton 1908:430), great chiefs were sometimes buried rather than cremated, which was considered a great honor (Emmons 1920–1945, ch. VI:21).[41] It appears that the rationale behind this practice was the same as the one that justified the preservation of the heads or scalps of prominent aristocrats and leaders, mentioned in Chapter IV. Like the shamans and the brave warriors, the highest aristocrats were the Tlingit supermen, to whom the fundamental principles of purity and pollution did not fully apply.

Attitude Towards Death and Relations Between the Living and the Dead

What was the Tlingit attitude towards death and how did they perceive the relationship between the living and their ancestors? To begin with, in this society of hunters and warriors where everybody had to take part in mortuary rituals, death was a common experience. The notion that death was always near and that a thin line separated it from life was expressed in a popular story about a boy who refused to listen to the elders' warning about the world being "as narrow and as sharp as a knife." Instead of being careful, he began to stamp the ground with his foot telling his grandfather, "See how I stamp the ground. There is plenty of room; I cannot fall off." While saying these words, something sharp went into his foot and the next day he died (Jones 1914:181–182; compare Boas 1895:319).[42]

Did the Tlingit fear death? There is no simple or definite answer to this question, since few statements on this subject were ever recorded, particularly in the nineteenth century. However, what evidence there is indicates that the Tlingit were rather calm, stoic, and fatalistic about it. Many elderly or severely ill persons have been reported to predict the time of their death and usually accepted it with resignation and self-control. Trefzger, an American who spent the entire first half of this century living among the Tlingit, says, "I have talked with thousands [?] of Indians and have never found one who feared death. When an Indian makes up his mind to die, he is going to die" (1963:27; compare Wilbur n.d.:518–519; Kan 1979–1987).

The warrior ethos glorified those who died defending the lives and honor of their matrikin and death was clearly preferred to slavery, poverty, or the miseries of old age.[43] Thus we know that a well-known Sitka chief, who was sick and almost totally blind during the last nine years of his life, finally decided to die and refused to accept any food or medication. American doctors tried to force-feed him, but his relatives strongly objected (*The Alaskan*, February 22, 1890). More recently, an old woman was found dead in her cabin, lying composedly on the bed, her face blackened with soot from the stove. It was believed that she had known herself to be dying, and had thus prepared herself for death, using the same color that a warrior going into battle would use, to show that she was not afraid (de Laguna 1960:77).

The Tlingit appear to have been less concerned with the prospect of leaving this world than with a possibility of dying a bad death, which would prevent the body from being cremated and from being properly honored by their survivors. Many elderly people had their funeral attire ready, long before they passed away. They would also often ask to have those clothes put on them before the onset of death (Jones 1914:149; McClellan 1975:299; Kan 1979–1987).

The emphasis on balance in social relations and on retribution and compensation for every wrong committed against oneself and one's matrilineal group by members of another one was reflected in a tendency to attribute many of the deaths to some sort of an agent. It is true that death of old age was seen as natural and that an expression "his/her time has come" was used for such deaths (Olson 1967:86). However, accidental deaths, deaths that followed a debilitating illness, and deaths of younger people tended to be blamed on an agent, who could be human (enemy, witch), superhuman (shaman's spirit, spirit of illness), or nonhuman (water).[44] Even when death was not attributed to a human or other-than-human agency, the language itself emphasized the need to search for an agent rather than accept death as resulting from some impersonal force. Thus drowning was referred to as "being killed by water" (de Laguna 1972:766).

What were the thoughts that could reconcile a Tlingit with the prospect of dying? First and foremost, there was the belief in reincarnation and the immortality of several of his spiritual attributes. Second, there was the hope of meeting one's departed relatives once again (Emmons 1920–1945, ch. VI:14). Most importantly, a dying person, particularly a member of a large kinship group and a person of some distinction, could expect not to be forgotten, but to live on as part of his group's *shagóon*, since his name, regalia, and other attributes of his social identity would be perpetuated by his matrilineal descendants. He could also hope to be able to visit his living relatives in their dreams and visions, and periodically receive gifts and food from them.

In Tlingit culture, the dead were clearly prominent in, what Hallowell (1955) calls, "the culturally constituted behavioral environment" of the living. With the exception of the ghost and mainly during the wake, there was relatively little fear of the dead or desire to keep them out of the world of the living, especially compared to many other North American Indian cultures (e.g., Hultkrantz 1953). Occasionally spirits which felt insulted or neglected by their living matrikin caused their illness or even death (e.g., Swanton 1908:462–463). More often, however, an unhappy spirit would appear in its close matrilineal relative's dream, asking for food, water, or warm clothing. It was then the duty of the living to organize a memorial feast, similar to those that followed cremation but smaller than a memorial potlatch, where the things requested by the deceased were cast into the fire and given to members of the opposite moiety (Olson 1967:65). However, unlike the classical East Asian and African ancestors, the Tlingit dead rarely interfered directly in the life of the living as the guardians of law and morality. Neither did they play the role of the major benefactors of their individual living kin. Instead, they served as the source of *shagóon*, the origin and destiny of their matrilineal descendants.[45]

Despite this closeness, the living and the dead had to maintain a certain distance. The forms of their interaction were clearly circumscribed, and their violation was severely punished. Thus, in the mythical era, when interaction between spirits and human being was much more common, the dead did act as benefactors, returning periodically to supply their descendants with food, wealth, and supernatural power. As long as the living maintained a certain distance from the ancestors, everything went well. However, most myths end in a tragedy—the living wish to see their ancestors or visit their homes and thus force the spirits to leave them forever (e.g., Velten 1939). Similarly, mythical marriages between the living and the dead end in the spouses' separation (Swanton 1909:247–250). The most serious violations of proper forms of interaction between the living and the dead were committed by the witches believed to visit cemeteries in order to speak to and have sexual intercourse with the dead. Numerous examples of the association between witchcraft and death exist.[46]

Nowhere else were the closeness and the reciprocity between the living and the dead so clearly expressed as in the mortuary and memorial rites themselves.

chapter six

THE DECEASED, THE MOURNERS, AND THE OPPOSITES
Actors in the Ritual Drama

Taking my cue from Hertz, I focus my symbolic analysis on the inter-relationship between the transformations that the corporeal and the noncorporeal attributes of the deceased as well as the survivors under-went in the course of the funeral. Unlike Hertz, however, I separate the living participants into two categories—the mourners and their op-posites—since their respective roles in this ritual were so radically different.

The Deceased

In the previous chapter, I demonstrated a correlation between the Tlin-git ideas about the need to maintain the purity of the human body and control over its outside by the societal values and norms internalized by its inside, and the use of fire to quickly destroy the flesh and release the hard and heavy bones as well as the immortal nonmaterial com-ponents of the deceased. This need for a speedy disposal of a dangerously polluted and polluting body seems, however, to contradict the lying-in-state ceremony, which was elaborate and usually lasted longer than the time needed for the corpse to begin to decompose.

To interpret the meaning of this prolonged wake, we must carefully examine the treatment of the dead body itself. On the one hand, as Hertz (1960) pointed out, the fate of the corpse often serves as a model for the fate of the soul. On the other hand, "close attention to the combined symbolic and sociological contexts of the corpse yields the most profound explanations regarding the meaning of death and life in almost any society" (Huntington and Metcalf 1979:17; compare 54). Even though the latter is something of an overstatement, it does apply fully to the Tlingit, so preoccupied with the purity and harmony of the living body. By focusing on the location of the corpse in the house, the nature of the artifacts with which it was decorated, and the interaction between the deceased and the survivors, we learn a great deal about the Tlingit view of the relationship between the person and his or her kin group, death and the social process, mortality and immortality.

The Decoration of the Corpse

The threat of pollution emanating from the corpse was made clear by the taboo on touching it, imposed on the deceased's matrilineal relatives. Being a material entity (outside) no longer animated and protected by its spiritual attributes (inside), the corpse was not only a source of danger to others but itself vulnerable to evil forces. Thus, witches were supposed to be drawn to it, in their desire to both harm the deceased and steal some small part of the corpse, for use in harming others. Only a constant vigil provided by the deceased's opposites and the fire kept burning in his house around the clock could protect him. The presence of the corpse in the midst of the living altered their social world completely, with all their routine activities suspended, reversed, or seriously curtailed (see below).

However, the corpse lying in state was more than just the dangerous outside no longer controlled by the inside. It was a visual representation of the transformations the deceased's immaterial attributes were undergoing. Thus, by decorating and manipulating the dead body, the living helped the spirit of the deceased in its journey to s'igeekáawu aaní. Some of these acts have been described in the previous chapter, but a few additional important ones should be mentioned. The crying songs performed by the matrikin of the deceased were said to be sung "under the foot" of the spirit, creating a trail for it by clearing the underbrush (McClellan 1975:373). They were performed every night of the wake, each of them marking a new stage in the spirit's journey. Although no direct evidence was found in Tlingit ethnography for the idea that these songs also actually guided the spirit, it is available for several closely related groups, such as the Tahltan. In their funeral, the mourners lifted their sticks and pointed them towards the east, the direction of the land of the dead, while singing, "This way is the trail. This way it goes. Don't miss it. The trail goes right to the east where the sun gets up" (Teit 1956:154–155).

By placing the deceased in a reclining rather than horizontal position, the mourners made it easier for the spirit to rise and leave for its journey into the interior, while the location of the deceased in the back of the house emphasized the direction that journey was supposed to follow. In the discussion of the two villages of the dead (Chapter V), we have already seen this use of the visible/corporeal to represent the invisible/spiritual, as the central element of the Tlingit world view. In the context of the funeral, it was expressed in the notion that the well-being of the corpse was a guarantee of the survival of the spiritual attributes of the deceased. This would explain the fear of any physical harm to the corpse, noted by several European observers. Thus, when a certain Klukwaan man was about to be killed by his enemies on the porch of his house, his mother appealed to them to let him descend to the foot of the steps, so that his dead body might not fall and be bruised (Willard 1884:81). Like those of dead animals and fish, human remains had to be maintained whole, so as to ensure proper rebirth and well-being of the deceased's new incarnation (compare Chapter II).

Considering a strong fear of pollution emanating from the corpse, how can we explain the Tlingit wake which lasted four days when the deceased was a commoner or an aristocrat of lower rank, and eight days if he was a high-ranking *aanyádi*? One could say that the wake was justified by the eschatological beliefs about the amount of time needed for the spirit to reach the distant village of the dead. The journey took several days, each one being marked by each night of the wake and each of the four major crying songs performed by the mourners. Cremation, with its own set of four crying songs, marked the completion of this journey (Olson 1967:59).[1] Occasionally the spirit would return and reanimate the dead body before it was cremated. Could it be that a four to eight day long wake was a practical solution to the problem of ensuring that a comatose person would not be mistaken for a dead one and prematurely cremated?

Eschatology and common sense do give us part of the answer but not the whole story. How, for example, could we explain a longer wake for an aristocrat? Of course, since his dead body was seen as being harder, heavier, and purer than that of a commoner, it could be displayed for a longer period of time. Thus, ethnopsychological and ethnosociological ideas also appear to be behind the lying in state ritual (compare Hertz 1960; Huntington and Metcalf 1979:63–67) but still do not explain what the survivors could possibly gain from a lengthy wake, if it posed such a danger to them.

Only an examination of the symbolism of the artifacts used to decorate the corpse and other verbal and nonverbal symbolic acts involved in the wake can provide answers to this question. One interesting fact was a concerted effort to mask and literally cover up the impure and polluted body with the artifacts representing the "social being grafted upon the physical individual" (Hertz 1960:77) and, hence, deny or at least retard the onset of death. Thus the corpse was displayed in a sitting or reclining position and was wrapped in several blankets. The face was painted with a representation of the deceased's crest, "so it won't look as if he was dead," as one of Emmons' (1920–1945, Shukoff's Account:16) informants put it, or would make him look like a sleeping person (Kan 1979–1987). While the mourners' faces were painted black, red—the color of life—was used to depict the crest designs on the face of the deceased.[2] Similarly, his festive garments contrasted sharply with the dark color of the mourners' attire, while his well-groomed hair was juxtaposed to their shorn hair.

All of the main personal possessions of the deceased, blankets and other wealth items donated by his lineage or clan, as well as the sacred regalia depicting his crests were displayed around the corpse. Its location in the most conspicuous and sacred area of the house, associated with its leader and ancestral paraphernalia, indicated that the deceased was treated with utmost "respect" and was in a position superior to all of the other members of his matrilineal group. While the head of the house had his quarters in that area and his closest matrikin frequently sat there, for a commoner, death was the main opportunity to move from the front to the back of the house, just as it was one of his rare chances to wear the sacred regalia of his group.[3] The wake was the time when society paid the individual its greatest respect and when a glorified image of his social persona was presented through various symbolic media. Thus the personal possessions of the deceased reflected his social roles of hunter, warrior, carver, house head, and so forth and made a statement about his success in accumulating wealth. The gifts brought by his matrikin for display around the deceased signified that he was highly esteemed.

My initial interpretation of the contrast between the appearance and treatment of the deceased and of his matrikin was that the latter, whose life was restricted by so many taboos, were socially dead, while the former was presented as being the center of sociality, hence symbolically alive (Kan 1982:210). However, a more careful examination of the nature of the decedent's decoration and regalia suggests that these items were similar but not identical to those used by the living aristocrats on ceremonial occasions. Hence the decorations and regalia reflected a more complex and ambiguous view of the deceased as being simultaneously alive and dead, at the height of his glory as well as on the threshold of his departure from the world of the living.

Thus, Emmons (1920–1945, ch. 2:25; 1916:17) tells us that the type of design painted on the deceased's face was reserved mainly for the dead and was considered more important than any other, since it represented his moiety rather than clan or house. This suggests that, in this moment of the person's greatest glory, the most fundamental aspect of his total social identity was emphasized while some of the basic distinctions dividing members of Tlingit society were transcended. This practice might be connected with the idea of the deceased's journey back in space towards the ancestral home of his people and back in time to the era preceding the Great Flood, when clans did not exist yet (compare Chapter V).

Some of the descriptions and drawings and photographs of the wake indicate that the deceased wore the conical wooden or woven root headdress called [aan ḵáawu] s'áaxw, "[chief's] hat" (e.g., Krause 1956:157; Kamenskii 1985:34; see fig. 3). This was the most valuable representation of a matrilineal group's crest, carefully guarded by its leader and worn by him or by a few selected aristocrats only during potlatches and some other highly auspicious occasions. More often, however, the [aan ḵáawu] s'áaxw was placed near the dead person's body while another type of headdress adorned his head. It was called shakee.át (see fig. 3) and consisted of a frontal relief crest animal, often surrounded by abalone shells, surmounted by sea lion whiskers and flicker feathers, with a long train of ermine skins hanging down the back. Held in place by the bristles or feathers was eagle down that the wearer shook out when dancing, creating white, fluffy drifts that covered everything like snowfall. As Jonaitis (1986:20–21) points out, despite the use of such valuable materials as ermine skins and abalone that suggested great wealth, this headdress was not quite as prestigious as the [aanḵáawu] s'áaxw (Jonaitis 1986:19). Unlike the conical crest hat, derived most likely from war helmets, which seem to have originated among the Tlingit themselves, and could be worn only by men, the shakee.át was said to have been copied from the Kwakiutl or the Tsimshian and to have become popular only in the middle of the nineteenth century among men as well as women (Jonaitis 1986:19; see also de Laguna 1972:492).

Another item of the ceremonial attire adorning the corpse was the so-called "Chilkat blanket" (naaxein; see fig. 3), a magnificent twined textile used by high-ranking persons for ceremonial dancing during potlatches and peace-making rites (Emmons 1907; Samuel 1982). While one blanket was wrapped around the deceased's shoulders, in the same manner as it was worn by the living, another one was invariably laid flat over his lower limbs. Additional Chilkat blankets as well as skins and ordinary blankets adorned the wall behind the body. The funeral was the only occasion on which the Chilkat blanket was displayed on a flat surface, with all of its geometric designs visible (compare Holm 1983:58–59; Jonaitis 1986:22). Sometimes it was cast into the funeral pyre, but more often it was used to wrap the cremated remains and was hung on the front of an aristocrat's gravehouse, once again being displayed on a flat surface.

What distinguished the shakee.át and the naaxein from the [aanḵáawu] s'áaxw and other ceremonial garments representing the wearer's crest was not only the fact that the first two could be found outside the Tlingit society but that they were traded from one Northwest Coast group to another and that, by the second half of the nineteenth century, they had become potlatch gift items (see Chapter IX). A few whole Chilkat blankets were given to the highest-ranking guests, while the rest might receive small strips. These greatly coveted strips were taken home and made into ceremonial garments such as aprons, leggings, and so forth. Occasionally, the strips of one blanket were reassembled to form a shirt, but there was little attempt to match the designs (Emmons 1907:346; Samuel 1982:35). Emmons and others also reported that the geometric elements used to depict a crest were so obscure that, in the end of nineteenth century, only the owner could identify it.[4]

All of this indicates that, while the Chilkat blanket remained a crest-bearing ceremonial garment, it could be passed from its original owner to an aristocratic member of another clan, who could not claim the crest represented on it. Similarly, if a *shakee.át* changed hands in a potlatch or a marriage transaction (e.g., de Laguna 1972:461), it could end up among people who had nothing to do with the crest adorning its front. It also seems that, unlike the conical crest hat and some other regalia representing crests which were collectively owned and, under normal circumstances, could not be alienated, the *naaxein* and the *shakee.át* were in the process of becoming the personal property of the wealthy and high-ranking aristocrats (see Chapter IX).

The reason for placing the more precious and prestigious conical crest hat near rather than on the corpse might have been the fear of pollution which could be masked but not denied by this elaborate ritual. At the same time, a preference for the Chilkat blanket and the *shakee.át*, could have something to do with the fact that they represented primarily the deceased's actual or temporary high social status and prestige and only secondarily his crests. Of course, his lineage, clan, and moiety identities were also represented by the design on his face, the regalia displayed near him, and the rear house screen and posts. Being more closely associated with the aristocrat's body and treated more as his personal property, the *naaxein* and the *shakee.át* were the more likely candidates for destruction in the funeral pyre. To burn the conical crest hat and other regalia claimed by the entire matrilineal group was too radical an act, carried out only on those rare occasions when the dedication of a new crest object, a very expensive undertaking, was planned (see Chapter VII).

I might add that despite the emphasis on the lineage, clan and moiety affiliation of the deceased made by the artifacts decorating the corpse, his paternal identity ("complementary filiation") was also represented. This was done by placing some of his father's clan regalia near the body and by performing some of its songs during the wake.[5]

Slave Sacrifice

When a chief or another high-ranking *aanyádi* died, it was customary to kill one or several slaves during the wake and cremate them along with him. The explicitly stated rationale for this act was to allow the deceased to use slave labor and enjoy high status in the *s'igeeḵáawu aaní*. Usually one or two (and occasionally more) slaves owned by the deceased himself were killed, but when a person of very high rank died, his matrikin and even his close affines donated their own slaves for that purpose (Markov 1849:37). Thus, when Shḵ'awulyéil, a famous chief of the Kiks.ádi clan of Sitka, died some time in the mid-1800s, five slaves were killed and one set free just before his body was cremated. Three of them were donated by his high-ranking Kiks.ádi relatives and the others by three Kaagwaantaan aristocrats, who offered them in the name of their Kiks.ádi wives (Olson 1967:52).

The manner of killing the slave was determined by the circumstances of his master's death (Veniaminov 1984:426). Thus, if the latter had died of illness or old age, the victim was usually killed by being laid down on the floor and having a log placed on his neck, on the ends of which several affines of his deceased master would sit. Sometimes he was simply hit on the head with a special stone club, which came to be known among the Europeans as the "slave-killer" (Emmons 1920–1945, Shukoff's Account:5; for illustration see Niblack 1888: plate XLVI). If the deceased was a victim of drowning, the slave was killed and thrown into the water instead of being cremated. Once the slave had been chosen for the sacrifice, his fate was linked to that of the deceased and he was marked as socially dead. The two had to depart from this world at the same time and travel to the *s'igeeḵáawu aaní* together. Hence if such a slave ran away and was caught or voluntarily came back after the cremation, his life was spared and he was usually set free. Thus, for example, when a young Haida man, selected to be killed at the funeral of a Sitka chief in 1868, escaped and found refuge among the American troops inside the fort, the Tlingit were willing to exchange him for four other slaves (Teichmann 1963:240–243; compare Markov 1849:36).

Death by cremation was considered an honor for the slaves, since the usual manner of disposing of their dead bodies was to throw them on the beach to be carried away by the tide. This postmortem treatment and other characteristics of the slaves, some of which have already been mentioned in Chapter IV, marked them as nonpersons. Thus, ironically, their sacrifice at the funeral of a high-ranking *aanyádi* restored their personhood and, in some way, equalized them with the free persons. The slaves' lives were at the mercy of their masters and they were generally treated like property. In fact, they were a standard measure of value, similar to blankets and copper shields (see Chapter IX).[6] Most slaves came from other tribes and were obtained through warfare and trade, and only the wealthy aristocrats owned them (Emmons 1920–1945, ch. VI:25; Kan 1979–1987).[7]

Slaves were killed on other occasions related to death (such as the potlatch) or to the "washing away" of an aristocrat's shame. The funerary killing or freeing of such a valuable commodity as slaves, demonstrated the dead person's and his relatives' wealth and the high esteem in which the relatives held him. On other more happy ceremonial occasions when large amounts of property were given away, such as the celebration of a high-ranking girl's completion of her puberty confinement, the birth of a child to high-ranking parents, or the piercing of their children's ears, slaves were more likely to be set free rather than killed (Veniaminov 1984:426). From their owner's perspective, the manumission of slaves was equal to their sacrifice, since in both cases valuable property was dispensed with.[8]

In addition to the abovementioned reasons, the killing of slaves at the funeral of a high-ranking and wealthy person had other, more covert meanings, which had to do with the destruction of human life. Despite the view and the treatment of slaves as nonpersons, their human nature could not be denied easily. First, high-ranking slaves were frequently redeemed by their matrikin and restored to their original status.[9] Second, strong attachment often developed over the years between an aristocrat and his slave. Third, if a slave who had been set free did not want to leave his master, he could be adopted into the lineage of the latter (de Laguna 1972:473). There is some evidence that the killing of a slave, particularly a favorite one, was not an easy thing to do emotionally (de Laguna 1972:471). This might explain why, according to some sources, the slaves to be killed in a potlatch were often purchased immediately before the occasion and were not used for economic purposes (Oberg 1937:116–117).[10] Finally, linguistic evidence points to the ambiguity of the slaves' status as both human and nonhuman. Thus, according to Boas (1917:93), in counting slaves, one could use either the form of the numeral applicable to persons or that used for objects.

All this indicates that there was some discrepancy between the beliefs about slaves, on the one hand, and the actual attitudes towards them and their sacrifice, on the other. Consequently their sacrifice in the funeral dramatized the social and cosmological crisis brought about by a high-ranking aristocrat's death.

The Deceased and His Matrilineal Ancestors in Oratory and Song

Similar to the abovementioned nonverbal statements, the speeches and songs performed during the wake expressed the beliefs about the changes the deceased was undergoing. While the speeches delivered by the mourners as well as their paternal/affinal kin made references to the deceased's biography and, by focusing on his contributions to the well-being of his house and clan, rather than on his shortcomings or idiosyncrasies, constructed an idealization of his life's career, the main underlying theme of the funeral oratory as well as the mourning songs performed during the wake was the beginning of the process of transformation of the deceased into a venerated ancestor. Thus to deliver a eulogy was "to speak of the ancestry [shagóon]" of the deceased (Olson 1967:60). Whereas the texts of the eulogies have never been written down,[11] a few condolence speeches made by the mourners' affines as well as a sizable number of the so-called crying songs (sing. gaax daasheeyí) or "song about one's feelings"[12] have been recorded, primarily by Swanton (1909:390–415), de Laguna (1973:1152–1176) and myself (Kan 1979–1987).

Because the structure and meaning of the condolence speeches is discussed below, I will address them here only briefly. Whenever the deceased was mentioned, his reunion with his departed kin in the s'igeekáawu aaní was emphasized. For example, in the following speech delivered by the husband of a deceased woman, the mourners are told not to mourn, because "She is not dead. Her paternal aunts are holding her on their laps. All her paternal uncles are shaking hands with her" (Swanton 1909:372).[13] Thus, in the village of the dead, the paternal kin continued to play their usual role of comforters who "pitied" their "children" (see below).

In contrast to these speeches which were composed for the occasion, although drawing on traditional images and themes, many of the crying songs were believed to have been composed many years

earlier by the mourners' human ancestors or mythological figures associated with their clan, while only some were created by the present
mourners themselves wishing to express their feelings (see below).
Like any other ancestral possessions, the former had a higher value.
Some of these songs made direct references to the matrilineal ancestors
of the deceased waiting to welcome him in the afterworld. For example, the song performed by a Kaagwaantaan clan during cremation
had the following words: "My sister's son has been led to the place
where people, who have been killed, go. His maternal uncles have
already made a house for him there" (Swanton 1909:407).

Because the songs of mourning rarely, if ever, mentioned the
deceased by name, using kinship terms instead, they could be used
generation after generation. The performer simply chose a kinship
term appropriate for his or her relationship to the deceased. Frequently
a particular song was chosen because it mentioned the same cause of
death as was involved in the present case, with drowning and violent
death being the most common. A typical crying song dramatized the
loss suffered by the mourners by increasing it to cosmic proportions, as
in the following one composed by a man whose mother and maternal
uncle had died: "The sound of your death, my maternal uncle, will
come down through Chilkat river. The clan's drum has fallen down,
my mother. Take the drum out from among the clans so that they can
hear my mother" (Swanton 1909:409).[14]

In the mourning songs, the present loss was compared, explicitly
or implicitly, with the previous deaths that had occurred in the same
matrilineal group. Thus, for example, one popular crying song belonging to a Sitka clan is believed to have been composed by a woman of
that group, after her canoe with her baby had been carried away by the
tide. In this song, the woman mourns her beloved child's death and
compares it to the tragic deaths of several of her clan ancestors, killed
while travelling in a canoe during the war with the Russians in the
early 1800s (Olson 1967:44–45; Kan 1986:198). The canoe carrying the
dead bodies links the two tragic events and invokes an image of loneliness and of being lost, a state greatly feared by the Tlingit. When the
matrilineal descendants of the song's author performed it during a
funeral (or a potlatch), they lamented the deaths of all of their
matrikin, both the recently deceased and those of long ago, including
the unfortunate infant and the brave warriors.

In both the funeral oratory and the crying songs, frequent references were made to the *shagóon* of the mourners' lineage and clan,

whether a certain landmark or a crest, for example, "When I look at the mountains of my grandparents' land, I imagine that my grandparents are still alive" (Kan 1979–1987). The power of the crying song lies in its ability to unite the mourners' totemic creature, a crest representing it, their departed ancestors, and their most recently deceased kinsman, thus expressing one of the two most fundamental principles of the Tlingit sociocultural order, the unity, solidarity, and immortality of the matrilineal group.

The Mourners

As we have already seen, the fate of the deceased depended heavily on his matrilineal relatives' conduct during the funeral. It was their sacred duty to carry out all their ritual tasks properly because, as Krause (1956:192) found out, "Only when the survivors observe all the mourning rites carefully does a soul easily find the path to the land of shadows. Otherwise the soul must wander around a long time before it reaches its goal." Any incorrect behavior on the part of the mourners was supposed to have dire consequences for the spirit travelling to the s'igeekáawu aaní. Thus, for example, excessive crying was discouraged, since it was believed to cause rain and sleet to fall on the spirit's trail.

The funeral was supposed to be watched by the spirits in the village of the dead, who took it to be a statement about the deceased's worth. A person whose funeral was not carried out properly, i.e., without sufficient "respect" shown to him, could not expect to be treated with "respect" by his fellow-spirits (Jones 1914:136). The more wealth was displayed, burned, and later distributed to the opposite moiety—the better the deceased was equipped for his new life in s'igeekáawu aaní. If he received little food, the deceased was "ashamed" to face the other spirits there (Swanton 1908:431).

Similarly, if the mourners showed a lack of generosity during the wake by not surrounding the deceased with large amounts of property, they embarrassed him, and themselves as well, in the eyes of the living—members of other clans, and especially those of the opposite moiety, entitled to receive that property at the end of the funeral.

For the duration of the entire mortuary cycle, and particularly during its most intense period between death and cremation, the fate of the deceased and that of his matrikin were closely intertwined.

Being physically linked to the deceased in life through shared corporeal and noncorporeal entities, they had to be separated from him in death, so as keep themselves from dying. The opposite moiety members were much less vulnerable, but even they had to purify themselves after carrying out their mortuary tasks (Kan 1979–1987).

The death of any Tlingit, with the exception of a slave or a *nichkakáawu*, had an immediate effect on his house and the matrilineal group associated with it. The passing of a free person was announced by the sound of the box drum beaten inside the house of the deceased. Although the box drum bore the same name (*gaaw*) as the smaller tambourine, in the hierarchy of musical instruments the former was considered to be higher (Jonaitis 1986:98). It was beaten with a fist or special tapping sticks and produced a loud sound. In times of death, it was beaten in a slow tempo, described by the verb *ji-si-taan*, "to pound," rather than *ya-gwaal*, "to beat" or "to tap," which is used to refer to the faster beating of the box drum, and particularly the tambourine (Story and Naish 1973:26–27). This practice explains such terms for the wake as, "they are sounding the drum" (Peck 1975:70) or the "drum-beating ceremony" (Shotridge 1917:106).[15] In addition, if the deceased was a high-ranking man, his brother-in-law announced his death by calling out loudly from the porch of his house.

The most immediately affected were the lineage kin of the departed. As soon as death was announced, they moved out of their house, while their opposites prepared the body for the wake (Emmons 1920–1945, ch. 6:14). This was the only occasion on which the winter house would be abandoned by its owners. Later on they returned to remain with the deceased until cremation, but no cooking was done in their house. Instead, the food was cooked and brought in by their opposites. Finally, during the wake the corner posts representing the lineage's crests remained draped and were uncovered only during the time of the special, ritualized wailing that took place every night.

The extent of the involvement of the other matrikin and the affines of the deceased in the wake and the duration of this ceremony were directly correlated with the deceased's own rank and status as well as that of his lineage and clan (compare Hertz 1960; Hunting and Metcalf 1979:69–71). In the case of a high-ranking decedent, the population of his entire village stopped its mundane activities and remained awake for a day or more, periodically visiting the house of mourning.[16] In addition, all of the members of his own moiety stopped working for eight days (Wallis 1918:79–80). When an aristocrat passed away, an atmosphere of tension and gloom set in. Thus, according to Olson (1967:49), when the head of a clan or his close relative died, everyone was alert to see if something out of the ordinary would take place.[17] The higher the status of the deceased, the greater was his matrikin's effort to establish the cause of death and, if a culprit was singled out, to avenge it.[18] An aristocrat's death, as we have seen, called for the death of slaves; in addition his male relatives might go on a war raid to kill some enemies and capture others to be sacrificed for his benefit (Swanton 1909:54–55; Olson 1967:110). In light of a strong emphasis on the unity and solidarity of the matrikin, it is not surprising that any death, particularly that of a person of high rank, sent shock waves throughout his entire house, clan, and even the other localized clans of his moiety.

Mourners in a State of Liminality

The mourners' separation from the mundane reality of everyday life was dramatically expressed by the various rules and taboos imposed upon them, including wearing old and dark-colored clothes and short hair, as well as fasting followed by abstention from most foods, sexual relations, idle talk, and work. For the duration of the wake, the mourners were socially dead, their condition marked by immobility and curtailed social activities. In addition, with their dark-colored and worn out clothes as well as their charcoal-covered faces, they were symbolically dead as well.[19] Their appearance, of course, contrasted sharply with that of the deceased. Face painting and haircutting were powerful expressions of the mourners' state of limbo between life and death, since they downplayed the regular social distinctions between people. Short hair was an especially dramatic sign of this, since long hair distinguished a free person from a slave. In addition, women's hair was seen as one of the main attributes of feminine beauty.[20]

Besides giving up part of their bodies' outside layer, the mourners temporarily gave up their physical beauty and the pleasures of life and parted with a substantial portion of their wealth. Another characteristic of the mourners was their helplessness. Just as they could not touch the corpse, they were not supposed to cut their own hair—shearing was done by their opposites. They were not allowed to touch their own polluted bodies either and had to use a scratching stick or a special stone instead.

One of the explicit objectives of these observances was to protect individual mourners and their entire kin groups from illness, death, and bad luck. The idea that many of the mourning observances were a form of self-sacrifice was clearly stated by one of de Laguna's informants, who offered the following explanation of haircutting:

> That's a law, you know. If we don't cut our hair, we [are] going to have some kind of trouble. We cut it off in place of that. Some bad luck, you know . . . something's going to happen to that [another matrilineal] relation again. That's why in olden time they cut your hair in place of that other trouble. (1972:537)

Many of the key features of the mourners' conduct were similar to those observed by the initiates in other rites of passage, such as childbirth, menstruation, and puberty or by persons who made a temporary but radical transition from their normal social state, such as the peace hostage, the shaman, and the warrior preparing for battle. What did all these rites have in common? In one way or another, they either involved a transition from life to death or were connected either with destroying life or with giving it (as in the case of the female rites). For example, the shaman died symbolically and was reborn during his quest or seance in which he might restore a patient to life or kill a rival shaman, while the warriors left their home (inside/center), where they had been born and where they were safe, and ventured into foreign lands (outside/periphery), where they could either be killed or would themselves become killers. In all of these cases, the transformations that the initiate/ritualist underwent had an important impact on the fate of his or her matrilineal kin and the universe in general.[21]

The mourners' state clearly corresponded to the one that Turner (1967:93–111) (following Van Gennep) described as "liminal." As he pointed out, the symbols associated with such states are in many societies often drawn from the biology of death, decomposition, catabolism, and similar physical processes. This association is particularly true, of course, of the mourners.

The function of their observances as protection against the polluting corpse and the dangerous ghost is a common phenomenon in mortuary rituals throughout the world. What is more unusual, however, is the Tlingit mourners' use of these practices to try to achieve spiritual power and good fortune. The key to their ritual conduct, and to that of all persons undergoing a rite of passage in this culture, were the concepts of *ligaas*, "it is taboo/danger/bad luck" and *laxeitl*, "good luck". To violate mourning rules was *ligaas*, while to follow them properly brought good luck and wealth, and ensured health and long life for the mourners themselves as well as the future members of their matrilineal group. Their liminal state allowed the mourners, like other Tlingit neophytes and ritualists, to make their bodies harder and more pure, and thus ensure *laxeitl* (see Chapter II). Turner emphasized these "positive aspects of liminality," when he spoke about "undoing, dissolution, decomposition" being accompanied by "processes of growth, transformation, and the reformulation of old elements in new patterns" (1967:99).[22]

Thus, according to one of de Laguna's (1972:536–537) informants, participants in the late nineteenth-century funerals in Yakutat wished to be "good people, have lots of money and good living." They also treated the female mourners' hair in a special way. Part of it was buried in a hole under a dead tree. The rest, in four strands, was draped on branches of a young tree. After eight days, it was removed and put in a hole under the tree. All of this was done to ensure the hair's good growth. At the end of the mourning period, members of the opposite moiety washed the female mourners' hair with blueberries to prevent it from turning grey in old age (see below for further discussion of the female mourner's body).[23]

An aristocrat's death gave the mourners a greater opportunity to seek *laxeitl*, since, as I have explained earlier, it created a greater social and cosmic crisis. Thus several sources mention a special ceremony involving the mourners' marching at dusk with tree branches throughout the village and performing a ritual of "lifting the sun":

> Just as the sun neared the horizon all held their canes out straight with the small end toward it and moved them slowly upward to keep the sun up a little longer. Then each would give utterances to some wish or prayer, such as these: "Let me be rich. Let me kill seal." (Swanton 1908:430; compare Olson 1933-1954, notebook 1:48)

In light of our discussion of the symbolism of aristocratic status, this association between the death of a high-ranking person and the setting sun (also a liminal phenomenon) makes a lot of sense.[24]

The Tlingit funeral represented a clear example of a close association between and a mutual influence of the "physical and the social bodies" (Douglas 1973:93). The transformations the deceased and his matrikin underwent clearly paralleled each other and can be represented schematically, following Van Gennep's (1960) model of the rites of passage:

The Deceased

1. Separation: the body had been washed, dressed, covered with crest designs, and surrounded with crest-bearing objects and wealth;

2. Transition: the body in state, spiritual attributes of the deceased separated from the corpse, but remain in the house; the dead flesh (the outside) is covered with attributes of the decedent's social persona / shagóon; the corpse is taken outside and cremated; and cremation destroys the flesh and releases the bones and the noncorporeal entities which survive;

3. Incorporation: bones are deposited in the gravehouse; ghost and two spirits are installed in their respective domains.

The Mourners

1. Separation: the mourners cease regular activities, don old clothing, and have their hair cut;

2. Transition: the mourners are in proximity to the corpse, converse with the deceased, and are subject to mourning observances (i.e., being neither dead nor alive);

3. Incorporation: the mourners return to the house after the cremation, dress festively, and are no longer subject to most of the mourning rules.

This scheme also reminds us of Hertz's (1960:64) comment about the "parallelism between the rites which introduce the deceased, washed and dressed in new clothes, into the company of his ancestors, and those which return his family to the community of the living" (compare Huntington and Metcalf 1979).

Ritual Expression of Grief

In addition to trying to protect themselves from pollution and achieving laxeitl, the matrikin of the deceased used mourning observances to express their grief. My reconstruction of the mourners' behavior and experience in the funeral is inevitably incomplete, since most of the data available for the nineteenth century deal with the public and more ritualized forms of expressing grief. We do know that individual mourners cried and wailed in private and that their public conduct did not always correspond to cultural norms. However, with the emphasis placed by the Tlingit on self-control and self-restraint and on ritualized rather than spontaneous expression of emotion, the information available on public mourning seems rather comprehensive. What we can reconstruct is *the native theory of grief and mourning*, a model which guided an individual mourner's public behavior and against which it was judged.

In the Tlingit view, grief developed inside the mourner's body, independent of his or her will. It was described as the "pain inside one's *toowú*." Thus "I am sad" or "I am in sorrow" was rendered as *ax̲ toowú yanéekw*, literally "my inside hurts." Grief was also described as a "weight" inside the body. It was said to emerge *spontaneously* from this inside container and could be expressed in more idiosyncratic behavior, such as violence against oneself or others, and crying, as well as in more formalized conduct, including singing and oratory. Thus, Swanton (1908:437) was told that,

> If a man's near relative, such as his mother, died, it is said that a song was made up inside of him, where it worked until it came out. It is not through a man's own will, but the way Raven made people that brings forth a new song when people are called together after one has died.

Accounts of nineteenth century funerals do indicate that expressions of grief were often violent: mourners often shrieked, wept uncontrollably, inflicted cuts and bruises upon themselves, and even tried to throw themselves into the pyre (Khlebnikov 1976:29; Veniaminov 1984:420; de Laguna 1972:532). According to several sources, they even occasionally committed suicide and, in the post-contact era, "stupefied themselves with liquor" (Jones 1914:9). As Jones (1914:120), who labored among the Tlingit as a Presbyterian missionary for many years, put it, "No people of the world have keener anguish over the loss of loved ones than the [Tlingit] natives of Alaska. We have heard wailings from them that would melt the hardest heart to tears."[25]

Even if some of these descriptions are not based on first-hand observations while others tend to exaggerate and/or mistake orchestrated wailing for a spontaneous expression of sorrow, it is clear that some mourners did lose self-control. Such behavior contrasted sharply with the emotional restraint characteristic of daily life, which impressed many Western observers. Krause spoke of the Tlingit reserve, dignity, self-control, and amazing endurance of pain and other hardships (1956:110). He claimed that few signs of strong affection were displayed, except towards small children (Krause 1956:112). The mourners' conduct clearly marked the funeral as a special social event, where norms of everyday behavior were modified and even violated.[26] Grief mixed with anger made the mourners act violently not only against themselves but against others as well. Thus, in Shotridge's words, "A grief-stricken man would oftentimes resort to some means which he believed to create some sort of a relief of the pain of bereavement . . . which oftentimes led to taking in hand the life of a slave, or destruction of property" (n.d.:n.p.). The violence could also be directed outside the mourners' community, as in the case of a high-ranking deceased's kin going on a war raid and killing the first person they happened to encounter.[27]

These less restrained, more idiosyncratic expressions of grief occured throughout much of the funeral, beginning with the announcement of death and reaching their climax during the corpse's removal from the house and its cremation, when the mourners saw the body of their relative for the last time. Although such behavior was expected, excessive grieving was discouraged as being detrimental to the deceased (as noted at the beginning of this subsection), the mourners (who could get sick or kill themselves), and their present and future matrikin (whose deaths could be caused by their forebears' excessive grieving) (de Laguna 1972:532–533).[28] Thinking too much about the deceased was also seen as dangerous to the mourners, who could lose their minds or decide to join him.[29] Among the Inland Tlingit, members of a bereaved family used to mark their temples with hellebore to prevent such thoughts from becoming an obsession (McClellan 1975:396).

More typical than this violent and unrestrained expression of grief was the more formalized wailing, weeping, and lamenting, as well as speaking about the deceased's life and addressing him directly. With the exception of eulogies delivered mainly, if not exclusively, by men, all of these other acts were performed by women throughout the entire wake, interrupted only by the much more formalized nightly mourning ritual attended by both the high-ranking members of the mourners' clan and moiety and their affinal/paternal kin (Emmons 1920–1945, ch. VI:16).[30] The key role of crying in the expression of grief is clearly indicated by the noun _gaax_, "crying," used to refer to the wake. The verb _gaax_ can be glossed as "cry, weep, lament, mourn." The mourners themselves were referred to as _gaaxni_, "criers" (de Laguna 1972:533–536). Unfortunately, very few of the funeral laments have been recorded. Emmons reported one, which he described as follows:

"the talk is low and is a song or a chant;" it was addressed by female mourners to their deceased chief:

> When you were alive you used to look after us and help us so, now you have left us forever, you will never see us again, but you will see your fathers in another world who have been waiting many long days for you, but do not forget us for we will see you in the future. (1920–1945, Shukoff's Account:17)

This chant was both an expression of the grief of the mourners faced with the inevitable parting with their matrilineal relative and an effort to comfort the deceased himself by promising a reunion with his beloved paternal kin.[31]

Another genre were the songs the mourners themselves composed for the occasion, in which they addressed the deceased using an appropriate kinship term. The imagery here is rather simple, expressing the feelings of loneliness and sorrow. Such songs became the property of the composer, but were often passed down to his or her matrilineal descendants and transformed into a lineage- and/or clan-owned mourning song performed at funerals and even memorial potlatches. The following song reported by Emmons (1920–1945, ch. VI:18) could well have been one of them:

> I am sorry, my brother
>
> When you go.
>
> I will see you again, my brother.
>
> May be I die soon.[32]

Many of these songs described the afterlife and, thus, both directed and helped the deceased, and comforted the mourners by emphasizing the survival of his spirit.

Mourning songs performed during the more formalized nightly rituals attended by members of the opposite moiety had a higher value. They were called "sad songs" (*toowúnóok daasheeyí*, from the verb [*kaa*] *toowú + ya-néekw*," to feel sad"), "heavy (i.e., serious) songs" (*yadali sheeyí*), or "songs about feelings" (de Laguna 1972:569; Kan 1979–1987). Four (or eight) of them marked the stages of the spirit's journey to *s'igeekáawu aaní* and were especially precious. Each matrilineal group possessed its own set, used generation after generation. A few of these songs have been recorded by Emmons (1920–1945, ch. VI:18):

> Come back, come back,
>
> My brother.
>
> From the spirit land.
>
> Come back.

As if it were possible to hear thy voice
Once more in thine house,
My brother.
I listen for thee in the early morning.

Another example of a song of mourning is the one composed by a man called Hayiaak'w about a drifting log found full of nails, out of which his lineage house was eventually built. It was used when a feast was about to be given for a dead man and the mourners had blankets tied up to their waists and carried canes (Swanton 1909:395):

I always compare you to a drifting log with iron nails in it.
Let my older brother float in, in that way.
Let him float ashore on a good sandy beach.
I always compare you, my mother, to the sun passing
    behind the clouds.
That is what makes the world dark.

The most valuable of the crying songs used in funerals were those that made references to the mourners' crests. They were believed to have been composed in the mythical past by the ancestors of the present owners. They were called "long ago songs" (ch'áakw daasheeyí) and, because of their value, were often reserved for the memorial potlatch.[33] Some valuable songs were used in both the funeral and the potlatch. In fact, sources reporting them do not always indicate the occasion on which they were performed.

One such song was collected by de Laguna (1972:1171–1172) in Yakutat. It is owned by the Shangukeidí clan and is believed to have been composed by a young boy of that group who had been lost and saved by a thunderbird. After returning to his clan, he built a house with a screen decorated in the same manner as the thunderbirds' cave in which he had dwelled. The screen depicted a thunderbird, which his clan adopted as its crest. The song is performed at every funeral of a Shangukeidí and has the following words:

Whenever I hear the sound of thunder[bird],
I become hurt.
This sound reminds me of my [lost] maternal uncle and brother.
I am surprised when I hear thunder.
It sounds like the relatives I lost.

Another interesting mourning song, which could have been used in funerals as well as memorial potlatches, is reported by Garfield and Forrest (1961:20). It belongs to a certain house of the Wolf moiety which claims the wolf as one of its crests. One day, when the ancestors of that house were fishing, they came upon a wolf swimming ashore. The wolf was tired and so his tongue was sticking out. Men pulled him ashore and took him to their village. The wolf stayed with them, hunting and always bringing them plenty of meat. It came to be regarded almost as a member of that house. Not long before its death, a dream came to one of the men of the group. In the dream, the wolves, "wolf people," appearing as human beings, were singing a mourning song for their relative:

> He did what his forefathers have done.
>
> He did what his forefathers have done.
>
> My uncle has crossed the great divide.
>
> Now I have given up all hope since he is gone.

Because this is a lament for their dead relative, members of that group sing it only as a mourning song. They also have a house post depicting a Tired (Panting) Wolf, their house crest.

Let us now look at the characteristics of these songs, in order to establish how they were supposed to express the mourners' sorrow.[34] Crying songs were often composed in response to some tragic event that caused the death of the composer's matrilineal relative. Thus, a beautiful and sad funeral song claimed by the Teikweidí clan, which claims the brown bear as its crest, was believed to have been composed under these circumstances. A man named Kaats' married a female bear and had cubs with her who grew up and one day killed him. At that time his bereaved wife composed the song:

> You left me for good, my old husband.
>
> Where have you gone?
>
> Where have you gone?
>
> My husband. (see Emmons n.d., notebook 3)

Other examples of this genre include a song composed by a man who accidentally killed his brother; in it he addresses the victim, "My younger brother, where are you / Why did I do it / Come back to me." Another sad song was composed by a woman about her drowned relatives. One mourner composed a song during an earthquake, when the earthquake displaced the remains of his maternal uncles from their tombs. Songs were often composed about one's relatives that had drowned or had been slain in war. Some songs came to the mourner in a dream or were heard by him in the sound of the waves and other natural phenomena (Kan 1979–1987).

Mourning songs always addressed one or several members of the composer's/singer's own clan. For example, the death of the composer's brother reminds him of the loss of his maternal uncles; in the song he creates, the first stanza laments the former and the second the latter. Only the dead members of one's clan could be addressed. The composer/singer never referred to himself by name and, hence, the song could be used by other members of his matrilineal group. In subsequent performances, different kinship terms could be substituted for the original ones. A song considered beautiful and moving became clan property and part of its mortuary repertoire. Since many of the same songs were used generation after generation, in the minds of the people they became associated with their own specific relatives they had lost. Hence, in a group of mourners singing a song together, different individuals might be mourning different dead kin. One of Emmons' informants (1920–1945: Shukoff's Account:17) pointed out that the Europeans were wrong in thinking that the Tlingit hired mourners to cry, instead "other women"—matrikin of the deceased as well as their affines—"may come to sit and cry through memory of their own troubles."

The structure and imagery of a typical mourning song is indicative of its intended message and effect on the mourner. It emphasizes an interconnection between individual members of a matrilineal group, their living and dead relatives, as well as their crests. Thus, for example, one of the above-mentioned songs deals with the composer's feelings caused by the death of his brother. This loss makes the composer lonely—he expresses his sorrow by referring to his lineage house that had been destroyed. Hence, a connection is established between the lost matrilineal relative and the house the composer had once shared with him. The log's safe landing on a sandy beach is juxtaposed to the relative's death. The song expresses the composer's wish to see his brother again or at least to know that he is in a good, comfortable place. In the second stanza, the death of the composer's mother is compared to the hiding of the sun, i.e., darkness, absence of light, death. Through the use of metaphor, the loss of a relative is magnified to cosmic proportions. Thus, the song establishes a homology between the deaths of close matrikin, important events in the history of the composer's matrilineal group, and natural calamities.

Crying songs were supposed to be an expression of the composers' innermost feelings and were expected to move other mourners to tears. They were highly introspective: the composer constantly referred to his feelings (*ax toowú;* compare de Laguna 1972:567). In the past as well as today, mourning songs have been accompanied by sobs and wails. As de Laguna points out, "Long after the death they might be renewed, for example, at potlatches or on any other occasions when the dead were called to mind" (de Laguna 1972:532–533). Thus one of her informants told her that when she was a child her grandmother used to go outdoors and take her in her lap, while she sang and wept for hours over the death of an uncle who had died many years ago (de Laguna 1972:532–533). "It is still common for individuals, especially women, to sing when alone, the tears streaming down their faces at remembrance of the dead with whom the music is associated in their minds" (de Laguna 1972:561). During the recording of one of the mourning songs, the singer explained (de Laguna 1972:1163): "It's just the way I feel too, sometimes—like that song composer. Sometimes I get the same feeling. And I'm just singing to let the people know that I have the same feeling for my relatives."

The mourning songs' style strengthened their sad message. Their tempo was slow and heavy. In fact, while the more recent songs, composed in the late nineteenth and the early twentieth centuries, are more tuneful and more dependent upon the sense of their words, the older songs—more valuable because of their association with the earlier ancestors, including the nonhuman crest animals and mythical beings— used unfamiliar archaic expression and conveyed little information. The singers were often uncertain of their meaning, although they knew the basic general idea of the songs. As de Laguna (1972:566–567) explains,

> Just as the words of the old songs so often convey so little explicitly, so too their tunes are generally limited in range to a few notes. It is as if time had drained them of words and melody, leaving only the emotional significance to be conveyed by the several voices intoning in harmony and the insistence of the long drawn-out phrases reiterated to the slow heavy beat. *This is particularly true of the old mourning songs and dances chanted at funerals.* (italics mine)

The mourners' feelings were expressed not only through singing but through movement of the body as well. Most Tlingit songs performed on ceremonial occasions were accompanied by dancing. In the case of the mourning songs, the dancing involved a slow movement; the mourners performed without moving their feet and with their bodies swaying to and fro, their arms moving from side to side, and their knees dipping (de Laguna 1972:567; Peck 1975:56; Kan 1979–1987). Female mourners wore long earrings, which swayed slowly as they danced. Like the mourning songs themselves, this type of dancing was supposed to help the mourners forget their sorrow. Songs and dances performed at funerals and memorial potlatches were structured and patterned. The songs were always performed by choruses of men and women.

The formalized expressions of grief, particularly in the mourning songs, is a good example of the centrality of the kinship group in Tlingit culture and the person's life and experience. Grief was an emotion that had to be shared with others. In fact, a song that expressed the innermost feelings of the singer could be used generation after generation, by his own clan and even other clans, who might ask for permission to do so. Just as the individual shared many of the aspects of his social identity with the group and inherited many of them from his clan ancestors, so could a song of mourning composed by a specific mourner for a specific occasion become part of the permanent sacred property of his group. That must be the reason why the composer did not refer to himself by name and why kinship terms referring to the deceased could be substituted. The causes of death and the metaphors used to depict the demise of the relative being mourned were usually common occurrences in Tlingit life, for example, drowning or death in battle. That is another reason why they so often became clan-owned property. However, despite this emphasis on standard imagery and tunes, there was plenty of room for individual creativity. A song that moved the audience, that was remembered and became part of its ceremonial repertoire, had to be especially eloquent in expressing emotion and in using crests (compare Dauenhauer 1975).

The following example, which illustrates the power of the cultural form over spontaneous expression of emotion, confirms my argument about the relative rigidity of the Tlingit etiquette, particularly for the aristocracy. Olson (1967:50–51) reports a story of an aristocratic woman who returned home to find out that her son was dead. When first told about the tragedy, she managed to maintain a reserved demeanor and answered, "All right. I have heard." As she entered the house and saw the body of her son propped up in the back of the house, she went down the steps, dancing and singing in Tsimshian (to indicate some Tsimshian ancestry that she had), "I am stunned. I am stunned." Only after that did she start weeping and wept for days. She composed mourning songs for all of her children who had died, and these songs are still sung today at funerals and potlatches.

Differentiation of the Mourners

The influence of social norms and ethnopsychological ideas on the mourners' conduct was also evident in their differentiation according to gender and rank. Thus the female mourners were supposed to spend more time near the corpse than their male matrikin, who were busy discussing the funeral arrangements with their affines.[35]

The men's mourning was expressed primarily during the formalized nightly "cries," in which they appeared carrying long staffs. The latter were used to strike the floor in time with the mourning songs. According to some accounts, all of the male mourners carried them, while other reports suggest that only the aristocrats did. In the latter case, the staffs must have depicted the mourners' crests and were similar (or identical) to the wootsaagáa, a ceremonial staff carried by chiefs and their spokesmen during potlatches and other important ceremonies.[36] An anonymous author, who witnessed a funeral in Sitka in the 1880s, describes the following scene:

> A procession of about twenty Indian warriors [men], headed by old Anaxóots, the war chief of the tribe [head of the deceased's clan], filed through the small portal. Each carried in his hand a long slender staff made of hard wood and carved all over with fantastic figures. . . . These staves bore evidence of their great age by the high polish which they possessed, as well as by their smoky color and pungent odor. The warriors ranged themselves in line along one side of the house, facing the center, and immediately began a lugubrious death chant, keeping time by raising their staves about three inches from the floor and letting them drop together. (Niblack 1890:358)

Similar staves were used by the male mourners for striking a special wooden board to accompany the songs performed during cremation (Niblack 1890:359; Krause 1956:157–158).

The use by the male mourners of the wootsaagáa, the symbol of the matrilineal group's shagóon and the chiefly authority, not only emphasized their superiority over the female mourners, but reflected the notion that men and women had to express their emotions differently.[37] First, as I have already stated, women were expected to be less capable of controlling their emotions. Second, they were supposed to use their own body to express their grief. In contrast to women, male mourners had to restrain their bodily movements and use a material object representing their *shagóon* instead.[38] Thus, according to Krause (1956:156), during the distribution of gifts immediately following a funeral he had witnessed, ten to twelve men of the clan of the deceased kept time by striking the floor with long poles grasped with both hands, while mourning songs were performed. During the same performance, the women mourners rose several times and "accompanied the songs with peculiar, but beautiful, motions, a rocking with the knees and the willowy bending of the upper body."

While aristocratic members of the matrilineal group of the deceased were supposed to be immobilized by the mourning rules which they shared with their matrikin, they retained their leadership role in the funeral, presiding over the periodic formalized cries, the distribution of gifts to members of the opposite moiety, and other important aspects of the ritual (see next chapter).

The Opposite Moiety

Prohibited from touching the corpse, the matrikin of the deceased turned to the opposite moiety for help. They were rarely refused, since the performance of funerary services for one's paternal/affinal relatives was a sacred duty, fundamental for the functioning of Tlingit society. In the funeral, the local opposites predominated, since there was usually not enough time to wait for the out-of-town ones to arrive. Their ritual acts, which might be called "services of affliction" (compare Goody 1962:64 and following), were ranked, with the most prestigious ones assigned to persons of higher status and the closest paternal/affinal kin of the deceased. Male opposites were entrusted with the duties seen as somewhat more prestigious than those performed by the female ones.

Opposites as Mediators

Women usually washed and dressed the body and painted the face, while men protected the corpse against witches. The men also took the body outside at the conclusion of the wake, built the pyre, and cremated it. Following cremation, the women gathered the bones and wrapped them up, while the men built the grave house and placed the remains in it. Either one of the sexes would cut the mourners' hair, while the female opposites prepared the food for them. Both sexes helped the mourners with the singing. Male opposites dominated the oratory of condolence and received more tobacco in the smoking ceremonies.

These acts protected the mourners from the danger and pollution emanating from the corpse and mediated between them and their deceased relative, or more generally, between *pollution* and *purity* and between *death* and *life*. They prevented the mourners from touching not only the corpse itself but their own polluted bodies. Finally, in the course of the wake, and especially during the subsequent memorial feasts, the opposite moiety served as the channel through which tobacco and food could be sent to the recently deceased and other matrilineal ancestors of the mourners.

This mediatory role of the ego's affinal/paternal kin was crucial throughout his or her entire life cycle. Thus, the ego's father's sister assisted in the delivery, while the father's brother built the cradle. During the first menstrual seclusion, the girl's paternal aunt visited her, along with her mother and maternal grandmother. The ego's ceremonial regalia were made by his or her opposites, with men carving staves, helmets, house posts, and other wooden objects and women making ceremonial garments. If the person were a high-ranking aristocrat and had to build a new house, his brothers-in-law performed the work.[39]

Throughout his or her life, the person wore a series of garments and moved from one container to the next, all of them made by his or her opposites. Even the funeral pyre and the box for the cremated remains were containers, and these were constructed by members of the opposite moiety. The association of the opposite moiety with these containers is indicated by the terms used for addressing the opposite moiety on ceremonial occasions. Among them were: *ax̱*, "my," *daakeitx̱'í*, plural of *daakeidí*, "box, shell, container, womb, grave, coffin." These terms were translated as "my outside box, my outside shell, people I came from" (Olson 1967:13; Swanton 1909:374; Stone 1971:44). Another term commonly used in formal oratory was *ax̱ daakanóox'u,* "my outside shell" (Swanton 1909: 372–373; Kan 1979–1987).[40]

Another way of looking at the meaning of the funerary services provided by the opposites is that they handled the deceased's polluted outside, allowing the mourners to concentrate on his pure inside, i.e., those aspects of his total social persona that were immortal and derived from his matrilineal group's *shagóon.* Just as the existence of the opposite moiety as the pool of affines prevented the person from engaging in incestuous relationships, it saved him from touching his own dead matrikin.[41]

This help offered to the mourners by their opposites was presented as an expression of the love that fathers were supposed to feel towards their children. The crucial role of the father in the construction of the ego's total social persona has already been discussed. I might add that, unlike the ego's maternal kin who acted as harsh disciplinarians, the father was seen as somebody who pitied the child and did not punish it.[42] In Tlingit ethnopsychology, *love* and *pity* were the key emotions that characterized the relationship between the father and his child, and were frequently used in oratory. For example, a person trying to make peace between feuding individuals or groups would appeal to them by saying, "Have pity on my children" (Olson 1967:14). The father/child closeness was emphasized by the practice of allowing the warrior to wear a helmet representing his father's clan crest and even to borrow such a crest for wearing in a potlatch (Olson 1967:108; Kan 1979–1987). The ultimate expression of the father's love was his lending of his crest for his child's lying in state ceremony, mentioned earlier.

In addition to performing the necessary funerary services, the mourners' opposites offered moral support by their presence, their help in singing the crying songs, and, most importantly, by ritual oratory, which expressed their paternal love and pity most dramatically. Because oratory is the subject of a separate paper (Kan 1983) and is also examined in Chapter VIII, I will discuss it here only briefly (see also Dauenhauer 1975:185–204).

Unfortunately, very few condolence speeches given during the funeral have ever been recorded. At the same time, there are a number of examples of a similar kind of oratory presented by the mourners'

opposites in the memorial potlatch (Swanton 1909:374–389; Dauenhauer 1975:185–201; Kan 1979–1987). Although we do not know exactly how different the speeches delivered at funerals were from those
given at potlatches, it is my impression that their basic structure and
imagery were quite similar. The latter seem to have been more
elaborate and more concerned with invoking the speaker's crests and
ancestral myths. The former's main goal was to remind the mourners
that their opposites had suffered similar losses in the past and could
thus fully understand and sympathize with them. They also emphasized that the mourners had to remember that they could rely on
their paternal and affinal kin for help and comfort. As one speaker put
it in his address to the matrikin of the deceased, "When my father's
father died you came to comfort us. Now I am here. You see it, my
father's clansmen, my grandparents. Do not mourn too much!" (Olson
1967:59–60).

Each speech of condolence opened and closed with what Dauenhauer (1975:186) calls a "genealogical catalog," an invocation of all of
the kinship terms appropriate for addressing the mourners.[43] These
kinship terms were seen as powerful words of comfort, because they
presented the speakers as the mourners' fathers and affines full of love
and pity for them. The opposites also comforted the mourners by telling them that their own matrilineal ancestors were now welcoming the
newly departed person into the village of the dead. As one elder put it
in a recent speech addressed to the matrikin of the deceased:

> We know that you are suffering a great deal, my fathers, my in-laws. But you
> should feel better knowing that our own departed maternal uncles and aunts
> are welcoming the relative you have just lost, their paternal nephew, with the
> open arms. They are waiting to embrace and caress him, their beloved paternal
> nephew. (Kan 1979–1987)

Here is a sample of a typical condolence speech which would have
been delivered during a smoking feast held during the wake. It was
recorded in the early 1900s by Swanton (1909:372–373) from chief
Katishan of Wrangell. In this case, the first speaker is the husband of
the deceased woman. According to Katishan, he would say something
like this:

> Yes, yes, my grandparents, we remember you are mourning. We are not smok-
> ing this tobacco for which you have invited us. These long dead maternal
> uncles of ours and our mothers are the ones who smoke it. Do not mourn, my

grandparents. She is not dead. Her paternal aunts are holding her on their laps. And all of her paternal uncles are shaking hands with her. Our [dead] chief has come back because he has seen you mourning. Now, however, he has wiped away your tears. That is all.[44]

One of those giving the feast would now reply:

I thank you deeply, deeply for the things you have done to your grandparents with your words. A person will always take his outside shell [*daakanóox'u*] to a dry place. So you have done to this dead of ours. All these, your grandparents, were as if sick. But now you are good medicine to us. These words of yours have cured us.

By emphasizing that they were only representing or incarnating their own deceased matrikin, the speakers comforted the mourners by constructing an image that linked together four categories of persons: the living mourners/hosts and their opposites/guests, and the dead matrikin of each group. The current loss suffered by the hosts was placed within a perpetual cycle of births and deaths, in which the two moieties offered help and condolence to each other. This was an effort to render death more predictable and may be less threatening. The opposites' help was compared to the aid offered to mythical protagonists by superhuman creatures as well as to beneficial actions of ordinary human beings, for example, "taking one's outside shell to a dry place."

The emotional comfort provided by the mourners' opposites was also compared to medicine and other forms of physical comfort and healing that affected the grieving persons' inside (*toowú*). Thus to describe comforting, encouraging, and cheering up the Tlingit used *ḵaa toowú yaa-x' + si-haa*, "erase something from the person's inside," *ḵaa toowú + li-t'aa*, "warm the person's inside," and *ḵaa toowú + li-tseen*, "strengthen the person's inside" (Story and Naish 1973; Kan 1979–1987). The guests were also described as having given the mourners "good fortune" or "blessing" (*laḵeitl*), an act usually associated with benevolent superhuman creatures.

Besides this ritualized condolence, the mourners' opposites offered them informal comforting. Unfortunately, we do not know much about this. A visit from the opposites, a handshake or a word of comfort offered in private must have been important in assuaging the mourners' grief, just as such gestures certainly are today. However, ideologically, they were valued lower than the ritualized forms of condolence, just as the informal mourning was placed below the formalized one.

The Widow

Among the mourners' opposites taking an active part in the funeral, an anomalous position was occupied by the spouse of the deceased. Although not a member of the latter's matrilineal group, the widow or widower behaved like one, observing a variety of mourning taboos. This was particularly true of the widow whose mourning observances were more prolonged and elaborate than those of either the widower or any of the deceased's matrikin. At the same time, the identity of the dead person's spouse as a member of the opposite moiety was not completely denied, so that he or she was generously remunerated at the post-cremation memorial feasts and especially the potlatch. The discussion of the uniqueness of the role played in the funeral by the spouse of the deceased, particularly the widow, sheds light on Tlingit ideas about marriage, the relationship between spouses, and the role of women in the sociocultural order.

During the entire funeral, the widow or widower remained in close proximity to the deceased and was required to sit motionless and quiet next to the body.[45] The only food that reached the deceased during this time was that which his or her spouse burned. Whenever he or she partook of any food or water, a small portion of it was placed at the edge of the fire for the spirit. In fact, this observance continued for quite a while, sometimes even until the memorial potlatch itself (Olson 1933–1954, book 10:3). Thus the spouses continued sharing their meals, as they had done in the past.

While the data on the widow's mourning is extensive,[46] we have very little information on the specifics of the widower's conduct. This suggests that his mourning was not as prolonged and intense, and that he was much less restricted in his conduct. The fact that he could be asked to deliver a major speech at his wife's funeral reinforces this impression (Swanton 1909:372–373).[47]

In addition to fasting and abstaining from sex, work, idle talk, and other mundane social activities, the widow used several special rocks which were supposed to "anchor her down," that is, prolong her life and ensure that she remained loyal to her future husband and would not run around with other men. One large polished rock was kept under her pillow and another small one was used to rub her mouth.

The former must have symbolized her deceased husband, while an additional rock was said to represent the life of her future spouse. All her food was placed on another large rock before she could partake of it. This was supposed to make her mouth heavy, that is, to prevent her from becoming a gossip who "caused trouble with her mouth"(Kan 1979–1987). The widow was not allowed to use sharp objects and scratched her skin with a special stone or stick instead of her fingernails. She also performed a number of magical operations aimed at ensuring her long life and beauty. For example, washing the hair with the juice of blueberries was aimed at keeping it black well into old age. The close physical and social tie between the woman and her husband was manifested primarily in their sharing of food and sexual relations. And, in fact, they continued these forms of interaction after one of them died. That is, until cremation the widow continued to feed her husband and sleep with the rock which, I think, symbolically represented him.

The proper performance of the rules of mourning was believed to ensure that the woman lived a long, healthy and prosperous life, found herself a new husband, and had more children with him. On the other hand, by violating them she endangered her future life. Thus, for example, a certain widow who talked too much during the funeral became afflicted with a mouth disease (Kan 1979–1987). The widow's conduct was also believed to have a strong effect on the life of her children, her new husband, and her own as well as her husbands' matrikin. Between the time of her spouse's death and his memorial potlatch she was said to be in the hands of his matrikin whom she referred to as "my masters." In fact, the widow was called *l s'aatí shaawát* ("woman without a master"; Olson 1967:20–21).

At the same time, her husband's personal property remained under her control, until after the funeral when she called his lineage members to her house and distributed it among them. If she wished to show the special intensity of her grief, she added some of her own wealth to it (Shotridge 1917:109; Olson 1967:20–21; de Laguna 1972:539; Kan 1979–1987). Thus, like other paternal/affinal kin of the deceased, the widow mediated between him and his matrikin by handling polluted objects—in this case, his personal property, which could pass to his survivors only through her hands.[48] However, if the matrikin of a woman's late husband provided her with a new spouse, much of this property was passed on to him and thus remained in her household. While the widow was gradually freed from mourning, starting with the cremation,[49] her final release occurred at her late husband's memorial potlatch, when his matrikin replaced the black paint on her face with red and announced who her next spouse was going to be.[50] If they were not happy with the way she mourned, they could indicate so symbolically and let her go. Thus, in the late nineteenth century, when a certain widow had an affair with a white man, her disgrace was indicated by a boy dressed in European clothing coming out and playing a hand organ during the memorial potlatch in honor of her late husband (Olson 1967:66).

In addition to ensuring her own well-being as well as that of her matrikin and affines, the widow's proper observance of the rules of mourning was seen as an expression of sorrow. For example, the black paint used to cover her face allowed the deceased's matrikin to see whether she shed enough tears during the funeral, since tears left white streaks on her cheeks. I might add that, because men and women were seen as having a different degree of control over their emotions, the widow was expected to express her sorrow more violently than the widower. According to some accounts, widows might bite, cut, and bruise their bodies and occasionally might even throw themselves against the funeral pyre, although not to kill but only to burn themselves slightly (Emmons 1920–1945, ch. VI:15–16).[51]

The widow's mourning included many of the major taboos and magical practices observed by the pubescent girl in her first menstrual confinement, which were more elaborate than those imposed on other types of initiates and ritualists in a liminal state (see Drucker 1950:209–212, 276–277; de Laguna 1972:518–523).[52] Both the pubescent girl and the widow were considered ligaas and both of them tried to ensure that they, their matrikin and affines had laxeitl in the future. The Tlingit themselves were aware of the similarities; they also compared the two stages in the woman's life to her first childbirth, which involved many of the same observances. As an Inland Tlingit informant put it, "It's like you are [be]coming woman again" (McClellan 1975:380).

I believe that the similarity between and the emphasis on the two rites of passage in Tlingit culture was a reflection of the special role played by the woman in the social order. First of all, in this matrilineal society, the woman was responsible for perpetuating the descent line and ensuring its purity. The latter explains the importance of premarital chastity, especially among the aristocracy, and the fact that the female puberty rite was much more elaborate and culturally significant than the male one.[54] As de Laguna's (1972:514) informant put it, comparing male and female puberty observances, "Girls—it's stricter, because girls from the time they start growing [are] getting ready to get married. They have to live just right."

What the pubescent girl, the parturient woman, and the widow had in common was their key role in biological and social reproduction, an actual creation of a new life or a potential for doing so. With the Tlingit emphasis on remarriage and fecundity, the widow, even an older one, was seen as a potential giver of life. In addition to perpetuating the matriline, the woman was the main link and mediator between the two moieties. Hence the puberty ritual marked and celebrated the young girl's physical maturity which made her marriageable, while the widow's observances emphasized her eligibility for remarriage. However, because the parturient woman was already married, her observances were less elaborate than those of either the pubescent girl or the widow.

The death of a woman's spouse created a delicate situation, since it broke the affinal link between two matrilineal groups of the opposite moieties. The dead man's matrikin were anxious to retain the widow and provide her with a new spouse, preferably a close matrilineal relative of his. Hence, the Tlingit practiced levirate and sororate and required the deceased's heir to marry the widow, regardless of her age. To marry her late husband's kinsman was not only the widow's duty but her privilege as well. She expected her late husband's matrikin to provide her with a spouse, and if the matrikin did not, she felt insulted and demanded retribution. To let such a woman go was considered a disgrace and would often precipitate a violent confrontation with her own matrikin or at least a generous compensation given to them.

The idea that the woman rather than the man was the key link between moieties is indicated by the fact that a widower found it easier than a widow to remarry into a matrilineal group other than the late spouse's.[54] Of course, in the native view, the men also had more autonomy than the women (see Chapter II). It also appears that the rule of virilocal residence reinforced the woman's image as a mediator who left her own matrilineal group and settled in her husband's.[55] The crucial role of the woman in establishing and maintaining ties between two matrilineal groups is further emphasized by a special relationship of reciprocity between brothers-in-law. The two men were supposed to exchange gifts and ritual services throughout their lives, with the woman acting as an intermediary between them. A special form of this gift-giving was called _k̲éenás_ and involved an initial gift made a man to his wife's brother (or sometimes maternal uncle) and delivered by her. This gift was rather modest but required a more generous return one.[56] It appears that the size of the return gift was not set but was supposed to reflect the feelings of the donor towards his sister and her husband (Kan 1979–1987). It is significant that the latter was usually favored in this exchange, which was interpreted as a way of making the husband respect his wife more and treat her better.[57] _K̲éenás_ also allowed an adult man to express his feeling towards his sister, which he could not do directly because of the brother/sister taboo. Although _k̲éenás_ also existed between sisters-in-law, the amount of wealth exchanged was much smaller and the relationship itself considered less significant than the one between brothers-in-law.

If the woman's role in the social system was so crucial, one might ask why she was often blamed for interpersonal and intergroup troubles and hostilities and why her body was seen as polluting and dangerous to the man. The answer lies in part in an ambiguous position of the in-married woman, whose primary loyalty was supposed to remain with her own matrikin but who frequently developed close ties with her husband and his lineage mates among whom she spent the rest of her life. The close relationship and identification between the spouses was recognized and symbolically expressed by the special belt worn by the wife whenever her husband was away on a dangerous mission, referred to as his "life" (compare the belt worn by the widow).[58] The wife would also often imitate the activity her husband was engaged in, for example, fighting, hunting seal, and so forth. Some of her observances, for example, restrictions on movement and speech, resembled those of the widow. If the husband was injured or lost his life, the wife's misconduct was often blamed.

The woman was also more likely to be blamed in case of adultery. In fact, the splitting of matrilineal groups was frequently blamed on the in-married women who were supposedly responsible for jealousy and hatred between matrilineally-related males competing over them. Woman's gossip and backbiting was also frequently invoked as a major cause of both intra- and intergroup hostilities, including wars between members of the two moieties.[59] This double loyalty of in-married women was not entirely a fiction, since we do know of actual cases where women sided with their husband's matrikin against their own.[60] The woman's relationship with her brother, who epitomized her matrikin, was just as ambivalent that with her husband. It was both very close, because she saw her brother as her major protector and supporter as well as disciplinarian, and yet very distant, since upon reaching puberty the two were strictly prohibited from being alone together, speaking directly to each other, and so forth (see de Laguna 1972:482–485).

The structural position of the Tlingit woman partially explains the ambivalent perception of her and the Tlingit fear of being polluted by a woman's body. This ambivalence and this fear are also based upon beliefs, widespread among North American Indians, that menstrual blood and other female bodily fluids repelled animals and brought male hunters bad luck (Drucker 1950; 1965; Hulkrantz 1979).[61]

The paradox of the woman's status in Tlingit society is further illustrated by a discrepancy between a somewhat subordinate role of women in public life and potlatches and a much greater role played by them in the more informal daily economic activities and politics.[62] Statements made by western observers throughout the nineteenth century attest to the fact that Tlingit women had a great influence on their husbands, especially in trading (e.g., Khlebnikov 1976:28; Jones 1914:138). De Laguna (1983:81) has recently suggested that "in economic, political, and ceremonial [?] matters, Tlingit women have more authority than is usually recognized, perhaps even the final say."

This inconsistency characterizes the status and role of women in other societies in the region as well as in other parts of the world (e.g., Ortner and Whitehead 1981).[63] It appears that, in order to maintain male doninance in social and political life, men often try to compensate for their inability to create life by restricting women's access to the domain of the sacred, which men themselves control (compare Keesing 1982:218–229). In other words, having a subordinate role in biological reproduction, men try to control the social one.

As Ortner and Whitehead (1981:19) suggest, in societies based on rank men play the dominant role, while women constitute a "dependent rank." This seems to be the case even among the Tlingit, where the woman's status was fairly high compared to many other societies. The theory of the person, and particularly ideas about purity and pollution, as well as the control of the "inside" over the "outside," served as an ideology justifying the Tlingit woman's somewhat subordinate role in social life (see Chapter II). In the final analysis, many of the same criteria that differentiated aristocrats from commoners were used to establish a fundamental difference between males and females (see Chapter IV; compare Ortner and Whitehead 1981:16–17).

The Naa Káani

The special role played by the wife of the deceased in the funeral is further illustrated by the assignment of the most important and honorable "services of affliction" to his real or classificatory brothers-in-law, the *naa káani*, literally, "clan's siblings-in-law."[64] The latter also assisted the clan in various delicate and important ceremonial activities outside the mortuary complex. For example, the *naa káani* served as intermediaries and negotiators whenever their affines tried to end hostilities and make peace with another matrilineal group.[65]

In the funeral itself, the *naa káani* were the ones who guarded the corpse, took it outside, and cremated it. The fact that the "clan's brothers-in-law" were seen as playing a special role in the funeral, that is, being more closely identified with the deceased and his or her matrikin than other opposites, is further indicated by the fact that the term "widows" is applied to them. This is another example of the key role of the woman in creating affinal relations between men. In fact, the relationship between brothers-in-law was considered so important that, unlike the widow who stopped calling her deceased husband's matrikin *ax̱ káani,* "my in-laws," after the funeral, the widower continued using that term unless he remarried a member of a different matrilineal group (Durlach 1928:33). In the funeral, and especially the potlatch, the brothers-in-law of the deceased would often contribute wealth in the name of their wives to the pile assembled by the mourners and might even offer their own slaves for the sacrifice (see the beginning of the "Slave Sacrifice" subsection, earlier in this chapter).

Conclusion

In this chapter and the previous one, I have shown how the treatment of the deceased in the funeral involved, on the one hand, the masking of the impure and perishable flesh followed by its destruction and, on the other, the freeing of the pure bones and of the immortal noncorporeal components of the deceased, helping them in their journey to the *s'igeekáawu aaní,* and transforming the deceased into a respected ancestor of his matrilineal group. The total image of the deceased constructed in the wake was an ambiguous one. While it emphasized his social status and lineage and clan membership, it could not completely deny his individuality. Death was still too close for the chief mourners to accept a culturally constructed illusion of a depersonalized ancestor. Even though their eulogies and laments focused on those aspects of his total social persona that were derived from his matrilineal group's *shagóon*, they did make some references to the more idiosyncratic features of his biography and personality. Similarly, while the survivors were encouraged to express their grief collectively and through the medium of the ritualized forms of mourning, they did grieve more privately and idiosyncratically.

The tragic irony of the Tlingit funeral was that the individual reached the peak of his social career when he was no longer living and his body was in its most polluted state. Ambivalence also characterized the relationship between the deceased and his matrikin. The latter were expected to help and honor him by their ritual conduct and, at the same time, protect themselves from the pollution emanating from the corpse. They had to stay close to the body, yet could never touch it. They told the ghost to go away, but encouraged one of the two spirits of the deceased to return as soon as possible by being reincarnated. And while the mourners' loss was a terrible danger and an emotional blow to them, it was also their major opportunity to seek superhuman power and good luck.

This contradiction is inherent in the mortuary ritual since it tries to mediate the insurmountable opposition between life and death (compare Danforth 1982). As Hertz pointed out, this is particularly true of a funeral that is part of a larger mortuary cycle, in which the final transformation of the deceased and the mourners is not completed until the rites of secondary treatment. This, of course, was the case with the Tlingit funeral. Even though it clearly included the three stages of Van Gennep's scheme of the rite of passage, it was simultaneously the first stage in the larger cycle culminating in the memorial potlatch.[66] Until the potlatch, the transformation of the deceased's material and spiritual attributes was considered unfinished. Similarly, his matrikin remained in a state of liminality, even though the mourning rules were relaxed. Until the potlatch, their ties with the deceased continued to be closer than with the rest of their ancestors. Finally, their relationship with their opposites remained ambiguous as well, until they thanked and remunerated them for the services of affliction.

This liminal nature of the funeral was best exemplified by the offerings made to the deceased in it. For most of the wake, the deceased could only be fed by having the surviving spouse place some of his or her own food into the fire. At the smoking feast, which took place either just before or immediately after cremation, the spirit received tobacco along with the other departed members of his matrilineal group, whose names were invoked. Finally, in the post-cremation feasts, food and clothing were given to him as well as to the other matrilineal ancestors of his lineage/clan. The number of these ancestors increased significantly in the potlatch when the deceased himself was finally transformed into an ancestor.

chapter seven

GRIEF, MOURNING, AND THE POLITICS
OF THE FUNERAL

If we limit the discussion of the Tlingit funeral to a symbolic analysis of the transformations its living and dead participants underwent, we risk painting a picture of a smoothly running ceremony, in which the mourners and their opposites were unified in their concern with helping and honoring the deceased and in their collective expressions of sorrow. The mourners in this picture appear passive and dependent on their affinal/paternal kin for funerary services and condolence. The ritual then becomes nothing more than an expression of eschatological and ethnopsychological beliefs which could be assigned exclusively to the domain of "religion." Such a picture is not incorrect, since much of the funeral was, in fact, focused on these issues, which were discussed in Chapters V and VI. It is, however, incomplete and limited to the native ideology, i.e., the image that the mourners themselves tried to project.

What this image tried to downplay was the political aspect of the funeral, i.e., its central role in the rank- and status-enhancing efforts of the participating individuals and kinship groups. By looking at the political process couched in the rhetoric of grief, mourning, and love and respect for the deceased as well as at the mourners' backstage activities, we should be able to explain why and show how the funeral built the foundation for the memorial potlatch—the major arena in which changes in the distribution of power and prestige in Tlingit society took place.

Like the other ceremonies constituting the mortuary cycle, the funeral was the main opportunity for the matrilineal group to display the representations of its sacred collective heritage (*shagóon*), from crests to songs. Prominent among these representations was the decorated corpse itself—the focus of the ritual. The funeral was also one of the major contexts in which the matrilineal group's wealth could be demonstrated to members of the opposite moiety. Hence, the group's place in the social hierarchy was tied to the effectiveness of its performance in the mortuary rituals of every one of its members. At the same time, any mistake made during the funeral had dire consequences for them, not only because of the supernatural repercussions discussed earlier but because a mistake lowered their status and prestige.

In light of this, it is obvious that the funeral had to be carefully planned and carried out. To ensure that, the aristocracy, the guardians of the matrilineal group's *shagóon*, had to involve itself significantly in the planning and execution of the funeral. The existing data demonstrates this very clearly. Despite the fact that in their mourning, the matrikin of the deceased were more unified than in their daily life, the Tlingit funeral, unlike mortuary rites in some other societies, did not obliterate the fundamental age, gender, and rank distinctions that dominated social life. Just as the men and the women played different roles in this rite, a division of ceremonial labor also existed between the aristocrats, who planned and supervised the funeral, and the rest of the participants. Although, as mourners, the *aanyátx'i* were supposed to be passive and immobile, as leaders of the mourning lineage or clan, they were very busy, presiding over the formalized daily cries, the distribution of gifts to members of the opposite moiety, and other important aspects of the funeral.

Whenever a free person, and especially a high-ranking one, died, important decisions had to be made by his matrikin. The opposites who were to act as funeral workers had to be chosen very carefully on the basis of both their relationship to the deceased and his immediate matrikin, and their rank and status. The funeral could be used to affirm or modify the mourners' alliances with members of the opposite moiety, since those who performed the services of affliction had to be among the chief guests in the subsequent memorial potlatch.

Similarly, the identity of each mourner who was to play an important role in the funeral had to be established, with the degree of his or her relatedness to the deceased as well as rank, wealth, and ritual expertise taken into consideration. The songs to be performed and crests to be brought out also had to be chosen carefully, since each one had its own value and its use called for a specific amount of property to be displayed and distributed to the opposites. The amount of wealth each mourner would contribute also had to be discussed, so that it would match his or her specific role in the ritual. Finally, the death of any free person involved a transfer of at least some personal property as well as names (of which the ceremonial title[s] was the most important), regalia, and other aspects of his *shagóon*. This transfer was more significant when a male aristocrat died. The demise of a house or clan head involved an important additional issue—the selection of his successor.

To make all these decisions, the leaders of the mourning group met prior to the wake and continued their behind-the-scenes discussions throughout the funeral. Disagreements undoubtedly arose but they had to be resolved outside the ritual sphere, in order not to embarrass the mourners and in order to present a unified front to their opposites. Competition had to be restrained, to avoid violating the ethos of matrilineal solidarity and of love and respect for the deceased. Unfortunately we know little about these backstage activities.[1] Although the basic features of the mourners' roles in the funeral were established prior to it, there remained some room for them to negotiate and enhance their status and prestige by contributing more wealth, performing the more honorable ritual tasks, and dramatizing the effect of the loss on their emotions.

I must emphasize that aggrandizement of status and concern with prestige were not as prominent in the funeral as in the subsequent mortuary feasts and especially the potlatch. For some of the participants, their grief was too intense and overwhelming to focus on the more practical political matters. In fact, even though grief and other death-related emotions are difficult for us to measure, they should not be ruled out as an important factor which influenced the mourners' conduct. Thus I have seen mourners moved by grief who contributed more generously to their relative's funeral than one would expect on the basis of their position in their matrilineal group or their pocket-book (Kan 1979–1987).

At the same time, the rules of propriety and the restrictions imposed upon mourners by the mourning observances prevented those mourners who experienced little or no grief from acting too competitively. The mourners had to show moderation in using the funeral to enhance their status and prestige.[2] Thus the scale of the funeral had to correspond somehow to the deceased's and his matrikin's position in the social hierarchy. As Shotridge, a Tlingit aristocrat, pointed out, "should relations make much ado over the burial of a man of no account people would laugh at them" (Wallis: 1918:79).[3] Similarly, while the rank and wealth of a mourner were crucial in determining his or her financial contribution, the nature of his or her kinship relationship with the deceased could not be ignored. Thus, it would have been improper for the deceased's sister's daughter to contribute more than his mother.

The key rule of the funeral was that the mourners had to present their prestige-oriented actions as expressions of their grief and "love and respect" for the deceased. Only by skillfully using the mortuary rhetoric and symbolism could they accomplish their "political" objectives while maintaining an image of the moral selves who experienced culturally appropriate emotions and performed their funerary tasks with perfection.

This complex interplay between genuine grief and other, more ambivalent attitudes towards the deceased, ritualized mourning, and status-aggrandizement is best exemplified by the process of selection of his successor and the role assigned to the latter in the funeral. My discussion will focus on the death of a *hít s'aatí*, "head of the house," literally "master of the house," since it often involved major negotiation and competition between the mourners and because a fair amount of data is available on the subject.

Immediately after an incumbent's death, adult males of his house gathered and discussed the issue of succession as well as the details of the entire mortuary rite (Kamenskii 1985:34; Kan 1979–1987). Whenever two or more men would vie for the successor's position, each stating that he was the right person to conduct the mortuary rites, since he had the pedigree, the knowledge, and the wealth to do so, the choice had to be made prior to the funeral, so that there would be no major disagreement during that rite or in the memorial potlatch.[4]

Theoretically, the most likely candidate to replace the deceased incumbent was his younger brother, especially if the latter resided in the same house. Although a man was likely to be higher in rank than his younger brother, the difference was not supposed to be very big (Oberg 1973:31). However, if the younger brother of the deceased was advanced in age or had no interest in assuming the title of the *hít s'aatí*, the headship was passed further down along the line of brothers and finally came to the dead man's oldest sister's son.

According to Garfield (1939:179), who studied succession among the neighboring Coast Tsimshian, myths and direct questioning of informants generated the answer that the sister's son usually succeeded. But when actual cases were examined, it became clear that a brother had a legal precedence over a sister's son. In her own words,

> In most houses there were a number of men's names which carried with them use-ownership rights and prestige of sufficient value to satisfy their owners. When the head of the house died, his own younger brothers already possessed important names and had established their reputations through potlatching and did not care to step up, although they could if they wished. Instead they usually agreed to a nephew taking this position. (Garfield 1939:179)

The actual cases recorded by Garfield show that in about half of them, brothers succeeded, and nephews in the other half. The same is true of the Tlingit data (de Laguna 1960; 1972:315–326; Kan 1979–1987).

The reason that a number of sources mention the dead man's sister's son as the successor is that brothers of the house chief often split off from the original lineage and established separate junior houses of their own, instead of waiting for the death of the head of the original house. Fission, as we have seen, was the only form of resolving a conflict between two men of the same generation vying for the headship of the house. Such conflicts could occur as a result of competition over the position, the name, and the ceremonial paraphernalia entrusted to the deceased house chief. However, strong efforts were made to resolve them or, at least, prevent them from being brought into the funeral. It would have been an embarrassment for the house if one of its senior men refused to take part in a lineage mate's funeral.

In addition, frequent references to the maternal nephew as the likely successor are explained by the fact that the relationship between a senior man and his sister's son was the main idiom of hierarchical relationships within the matrilineal group. The maternal uncle was the authority figure for his nephews, who were supposed to dwell with him upon reaching the age of eight or ten. Not all of the men grew up in their maternal uncle's house but this was the ideal, particularly among the aristocracy. The uncle trained his nephews to be true men in accordance with the ideal of a tough, brave warrior/hunter. This training involved physical punishment and hardening exercises (e.g., staying in icy cold water and then being hit with branches). The nephews were said to "make their maternal uncle rich," by working for him and giving their catch to him. When it came to such ritual services for the opposite moiety as totem pole raising or house building, the actual work was done by the nephews while their uncle received the lion's share of the remuneration. The most honorable way to die was to volunteer to be killed in place of one's uncle, after the latter had been chosen by the enemy as a victim for the ceremony of balancing the losses, which was a prerequisite for peace between the two parties engaged in violent conflict.[5]

In return for his loyalty and subordination, the young man received from his maternal uncle the necessary knowledge for participating in the ceremonial/political life. Ideally, he could also use his uncle's personal property without asking for permission. According to some of the sources, he could even engage in sexual relations with his uncle's wife, and although the uncle might object, he was not supposed to punish the younger man too harshly. Thus one could say that the nephew's sexual maturity was dependent on his uncle. Theoretically, adultery did not exist within the house. Sexual relationships between a man and his house mate's wife was described as "eating out of the same dish." Very frequently the husband of a woman designated the young man, traditionally one of his real or classificatory nephews, who was to marry his wife in the event of his death (Kan 1979–1987).[6]

The ultimate expression of a house chief's authority over his close junior matrilineal relative was his control over the ceremonial name that he could bestow upon or withhold from the latter. The name, as I have shown, was the main index of the rank and status of its carrier. Thus the senior could control the junior's advancement in the social hierarchy. The head of the house also controlled the use of the crest objects in the ceremonial context. Since crest objects had different values, by allowing his junior lineage mates to use certain regalia, the house head publicly stated what the current status and rank of the user of the crest object was.[7]

Relationships between two brothers of different ages resembled those between a man and his sister's son, although the older brother did not have as much authority over the younger one.[8] Like the maternal uncle, the older brother could make the younger one marry his wife, if he himself did not wish to continue the relationship. Sexual relations between a man and his brother's wife seem to have been acceptable (de Laguna 1972:489) and levirate was an important law that was rarely violated.

The overall relationships between the senior and the junior male matrikin were very close, yet undoubtedly ambivalent. This might explain the male's practice of covering his mouth whenever conversing with his maternal uncle or sister's son. The Yakutat people explained it as a show of great respect the two men had for each other. There is also some evidence that the relationship between them involved ritual avoidance, which might be explained as a mechanism for reducing tension in their relationship (de Laguna 1972:479–481). Similarly, it appears that some form of avoidance characterized the interaction between two brothers (de Laguna 1972:485).[9]

A man was supposed to be proud of his older brother's or maternal uncle's accomplishments, yet he was often jealous of them and/or resented their authority. As I have shown in Chapter III, the ideal of matrilineal unity and solidarity was often contradicted by the reality of social life, with very few legitimate means of resolving such conflicts being available. Hostility between two closely related male matrilineal relatives, one of whom was senior to the other, was also encoded in and expressed through mythology. It is not an accident that Raven, the Tlingit Creator-Transformer, is born despite his evil maternal uncle's wish to kill all of his sister's children and that he begins his exploits, so beneficial to mankind, after he has defeated his uncle. A number of versions of this Creation myth agree upon the basic plot,[10] in which the original ruler of the universe kills one of his sister's male children after another, fearing that they would gain access to his wife and would overpower and replace him. Born miraculously after his mother swallows a rock, Raven has sexual relations with his uncle's wife and survives all of the tests the uncle sets up for him in order to kill him. Although the myth does not mention Raven's killing his uncle, the replacement of an evil and greedy senior kinsman by a junior one, who shares his uncle's possessions with the rest of mankind, is clearly its main theme. What the wicked uncle tries to do is prevent the world from acquiring its present shape and eliminate social reproduction. He maintains the universe in an unformed state of chaos and stasis.[11] This myth shows that social time replaces stasis and cosmos replaces chaos, as a result of an intergenerational struggle and the victory of a junior member of the matrilineal group.

In real life, to assume the title and position of his predecessor, the successor had to "finish the body," that is, to sponsor his mortuary rites, from the funeral to the final memorial potlatch. In addition he was usually required to marry the widow. Many of the personal possessions of the deceased became his property as well.[12] Ideally the successor had to be a mature man in his mid-thirties, so that a reasonably certain evaluation of his qualifications could be made. Sponsoring the mortuary rites of one's maternal uncle or other senior house relative was both a duty and a privilege as well as the goal of every Tlingit male who had any ambition to enhance his position in the social hierarchy. This act could also be seen as the proof of his maturity and manhood. Hence when westernization began to interfere with the men's right to finish the bodies of their senior matrikin, they saw that as a threat to their sense of selfhood. One Yakutat man described to de Laguna (1972:481) how he protested the fact that his sister and her white husband purchased the gravestone for his maternal uncle. In his words, "I am the one that's supposed to fix up my uncle's grave. It's just like I haven't strength enough to do it. . . . My mother preached to me about my uncle, 'You take care of your uncle's body. When you're poor you can't afford it.'" The informant added that his mother wanted him to be a strong man, "so he could take care of his own people's death expenses" and concluded that "It's an awful insult if you can't fix your uncle's grave." We might say that a man could not achieve the position of a mature adult within his matrilineal group until he had sponsored or at least actively participated in the mortuary rites of his senior maternal kinsman.[13]

An examination of the main qualities the successor was expected to have reveals the same combination of *ascription* and *achievement* that I have proposed in the discussion of the basis of aristocratic status (Chapter IV). The rule of primogeniture was clearly of great importance.[14] Occasionally it resulted in the selection of a young and inexperienced man. In that case, the head of another house of the same clan was chosen to make speeches and manage ceremonies, lest the novice shame his clan by making blunders. In the potlatch, the older man would deliver the speeches but the answering ones would be addressed to the younger one (Olson 1967:6). If the deceased had named his successor before he died, his wish was usually deferred to, unless the candidate was totally unacceptable to the members of the group involved.

Wealth and the ability to accumulate it were other important criteria for the selection of a successor. The latter was expected to begin accumulating property while the deceased was still alive. In fact, the older male would usually help the young man get started.[15] The young man's wealth was a demonstration of his success in hunting, trade, and warfare. Sometimes possession of great wealth overrode the concern with the proper kinship ties between the deceased and his successor. Garfield's (1939:180–181) comment on how this worked among the Tsimshian applies to the Tlingit as well:

> Circumstances sometimes favored a man, who through some advantage seized and maintained possession of a position. Absence of the senior heir at the time of the death of the holder, lack of ready wealth with which to carry out the obligations, war and other conditions of unrest in the tribe have been turned to the advantage of a man wanting a name for the special privileges attached to it. . . . When there was a dispute the man who could get his wealth together first and take charge of his predecessor's funeral was most apt to be recognized. In order to do this he had to have the support of most of his relatives, since few men had sufficient means to assume such responsibilities single-handed.

Other important criteria for selecting the incumbent's successor included leadership potential, eloquence, high morality, wisdom, and the knowledge of the sacred traditions of his own and other matrilineal groups. According to Olson, a potential heir who was rich would be preferred over one who was merely wise and the wise one would be appointed speaker. "Yet in the native mind this would be an extremely unlikely situation, for if a man is wise he will also be wealthy!" (1967:6).

Finally, the successor was supposed to have shown "great love and respect" to the deceased in the past. If he had not demonstrated his feelings by working for and taking care of the incumbent while he was still alive, the latter could choose any other adult male residing in the house, and if they were not respectful enough, he could even turn to a man from a related house of the same clan.

The same feelings had to be shown by the successor in his role of the chief mourner. Only by carrying a heavy burden of mourning observances and funerary tasks, was he able to legitimize his role as the new house head. The chief mourner led the formalized daily cries, and presided over all of the other major ritual activities involved in the funeral. Speeches of condolence delivered by the opposites were addressed to him, and he was the first one in his matrilineal group to respond to them with words of gratitude. His contribution to the amount of wealth to be distributed to the guests at the conclusion of the funeral had to be the largest. Following the funeral, he finally acquired much of the personal wealth of the deceased and began his career as the new *hít s'aatí*. His final assumption of the attributes of his predecessor's social persona did not take place until the memorial potlatch which he had to sponsor. The successor also had to pledge to marry his predecessor's wife. For an older man, such a pledge meant adding another woman to his household, and for a younger, marrying a woman much older than himself.[16] In Yakutat, the nephew of the deceased was expected to distribute the meat of any seals (or other game animals) which he killed to the opposite moiety members in his village, until his maternal uncle's grave had been fixed (de Laguna 1972:538). The mourning rules imposed upon this man were more stringent than those to which any of the other of his participating matrikin submitted. He had to spend, near the corpse, much of the time between the cries. At one particular mortuary feast immediately following cremation, reported by Olson (1967:60–61), the successor sat down in the rear of the house, at the side of the box on which the crest hat of his predecessor rested. During the wake, he would be the one to address the deceased. Thus when he wished to announce the end of a particular cry, he would ask the spirit of his predecessor "to step aside and let his fathers leave" (Olson 1967:60–61).[17] Between the funeral and the memorial potlatch, the chief mourner continued to appear in public dressed in the mourner's attire; in private he, along with a few other close matrikin of the deceased, continued to observe such mourning rules as, for example, abstaining from certain types of food.

In light of our earlier discussion of how the mourners' conduct during the wake affected their and their matrikin's future, it is obvious that the fate of the entire matrilineal group of the deceased depended on the chief mourner's strict adherence to the proper rules of mourning. This, however, was not the only reason why his appearance and conduct during the funeral and in subsequent feasts preceding the memorial potlatch was subjected to scrutiny by his own matrikin as well as their opposites involved in the funeral. The chief mourner's ritual actions were interpreted as messages about his grief as well as his plans about the upcoming memorial potlatch he had to sponsor. It is remarkable how information about prestige-oriented activities of the chief mourner was conveyed to the audience through metaphorical statements he uttered and symbolic acts he performed, all of which had to do with his mourning and were supposed to reflect his grief.

Here are some of the examples, most of them reported by Olson (1967:60–61), in an account of a hypothetical mortuary cycle of a high-ranking person. While the corpse was carried away to be cremated, the chief mourner might sing a song. The listeners noted his words carefully to determine if he intended to give a feast soon. During the feasts conducted immediately after cremation, he sang the last series of special mourning songs and, during the very last one, his opposites listened carefully for some reference or sign indicating feasts to come. If, after giving a memorial potlatch, the chief mourner continued to paint his face black when attending the potlatches of others, it meant that his deceased predecessor "was still on his mind," i.e., that he might give another potlatch in his memory.

This use of metaphors referring to one's grief and mourning to make status-enhancing statements was part of a general Tlingit tendency to use formalized rhetoric rather than ordinary speech in the ritual context (see Part III), especially during reciprocal exchanges between moieties. It is as if references to grief and mourning legitimized the mourners' actions designed to maintain and/or raise their status, by means of remunerating their opposites for mortuary services with food and gifts.[18]

Many of the symbolic acts performed by the deceased lineage kin were, in Turner's terminology, "multivocal" and could, thus, serve as statements about the mourners' emotions, their efforts to maintain order and balance in the cosmos, and their political goals, or all of the above at the same time. A good example of this was an occasional destruction by the mourners of one of their crest objects. The precious item was cast into the funeral pyre, along with the deceased's personal property. This radical act was carried out only when a high-ranking aristocrat died and was seen as the ultimate expression of the survivors' grief. In fact, several of my informants reminisced about some past funerals in which their own kin, overwhelmed by sorrow, acted that way (Kan 1979–1987). However, this act was also a major strategy to raise the mourners' rank, since it justified the commissioning and dedication of a replacement for the destroyed object.[19] Such dedication could only take place in a potlatch and had to be accompanied by a lavish distribution of wealth to the opposite moiety. Because of its expense, only wealthy kin groups could afford this ambitious political maneuver. Similarly, when the head of the house/lineage died, his successor would sometimes tear the entire house down and build a new one, in order to show his grief and build a memorial to the deceased, but also to raise his own and his lineage's rank, status, and prestige.

In light of this ritual ambiguity, it is an interesting question whether the sincerity of the deceased's successor and of other mourners was important at all or whether it was only the proper performance of the formalized mourning that mattered. I believe that, despite a heavy emphasis on ritualized behavior and in fulfilling one's duties as a mourner by sponsoring a respectable funeral and subsequent memorial rites, the participants made some distinction between true and feigned grief. Although the Tlingit have always been aware of a possibility of pretense and pro forma mourning, such behavior was not condoned. It is true that the sincerity of the grief felt by the deceased's junior matrilineal kinsman was not the main criteria for making him his successor, but it did increase his chances. Such sincerity was approved of and contributed to the chief mourner's status and the respect he enjoyed in the community.

Condemnation of insincere mourning is evident in numerous remarks made within and without the context of the mortuary rites by the Tlingit I have known. In addition, examples from mythology support my argument. Thus, in one of the episodes of the cycle of creation myths involving Raven, the latter tricks the deer into killing himself, devours him, and then pretends he is in mourning. Katishan, Swanton's informant who related this myth, commented that, "This episode is brought up when one who was the enemy of a dead man is seen to act as if he were very sad in the house where the body lies" (1909:107). A similar notion is expressed in a story told to me by one of my closest elderly friends and informants. In it, an old head of a house decides to test his nephews, so as to determine who would make the best successor to him. He pretends to be dead and is placed in the back of his house. As his nephews come in, he watches them and listens to what they say. All of them promise to be the best successors and heirs to the deceased, to enrich, and to raise the status of the house. Only the youngest, however, who has the smallest chance to be chosen, acts sincerely and cries over his uncle's body; he also promises to give him the most respectful funeral that he can afford. Of course, he is the one the uncle selects to be his successor (Kan 1979–1987).[20]

The polar opposite of the bereaved man crying over his maternal uncle is the witch, who first kills his matrilineal relative and then attends the funeral pretending he is in sorrow. In some accounts of alleged witchcraft cases, the witch is the potential heir himself who, moved by jealousy and a desire to take over the victim's position, kills his senior relative.

The Tlingit clearly recognized that not all of the mourners were sincere and that many simply went through the motions. Nevertheless, they expected at least some correlation between grief (as an emotional state) and mourning (as its formalized outward expression). Those whose mourning seemed to be an emotional experience gained additional moral capital, which enhanced their prestige.[21]

This interplay between the symbolic and the sociopolitical aspects of the ritual continued throughout the entire mortuary cycle, with the latter gradually becoming more important. In the potlatch, they took the center stage.

part three

THE POTLATCH

chapter eight

POTLATCH AS A MORTUARY RITUAL

The Deceased Person Commemorated in the Potlatch

A person's cycle of mortuary rites was not considered completed until a memorial potlatch had been sponsored by his matrikin. Up to that time, the dead body was referred to as unfinished. To be finished, the bones and ashes had to be placed in a new container—a box, a grave house, or a mortuary pole. Hence one of the characterizations of the memorial potlatch, that Veniaminov (1984:421) recorded in the 1830s, was that it involved "raising the dead," i.e., putting them in mortuary posts and other new containers located above the ground. Like all the other mortuary services, this one had to be performed by the mourners' opposites, for which they had to be generously remunerated. The only proper way to do that was in the potlatch.

Since a potlatch worthy of its name involved consuming and giving away a large amount of food and wealth, its timing depended heavily on the mourners' ability to accumulate them. In most cases a person's memorial potlatch occurred one or several years after his death, but a longer period of time could elapse before the survivors were ready. A person of lower rank could be commemorated in his own modest memorial feast but quite often he was included in one organized for his close matrilineal relative of higher rank. This means that the cycle of mortuary rites of a commoner might often be longer than that of an aristocrat.[1]

A lack of strict timing for the potlatch suggests that it was not necessarily directly instrumental in transforming the corporeal and noncorporeal elements of the deceased. I found no evidence indicating that the person for whom no potlatch had ever been given remained a hungry ghost forever or that one of his spirits could not come back to this world to be reincarnated. Similarly, his remains could presumably stay in their temporary container, but somehow this was not right. In any event, some connection between the deceased's transformation and his final mortuary ritual did exist. One year after death was the ideal timing for the potlatch, while two or three were also acceptable. Anything beyond that seems to have been looked at somewhat critically. From the point of view of the deceased's fate, the failure of his matrikin to give a potlatch was a show of disrespect to him. His own fellow spirits in the village of the dead would despise him and so would his living opposites.

What the potlatch definitely did was to mark, legitimize, confirm, and celebrate the end of a long process of transformation of the deceased's social persona (compare Hertz 1960).[2] Thus until the potlatch, the mourners continued feeding the deceased by throwing food in the fire, every time they had a meal. If not fully satisfied, the ghost (or the spirit?) might also visit them occasionally, appearing in their dreams and visions. This did not seem to be a frightening experience—the deceased's visit simply made the living feel sorry for him. To appease him, a small feast would then be held in which food was given to members of the opposite moiety, since this was the only way to send a more substantial nourishment to the village of the dead. The potlatch itself was the last time when the ghost (or the spirit?) was supposed to join the living in their feasting and celebration. Hence other common terms for this ritual included: "to invite the dead" (Kan 1979–1987) and "to feed the dead person" (*ḵaa naawú x'éix at duteex*; N. Dauenhauer in Veniaminov 1984:419).

The ideal timing of the potlatch recognized the decrease of the mourners' grief a year or two after their loss, expressed in the notion of their final separation from the ghost. The close kin of a deceased woman clearly expressed this notion to me a few days before the potlatch in her memory. The relative said that they felt she was now leaving them forever. Their feeling were ambivalent—happiness that she had finally found rest and sadness that they could no longer maintain a close relationship with her (Kan 1979–1987).[3]

While the ghost presumably settled for good in the cemetery, the spirit found its permanent place in his lineage house in the distant village of the dead. Finally, another spiritual entity came back to the living by being reincarnated in a close matrilineal descendant of the deceased, born soon after his death and named in his potlatch. Obviously, if the ritual took place within a year or two after death, this public confirmation and celebration of the infant's social identity was correlated perfectly with the finishing of the body. The rebirth of the deceased was also confirmed and dramatized when, immediately after the naming, the participants addressed the baby with kinship terms appropriate for its deceased namesake, saying something like this: "Welcome, my dear maternal uncle! It is so good to see you again!" (Kan 1979–1987). Along with the name, the infant was supposed to inherit the deceased's physical characteristics, personality, and some ceremonial regalia and prerogatives.

Other aspects of the dead person's social identity, such as his ceremonial titles and some of his regalia, were bestowed upon his other close matrilineal relatives in the course of the potlatch. Some of his more valuable personal possessions that had not been cremated with the body or distributed earlier among his matrikin by the surviving spouse, could also be presented as gifts to the guests during this ritual.

The presence of the deceased in the potlatch was indicated by various verbal statements and symbolic acts. One of them was the dressing of one or several of his descendants in his ceremonial regalia. This was a dramatic moment, since the regalia were displayed in public for the first time since their owner's demise. It is as if they were now pure and could be worn by the living. They were believed to retain part of his social persona and, at the same time, to represent the *shagóon* of his matrilineal group. Thus, in one of the potlatches I attended, a shirt belonging to the deceased which depicted his clan crest was placed on his younger brother. This elicited the following statement from the guests' leading spokesman given the honor of performing the dressing, "This shirt belonged to X. I used to be very happy to meet him in the street whenever I visited this community. Now I feel as if I have met him again" (Kan 1979–1987). Sometimes the deceased was addressed directly, as in a nineteenth century potlatch described by one of Olson's (1967:62) informants. There, at the end of the first day, the chief host indicated that the ceremony was adjourned by asking the deceased to step aside and let the guests go by.

The act of feeding and clothing the dead person through the fire was another reminder of his presence in the ritual. Thus, as the dish containing food for him was placed in the fire, the chief host named the recipient by saying, for example, "ax̲ tláa, x̲'éidei, "put into my mother's mouth." As it burned, he added, "For So-and-So, that she may benefit from it" (Olson 1967:64).

In the speeches delivered by both sides, the deceased's biography was still alluded to, but increasingly he was presented as one in a long line of ancestors of the hosts. After the potlatch, he was not supposed to be mourned any longer, his image fading away as the elements of his social persona were being appropriated by his descendants.

While the existing data indicate that the participants thought the deceased was actually taking part in the potlatch, the Tlingit did not use any of his remains to make this presence more tangible. Instead, they relied on their memory and the ceremonial oratory and other performative genres as well as the sacred lineage- and clan-owned regalia and paraphernalia, once used by the deceased. In contrast, their neighbors to the south made the deceased's presence more tangible. Thus, the Coast Salish displayed his hair or fingernails or even his wooden effigy during the memorial potlatch (Barnett 1955:218–220). The Kwakiutl and the Bella Coola memorial potlatch featured an appearance of a dancer representing the deceased, who wore a mask depicting his ancestral crest (McIlwraith 1948, vol. I:187; Curtis 1915:57; Drucker and Heizer 1967:131; see Chapter X).

The Hosts' Matrilineal Ancestors

Unlike the funeral, which focused mainly on the deceased himself, the memorial potlatch was an opportunity for the hosts to memorialize, honor, and please all of their departed matrikin. From the initial part of this ritual, when the hosts mourned all of their lineage (or clan) ancestors, to the subsequent speeches in which their virtues were extolled, the recently deceased increasingly blended with his matrilineal ancestors.[4]

In the beginning of the potlatch proper, each host had an opportunity to mourn his or her own deceased relative(s). One of the dramatic and emotionally effective forms of expressing grief were the previously described heavy or crying songs (see Chapter VI). Some of them were the same as those performed in the funeral, while others, often the older and the more precious ones, were reserved for the potlatch. The subject matter of most of these songs was the tragic death of the composer's/performer's matrilineal ancestor(s). As in the funeral, by choosing a song that described a certain manner of dying (e.g., drowning or being killed in battle) and by substituting kinship terms, the singer could express his or her feelings about a particular deceased relative. As one of de Laguna's informants put it:

> There is a song composed if you lost your brother. That's a song you are going to sing. There's [sic] so many songs. If I lost a mother, there's already a song composed about it, so many years ago. . . . They had so many songs . . . some of them pretty sad. Somebody got shot and killed . . . a brother drowned . . . song's already there, so you wouldn't get stuck. (1972:632)

The memorial potlatch was the main occasion for offering food, water, clothing, and other gifts to all of the dead members of one's matrilineal group, believed to be present in the house during the entire ceremony, and especially those who were still remembered by the living participants. The clearest indication of this notion was an invocation of their names, just before the distribution of wealth. Apparently, only those ancestors whose names were called out could definitely receive the things offered; thus, the hosts made a special effort not to omit anybody, by going back as far in time as they possibly could,[5] because the fate of dead who were not named was unclear.[6]

Despite the importance of giving offerings to the dead by burning, most of the food and gifts reached the hosts' matrilineal ancestors through the guests, members of the opposite moiety. While the latter were given the material substance of each present (i.e., the "outside"), the former received their noncorporeal essence (the "inside"). The custom of inviting the dead to the potlatch was believed to have been established by Raven himself, during the time when he was shaping the world into its present form. The only recorded account of this event could be found in Veniaminov (1984:421f):

> The Tlingit say that they hold the memorial feasts for their deceased relatives because when Yéil [Raven] was living among them he at one time invited the spirits of the dead to his house as guests. When they had assembled, he placed various dishes in front of them, but nobody touched them, though the host pressed the food upon his guests very assiduously. Finally one of the guests said to him, "Host, your guests cannot eat this way. If you wish them to eat, then place everything in the fire and then see what happens." At once the host

did as he was told, and when the food began to burn, he saw clearly that the guests were eating and were very pleased.

> However, after they had departed, he found that everything—the dishes and food therein had been left intact. Therefore, nowadays the Tlingit hold the memorial feasts for their departed relatives, in order to feed them. The difference is that they throw only a small portion into the fire and [their guests] eat the rest.[7]

The notion that all of the potlatch food and gifts were destined for the dead explains why they were said to "be burned," "die," or "be killed" in that ritual.[8] Once they had been set aside for the distribution, not a single item could be used by the hosts. The pervasiveness of this belief was revealed to me when a Tlingit friend, who seemed rather uninformed about the traditional ideology of the potlatch, told me, "Even if some of the money or gifts is left over after the distribution, the hosts can't touch them—they already belong to the dead" (Kan 1979–1987).

The opposites' curious role as the channel through which the hosts could supply their own dead matrikin with the necessities of life was part of their larger function as the mediators between purity/life, on the one hand, and pollution/death, on the other, outlined in Chapter VI. The idea that the guests played such a role was expressed directly in a variety of ways. Thus, they were invited to occupy the seats belonging to the illustrious ancestors of the hosts and to use their ceremonial spoons and dishes. Swanton (1908:441–442) described this as follows:

> Around the floor of the house were laid all those mats that the [maternal] uncles and mothers of the hosts had formerly used for their guests to sit upon, and one chief had hung up his mother's blanket behind the guests so that they would feel happy. When the guests came they said to them, "up to the rear of the house. You will sit on my mother."

Before each dish and gift item was passed to a guest, the donor invoked the name of a particular ancestor of his, to whom he wished the offering to go. The living recipient of this offering responded with "haadé," "hither" and the item was passed to him. When food was given out a special phrase was added: "So-and-So, to his mouth," with the name of the deceased as well as the living recipient being invoked. In addition, according to some accounts (e.g., Krause 1956:162), a significant portion of the food was put directly in the guests' mouths by the hosts, which reinforced the notion of the food's being literally sent to the spirits via the living guests.[9]

In addition to serving as a channel through which the hosts could send food and gifts to their own deceased matrikin, the guests represented and incarnated their own matrilineal ancestors whose names they carried and whose regalia they wore. They emphasized this in every speech in which they thanked the hosts for their generosity, e.g., "It is not really me that reached for this food, it is my departed maternal uncle So-and-so." Thus, like the funeral, the memorial potlatch involved an exchange and cooperation between the four categories of participants: the living hosts and guests, and their respective dead matrikin. In the recent potlatches I attended, this notion was beautifully illustrated by a special ceremony in which the leading hosts were being dressed into their ancestors' crest-bearing regalia. The honorable task of clothing them was given to the leading guests, many of them close paternal and affinal relatives of the people they dressed. As each guest lifted the sacred regalia, he or she said, "It is not really me but my beloved mother that is putting this shirt on you" or "I am placing this staff in your hand, my brother-in law, on behalf of/in memory of my maternal uncle So-and-So" (Kan 1979–1987). Thus the material manifestations of the hosts' *shagóon*, which survived their living owners and were used generation after generation, united the living and the dead of both moieties in this emotionally charged moment, when opposites embraced each other and when the living, in the words of one of my informants, could feel the "weight of their ancestors on their shoulders" (Kan 1979–1987).

As I have mentioned earlier, the nineteenth century Tlingit preferred to use the symbolic medium of the manifestations of *shagóon* to bring the dead into the potlatch rather than impersonate them as some of their neighbors did. As pure spirits, the dead were invisible. For some of the nineteenth century participants and for many of the modern ones, the presence of the dead was more metaphorical than real. One informant expressed this by telling me that he could *almost* hear his mother's voice when her clan mates performed her favorite song and *almost* see her when her ceremonial garment was worn by another woman (Kan 1979–1987).

Nevertheless, I found a few fascinating glimpses of the more direct references to the spirits' presence. Thus, Emmons' (1920–1954, Shukoff's Account:9) informant Shukoff made an intriguing statement, in his explanation of the mid-nineteenth century potlatch, when he said that the hosts "dressed" the guests by giving them pieces of blankets.[10] An even more interesting piece of information was given to me by an elderly Tlingit man, who described a potlatch he had attended as a child in the early 1900s, in which a bucket of berries was pulled up to the roof through the smokehole by young men sitting there. They then took it to the woods and ate it there, which was referred to as "the dead eating the food" (Kan 1979–1987). An additional fact supporting my argument about the presence of and the key role played by the dead and the death-related rhetoric in the Tlingit potlatch was the custom of killing a slave on the beach at the time of the guests' arrival and wiping the path they followed to the hosts' house with his blood, which was referred to as "killing a trail for the guests" (Emmons 1920–1945, Shukoff's Account:7). Though not entirely clear, this dramatic act does seem to illustrate the central concept of the potlatch, that the guests were the mediators between the hosts and the land of the dead. The fact that the potlatch could only be conducted during the hours of darkness, the time when the spirits were awake, is another indicator of its focus on the dead. In the potlatches I attended, whenever the hosts where unable to complete the ritual before sunrise, a special song was performed asking Raven to permit them to go on without any harm to them (Kan 1979–1987; compare Olson 1933–1954, book 1:20). Finally, the presence of the dead seems to be the best explanation of the bad luck that was supposed to afflict the hosts if they made any errors in their performance.

To further support my argument, I turn briefly to the western Subarctic Athapaskans and the Eyak, with whom the Tlingit are believed to share a common origin and culture. A detailed discussion of the "Proto-Athapaskan" mortuary complex is in Chapter X. Here, however, I would like to give a few suggestive examples. What we see are beliefs and ritual practices that are essentially similar, although, as I have said earlier, the Athapaskans made the presence of the dead much more tangible and dramatic than the Tlingit.

Thus, for example, among the Ingalik, when messengers were sent by the potlatch host to invite people from another village, they did not stay in the latter's *kashim* (men's house) for long, because it was conceived as the *kashim* in the village of the dead (Osgood 1958:138). Throughout the Ingalik, Koyukon, and other Athapaskan potlatches, the guests frequently spoke as and were addressed as if they were the hosts' own dead relative(s) being honored. Jetté (1911:712), who provides us with one of the earliest detailed account of an Alaskan

Athapaskan feast of the dead, suggested that, judging by the content of the Koyukon mourning songs as well as other observances, "it would seem quite probable that the primitive [original] purport of this performance, was to call back the souls from the land of the dead."

The most clear expression of this idea was the Koyukon practice of dressing the guests in the new festive garments which the hosts had made to commemorate their own dead matrikin. Carlo, a Koyukon woman, describes this custom, as observed during her childhood and continued in the 1970s. The guests chosen to be dressed are those who took the most active part in the funeral. At the conclusion of the feast, after they have exchanged their own old clothing for the new parkas and other items, they leave the house, representing the dead leaving their village forever:

> They are not supposed to look around. . . . The saying is that if you look back, because you represent the dead person it means you are looking for someone to take with you, especially the one that dressed you or a relative of theirs, so the last thing the person is told as he gets ready to go out is, "Do not turn around or look around as you are going out. This going out is supposed to be the dead person leaving the village for good." A lot of people at this time would cry, thinking of their loved ones that are to be leaving them forever. (Carlo 1978:67; compare Osgood 1958:141; Loyens 1964:136; Kroul 1974; Sackett 1987)

The Eyak, whose culture might be seen as occupying an intermediate position between the Interior Athapaskans and the Tlingit, did not go as far as the Koyukon. They did, however, address the potlatch guests using the names of the hosts' own matrikin who had died recently and had not yet been reincarnated in a namesake. In addition, the guest who was addressed in this manner and given food that was supposed to feed the donors' own clan ancestors, stated that the food was not for him but for his own dead matrilineal relative who had not yet been reincarnated (Birket-Smith and de Laguna 1938:156; 171).[11]

No matter how the dead were brought back into the Tlingit potlatch, the important thing is that their presence was essential and that it emphasized the commemorative nature of this ritual. Throughout the potlatch, the living displayed their ancestral regalia and performed their ancestral songs and dances. By donning their matrilineal ancestors' regalia and singing their clan songs, the hosts brought the spirits back to life. Thus, the dead, who no longer had a corporeal "outside," were revitalized through the actions of their living descendants who donned their garments, that is, the pure, immortal layer of the ancestors' "outside." As two Tlingit authors have recently put it:

> The memorial . . . ceremonies of the Tlingit are timeless rites in which those living imitate the life of their ancestors. We are the life of our ancestors. We are the crests of our ancestors. Thus we are obligated to give the crests, the names, and the lives of our ancestors dignity. (Littlefield and Littlefield 1980:2)

In return for the right to use the various manifestations of the ancestral heritage passed down through the matriline, the living supplied the dead with food, clothing, and other necessities. Most importantly, by periodically placing their remains in new containers, invoking their names, and inviting them to the potlatch, the living honored the dead and kept their memory alive. As long as the dead were remembered by the living, they remained immortal. Thus, matrilineal continuity—the basis of social reproduction—depended on the human ability to *remember*.

The Mourners' Unity in Common Sorrow and Shared Glory

As I have mentioned earlier, the closest matrikin of the deceased and especially the chief mourner continued to observe the rules of mourning until the memorial potlatch. These mourners remained incomplete persons, still tied to the deceased and indebted, and thus subordinate, to their opposites. In public they still wore old clothes and black paint on their faces; they abstained from certain potent foods and tried to avoid festivities. According to Swanton (1908:441), they slept with the blankets gathered up around their waists, in the way they did during the wake. Similar to the wake, the liminal period between the funeral and the potlatch was both a dangerous and potentially propitious time, when the mourners could wish for wealth, long life, and, more specifically, success in potlatching.

When obligated to attend potlatches sponsored by others, the mourners would usually indicate their special condition. For example, in a recent potlatch the hosts' clan mate, still in mourning for her own relative, for whom a potlatch had not been given yet, was asked to sing one of her clan's crying songs. She agreed but did not complete it, which was explained by the chief host as follows, "Her feelings are still in a storm, that is why she is still mourning and has not yet given a potlatch for her beloved relative" (Kan 1979–1987).

Similar to finishing the body of the deceased, ending mourning was a major explicit objective of the memorial potlatch. Despite the importance of the practical considerations (e.g., the accumulation of sufficient wealth) for the timing of this rite, the deceased's matrikin preferred to hold the potlatch when the were emotionally ready to do so.[12] The public ending of mourning was dramatically expressed in the ritual of "pushing away the sorrow," performed in the initial part of the potlatch. This was, in many ways, a replay of the funeral, hence the same terms were used for both of them: *gaax̱*, "cry," *wudanaaḵ*, "to stand up," or *gaaw wutaan*, "to beat the drum" (Kan 1979–1987). During the *gaax̱*, the mourners recreated the funeral by appearing with their faces painted black and/or with black kerchiefs tied around their foreheads. The guests encouraged them "not to hold back their tears," that is, to express their grief by crying, wailing, and singing the four special heavy crying songs of their clan. These were the old ancestral songs, the most valuable of all those owned by each matrilineal group. Contemporary Tlingit refer to these songs as "very sensitive," and say that the singers have to be "specially prepared" for singing them, that is, purify their bodies and minds for this performance and continue their mourning observances until the *gaax̱* is finished (Kan 1979–1987). Swanton (1908:437) was told that the singers "received special strength" through them, which suggests overcoming grief and/or obtaining spiritual strength (compare Chapters II and VI). The songs triggered painful memories and brought back the emotions experienced during the funeral. Loud sobbing as well as quiet keening could be heard as the mourners jointly relived their losses.

This symbolic expression of sorrow was the last collective public statement of the mourners' feelings towards the deceased. It was followed by four prolonged "oo" sounds, said to expel grief from the mourners' "inside." In the potlatches I attended, the sound was repeated after the song leader who hit the floor with his pole and thrust it upwards and away from his body four times. The leading male mourners did the same with their own canes and staves. Olson (1967:61) reported a similar ceremony, in which the male mourners clustered together, knelt on the left knee with their dance poles in their hands and, as the drum was beaten, gave a series of prolonged cries of "oo," not moving for several minutes. At the fourth "oo" they thrust their poles upward and to the left "pushing away the sorrow." At the conclusion of this act, the guests usually stood up and stretched their arms with the open palms towards the mourners, to express their sympathy and support (Kan 1979–1987).

In light of our discussion of the Tlingit theory of emotion (Chapter VI), it is clear why grief had to be expelled from the body. Whether it was the singing of the crying songs, the condolence oratory, or the ritual of pushing away grief, the Tlingit treated sorrow as a physical substance that had to be destroyed. Here is another example of the use of metaphor and symbolic action to eliminate grief. In one of the accounts of a typical nineteenth century potlatch, recorded by Olson (1967:62), "At the end of the last of the four songs sung by the nephew of the deceased at the potlatch for him, the hosts (men) shed their coats (in lieu of blankets) and held them before the fire, thus 'drying their sorrow'." Here an opposition between "wet" and "dry" was used to represent the one between "sadness/crying" and "joy/end of sadness/end of crying." Following this part of the potlatch, the guests delivered their speeches of condolence to "balance out the efforts of the hosts and to help remove the grief" (Kan 1979–1987; see below).[13]

Once this collective expulsion of grief had been finished, the hosts were expected not to remain sad any more. At least, they were not supposed to dwell exclusively on that feeling. Individual hosts/mourners could still sing "crying songs" in memory of their own deceased matrikin, but the general tone of the ceremony changed dramatically from sadness to joy. As the chief spokesman for the hosts announced in a recent potlatch, "The sorrow is finished now. We are going into a different ceremony, we are going to have fun. Do not mourn any more, my clan relatives" (Kan 1979–1987). Sometimes the hosts utilized their crest objects to express this change. Thus, in another recent potlatch, two carved wooden salmon, the hosts' major crest, were displayed on the wall in the back of the hall, with their heads pointed downwards to show how the hosts felt. After the completion of the rite of pushing away grief, their heads were turned upwards to make them "look happy" (Kan 1979–1987). This dramatic change in the hosts' condition was emphasized by the joyful feeding of the guests and the singing of love songs, which began immediately after the completion of the *gaax*. While resembling the funeral, the potlatch *gaax* was even more formalized, with the crying songs clearly preferred to unrestrained weeping. Of course, most of the mourners by now had achieved a certain distance from their loss and could control themselves better.

In their collective expression of sorrow, the hosts were strongly unified. They spent a lot of time rehearsing the singing, dancing, and other aspects of the potlatch, so as to act harmoniously and flawlessly in the presence of their dead matrikin and opposites. Their standing together in the front of the house (the place of the lowest status) in a single row, dressed in old clothes worn during the funeral, and the joint expelling of sorrow emphasized the value of matrilineal unity and solidarity. They were also united in their verbal and nonverbal expressions of love and respect for the opposite side. Throughout the potlatch, the hosts often referred to themselves as ravens or eagles and made the sound of those birds, thus emphasizing the most encompassing level of their matrilineal identity and the broadest common denominator that united them (compare the moiety design painted on the face of the deceased, discussed in Chapter VI).

Each member of the host group had an opportunity to express his or her feelings towards the recently deceased person, the other matrilineal ancestors, and the opposites, and to make a personal contribution to the common pile of gifts prepared for distribution to the guests (de Laguna 1972:632–633; Kan 1979–1987). Even when a small donation was made by somebody, no open critical remarks were allowed to be made about it. When the hosts decided how much wealth each guest was to receive, such a poor person could take more property out of the joint pool than he had contributed. Chiefs and wealthy hosts would also add their own property to his donation, so as to make it appear more respectable (de Laguna 1972:639; Kan 1979–1987). Small children were also encouraged to make a contribution and participate in the singing and dancing. Wealth was even contributed on behalf of some mourners who happened to be absent. All this suggests an emphasis on the participation of each social persona of the matrilineal group, represented by his or her name, regardless of age of physical presence (compare Mauss 1938).

The hosts were also united in the display of their ancestral crests and performance of their clan songs. The latter were usually the ancient songs believed to go back to the time of the original migration of the group's ancestors to its present territory. Although resembling the crying songs in style and content, these "national" songs, as the Tlingit call them in English, expressed the singers' pride in their *shagóon* and confirmed their claims to particular crests and territories, often mentioned in these songs. The most valuable songs were those mentioning the performers' main crests and, for that reason, called *at.óow daasheeyí,* "song about crests" or "sacred possessions." As de Laguna (1972:634) explains:

> These are traditional songs (and perhaps dances) that are supposed to accompany the exhibition of each sib [clan] heirloom of this kind: hat, helmet, blanket, drum, and so forth. Sometimes the chief himself displays the emblem or calls his nephew to do so, and sometimes he calls on his paternal grandchild. The greater the importance of the object displayed and of its song, the more wealth would be contributed when it was shown, and this in turn enhances the value of the object and the prestige of the sponsor and of the junior who exhibits the crest. Even a house screen may have its song.

The words of such songs were not themselves sorrowful but, like the mourning songs, their rhythms were slow and heavy and the tunes solemn. They were felt to be sad because of their association with so many potlatches and so many dead singers (de Laguna 1972:632). In my opinion, however, this sadness was often combined with and assuaged by pride in one's *shagóon* (see Conclusion).

A good example of the complexity of the crest symbolism and the use of these sacred regalia in the potlatch is the following account of an Interior Tlingit potlatch:

> when the Old Yenyedi of Teslin potlatched recently they wore regalia in which the Wolf, their chief crest animal, was represented on beaded dance shirts and by a huge black mounted wolf skin. Claims to the Grizzly Bear were shown by a headband with grizzly bear ears attached, their Eagle affiliation by beaded dance bibs with eagle designs, and their rights to the Killer Whale by a whale outlined in pearl buttons on a dance blanket. The story of their ancestor's encounter with a supernatural Wolf was constantly referred to in subtle rhetoric and their various mourning songs were rich in the imagery of wolves. The wealth to honor the departed was carried into the hall on driftwood and willow boughs and then distributed from them in order to reaffirm local sib [clan] claims to the Nisutlin River. Finally at the end of the potlatch, all the hosts howled like wolves. (McClellan 1954:89; see fig. 9)

The house itself, the scene of the potlatch, was the host lineage's major crest presented to the opposites in its highest moment of glory. No wonder that for the duration of the potlatch, the house could be referred to only by its crest name rather than the name of its current head which was occasionally used in day-to-day conversation (Khlebnikov 1976:31). In some communities, the main representation of the house crest, usually kept inside, was displayed outside, on the porch or above the entrance (see fig. 10).

Fig. 9. A potlatch performance illustrating the myth of the acquisition of the bear crest by the clan of Chief Shakes of Wrangell. A sketch by A. P. Niblack, 1885–1887. Niblack 1890, pl. LXVIII, fig. 354.

Besides displaying its old names and crests and thus legitimizing their claims to them, the hosts could dedicate new ones. In fact, the potlatch was the only opportunity to do that, since the dedication required the presence of the opposites and a distribution of wealth among them. A potlatch usually called for the creation of new songs and the coining of new names that referred to the events surrounding this ritual itself. Thus the songs mourned the deceased being commemorated while the names immortalized some remarkable act performed by the hosts. For example, if they gave away eight valuable copper shields (*tináa*), they might name one of their high-ranking members "Eight Coppers" (compare de Laguna 1972:636).[14] While these new manifestations of the hosts' *shagóon* were not as valuable as the old ones, their significance gradually increased, as they were displayed in more and more potlatches. The lineage house itself was often renovated or rebuilt and dedicated in the potlatch given in honor of its deceased chief, whose memorial it became.[15]

Thus the memorial potlatch not only reproduced the existing *shagóon* of its sponsors but allowed them to expand their collective

Fig. 10. An interior house post displayed on the porch of the Wolf House of Chief Anaxóots during the 1904 Kaagwaantaan potlatch in Sitka. Photo by E. W. Merrill, 1904. Alaska Historical Library.

heritage. A death-related rite became a reaffirmation of life, and more specifically of the continuity and immortality of the matrilineal group. It was the highest point in the life of its hosting lineage/clan, when its living and dead members were brought together in a celebration of their shared history and identity which took place in the presence of their opposites.

Ritual Services Offered by the Opposites

Despite the significance of the interaction between the living and the dead members of the mourners' group, much of the potlatch was focused on the relationship between the hosts and the guests. The crucial role of the *guneitkanaayí*, "opposite side," literally "the strangers' group," was emphasized by the major term for the potlatch: *ḵu.éex'*, "invitational ceremony," from the verb *ya-eex'*, "to call out, to invite" or *ḵu.éex' tlein*, "big *ḵu.éex'*." An English term "pay off," used by many of the Tlingit today, also underscores the reciprocity between the two sides as the focal point of this rite.

In fact, in the potlatch, the mourners/hosts were more concerned with their relationships with the opposite moiety than in the funeral where much of their attention centered on the deceased himself. The ritual services offered by the opposites throughout the entire mortuary cycle placed the mourners in the position of receivers indebted to their givers. With the balance in intermoiety relationships being central to the entire culture, this situation could not persist indefinitely. At some point, preferably not more than a few years after the funeral, the opposites had to be generously remunerated ("paid off") and thanked. The hosts' gratitude was expressed not only through feasting and gift-giving but also through oratory, singing, dancing, and other forms of entertainment. In return, the guests, acting as the intermediaries between the hosts and the hosts' matrilineal ancestors, as well as the incarnations of their own matrilineal predecessors, comforted and entertained the mourners. Most importantly, by their participation, and especially in their acceptance of food and gifts, they acted as the witnesses of the hosts' glory, confirming the legitimacy of the hosts' claims to crests and other tangible and intangible resources. This role was most dramatically expressed in the naming ceremony. After one of the leading hosts announced each of the names, the guests had to repeat it three or four times. To underscore the significance of this act, the hosts distributed their gifts to the guests immediately after it. As one informant put it, without the presence of the opposites, the hosts' words and actions would have been "floating aimlessly in the air" (Kan 1979–1987).

From the perspective of the mortuary cycle itself, its completion depended entirely on the mourners' opposites who constructed the permanent receptacle for the cremated remains, thus "finishing the body." Those opposites who had earlier performed crucial funerary services were entitled to a prominent role in the potlatch as well. At least some of these persons were supposed to be the close paternal/affinal relatives of the deceased and of his lineage, whose ritual roles were presented as the ultimate expression of their love for their spouses, fathers, children, and siblings-in-law. However, a truly big ku.éex' required the participation of a substantial number of out-of-town opposites. While their selection was guided, to a large extent, by the hosts' political (i.e., alliance-building and status-aggrandizing) objectives (see Chapter IX), they too were cast in the role of the loving fathers and affines. In fact, some of them were closely tied to the hosts through marriage.

This emphasis on harmony and cooperation of loving opposites is best illustrated by the special tasks assigned to the close paternal/affinal kin of the hosts and the generous remuneration they received. We have already seen the key role played in the funeral by the deceased's spouse, especially the widow (Chapter VI). In the potlatch the widow/widower was treated with special care, seated among the highest ranking guests and given lavish presents. In fact, a symbolic marking of his or her final release from mourning, mentioned earlier, and the announcement of the identity of his or her new spouse could be seen as the greatest gift the hosts could offer. The rhetoric of this act emphasized that the widow/widower was rewarded for her/his great love as manifested in proper and emotionally intense mourning. From now on, the surviving spouse's social persona was no longer linked to that of the deceased.

Of all the guests, the most important role was played by the hosts' *naa káani*, "siblings-in-law," especially the male ones. In the funeral they protected the mourners from the polluted corpse; while in the potlatch they were entrusted with the most delicate tasks of mediation between the hosts and the guests. Thus months before the potlatch, the *naa káani* were sent out to invite the out-of-town guests, a job that required a great deal of diplomatic skill and ritual expertise. In the potlatch itself they acted as ushers and, most importantly, as the distributors of food and gifts. Thus they served as a buffer between the hosts and the guests, deflecting criticism of unfairness from the former.

The chief hosts' spouses and other close affines went beyond the contribution of ritual services and offered substantial wealth of their own to build up that of the potlatch sponsors. Here the above-mentioned practice of *kéenás* (Chapter VI) played a crucial role. As Olson (1967:17) explained:

> A man wishes to give a potlatch but would like more wealth before doing so. He sends his wife to her clansmen with small gifts. Before the time of the potlatch they send their "brother-in-law" return gifts amounting to many times the value of the gifts received.

Swanton (1908:438) confirmed this practice and gave an example of a man planning to host a major potlatch who obtained $2,000 from his wife's clansmen, thereby increasing his own contribution by 50 percent. Drucker (1950:233), who reported this practice among the Tlingit, as well as the Haida and the Tsimshian, called it a loan. This might have been the case among the other two groups but not the Tlingit. While expecting a handsome return, the hosts' close affines emphasized that their contribution was a sign of their "love and respect" for the mourners and for the departed person. There was also no fixed rate of return as reported for the Kwakiutl (Drucker 1950:233).

Contributions of food and wealth made by men and especially women to their spouses' potlatches were quite significant. They increased in the post-contact era when both genders found new sources of wealth, including money.[16] Thus in a famous potlatch in Sitka in 1904, the chief host's wife gave him $500 she had earned by making and selling spruce root baskets, moccasins, and other items to American tourists (Kan 1979–1987).[17] Spouses, in-laws, and children of the hosts could also show their "love and respect" by refusing to accept the gifts they were presented with. This was usually done with such words as "I give myself up for my husband" or "I give it [return the gift] for the face of my father" (Kan 1979–1987; compare McClellan 1954:84).

In addition, the hosts' children, who also assisted them in the distribution of food and other less glamorous tasks, emphasized their devotion to their parents by refusing to eat with the guests, saying that they were "tired of their fathers' food." Such self-deprecating statements were common in the potlatch and their aim was to flatter rather than criticize. In this particular case, the children emphasized their fathers' generosity. The children's devotion and closeness to their parents, as well as the children's humility, were further underscored by their sitting among the hosts, near the door (referred to as sitting "against the dogs running out"), rather than in the place of honor—the back of the house (Kan 1979–1987).

Another important form of ritual assistance offered to the hosts by their closest opposites was their help in singing and dancing. Particularly honorable was the task of serving as the hosts' drummer, usually assigned to one of the *naa káani*.

Every special service and every form of help provided by the opposites were acknowledged by the hosts, who expressed their gratitude with such expressions as "you have given me strength," "you have helped me [or my mind] to regain balance," "you have lifted me way up" (Kan 1979–1987). The final recognition of these efforts came in the distribution of food and especially gifts.

While all of the guests acted as the channel through which the hosts supplied their ancestors with the life's necessities, the close opposites were the primary candidates for this crucial ritual service. Hence they were fed first and received the choicest food. They were also presented with a special dish referred to as *gankas'íx'i*, or *x'aan kas'íx'i*, "fire dish." Each fire dish contained the favorite food of a certain deceased member of the host group and was given to his spouse or other close paternal/affinal relative, who used to share his meals while he was alive. Before passing out the dish, the donor announced the deceased recipient's name, followed by the words "to his mouth," and then the name of the living recipient. The latter accepted the dish, thanked the donor, and said that he would share the food with the deceased (Kan 1979–1987; Worl 1984). According to modern-day Tlingit, who still observe this custom, (some of?) the food in the fire dish used to be burned by the recipient. This suggests that it represented an intermediate category between the offerings that were burned by the hosts and the bulk of the food and gifts given to the guests.

In the distribution of gifts itself, the first recipients were those opposites who had performed the mortuary services. Their help was publicly acknowledged by the announcement made before the presentation of every gift, e.g., "to So-and-So, such-and-such a gift, for helping us find the body of our beloved brother," "to So-and-So, such-and-such a gift, for building the gravehouse for our maternal uncle," "to So-and-So, such-and-such a gift, for his beautiful words of comfort offered to us today."

This special relationship between the hosts' and their closest opposites epitomized the harmonious and cooperative side of the inter-moiety relationships, in which balanced reciprocity was the leading theme. Much of this was eloquently expressed through the various forms of verbal communication that played a crucial role in the potlatch.

Exchange of Words

Analyses of the potlatch have traditionally focused upon the exchange of tangibles   material goods and food. Few anthropologists have heeded Mauss' insightful observation that what people exchange in societies like those of the Northwest Coast "is not exclusively goods and wealth" but rather "courtesies, entertainments, rituals, dances, and feasts" (1967:3).[18] Following the native view, I treat the various verbal genres, as well as dances exchanged by the potlatch participants as being just as important as the distribution of food and gifts. All of these exchanges can be seen as communicative acts expressing key cultural values maintaining or changing the social order. In the context of the Northwest Coast peoples' avoidance of direct expression of thoughts in public and in the ritual context in particular, the exchange of nontangibles acquired a special importance.

Oratory

Because the potlatch was a memorial ritual, the most important oral genre was the condolence oratory delivered by the guests, which the hosts responded to with their own speeches of gratitude. The function as well as the structure and basic imagery of these speeches was quite similar to those delivered by the mourners' opposites during the funeral (see Chapter VI).[19] My impression from a few existing recorded speeches and several informants' testimony is that the former were more elaborate and lengthy and, most importantly, placed a greater emphasis on the speakers' crests. As in the funeral speeches of condolence, the mourners' suffering was metaphorically linked to unfortunate events and tribulations of mythological protagonists or simply described as various forms of physical discomfort, such as being wet, lost, or hungry. The speaker made his crest responsible for mitigating these unpleasant or tragic experiences, while he compared the comforting actions of his matrikin to those of mythological protagonists who rescued the sufferers (see Kan 1983).

Let us take a hypothetical example in which the mourners' sorrow is compared to the suffering of the hero of a certain well-known myth, who had been abandoned by his family on an isolated beach and was miraculously saved by an eagle who lifted him on its wings and carried him to a safe place. The fact that the eagle happens to be one of the speaker's main crests helps create a link between the mythological episode and the mourners' present situation. The transformation of a crest into an animal that served as the addressees' helper and comforter was a common rhetorical device. Thus, for example, Dauenhauer (1975:192–193; 229–230) recorded a speech in which the speaker constructed a metaphor using the Frog Hat, one of his clan's most precious crest objects. The hat is transformed into a real frog which comes out of its den to take the mourners' sorrow and burrow down with it. In a potlatch I attended, one of the guests unrolled a ceremonial blanket representing a certain fresh water spring, a well known landmark owned by her clan. Pointing to this sacred possession of her matrilineal group, she told the mourners that her clan was offering them fresh water to quench their thirst and heal their wounds (Kan 1979–1987).

Crest objects belonging to the speaker were often described as towels for wiping off the hosts' tears, supports helping them to stand up straight, blankets to keep them warm, dishes to catch their tears, or boards to build protective walls around them (Kan 1983:52). The latter is a particularly dramatic and powerful image; the speaker means that he is willing to take apart his own house, his most precious possession, to protect his opposites. Frequent ritualization of metaphors based on the use of actual crest objects dramatized the oratory's comforting effect (on the ritualization of metaphors, see Sapir and Crocker 1977:101). The guests might even symbolically proffer one of their own crests to the hosts, so as to assuage their grief (de Laguna 1972:454–455). Thus in a recent potlatch, the guests responded to the mourners' singing of the crying songs by a performance of their own, in which a woman danced wearing a headdress representing her crest—the coho salmon. Her movements were described by the guests as "diving down with the mourners' sorrow" (Kan 1979–1987).

Elsewhere (Kan 1983) I have discussed in detail the structure of these speeches and the use of metaphors to mediate the opposition between life and death—and hence comfort the mourners by denying the finality of death. In this context, I would like to focus on the explicit as well as the more implicit meanings of the crests' use. By invoking their most sacred possessions, the guests not only emphasized their "love and respect" for the hosts and their desire to comfort the hosts as much as possible, but also elevated the present events to the mythical/sacred level. By using the objects once owned by their ancestors, the speakers placed the dead in the ritual domain, thus dramatizing the solemnity of the occasion and reiterating the historical depth of the ties between the two opposite matrilineal groups. For this reason repeatedly stated that they were only imitating their illustrious predecessors. This could mean that they were trying to emulate the ancestors, but more often the implication was that the latter were actually present, by being incarnated in their living descendants, as in the following statements recorded by Swanton (1909:383; 387): "my maternal uncle that had died long ago has come ashore to save you;" "your fathers that had died years ago have come out of the woods and have given your strength;" "it is not really me, but my [dead] maternal uncles and brothers who will be wiping the tears off your face, expelling sadness from your hearts, and shaking hands with you." (I recorded statements with a similar meaning Kan 1983:52–53.)

The invocation of the names of the guests' own dead matrikin was also supposed to comfort the mourners by reminding them that their opposites had suffered similar losses in the past. As one of the speakers in a recent potlatch explained, "I am telling you the names of my own clan relatives that are gone so that you would feel how much I sympathize with you. I am comforting you with their memory" (Kan 1979–1987). In fact, some of my informants stressed, in public and in private, that it was painful for them to recall their own losses, but that they did it to help their opposites. As one of them put it: "Everything has a time and a place. We do not speak of our dead loved ones without a special reason. Only on certain occasions we do that to comfort the opposite side. We put the names [of the dead] as medicine on their wounds" (Kan 1983:53).

In their responses, which tended to be shorter and less elaborate, the hosts thanked the guests for their words and reiterated the condolence speeches' imagery and message. They frequently referred to the change in their "inside" (*toowú*), brought about by the oratory's healing effect (compare Chapter VI). A special emphasis was placed on the opposites' role in replacing the speakers' own deceased matrikin, as in the following statement, "I have felt as though my maternal uncles had left me in a desolate place, so much I have been grieving, but with your help I have come back home" (Kan 1979–1987).

The mourners' reference to restored equilibrium in their feelings figured prominently in their response to the condolence speeches and emphasizes the crucial dimension of the potlatch as a ritual which reestablished proper relationships between the two moieties. "I will regain my balance" is an expression one frequently encounters in the mourners' speeches. While the hosts seemed to refer primarily to their feelings, there are some indications that they also implied that their relationships with the opposites were finally back to normal. As I have stated earlier, until the potlatch, the hosts were seen as being indebted to those of their opposites who had helped them during the funeral, and hence inferior to them.[20] To dramatize this transformation and thereby magnify their gratitude, the hosts elevated their personal drama to the cosmic level, as in the following statement: "Our sorrow has shaken us up like an earthquake, but your kind words have put everything back together again" (Kan 1979–1987). Another eloquent expression of this notion was made in English at a recent potlatch: "When sorrow comes, everything is like a jigsaw puzzle: nobody knows how to put it together. But when the customary ceremony is performed and kind words are exchanged, everything falls together (Kan 1983:56).[21]

Jokes

Having comforted the mourners with the heavy words of condolence, the guests shifted gears, so to speak, and, in the spirit of the general change in the potlatch's mood, began using jokes to make their hosts feel better.[22] Two major types of jokes were used in the potlatch: jokes targeting the speakers themselves and jokes jesting about the classificatory children of one's clan (*naa yátx'i*), that is, those members of one's own moiety who belonged to other clans and whose fathers belonged to the same clan as the joker's own father.[23] The former seem to have been less common in the past and did not constitute a distinct genre. They would typically refer to the speaker's own misadventures or embarrassing physical characteristics (e.g., obesity). Sometimes a speaker would even use his crest to construct a joke. Thus in a recent potlatch, a guest from the Bear Clan pointed out that although it was too early for bears to come out of their hibernation he had done so to attend this wonderful feast (Kan 1979–1987).

Jokes about one's *naa yatx'i* were more risque. These jokes were widely used outside the potlatch and were one of the very few interchanges in which one could joke with one's moiety kin. Among the central Tlingit, classificatory children of the same clan would often be seated together at the potlatch, so as to allow them to trade jokes and enliven the event.

Most often such jokes accused someone of sexual exploits and witchcraft. Particularly comic were jokes in which respectable elders accused each other of having sexual liaisons with each other's wives and of flying around at night as witches.

Potlatch joking and buffoonery might also take the form of a stunt in which the sons of a clan pretended to dance with a crest hat, the humor deriving from the fact that the dancers did not belong to the same clan in the first place and, in the second, were actually using a mask portraying a shaman's most dreaded tutelary spirit (Billman n.d.:7–8).

In contrast to the speeches of condolence, which comforted the hosts by presenting the ancestral myths and crests in a serious and solemn manner, this joking made them smile by poking fun at some of the most fundamental principles and values of the cultural order—

proper relations between matrikin, the taboo on witchcraft, and respect for one's crests. Such joking undoubtedly facilitated a release from the tension of the death-related ritual. It also tended to soften the effect of the hosts' loss, by casting the most sacred dimensions of the culture—the focus of the potlatch—in a humorous light.

We have little evidence that the hosts reciprocated with jokes of their own, although in 1979–1984 I did record some self-deprecating jokes they told themselves.[24] Instead, the hosts dominated another important type of ritual performance, the so-called love songs.

Love Songs

The Tlingit terms for these songs, performed after the initial sad portion of the potlatch, are *kusax̱án daasheeyí*, "love song,"[25] or *naa yátx'i daasheeyí* ('song about children of the clan'). The latter term is a precise description of this type of song: they were always addressed to persons whose fathers belong to the composer's/singer's clan. Thus, if the composer happened to be a member of the Kaagwaantaan clan, he would address his song to the *Kaagwaantaan yátx'i*, "the children of the Kaagwaantaan." To address an individual as a "child" of his father's clan meant to please and flatter that person by reminding him of his ancestry and the warm feelings that fathers and children were supposed to feel towards each other. Since members of one's fathers clan included persons of the opposite gender, categorized as paternal uncles and aunts, who were one's potential spouses, the love referred to in these songs was not only filial/paternal but heterosexual/romantic as well.

In fact the main reason for composing a *kusax̱án daasheeyí* was to express one's feelings toward one's sweetheart or spouse. These songs expressed and evoked love, longing, rebuke, appeals for sympathy, and leave-taking. For example: "I'm just wondering why. Every time I dream of Kaagwaantaan-children, it always ends with tears in my eyes. I just feel like crying." "Whenever I see you, *Jeeshk̲weidí*-children, strength of *toowú* [mind/soul] you always give me" (de Laguna 1972: 1291, 1301).[26]

Similar to the mourning songs, songs about clan children were highly introspective, with the composer constantly referring to his inner feelings (*toowú*). This might be the reason why so many late nineteenth-century love songs compared being in love to being drunk and made other references to liquor. Generally rather restrained, particularly when it came to public expression of love for a person of the opposite sex, the Tlingit might have felt more prone to express their feelings under the influence of alcohol, and might have thought that being overwhelmed by love was not unlike being affected by alcohol. Here are two examples: "It is only on account of whisky that you pity me. Why don't you also love me, children of Deisheetaan?" (Swanton 1909:404); "It is as if I were beginning to get drunk, when I just think about the children of Teikweidí. Sometimes when I think of the children of Teikweidí, I go out of my mind. I don't know why" (de Laguna 1972:1301).

Despite this emphasis on one's feelings, the composer/performer never revealed his own personal identity; only his clan affiliation was known. Neither did he single out the object of his affection. The love song always addressed the children. Nevertheless, people who knew the composer were often aware of the identity of the addressee. The impersonal nature of the love song allowed it to be used by other members of the composer's clan, long after his death, to address their own clan children collectively or individually. The central cultural theme of the inseparability of the individual and the group and the link between love and social identity was underscored by this important genre of the potlatch performance. As Dauenhauer puts it, in these songs,

> The domain of the individual is distinct from, but inseparable from the domain of society. Thus individual creative images are essential for a good composer, but equally important are the tribal [clan] images. Personal emotion is expressed to a specific individual by a specific individual, but the relationship is controlled by the marriage rules. (1975:153)

In addition to its content, the form of the love song—its fast, lively rhythm—contrasted sharply with that of the mourning song addressed to members of one's own clan. The emphasis on love, particularly heterosexual love between spouses, seems quite appropriate in a ritual aimed at overcoming sorrow and celebrating life's victory over death. Thus in the potlatch, the intermoiety relations were presented not only as a source of comfort and spiritual strength for the mourners, but also as a guarantee of biological and social reproduction. This use of the symbolism of love, marriage, and procreation in mortuary rituals is not uncommon (compare Huntington and Metcalf 1979 passim; Bloch and Parry 1982).[27] More unusual was the prominence of death among the themes of the love songs. They were often composed by a person on his or her deathbed and served as the final farewell. They were also created by a person mourning the loss of some beloved opposite. The composer might also appeal to the children of his clan for pity and compassion in time of trouble or emphasize that his love, particularly love that is not reciprocated, is killing him. For example:

> I am very glad you took pity on me, children of Wushkitaan.
> Now I am going up to the ghost world. (Swanton 1909:396)

> If you had died, children of Kaagwaantaan,
> I would have cut my hair for you.

> I love you so much, that I would have blackened my face for you,
> Children of Kaagwaantaan. (Swanton 1909:411)

> If one had control of death,
> it would be very easy to die with a Wolf woman.
> It would be very pleasant. (Swanton 1909:415)

> Come here to me. Let me love you for the last time,
> Children of Teikweidí
> I am going to die. Come here and let me love you for the last time.
> (de Laguna 1972:1297)

The death presented in most of the love songs contrasted sharply with the death that the sad songs described. The former was not as threatening, not as final as the latter. It always contained an element of optimism, hope, and humor, even if the words themselves are sad. While a love song might be originally created to mourn the death of one's father or wife, its subsequent performers might instead use it to joke with their opposites and to please them.

The rigid control of expression of emotion by the social order is made very clear here: one could not publicly mourn one's opposites and one's matrikin by using the same type of song. In fact, the emphasis on love between moieties was so crucial that, even if one wished to compose a song expressing displeasure with one's affines or paternal kin, one still had to use this genre. Thus, de Laguna (1972:1310) recorded a love song an angry man composed just before committing suicide, because of a bitter argument he had gotten into with his brother-in-law.

An important implicit message of these songs was clearly a restoration of intermoiety balance, threatened by death and the indebtedness of the mourners to their opposites. While much of the mortuary cycle was about funerary services, condolence, and remuneration of the funeral workers by the mourners and much emphasized the serious, solemn side of intermoiety relations, the love songs stressed its lighter but equally important aspect. In other words, while condolence oratory stressed the exchange of services of affliction between the two moieties, the love songs focused on the other side of that relationship—the exchange of spouses. For their "heavy" words of comfort, the mourners repaid their opposites with words of love, which were equally "heavy" (i.e., ritually significant), but expressed in a lighter form.

All of this was underscored by a standard response of the persons addressed in this type of song—they invariably got up and danced playfully, shaking their fingers (and sometimes hands) in a certain way. In fact, a special term for composing a love song, *shu-ka-dli-xoox*, is derived from the verb *ya-xoox*, "to call, to summon," and is translated by Story and Naish (1973:339) as "to call forth response from opposite side, by means of song." Usually the guests also reciprocated with a few love songs of their own.

The idea of the restoration of balance is also supported by the frequent use of this type of song in peace-making ceremonies involving groups from the two moieties. In both cases—the memorial potlatch and the ceremony of peacemaking—the opposites were acknowledging their dependence on each other, their being linked together in an eternal cycle of exchange. As one love song put it eloquently: "I will no more throw your faces away, Kaagwaantaan-children, because you are the ones who make the Wolf phratry [moiety] valuable" (Swanton 1909:398).

Conveying Love and Gratitude through Feasting and Gift-giving

The distribution of quantities of food and gifts among the potlatch guests has long been a fascinating and puzzling subject for European observers and anthropologists. Scholars who offered cultural materialist and ecological explanations of this phenomenon have looked at the items given out by the hosts simply as material objects, wealth, and subsistence products and argued that the potlatch served as a form of their redistribution (Suttles 1960; Vaida 1961; Piddocke 1965). Others (e.g., Benedict 1934) focused on the enormous quantities of objects given away and saw this generosity as an expression of megalomaniacal and other psychological characteristics.

Only recently have Northwest Coast ethnologists returned to Mauss' (1967) notion of gift exchange as a symbolic structure.[28] As Traube (1980:92) points out, "In the circulation of wealth and wealth tokens, where others had seen a flow of material goods accumulated and distributed for material ends, Mauss discerned a perpetual play of representations, an intermingling of persons, things, spirits, rights. . . ." One of the first among Northwest Coast ethnologists to rediscover Mauss and focus attention on the symbolic dimension of material objects and food was Goldman, who pointed out that the anthropologists' preoccupation with the use of large quantities of blankets in the late nineteenth-century potlatches "obscured for many scholars what had actually been the traditional pattern of a linked regard for both the quantity and the symbolic significance of each item of complementary property" (1975:134). In my view, the exchange of potlatch food and gifts was a rich and complex system of communication, in which material objects carried metamessages about eschatology, power, and rank, as well as success in subsistence activities, trade, warfare, and key cultural values and structural principles. Using the artifacts circulating in the potlatch system, the participants negotiated their social and power relations as well as expressed their feelings and attitudes towards each other.[29] Loving and grateful messages towards the opposite were more explicit than the competitive and status-aggrandizing messages, which are examined in the next chapter.

The notion that every object given to the guests expressed the donors' positive feelings towards them was fundamental to the potlatch. This belief explains why the hosts did not sit down to eat with the guests. To do so would be withholding some of the food destined for paying off the opposites. In his study of Kaluli ceremonialism, Schieffelin (1976:51) describes the guests behaving in a similar manner when feasting their affines:

> The social distance maintained between hosts and guests allows the gift of food to be a public demonstration of good faith in the relationship. In this context, for the hosts to eat some of the food they present to their guests would be, in effect, to take some of it back and throw a cloud over the relation they wish to affirm. Thus, even when the hosts do get hungry and eat, they tend to do so furtively after the guests have finished, and never from the same batch of food.

Food and gifts were perfect objects for expressing gratitude and affection since this was their role in daily life. In the potlatch, the gifts were said to "warm" and the food to physically "strengthen" (give *latseen* to) the guests, that is, remunerate them for the moral strength (also *latseen*) and for their own "warming" of the mourners' *toowú* with their words and deeds.

Furs, replaced by blankets or cloth in the postcontact era, were the most common types of gifts used. Furs were quite appropriate for "warming" or "covering up" their recipients in return for their kind words, which, in turn, were described as "covering up" the hosts like blankets (see above). Since European-made artifacts quickly replaced the indigenous ones, we have little information on the types of gifts used in the precontact era. Nevertheless, Russian sources agree that moose and deer hides (tanned and untanned) were most commonly used in the first half of the nineteenth century (Khlebnikov 1976:32; Krause 1956:132).

Despite the fact that sets of clothing are not mentioned in the early sources, we might hypothesize that in the precontact era the guests were actually dressed by the hosts, as is still done among the Koyukon Athapaskans mentioned earlier in this chapter. Emmons' informant Shukoff (1920–1945, Shukoff's Account:9) seems to confirm my hunch in the above-mentioned statement that the potlatch hosts "dressed the guests by giving them pieces of blankets." There are many references to the use of the strips of cloth, calico, and blankets to make shirts, dresses, and coats. Thus a Tlingit man, in his reminiscences about a major potlatch he attended in Sitka in 1877, mentioned that pieces of blankets were later made by the recipients into coats or shirts, quite regardless of color or matching stripes. In his words, "Such garments are considered to be very honorable indeed as they show that the wearer has been to many feasts and had received many presents" (Wilbur n.d.:442b). Olson reported (1967:65) that the part of the potlatch in which blankets were given out was called "putting on something given." An account of an 1898 Hoonah potlatch mentions towels, socks, stockings, suspenders, and other items of clothing were mentioned (Kan 1979–1987).

Animal skins, blankets and clothing appear to have served as a major symbol of love and gratitude, so that any generous gift from a member of the opposite moiety could be referred to as a "blanket." Thus, when an Inland Tlingit chief decided to express his great happiness about his daughter's giving birth to a son, he donated a piece of land to her husband's clan and gave the man a beaver skin robe. This was his way of thanking his daughter and son-in-law for his new grandchild. He also explained that he did not want the child to be cold. The land thus given was described as being "just like a blanket to their [the child's and the mother's] backs" (McClellan 1975:638). Traditional blanket symbolism explains why even today, when money has become the major type of potlatch gift, the hosts still try to give away some blankets and other items of clothing.[30]

Despite the attractiveness of this symbolic interpretation of the use of skins, blankets, and cloth in the potlatch, we cannot overlook an additional, materialist explanation. These were rather inexpensive items of standard size and value, which could be divided easily among large numbers of guests. Usually, after each guest had received one or several whole blankets, smaller pieces of blankets and of cloth were given out. Some sources suggest that the blankets received in the potlatch were not used in daily life but were stored in chests and circulated only as ceremonial gifts and payments (Oberg 1937:117). A recent Tlingit dictionary (Davis 1976:92–93) gives different terms for a "thin blanket for giving away" (l'ée) and a "blanket for wearing" (x'óow). In other words, these gifts represented symbolic rather than utilitarian clothing.

Besides presenting the gifts as garments which became part of the outer layer of the recipient's body, the hosts manipulated them, to convey the notion that they were giving away part of their own selves. Thus, those members of the hosts' group who were given new names, had their ears pierced, and were specially honored in other ways were often placed near or on top of the pile of furs or blankets, so that, as the Tlingit put it, "from underneath them the stuff came out" (Kan 1979–1987).[31] Some of the artifacts were rubbed on the faces of these hosts, just before being given away.[32] Placing the wealth in physical contact with the crest objects expressed the same notion, since the crest epitomized the hosts' social selves. Thus, the Kaagwaantaan who claim the wolf as one of their major crests might place their wealth on top of a wolf skin. In a potlatch I attended, the money prepared for distribution was put inside a headdress representing the hosts' major crest (Kan 1979–1987). By bestowing upon the opposites objects imbued with their own personhood, the hosts showed their love. Gift-giving was thus parallel to the exchange between spouses of bodily substances which ensured biological and social reproduction. The guests carried home physical manifestations of the hosts' love and elements of their personhood. The guests may also be seen as receiving something of the hosts' outside layer, in return for relieving them of the polluted bodies ("outsides") of their dead matrikin.

The idea that the gift itself contained some element of the giver's personhood was first stated by Mauss (1967:10), based upon his analysis of Northwest Coast as well as Samoan and Maori data. While I cannot comment on the latter two cases, I have demonstrated that he was right as far as the Tlingit and probably other Northwest Coast peoples were concerned. However, Mauss was in error when he argued that because the object was imbued with the donor's personhood, the gift retained a magical hold over the recipient and hence it was dangerous to keep it. Nowhere in the Tlingit ethnography do we find any evidence to support his contention that the gift was alive and strove to bring to its original clan and homeland some equivalent to take its place (Mauss 1967:10). As Gewertz (1984:192) has pointed out, "Subsequent ethnography has made us aware . . . that the meaning and intentions contained in objects of exchange are far more varied than the homogeneous reciprocal compulsion that Mauss suggested."[33]

Of course, the notion that the guests received only the material substance ("outside") of the artifacts given to them while the hosts' own dead matrikin received their spiritual essence ("inside") increased the solemnity of the event and, through the act of gift-giving, brought together all of the categories of the human persons inhabiting the social universe—the hosts, the guests, and the dead matrikin of each.

chapter nine

COMPETITION AND COOPERATION, HIERARCHY AND EQUALITY

In addition to its focus upon completing the mortuary cycle, the potlatch had a major political dimension. In Olson's (1967:59) words, it was not only a solemn *duty* of the deceased's matrikin but their major *privilege* as well, because "only by this means could the mourners, whether immediate family, household, or clan, maintain or raise their social rank." The sum total of the hosts' actions—the crests displayed, the wealth distributed, and the songs and speeches presented— established their current standing vis-à-vis other clans in their own and the opposite moieties. This jockeying for status began in the funeral but it reached much greater proportions in the potlatch where many more people from both moieties participated and where the concern with the death-related matters was not as dominant.

With more participants, ritual acts, and wealth involved, the potlatch required more preparation, rehearsal, and backstage negotiation than the earlier parts of the mortuary cycle (compare Chapter VII). Less constrained by their grief and by the mourning taboos, the hosts had more freedom to challenge each other's claims to rank and status. As in the funeral, much of this negotiation occurred prior to the ritual, to ensure that the hosts presented a unified front vis-à-vis their opposites. The general order in which each mourner spoke and/or sang and presented his or her contribution of wealth was established in advance, with the higher-ranking hosts following their lower-ranking kin. The chief host tended to be the last one to speak and made the most generous donation. By discussing his role with the rest of the hosts prior to the potlatch, he tried to ensure that they would not surpass him and thus embarrass him in the eyes of the guests.[1]

Rivalry among the Hosts

While all the hosts strove collectively to enhance the rank and status of their lineage, each individual was expected to do his or her best to advance in the group's internal hierarchy. Although the identity of the chief heir had been decided prior to the funeral, the fate of at least some of the deceased's titles and regalia was not sealed until the potlatch. Substantiating their claims to these strategic resources by references to their close kinship and emotional attachment to the deceased, as well as their wealth, the hosts used the pre-potlatch meetings to ensure that they and/or their close junior matrikin, rather than other members of their lineage, would receive the valuable titles in the course of the ritual. The same was true of their claims to the use of specific crest-bearing regalia owned by their lineage. The more intense competition obviously occurred among the aristocracy at the top of the lineage hierarchy where the use rights to the more valuable representations of *shagóon* were at stake.

The competitiveness and manifested inequality among the hosts increased as the potlatch progressed. As we have seen, the initial phase of the potlatch centered on mourning, the hosts were much more unified, and distinctions between them were not emphasized. However, for the rest of the ritual, when the issues of power, rank, and prestige became central, individual hosts' appearance and ritual action underscored their gender, age, and status differences. Despite the pre-potlatch negotiations and rehearsals, there remained room for the hosts within the ritual itself to try to outdo each other in word and deed.

Indicating the increased status consciousness of the potlatch is the fact that male and female hosts did not play an equal role. The former usually contributed more wealth, wore the most valuable crest objects, dominated the speech-making, and performed the most sacred dances and songs. Male hosts' contributions tended to be furs and blankets, while women primarily donated food. If they did contribute blankets, the quantity was usually smaller than the men's. Similarly, the older hosts, especially males, played a greater role in the ritual, acting as speakers and song leaders, while the younger ones served the food and performed other, less prestigious tasks.

The potlatch was clearly dominated by the aristocracy, whose greater wealth as well as superior ritual expertise and esoteric knowledge were essential for its success. In major potlatches, where the chief mourner was the head of the matrilineal group, it was his and the other leading hosts' duty to assist their matrikin in every possible way, from helping them select an appropriate mourning song to delivering a speech on their behalf. As one of de Laguna's (1972:632) informants put it:

> If I am of his [the chief's] tribe [clan], he is going to mention my name. . . . My big name. . . . "It's up to you, so-and-so." Then I always say a word to these people, which ones we invited. If I don't know what to say . . . I tell him . . . . The chief [then] does the talking for me. Then I start a song, my tribe's [clan's] song. And after I ended that song, I put up the money. . . .
>
> Chief always helps. That's what the chief [is] there for. . . . And if I am going to sing a song, I ask my chief, "Is it all right if I sing this song? I lost my brother." Maybe he says, "No, I got a better one than that." Maybe he says, "Yes."

As custodians of their lineage and clan crests, the heads of matrilineal groups determined who among their matrikin was to wear them, thus controlling their access to a major source of status and prestige. Similarly, the leading hosts presided over the giving of names, the most important element and marker of individual rank and status.[2]

Rivalry and inequality among individual members of the host lineage were usually much less intense than those between two lineages of the same clan, acting as hosts. The objects of this rivalry were the names, crests, and other collective possessions these lineages shared. While the house of the deceased was supposed to play the leading role in his potlatch, other houses of the same clan would usually contribute some wealth and take part in the ritual. Although it was inappropriate for them to try to outdo the chief mourner's lineage, they might try to display a certain crest or perform a particular song which the chief mourner's lineage claimed as its exclusive possession. Different lineages were also less likely to rehearse together, and hence, there was a bigger chance that a disagreement between them would emerge during the potlatch itself.

Another common form of intraclan rivalry was a refusal by the leading house of the clan to let a lower-ranking one use certain crests. As Oberg (1973:125) explained:

> If the local clan division is large and contains many houses, it often happens that one of the houses of lesser importance wishes to give a potlatch on a grand scale. This house has the right to demand any of the clan crests that it wishes to display, and the trustees of the crests will have to let them be thus used. The crests have definite value and, if the trustees and the clansmen generally do not think that the prospective potlatch giver has enough goods, they may refuse to give him the clan crest or crests. Disputes of this nature often occurred within the clan. The . . . clan of Sitka has two Raven hats, one being the original, and the other a hat made by one of the house-groups [lineages] which grew to great power in historic times. There was an effort to prevent this house-group [lineage] from getting too far ahead of the others by refusing to let it use the [original] hat, but it was strong enough to defy the clan members and to make a hat of its own.[3]

Other instances of this rivalry included a man's refusal to allow his younger brother to build a new lineage house and a clan chief's not allowing his nephew, a house head, to sponsor a potlatch in memory of the younger man's mother (Olson 1967:61).

Competition between hosts could only be expressed indirectly and subtly. Thus rival hosts rarely addressed each other; instead, they inserted their claims into the speeches addressed to the guests and used representations of their *shagóon* to make their point. In a potlatch held in the early 1980s, one of the chief hosts, who was struggling for the leadership position with the heads of other houses of his clan, spoke about the history of the ceremonial staff representing his clan crest (*wootsaagáa*) he was holding in his hand. Among many of the things he said was a statement that he planned to "maintain a firm grip on the staff," meaning that he had no intention of relinquishing his leadership position in the clan (Kan 1979–1987).

The hosts could not alter the content of the ancestral myths or the more recent history of their matrilineal groups, but they could carefully modify, emphasize, or play down certain kinship ties, so as to highlight their own link to certain prominent matrilineal ancestors. Because of the solemnity of the potlatch, it was difficult for other hosts to challenge directly the speaker's interpretation of the past. The only way they could do so was to present their own version through oratory. A skillful orator, who made a better impression on the guests, and/or the richest one, who could back up the rhetoric with generous gifts, was often the winner.

While the disputes and competition among members of the host lineage and clan were sometimes quite serious, they could often be resolved, softened, or at least glossed over by the rhetoric of matrilineal solidarity. An individual host's kinship ties with the deceased served as a restraint on his aggressive self-aggrandizement. Thus, it was considered inappropriate for a distant relative of the departed to contribute much more than the close ones did. The ritual etiquette—especially the emphasis on not "overdoing it"—also played an important role in checking the overly ambitious and selfish conduct of individual hosts. One could and was expected to try to raise one's standing in the social hierarchy but attempts to advance too far above one's current position were seen as being too pushy. To restrain one's ambitions and show respect to one's rivals was the mark of a truly refined person. To disagree openly with one's fellow clansmen was embarrassing, and only rarely did such disagreements result in a total breakdown of cooperation between matrikin. To walk out of a potlatch sponsored by one's clan was to disgrace oneself and the entire group. It seems that, by entering the ritual space, the disputants were already indicating some agreement on the distribution of power, rank, and prestige within their group. This tacit agreement did not pertain to different clans of the same moiety, which engaged in some of the most intense rivalry over rank, status, and prestige, usually expressed through competition over crests.

In most large-scale potlatches, the mourning clan was the only one acting as the host and representing the moiety. Other clans of its moiety could provide minor help, they might even be asked to participate, but they would very rarely dominate the ritual, unless the mourners' clan was so small and poor that it could not sponsor a respectable potlatch on its own. Thus two localized clans of the same moiety rarely sponsored the same potlatch. However, the validation of crests and claims to other sacred possessions made by the hosts in this rite were of great importance to other clans of their moiety. The latter often disagreed with them, particularly if the two clans happened to share a certain crest (see Chapter III).

Such disputes were very difficult to resolve. One of the competing clans could either ignore the use of their crest by the other one or challenge them to fight it out. If one of them was much weaker, it might simply move away to avoid embarrassment. Finally it could simply cease using the disputed crest altogether.[4] The fact that members of the opposite moiety had witnessed their competitors' claims and had agreed with them by accepting the gifts was important, since it made it more difficult for the rival clan to legitimize its disagreement with the potlatch hosts. Thus, even though intramoiety conflicts were the most difficult ones to resolve by means of the potlatch, they too were affected by it: without sponsoring one, clans could never legitimize their claims to certain crests and other prerogatives.[5]

The hosts' competition and cooperation with each other were both essential for their success. The individual's efforts to excel contributed to his entire matrilineal group's performance. At the same time, without cooperation such a complex ceremony could never get off the ground. Similarly, despite the centrality of the hierarchical relationships, they did not completely displace the egalitarian ones. Although competing against each other for much of the potlatch, members of the deceased's lineage acted as cooperating equals vis-à-vis other matrilineal groups of their own moiety. Moreover, they could never allow their internal rivalry to overshadow the fundamental opposition between the two moieties which underlaid the entire potlatch.

The Hosts and the Guests at "War" and at "Peace"

With all the emphasis on love and cooperation between the hosts and the guests, a great deal of subtle and not so subtle competitiveness was present in their interaction. The hosts' goal was not only to repay their opposites, thus restoring the proper balance in their relationship, but to surpass the standard set by the guests themselves at their own last potlatch in which many of the present hosts had participated. In the course of the potlatch, the hosts presented their opposites with an interpretation of the distribution of power and prestige in the social universe and tried to make them accept it, without antagonizing them. This was a delicate task which required a great deal of diplomatic skill and ritual expertise.

Beginning with the selection of the guests, every major aspect of the intermoiety relations in the potlatch had an important political dimension. Even as they called upon their opposites to perform the initial funerary services, the mourners had to keep in mind that the people they chose would end up as the prominent guests at their potlatch. Hence "services of affliction" could be assigned in such a way as to affirm some existing alliances, create new ones, or drop others altogether. Within their own community, the mourners had fewer choices, since the identity of the opposites with whom they had traditionally exchanged spouses and ritual services was fairly well established. In fact, some of the local lineages and clans expected to be called upon and subtly expressed dissatisfaction if they were ignored.[6] However, even close to home, the mourners could manipulate paternal/affinal relationships so as to legitimize their deviation from the local tradition.

The mourners had more choices with the performance of the potlatch-related ritual services to which the out-of-town opposites were usually invited and which included, for example, erecting the mortuary pole. Every lineage and clan of respectable rank had alliance relationships with a number of matrilineal groups in several communities which could be reactivated or allowed to lapse. Sometimes the deceased's matrikin began to recruit out-of-town opposites long before the potlatch, by asking them to contribute some wealth because they had not been able to perform the funerary services due to the distances they had to travel (see Swanton 1908:438–443). In the potlatch itself, the hosts' political objectives were illustrated by a common practice of assigning the most prestigious tasks involved in housebuilding and mortuary pole-raising to older chiefs who could not possibly perform the work themselves. Instead, the older chiefs reallocated these tasks to their own junior matrikin but still received the lion's share of the gifts. Similarly, in a major potlatch, the *naa káani* had to be selected from among the aristocracy.

By calling upon their opposites from other communities, the hosts not only strengthened their network of allies but also tried to impress their local rivals from their own and the opposite moieties with it. It should be pointed out that the participation of the nonlocal guests made the potlatch a more risky undertaking, since, compared to a ritual involving only the local opposites, there was less of a guarantee that the guests would reciprocate at a future potlatch of their own. Of course, such risk only added to the hosts' prestige.[7]

The delicate nature of intermoiety relations, especially those involving groups from different communities, is best illustrated by the dramatic arrival of the out-of-town guests. This arrival was invariably staged as a military confrontation. Prior to the potlatch, both sides engaged in "fasting, abstinence, and the manufacture of medicines, as if preparing for war" (Swanton 1908:438). As they travelled towards their host community, the guests acted as warriors on a raid. Sometimes this was mock warfare but occasionally powerful groups "plundered canoes and even towns of their provisions" (Swanton 1908:438).

The parallel between a war raid and the guests' arrival was particularly strong because most enemy attacks came from the sea.[8] The guests, who often arrived at dawn, pretended they were trying to sneak up on their hosts. The hosts, accompanied by their local opposites, were already waiting for the "attackers" on the beach. In the late nineteenth century, shooting in the air with guns and even small cannons became popular. A major exchange of verbal insults and mock fighting took place between the leaders of the two parties. As in a real military confrontation, a brave warrior from among the guests stood in his canoe in front of the chief host's house and asked "Who is the head (owner) of this war?" Another brave warrior representing the hosts responded "So-and-So, his true warrior I am. Him I represent." The hosts then began encouraging their chief (i.e., "the head of the war") to "attack his enemies." The chief was dressed and equipped for fighting. Two of his clan heads shouted, "Be strong! Do not retreat from your enemies until you are killed." The chief charged down the beach, crying "Huh, huh" in defiance.

Unlike a real warrior, however, he had a broken spear and a cracked bow. He pretended to use these weapons but when they failed or broke, he retreated in mock fear. His "enemies" in the canoes rapped on the gunwales with their paddles and cried, "Waw! Waw!" in derision, meaning he was a coward (Olson 1967:61–62; see also 71). In another account of this ceremony, the chief host first ran to the guests' canoes, drawing his bow as if he was going to shoot them, but then threw it on the ground, turned to the people on the beach, and said, "You think Stook is as foolish as that, to kill big game?" (Billman 1964:59; see Swanton 1909:71; Emmons n.d., notebook 10).[9] The notion that this was not a true war and that the host was to be the loser was emphasized from the very beginning of this ceremony. Thus, both Emmons (n.d., notebook 10) and Olson (1967:61–62) mention that the chief host emerged from his house dressed not as a warrior going into battle but as a person who volunteered to be killed by his enemies in the ceremony of equalizing the losses on both sides of a war, prior to making peace (see above). At the same time, he was acting as a coward, that is, the opposite of a true warrior.

Once the chief host had "lost the war," the ceremony turned abruptly from militarism to peace. He showed his guests great respect by taking off his shoes and walking into the water to meet them (de Laguna 1972:620). He then ordered his clansmen to carry the guests, sitting in their canoes, ashore. Thus the guests crossed a marginal area between water (their own domain) and land (the hosts' domain), without ever touching the boundary. The hosts might also perform the abovementioned ritual of "killing the trail for the guests" by sacrificing their own slaves and marking with blood the path from the landing to the potlatch site. Considered a sign of great respect (Emmons 1920–1945, Shukoff's Account:7), this practice might be interpreted as a demonstration of both the hosts' generosity and the marking of the liminal space crossed by the arriving guests as valuable and sacred.[10] The guests themselves emphasized their peaceful intentions by such statements as "we came here by the road of the sun," which Emmons' informant (1920–1945, Shukoff's Account:7) explained as implying that they came "with good faith" and to "have a joyous time."[11]

References to warfare continued throughout the potlatch. For example, the hosts referred to a dance contest as "a war dance,"[12] while the guests, wishing to emphasize that they were planning a return potlatch, said that they would "stand against" their present host (Olson 1967:97). If a person could not respond to a verbal challenge from the opposite side, he was said to be "knocked down with talking" (Kan 1979–1987). When wealth was about to be distributed, the chief host might appear dressed as a warrior to indicate that he was "brave," i.e., ready to give away large quantities of goods (Swanton 1908:439).[13] The host or the song leader would also encourage his singers with the exclamation "Gushwé!" which one Tlingit elder translated as "have courage to do the very best you are able to" (Wells in Billman 1964:61). In addition to bellicose rhetoric, this rivalry was expressed by the hosts' statements that were the opposite of what they really meant. For example, when the guests got tired, one of their chiefs might ask the head host for a recess. The latter would say "no," but then would order the recess himself (de Laguna 1972:631).[14]

This prominence of war symbolism and rhetoric in the potlatch has been noted by Tlingit ethnographers (e.g., McClellan 1954:96) as well as scholars who studied the Tsimshian (Boas 1916:539; Garfield 1939:200; 202), the Kwakiutl (Boas 1897 passim; Codere 1950; Drucker and Heizer 1967:125–129), and the Coast Salish (Haeberlin and Gunther 1930:14; Smith 1940:108; Snyder 1975:153). However, with the exception of Codere who devoted an entire monograph to this subject and, to a lesser extent, Drucker and Heizer, no attempt to interpret this phenomenon has ever been made.

Of course, the most immediate and obvious interpretation is that the mock battle in the preliminary stage of the potlatch was symbolic, first openly acknowledging and then denying the potential for violence. One might say, using Levy's (1984:227) term, that antagonism was hypercognized in the beginning of the potlatch, in order to downplay and overcome it during the rest of it. By casting himself in the role of a coward who was willing to lose the war, the host both flattered and honored his guests by acknowledging their superiority and emphasized that it was stupid to fight with the people needed as allies. Knauft (1985:247–248) has recently commented in a discussion of the use of violence in the early stages of the Gebusi feasts:

> It has often been noted that ritual communication takes place through physical demonstration; it concretely enacts its assertions rather than simply referring to them in discourse. This kind of analogic communication is especially evident in the affirmation of a positive state by demonstrating conclusively that its opposite is not true. Thus, rather than simply saying, "See! We're being hospitable and we're not angry!" the overcoming and transcendence of anger is itself concretely and unequivocally enacted.

A Tlingit elder asked by Billman (1964:56) in the 1960s about the meaning of the mock battle responded that, "The diplomatic relation of the two [parties] must be understood before action can take place. . . . There will be no more disagreement, but peace from now on."

However, the fact that references to war continued throughout the entire potlatch suggests that there was more to the similarity between fighting and potlatching. To support my proposition that fighting and feasting were two interconnected aspects of intermoiety relations I briefly examine the nature of Tlingit warfare and peacemaking. From the native point of view, revenge for insult or murder was one of the major causes of war (see Swanton 1908:449; Olson 1967:69; de Laguna 1972:581). The Tlingit did fight to obtain slaves, booty, and even territory, but contrary to Ferguson's (1983; 1984) recent materialist explanation of Northwest Coast warfare, an indigenous theory of justice and retribution, rather than a simple shortage of productive food resources, was a major contributor to the centrality of war in the social life of the Tlingit and their coastal neighbors. According to this theory, any insult or injury coming from a member of another clan had to be avenged. If it was a relatively minor one, a transfer of property from the guilty person's kinship group to that of the victim was sufficient. However, if an insult or injury were grave and especially if a murder had been committed, a life was demanded in return. The kin group of the culprit might agree to furnish such a life, but quite often they refused and this was the beginning of a feud which lasted until the offended group had been satisfied.

Two fundamental notions formed the basis of this practice. On the one hand, as Olson (1967:24) put it, "it would be difficult to imagine a culture where the dignity of the individual is more highly valued than among the Tlingit." On the other hand, relations between clans, especially those belonging to the different moieties, had to be maintained in a state of equilibrium. That is why, at the end of a war, the number and rank of the persons lost on each side were established and the group whose losses were smaller had to offer additional victims, as a prerequisite for peace. It is interesting that although insults and injuries frequently occurred between members of the same moiety, an attempt was usually made to fix the responsibility upon a member of the opposite one (de Laguna 1972:644; see Olson 1967:69). One of the reasons for this was a special emphasis on maintaining a strict balance in intermoiety relations.[15] In fact, among some of the Tlingit tribes, such as Yakutat, a formal peace ceremony could only be made between groups belonging to the different moieties (de Laguna 1972:594).

The sensitive nature of intermoiety relations in this society where warfare was endemic is well illustrated by this anecdote. During a potlatch given by the Tantakwáan Gaanax.ádi to the Wrangell Naanyaa.aayí, the chief host collapsed and died; the guests became frightened thinking they might be blamed and a war would begin (Olson 1967:85). Of course, war was more likely with groups residing in a different community than with the local ones, with whom stronger ties based on intermarriage and day-to-day cooperation existed.[16]

Warfare and potlatching had a number of important characteristics in common. Wealth and even crests could be obtained by capturing them from another clan.[17] Success in both of these activities brought glory and increased the prestige of individuals and groups. Both activities were highly formalized and involved the display of the participants' crests on their bodies.[18] Both of them required bravery and involved killing: an actual killing of enemies and capturing of their wealth in war and a symbolic killing of property, subsequently distributed among the guests in the potlatch. In war, the goal was to overpower the enemy with physical strength. In the potlatch, the hosts appeared humble and subservient, seemingly losing their war with the guests. Instead of gaining wealth, they gave it to their enemies. However, the power and prestige gained through potlatching were seen as more significant than the wealth lost, especially since it was expected to be recouped in future potlatches.

Though warfare was central in Tlingit culture, potlatching was preferable, particularly when the two groups were linked to each other through marriage.[19] One could not fight perpetually with one's opposites, because they were needed as affines and performers of funerary services.[20] Crests and other tangible and intangible property acquired through fighting were often less valuable and less legitimate than those items inherited from one's ancestors. The Tlingit preferred potlatching to fighting because they preferred peace to war and because the analogue for the potlatch was the peace ceremony. Indeed, the potlatch contains mock battles but only because the peace ceremony contains mock battles, and it is the peace ceremony which is the underlying model for the potlatch (see Olson 1967:81–82; de Laguna 1972:592–604).

Thus, while feasting and warfare were, in Lévi-Strauss' (1943) words, logically opposed aspects of a single mode of interaction, they were not equally valued. Unlike Codere (1950), I do not think that, in the post-contact era, potlatching simply replaced warfare. Although European interference undoubtedly reduced the level of fighting in the second half of the nineteenth century, the Tlingit continued to fight until the early 1900s, while the scale of their potlatches also increased.[21] The use of war imagery in the potlatch was not a survival from an earlier era dominated by warfare, as Codere argued, but a symbolic expression of potential conflict which the potlatch was aimed at overcoming (see Drucker and Heizer 1967:125–129; Walens 1981:39; Snyder 1964:397–401).[22]

Rivalry among the Guests

While symbolic warfare between the hosts and the guests tended to emphasize the transformation of potential hostility into cooperation, rivalry between the two halves into which the guests were always divided was much more serious, even though it was conducted through oratory, song, and dance. By dividing the guests and encouraging this rivalry, and also acting as the peacemakers and mediators between the two sides, the hosts underscored their own unity and their dominant role in the potlatch.

The two guest groups tended to occupy the two sides of the house. They were said to be "singing and dancing against each other," with each side watching the other one carefully for any mistake or any attempt to outdo it. As in the military and the peaceful/ritual confrontations between groups in the opposite moieties, the emphasis in this rivalry was also on the maintenance of a strict balance. As one native eyewitness explained, "Everything was equal between these groups of dancers. This was a sign of respect and honor to each other. If one group tried to add one more dance than another that meant they were trying to make trouble" (Wells in Billman 1964:60–61).

This rivalry was also expressed through the jokes about one's *naa yátx'i* mentioned in Chapter VIII. In this genre, the guests challenged each other with their wit, in order to cheer up the hosts and receive a larger gift. Despite some limitations placed on this type of verbal dueling (for example, joking with a *naa yátx'i* much older than oneself was discouraged),[23] some jokes caused bitter feelings. Thus, in the early 1800s, a man of the Kiks.ádi clan of Sitka went to Chilkat to attend a potlatch. There his *naa yátx'i* from a local clan taunted him about the humiliations his clan was suffering at the hands of the Russians. This is said to have given the Kiks.ádi "that fighting spirit," and to have provoked their successful attack on the Russian fort in Sitka (Billman n.d.:8). In fact, while informants usually deny that the word "hurting" used in describing the *naa yátx'i* joking means that one really tries to hurt the butt of one's jokes, some jokers undoubtedly used this genre to get at a person they disliked (Kan 1979–1987).

Some informants claim that this rivalry of the two factions of guests was "just for fun" (de Laguna 1972:614) and there is no doubt that it did add to the excitement of this ceremony. At the same time, the tension was quite high and, as Swanton (1908:435) was told, each dancer's performance was scrutinized so carefully that "the peoples' looks" could kill him. Occasionally this rivalry erupted into violence or could even result in a long-lasting feud between the two groups. For example, Golovin (1983:103–112), who visited Sitka in the 1860s, witnessed a violent confrontation between the two groups of guests at a potlatch sponsored by a Sitka chief, which resulted in thirteen injuries, three of them serious. Golovin was told that a year earlier one of the groups, composed of the local people, outsang the other one, which came from Yakutat. To avenge their humiliation, the latter acquired new songs from their neighbors in the Copper River area and came back to another potlatch (a dedication of a new house) in Sitka to demonstrate them. They had agreed in advance that in case the Sitkans should outsing them, they would attack and kill them, using the weapons they had hidden underneath their festive attire. The singing and dancing went on for a long time, with the Yakutat guests able to match every song performed by their local rivals. However, when the latter sang an Aleut song, the Yakutat people were left "open-mouthed." Their humiliation was clear and they fell upon their enemies with knives and fired guns at them. Even the chief host was hit by a bullet. Only the Russian authorities' intervention prevented this fight from developing into a more serious feud. Instead the matter was settled by the attackers giving much wealth to the clan of the injured.

While the amount of bloodshed involved in this particular incident seems rather extreme, the use of peace songs to restore calm between the rival guest groups in the potlatch suggests that there was a clear potential for violence in their competition. Another similarity with the ritual of peacemaking was the role of the *naa káani* who accompanied each of the two groups and watched for possible trouble (de Laguna 1972:615).

How was the membership in the two groups of guests determined? In their structural analysis of the Tlingit potlatch, Rosman and Rubel (1971:49–54) argued that they were the two clans linked to the hosts through marriage. In their view, the dual division of the potlatch guests supported their interpretation of the Tlingit marriage system as being of the father's sister's daughter type and linking a matrilineal clan to *two* clans in the opposite moiety.[24] While these two group were linked to the hosts through marriage, there is little evidence to support Rosman and Rubel's argument that they were the *only* or even the *major* affines of the hosts. Thus in a Kwáashk'i Kwáan potlatch given in Yakutat in 1905, the out-of-town guests were from an area where the members of the host clan who were memorialized in that particular rite had lost their lives (de Laguna 1972:613). Data from Emmons (1920–1945 passim), de Laguna (1972:613–614), turn-of-the century newspapers, and the people I interviewed indicate that even though the potlatch guests were usually divided into two groups, they represented more than two clans or lineages.[25] As McClellan (1954:86) suggested,

> No one explanation fully accounts for the varying rival alignments of the guests. Sometimes geographical locations may figure, or kinship consideration may hold together two sibs [clans] which were once historically united. On the other hand, the quarreling which caused sibs [clans] to split may dictate continued antagonism.

I would add that the dual division of the guests must have been influenced by the dual division of space in the Tlingit house itself (see Kan 1978). Its right side (looking from the inside towards the door) was associated with sunrise and had a higher status than the left one, associated with sunset. The former was offered to the out-of-town guests to whom greater respect had to be shown (see Olson 1933–1954, notebook 1:21). Finally, this tension was exacerbated by the suspicions that the out-of-town guests tended to provoke among the local ones.

The rivalry between the two groups of guests could not be allowed to disrupt the potlatch. To contain it, several rhetorical forms were used. If one of the rival groups wished to appease the other one, they might sing a love song addressed to the classificatory children of the latter, that is, to members of the host moiety (see Chapter VIII). An individual guest might also tell a rival that he was holding the man's daughter's hand, alluding to the fact that the daughter of a man from one of the groups was often the wife of a member of the other (Swanton 1908:440). Thus, appeals to the fundamental values of love towards one's children were used to transform war into peace.

The Hosts Challenging and Trying to Dominate the Guests

Once the guests had landed and entered the potlatch space, the hosts began using them for their own status-aggrandizing purposes. On the surface, the hosts acted with great humility—standing in the front of the house while seating the guests in the most prestigious area in the rear, feeding them while themselves refraining from eating, and frequently apologizing for not being able to live up to the standards set by their ancestors or for any possible offenses against the guests. The hosts looked and acted with particular modesty during the initial part of the potlatch when they cried collectively and wore their mourning attire. There they still appeared passive and dependent on the guests for help and condolence, as they had been during the funeral.

However, once the *gaax* was over, and the hosts donned their crest-decorated garments, brought out their crests, and began presenting them in speeches, songs, and dances, they changed from being rather passive receivers into being active givers, dominating the guests and challenging them to match this splendor in future potlatches. The biggest challenge of all was the hosts' distribution of food and gifts, since the guests could not reciprocate until their own potlatch, while they could respond immediately to the guests' verbal challenge. Some of this rivalry and boasting was subtle, carefully hidden behind the verbal rhetoric of "love and respect" for the opposite moiety, and some—particularly the showering of the guests with food and gifts—rather explicit.

Verbal Dueling

The riddles which tested the opposites' wisdom, esoteric knowledge, and extent of involvement in ceremonial life exemplified intermoiety rivalry couched in the rhetoric of love and respect. Riddles were exchanged throughout the potlatch, beginning with a verbal duel which accompanied the mock battle mentioned earlier. The aim of this verbal duel was to find out "who has got the smartest men" (Knapp and Childe 1896:54).[26] It appears that during the potlatch itself, the hosts were the ones who asked questions and the guests had to give answers. Those who guessed correctly received a special gift. The riddles used metaphors and other rhetorical devices to test the addressees' knowledge of the hosts' clan history, details of earlier potlatches, wars, and other events. Thus, for example, the chief host might put on his Raven crest hat and ask the guests, "Where has this raven been last year and what did he eat?" The correct answer would be, "This raven has been to Chilkat, where he ate lots of salmon skins." The reference here is to a particular potlatch attended by the host and the wealth he received there. The potlatch riddles contained a strong competitive element,[27] and also tested the knowledge that affines had about each other, as if to ensure the strength of their ties. In addition, the riddles allowed the hosts to confirm once again their claims to certain crests and other attributes of their *shagóon* and legitimize them by having the opposites verbalize those claims themselves.

The songs and dances performed by the hosts were another challenge to their guests. In the performance of the less serious, entertaining songs and dances, the two sides used their skill and imagination to upstage each other. Many of these songs and dances were obtained from non-Tlingit tribes as gifts or indemnity payments and, thus, also demonstrated the performers' diplomatic and military accomplishments. However, when it came to the more serious, prestigious, and valuable *(at.óow)* songs and dances depicting origin myths, crests, and other manifestations of *shagóon*, the hosts had a clear advantage. Through this medium, they made claims to tangible and intangible resources not only vis-à-vis their rivals in their own moiety but the guests as well. The latter did not share the hosts' *shagóon* and hence did not dispute these claims as the hosts' own moiety kin might do, but the guests still had to be convinced that these were legitimate. The guests demonstrated their agreement by their presence at the potlatch and by their acceptance of the gifts which followed these songs and dances. The hosts' performance displaying, validating, and increasing the value of their crests was at the center of the potlatch. The performance followed the initial grieving and preceded the distribution of food and gifts. While the guests could invoke their own *shagóon* by performing a few of their own *at.óow* songs and dances to comfort the hosts and express gratitude for the food and gifts, they had fewer opportunities to do so than the hosts.

Another performative genre which challenged the opposite moiety while appearing as a manifestation of love and respect was the so-called "spirit imitating songs" (sing. *yéik utee daasheeyí*; see Dauenhauer and Dauenhauer 1981:6–6a). These songs were accompanied by dances of a distinct style and were performed mainly by the hosts. There is some evidence that they could be performed in the early stages of the ritual as well as at its conclusion (Billman 1964:63). In these cases they served as a greeting, an entertainment for guests, and a form of farewell. A few informants said that the guests could perform *yéik utee daasheeyí* to comfort the mourners (Kan 1979–1987).

However, the most common time to perform the spirit imitating songs, at least in the recent years and possibly in the nineteenth century as well, was at the height of the potlatch, prior to or immediately after the giving of names and the distribution of gifts. This was a very serious performance, contrasting sharply with the love songs.[28] It also differed from the mourning songs and the songs about crests. *Yéik utee* songs were supposed to be the voices of the specific named spirits (e.g., the Wolf Spirit Song). They were the songs once used by the shamans belonging to the performers' clan. When used in shamanistic seances, they were sung by the men of the shaman's matrilineal group who helped him. They were quite old and were usually passed from one shaman to the next within the matrilineal group.

According to de Laguna (1972:632), in the end of the nineteenth century as shamanism became obsolete, the singing of *yéik utee* songs in memorial potlatches became more common, and the songs themselves began to be seen as clan property, so that in this century some informants refer to them as "national songs," similar to the *at.óow* songs.[29] Some of my own informants suggested that *yéik utee* songs were obtained from the land otters or the Tsimshian (Kan 1979–1987). The former, as I have said earlier, were the liminal, anthropomorphic monsters whose spirits served as the shaman's helpers. The latter were traditional enemies of the Tlingit, known for their elaborate "spirit dances" and shamanism.

According to Swanton (1909:436), masks—presumably the same as those used by shamans—were put on by the dancers performing *yéik utee*. In present-day potlatches, only *shaki.át* headdresses are used (see Chapter VI). The dancers hide their bodies and faces behind a blanket set up as a screen, so that only the decorated tops of their headdresses are visible to the audience. The rhythm of the *yéik utee* songs is slow, the songs are monotonous and somber, and the words themselves are often archaic and otherwise difficult to understand, because the language of the spirits was supposed to be understandable only by shamans. These characteristics make sense to the Tlingit: after all, these are the voices of the spirits. The dancers move slowly back and forth behind the blanket, shaking their heads energetically in time with the song performed by their matrikin. Eagle down may be placed on top of the *shaki.át*, so that with every thrust of the dancer's head some of it flies towards the audience, as a sign of peace and goodwill. *Yéik utee*-style dancing required a great deal of stamina, since the dancer had to maintain a crouching posture behind the blanket. Because it brought the performers into contact with the spirit world, this kind of performing was considered dangerous, so that the dancers (and possibly the singers as well) had to fast and observe other rules of purification prior to putting on the headdresses and masks.

I do not wish to deny an element of entertainment or minimize the importance of these songs as expressions of love and respect towards the opposites, but I would also emphasize the spiritual power emanating from them. The spirits invoked by them were compared to a "two-edged dagger," from which the opposites had to defend themselves by covering their faces with their hands (Peck 1975:73). This notion and the precautions taken by the dancers themselves indicate that these shamanistic songs and dances had not become completely secularized. Consequently, by performing them the hosts were demonstrating their collective spiritual power, derived from their shamans' control over superhuman persons of the universe.

In itself this power was neither good nor bad, but could either harm the guests or bring them a blessing (*laxeitl*), depending on their response. The proper way to respond to *yéik utee* songs was to acknowledge their power with one's own spirit songs and dances or at least with a speech that mentioned the spirits owned by one's own clan. By acting that way, the guests accepted the spiritual power emanating from the spirit songs, which meant that they received some element of the performers' selves. That is why, at the conclusion of the dance, the blanket that hid the dancers was used to wipe the sweat off their bodies and then given to the guests. What one was not supposed to do was to leave the *yéik utee* songs unanswered, or as the Tlingit put it, let the spirits "float and linger in the air" or "fall on the floor" (Kan 1979–1987). Once again, we see a strong emphasis on balancing the power exhibited by the two moieties in the ritual. At the same time, despite this emphasis, the hosts were the ones who initiated the *yéik utee* songs and used them to heighten the solemnity and significance of the giving of names and gifts.[30]

Finally, even the oratory of condolence and gratitude, the most nonconfrontational type of performance, served a major political goal, allowing the speakers to refer to the manifestations of their *shagóon* and thus increase their value which, in turn, raised their owners' rank and status. This was particularly important for the guests, since so much of the potlatch was devoted to the hosts' presentation of their own *shagóon*.

This combination of competition and cooperation, efforts to challenge and please the opposites, also characterized the exchange of tangibles—the climax of the potlatch.

The Burden of the Gift

Despite the importance of feasting and gift-giving as a major means of expressing and strengthening intermoiety cooperation and reciprocity, their implicit but equally significant function as the hosts' instrument of dominating the guests should not be ignored. In Tlingit culture, as in many others, gift-giving served not only to establish and reaffirm interpersonal and intergroup ties but was also to challenge the recipient to reciprocate with an equal or, preferably, a larger gift (see Mauss 1967; Weiner 1976). Because balanced reciprocity was the underlying principle of intermoiety relations, not being able to return a gift placed the recipient in an inferior position vis-à-vis the donor. This principle is operative even in genuine conflicts, for example, according to Oberg (1973:99),

> If a Tlingit wants to bring a potential enemy to terms, he invites him to a feast. When hunters or fishermen encroached upon the property of another clan, the clansmen could often bring about a settlement by inviting the poachers to a feast after which the visitors would be ashamed and leave the territory of their hosts in peace.

The ubiquity of reciprocity explains why the mourners were considered to be indebted to their opposites and, hence, below them in status, until the mourners "paid the opposites off."[31] Many scholars working outside the Northwest Coast believe that there was an obligation to return either the exact amount one had received at a potlatch or repay with interest.[32] In my view, the Tlingit did not consider it an interest-bearing debt, even though every individual who wished to maintain his or her honor and status tried to match and preferably exceed the value of the original gift.

While few references to a competitive destruction of property among the Tlingit could be found, the guests undoubtedly perceived the food and gifts given to them as a challenge. Thus when in the early 1980s, one of Sitka's leading clans of the Eagle moiety sponsored an unusually expensive potlatch, their main guests from a certain clan of the Raven moiety did their best to beat their former hosts by giving more wealth to them in their own potlatch held a year later (Kan 1979–1987).

Fish, meat, berries, skins, and other products and objects given to the guests served as signs of the hosts' success in subsistence activities. While the food and gifts spoke for themselves, we know of at least one chief who, inclined to brag, expressed this idea more directly, when he came out dressed in his deceased maternal uncle's regalia and spoke to his guests just before the distribution of presents:

> You all know that my [maternal] uncle was a great hunter, and also my ancestors were all great hunters. They killed a great deal of wild animals and wounded a great deal more. The latter have gone back to the woods and are alive at the present time. I am myself doing the same as my ancestors, and that is how I become rich and own many slaves. (Emmons 1920–1945, Shukoff's Account:8–9)

One of the hosts' important objectives was to create an impression of an endless supply of wealth. It appears that once the distribution had begun it could not be interrupted. In a potlatch described by Olson (1933–1954, notebook 1:21), distribution took two nights yet both sides remained in the house and did not sleep.

The hosts' dominance was also manifested in their efforts to force the guests to accept more gifts than they could carry home and consume more food than their stomachs could hold. A widespread Northwest Coast practice of pouring large quantities of fish oil on the fire to make it so large and hot that the guests could no longer stand it, while the roof itself might catch fire, was a powerful expression of the hosts' desire to display and brag about their wealth.

The most literal forcing of the hosts' generosity upon the guests was a common practice of overfeeding them to the point when they had to vomit. The hosts repeatedly encouraged the guests to eat as much food and drink as much oil as possible (e.g., Swanton 1908:440–441). In some accounts, the guests were said to vomit specifically into the fire, making it burn high and hence contributing to the hosts' glory (see Chapter V, for the discussion of the fire's symbolism).[33] If nobody vomited, it spoke badly about the food (Emmons 1920–1945, Shukoff's Account:20). Those forced to vomit were generously compensated for their embarrassment and suffering (e.g., Olson 1933–1954, notebook 4:54). Presented as the hosts' generosity and "love," overfeeding the guests was clearly a challenge to them. While some accounts indicate that it was treated as more of a joke (e.g, Swanton 1908:436–437, Olson 1967:12), others suggest that it was an insult for which generous remuneration had to be given (e.g., Olson 1967:38). Several sources refer to the guests being ashamed of having to vomit (Swanton 1908:437).

The hosts also used the food to encourage the guests to compete against one another. Special eating contests took place among the young male guests, similar to the song and dance contests among the two groups of guests.[34] Although the most high-ranking guests were supposed to eat the greatest amounts of food, their junior matrikin did the actual eating (Olson 1967:64). These young men would often challenge each other as well as their hosts, asking for foods that they knew the latter did not have (Olson 1967:101). In return, the hosts would mix different foods in one dish to make the food unpalatable. The guests' ability to swallow it was presented as a sign of bravery, on a par with their oratorical skills and singing and dancing abilities. If the contestants were able to eat the entire dish of food, they could hold it up and say "hu..." in derision; then an even larger gift would have been given to them (Olson 1967:64). It appears that eating contests involved a great deal of horseplay; the participants joked and threw food at each other (Swanton 1908:441).[35] Like the exchange of jokes between rival

guest parties, some of this competitive feasting resulted in bitter confrontations, with the hosts having to step in and calm the contestants.
Occasionally, the hosts themselves became the object of the guests'
anger. According to an old story told by the Gaanaxteidí of Klukwaan,
during the dedication of their Whale House, one of their Kaagwaantaan guests died of overeating. Payments were made to his kin but
they were not satisfied and subsequently retaliated by trying to kill a
Gaanaxteidí man at their own potlatch (Kan 1979–1987).

Thus, feasting represented another example of a mixture of competition and cooperation, friendly fun and serious rivalry. Of course, as
the providers of food and gifts, the hosts were in full control of this
aspect of the potlatch, and by accepting their presentations, the guests
accepted their subordinate position, which lasted until their own potlatch, in which their former hosts acted as guests. The food and gifts
the guests carried home reminded them for a long time of the hosts'
generosity and wealth.[36]

I must point out that competitive destruction of property or openly aggressive rhetoric were much rarer in the Tlingit potlatch than
among the Kwakiutl and some other Northwest Coast peoples.[37] A
potlatch was rarely given for the sole purpose of displaying wealth
and insulting the guests in speech and song, as Garfield (1939:208)
claims was done frequently among the Tsimshian. Boelscher's
(1985:125–167) presentation of Haida potlatching suggests a muted
rhetoric of rivalry, more akin to the Tlingit one.[38] Consequently, while
Mauss (1967:3–7) correctly identified the fact that behind the "volun-
tary guise" under which the gifts were given was a clear obligation to
reciprocate, his emphasis on the "agonistic" nature of the potlatch applied better to some of the central and southern Northwest Coast potlatches.

Differentiating the Guests Through Gift-Giving

In addition to serving as a demonstration of the hosts' wealth and a
mechanism of placing them above the guests as a group, the property
given out in the potlatch was used by the donors to reiterate, weaken,
or strengthen their relationships with the individual opposites. While
the thrust of the message of the unequally distributed food and gifts
was the hosts' current view of the hierarchical order of the guests, the
unequal distribution also reflected their attitudes towards about each
recipient. Contrary to the prevailing view, I argue that the quality and
the quantity of the gifts and food given to each guest were determined

by several additional factors besides his or her rank, even though the latter did play the major role.

In addition to being separated into two competing halves, the guests were differentiated according to gender, age, and rank, the same criteria that divided the hosts themselves. Just as the latter were united in their shared grief, so were their opposites during their collective singing and dancing, and especially the display of crests. Throughout much of the potlatch, however, the guests were sharply differentiated, more so than the hosts, whose greater unity reiterated their superiority.

The hosts' ranking of the guests began when their *naa káani* went to each of the opposites' houses and invited them by calling out their ceremonial titles. When they entered the hosts' house, the guests heard their names announced again and then were taken to their assigned seats, ranking of which was more or less standardized.[39] Leaders of the guests and other highest ranking members of the guest party took seats in the middle of the back of the house and along the sides of the house near the back. The seating arrangement juxtaposed aristocrats and commoners, old and young, men and women. The seats closer to the walls had higher status than those closer to the fireplace (see de Laguna 1972:625, fig. 70).

Not all of the guests may have been happy with their seats. As one native participant in a late nineteenth-century potlatch indicated:

> When a guest arrived and was not announced, he was expected to take his seat quietly in a corner, which he did unless he had lost his self respect. Then a big question arose in his mind: "Why am I seated in a corner?" Soon he discovered for himself that he had done some wrong. Then he knew that he had to bear his shame quietly. And so he learned his lesson while sitting in the corner. If the host saw a change in him he was placed again in his honorable seat. (Wells in Billman 1964:60)

This ranking of the guests continued throughout the entire potlatch, as individuals were called upon to orate, perform special ritual services (see Chapter VIII), and sing and dance, but especially as they received their food and gifts. Sources differ on the extent to which the aristocracy was treated differently from other guests. This disagreement probably stems from regional and temporal variation.[40] Thus, the Yakutat potlatches of the turn of the century, described by de Laguna (1972), appear somewhat more egalitarian than the Sitka ones of the same era (Kan 1979–1987), while in general, social differentiation increased from the middle to the end of the nineteenth century and then decreased again in the twentieth.

Food seems to have been more equally distributed, although Olson (1967:64) indicates that high-ranking guests (or more likely their junior male matrikin) had to consume and take home more food than others. When it came to gifts, aristocrats were clearly differentiated from their lower-ranking kin. In addition to being given slaves and coppers—special kinds of aristocratic gifts discussed below—they received larger quantities of better quality gifts. A high-ranking chief would often ask his brother-in-law to carry the gifts he could not carry himself, which was seen as a sign of the high esteem in which the hosts held him (Olson 1967:65). According to a late nineteenth-century account, calico and cast-off clothing were distributed among the poor people, while blankets were given to those who had wealth and position (Knapp and Childe 1896:112).

Sources also disagree on whether male and female guests received an equal share. Once again, the nineteenth-century Yakutat potlatch appears to have been more egalitarian in the way the two sexes were treated (de Laguna 1972), while the central and southern Tlingit seem to have made a distinction between men and women. Thus, Knapp and Childe (1896:121) claimed that in a Tongass potlatch given in the early 1890s, men received "a great many blankets," while women "went away happily" with dishes, baskets, berries, and beads (compare Oberg 1973:123).[41]

In addition to the recipient's rank, status, age, and gender, other factors determined the size and quality of his gifts. We have already seen in Chapter VIII how these were influenced by the nature of his paternal/affinal relationship with the deceased and the deceased's matrikin, particular the donor. In addition, the donor's attitudes and feelings towards him played a role as well. The important thing for the donor was to justify his generosity by referring to some special service or emotional support he or his matrikin had been given by the recipient during the time of sorrow.

The names of each donor and recipient, as well as the nature and the size of each special gift, as opposed to the ordinary ones distributed equally among all of the guests, had to be announced. This allowed the participants to make a mental note of the intricacies of intergroup and interpersonal relations.

Mauss was incorrect when he identified the potlatch exchange as being carried out by groups and not individuals; in his words, "the persons represented in the contracts are moral persons—clans, tribes, and families; the groups, or the chiefs as intermediaries for the groups, confront and oppose each other" (1967:3). The situation was more complex: each major gift was simultaneously given by the entire group, as well as an individual donor, and thus ideally represented the donors' collectively agreed upon evaluation of the recipient. Nevertheless, within the general guidelines provided by the group, each host retained some freedom to demonstrate his or her own personal feelings and attitude towards a particular guest. We should also remember that, despite the aristocracy's dominant role in gift-giving, each host could take more out of the total potlatch fund than he had contributed. Thus, each special gift was determined by the dominant cultural value of rank as well as collective sentiment and individual strategies and feelings. For example, a donor could present a beloved affine with more goods than the latter's rank or the role he had played in the funeral called for. A high-ranking aristocrat from a distant community, who had never provided the hosts with any funeral services before but with whose lineage they wished to begin exchanging spouses, might receive greater wealth than some other *aan yádx'i* who had been finishing the bodies of the hosts' matrikin for generations.

Such use of gifts was essential to the potlatch and hence requires further investigation. Unfortunately, most of the data on it comes from my own observations, which indicate an increase in the role played by the diadic relations of friendship and feelings in determining the size of the gifts given to selected guests. One must be careful in projecting this information onto the nineteenth-century potlatch, since there the recipients' rank and status played a greater role than today.[42] However, to dismiss emotions and personal idiosyncrasies and to see gift-giving as guided exclusively by the rigid rules of rank and status seems incorrect. Even the Kwakiutl, whose potlatch has usually been characterized as highly competitive, used gifts to show their grief and other feelings (e.g., Drucker and Heizer 1967:131; see also Chapter X).[43]

Aristocratic Gifts

Mauss described the Northwest Coast potlatch as being characterized by two major themes—"credit" and "honor" (1967:34). Both of these themes were clearly present, since at some point the guests had to pay off their former hosts. However, the Tlingit did not think of this as credit, since no exact calculation of how much wealth had to be returned was ever made. It was expected that they would try to exceed or at least match what they had received.

The only type of potlatch wealth requiring a direct return were precious objects owned and exchanged by the aristocracy (Olson 1967:66–67). Most important among them were slaves and copper shields (tináa); in addition, Chilkat blankets, abalone shells, and occasionally other exotic and valuable artifacts served in that capacity. Compared to the large number of animal skins, blankets, and other ordinary gifts distributed in the potlatch, only a few slaves and coppers were handed out and only high-ranking guests were their recipients. It appears that chiefs and other aristocrats of the highest rank maintained their own system of gift-giving based on, but partly separate from, the major one involving the rest of the potlatch participants. An examination of the symbolism of these precious commodities and the manner in which they were exchanged sheds additional light on the meaning and function of the Tlingit potlatch, and especially the aristocracy's role in it.

Slaves could be killed, freed, or given to high-ranking guests. As in the funeral itself (see Chapter VI), the former was done to send the spirit of the slain slave directly to the deceased in whose honor the potlatch was given. In addition, this destruction of property was seen as an indication of the donor's wealth and his disregard for an opportunity to obtain a return gift.[44] The latter rationale and motivation seem to have been stronger in the potlatch than in the funeral where concern with providing slaves for the deceased was much more pronounced.[45] Among the Tlingit and other Northwest Coast peoples (e.g., Garfield 1939:212), prior to the potlatch proper, slaves were sometimes placed in the hole prepared for mortuary or memorial pole or a house post and crushed to death by its weight when it was erected. Slaves, as we have seen, were also killed on the beach, prior to the guests' landing, as a way of honoring them (Swanton 1909:343).

The freeing of slaves was undoubtedly seen as equivalent to killing them: in both cases they no longer belonged to their owner. As Garfield (1939:274) explained in her discussion of a similar practice among the Tsimshian, by doing that the owner showed that he "had so much he did not need to give it away for some return at a later date." While in the post-contact era, and particularly after the American arrival, manumission gradually replaced slave sacrifice, it appears that in the earlier period the two practices coexisted. Drucker's Chilkat informant claimed that freeing a slave was even "bigger" than killing him, because he would go home, beget children, and thus "bring his tribe down," that is, lower its status by the taint of slavery (1950:218).

Slaves to be set free were symbolically killed by being touched with a weapon or a chief's ceremonial staff (Kamenskii 1985:36). Sometimes, before a slave was set free, blankets were placed on his back and/or face and then given to the guests (Olson 1933–1954, notebook 1:22). This, I believe, signified that part of the slave's persona was given to the guests and, hence, to the hosts' own dead matrikin as well. Similarly, a slave destined to be freed during a pole-raising was sometimes asked to make a mark on the pole or a representation of him might be carved on it (Wallis 1918:70).

Whereas slaves sacrificed during a pole-raising were killed by the pole itself, those destined to die in the potlatch itself were killed with the above-mentioned special club bearing a carved image of the owner's crest (see Chapter VI). The idea that it was the entire clan, epitomized in its crest, that performed the sacrifice was expressed most dramatically in a potlatch described by Olson (1967:63), where the slaves being led into the house had to hold the rope tied to the beak of the hosts' crest bird carved on top of the chief host's ceremonial hat. The victim's future was sometimes decided by the sound of the hosts' crest animal which the hosts uttered. If the sound was angry or sad the slave had to die, but if it was joyful he was set free. According to Veniaminov (1984:423), who reported this practice, the fate of the slave was decided at a council prior to the potlatch, but the slave was sacrificed at the highest point of the ritual, when the chief host emerged from his rear compartment dressed in his clan regalia. This ritualized uncertainty surrounding the fate of slaves in the potlatch might have been a way of adding drama to the potlatch and emphasizing that, despite slaves' treatment as nonpersons, killing them was emotionally more difficult than destroying other property (see Chapter VI).[46]

Finally, some slaves were given directly by the chief hosts to the leading guests. Sources disagree on how important and prestigious this act was. According to Oberg (1973:117), the giving of slaves as presents was of lesser importance than freeing them. On the other hand, Olson (1967:66), whom I trust more than Oberg, claimed that the giving of a slave was a great honor, so that only a great chief received one at a "great" potlatch.[47]

Tináa, known among Europeans as a copper, was a shield-shaped object roughly a yard long, two feet wide at one end and a foot wide at the other (see fig. 11). The metal in it was from 1/16 to 1/8 inches thick, sometimes hammered to a slightly greater thickness on the edges.

Fig. 11. a modern copy of a traditional tináa. *Miller and Miller 1967:126.*

Some coppers bore designs that have been scratched in a black coating said to have been derived from smoking in a fire. Others were painted black, the paint outlining the design which appears in burnished copper. Some had engraved designs mostly in the conventional Northwest Coast style. All coppers, without exception, had a groove running vertically in the lower half and transversely across the middle, forming a "T."[48]

Like slaves, coppers figured prominently in all of the Northwest Coast cultures as items of wealth owned by aristocrats and exchanged between them in the potlatch system. According to the native view, they were made of virgin copper pounded by hand. The main source of that material was the Copper River area inhabited by the Ahtna, an Athapaskan group. It bordered on the territory of the northern Tlingit who controlled the copper trade of the entire coast. Copper obtained there was used to make arrowheads, body ornaments, and most likely, small coppers. All of the large ones that have found their way into museums have turned out to be made of the copper imported by the Europeans (Keithahn 1964; de Widerspach-Thor 1981). It is not clear whether the few large coppers seen by early European visitors (e.g., Lisianskii 1814:150) in the end of the eighteenth and the beginning of the nineteenth centuries were made of the local or the imported material. Subsequently Europeans began trading ly Europeans began trading large amounts of copper and eventually flooded the market, so that the value of *tináa* declined dramatically. Until *tináa* became completely devalued in the second half of last century, the Tlingit continued to differentiate between those made of imported copper and what they believed to be the more precious authentic ones made of the local raw material (de Widerspach-Thor 1981:159–160). Whether the latter were in fact authentic or not does not really matter to us, since the important thing is the native view of them as such.

Coppers were the most valuable wealth items in Tlingit and other Northwest Coast societies, their value being measured in other, less expensive objects, such as animal skins and especially slaves.[49] Only aristocrats of high rank and great wealth owned them; rarely did a single person own more than a few (Olson 1933–1954, notebook 1:47). To accumulate *eight* of them was to attain the highest degree of wealth and status (Kan 1979–1987). Lisianskii (1814:150) said that slaves carried coppers in front of their masters and beat them like drums. Like slaves, they were the most prestigious and appropriate bridewealth items, with the high-ranking brides being described as carrying several (ideally, eight) coppers on their backs to their husbands' houses.

While coppers crossed clan and moiety lines, they were also seen as part of their owners' *shagóon* and were passed down in the matriline, especially when crests were depicted on them. The latter was supposed to add to their value (Niblack 1890:336). This representation of the crest as well as the terms used to describe the various parts of the *tináa* indicate that it was viewed as an anthropomorphic being. Thus, its vertical ridge was described as the "backbone," the horizontal one as "shoulders," and the lines drawn on both sides of the "backbone" were called the "ribs" (Olson 1933–1954, notebook 10:34). The top half was clearly the head zone in terms of both its form and proportions, and, when decorated, always portrayed a face. Holm (quoted in MacDonald 1981:233) calls it essentially a human form reduced to the bare essentials, while MacDonald (1981:233) adds (correctly, I believe) that it conveyed the concept of an animal or a human ancestor.

Coppers' association with and use by the aristocracy makes good sense, since both shared such important qualities as hardness, heaviness, and sheen (see Chapter IV).[50] In light of the symbolism of stones as the hardest and heaviest objects in the Tlingit world, I think it is not accidental that the eight coppers allegedly given to the potlatch guests by a certain chief when his pubescent daughter was being tattooed were referred to as "stones around the girl" (de Laguna 1972:637). The symbolic link between the *tináa* and the *aanyádi* is further supported by the practice of distributing pieces of copper owned by the deceased chief among the leading guests during the memorial potlatch given in his honor. The pieces themselves were called "bones of the dead chief."[51] This custom has been reported for the Kwakiutl, Bella Coola, Tsimshian, and Haida (Drucker 1951:237; Drucker and Heizer 1967:131–132; Garfield 1939:238; de Widerspach-Thor 1981:169). Drucker (1951:237) and de Widerspach-Thor (1981:169) claim that it was practiced by the Tlingit as well. In light of my interpretation of the Tlingit theory of the person (Chapter II), it is certainly tempting to believe them; unfortunately I have no evidence to substantiate their claims. The notion behind distributing the so-called bones of the deceased aristocrat seems to indicate that, at least among the northern groups which had moieties, the guests handled the polluted flesh of the deceased and built containers for his ashes and bones, and as their reward received the pure, indestructible essence of his body which survived the owner.[52]

Further association between a deceased aristocrat and his coppers is illustrated by the practice of placing a copper on his grave or carving its representation on his mortuary or memorial pole, common throughout the Northwest Coast (e.g., Boas 1966:98; Emmons quoted in Keithahn 1964:75; de Widerspach-Thor 1981:169).[53] Around the turn of the century, when slave sacrifice was no longer practiced, coppers were sometimes used as a substitute for slaves, as in a Tsimshian potlatch which took place in the 1920s. In it, a flagpole was raised instead of the usual mortuary or memorial pole. The chief host explained that in the past a slave would have been killed and his body placed in the hole; the chief host then placed copper shields against the base of the pole, named several leading guests, and gave the shields to them (Garfield 1939:212; see de Widerspach-Thor 1981:169–170).

Tlingit myths explaining the origin of copper and *tináa* connect them with the outside—the domain of powerful and potentially dangerous non-Tlingit peoples and superhuman creatures. Copper as raw material is described as being acquired from the <u>Gunanaa</u> (Athapaskans, literally, "other people" or "strange people") with whom the protagonist exchanges valuable knowledge, useful implements, and treasures (Swanton 1909:155).[54] While the origin of the first *tináa* is not clearly stated in Tlingit mythology, the acquisition of great wealth, and particularly of coppers, is clearly linked to strange human beings and superhuman creatures and monsters inhabiting the periphery of the universe. The chief among them was Gunaakadeit, a sea monster, half animal and half fish, who dwelled in a huge underwater house and seemed to control the sea's entire animal and fish population.[55] A fortunate man who happened to see this creature rising from the water could acquire great riches, provided that he prepared for this encounter by purifying himself and followed other rules (e.g., Olson 1967:110). Future chiefs were said to sight Gunaakadeit as well (Emmons n.d., notebook 7).

According to one account, the shape of the *tináa* represented Gunaakadeit's forehead (Waterman 1923:451). Most frequently Gunaakadeit, this master of wealth, appeared to people as a decorated house front with the crest represented on its front. It could also look like a giant box (possibly full of treasures; de Laguna 1972:821) or a beautifully decorated canoe, another wealth item occasionally given as a gift in the potlatch (Emmons 1907:333). Gunaakadeit's claws were said to be made of copper (Swanton 1908:166), and its fur had a coppery color like some species of salmon (Olson 1967:105). Gunaakadeit's association with salmon is indicated not only by his control over the underwater domain and his appearance, but by the fact that his wife and daughters were believed to dwell at the head of each salmon stream. Thus, he presumably controlled the annual run of this mainstay of the Tlingit diet. Seeing these relatives of Gunaakadeit also brought good luck (Swanton 1908:169).

As the chief of the water creatures and a giver of wealth, Gunaakadeit was a perfect symbol of the potlatch guests, who came in canoes from the outside and eventually reciprocated with their own gifts and made the hosts rich. This explains the use of Gunaakadeit as a metaphorical reference to the guests made by the chief host awaiting their arrival on the beach (Swanton 1908:119f). In addition, this creature was the original owner of all the major attributes of aristocratic, especially chiefly, status, which he gave to mankind. These attributes included the hat with cedar rings representing the number of potlatches sponsored by its owner, the *shakee.át*, and the Chilkat blanket (Swanton 1909:16, 172–173; see Chapter VI). It is interesting that in several accounts (ibid.), the Tsimshian are said to have been the first people to learn from Gunaakadeit about these attributes of chiefly authority and status. For the Tlingit, the Tsimshian were the master craftsmen, owners of valuable songs, dances and regalia, and powerful shamans—in other words, the kind of powerful outsiders with whom one fought as well as traded and intermarried. The link between Gunaakadeit and the Chilkat blanket is particularly significant, since the latter was also used as an aristocratic potlatch gift and was treated similarly to *tináa* (i.e., torn apart and given away; see below). According to a Tsimshian tradition also common among the Tlingit, the first woman to weave a Chilkat blanket learned the craft and the design from the Lynx, a cannibal wife of Gunaakadeit (Emmons 1907:329–330). MacDonald (1981; 1984) convincingly argues that Gunaakadeit resembled in appearance and was symbolically linked to painted house fronts, Chilkat blankets, and decorated boxes, all of which were treasured artifacts associated with the aristocracy and featured prominently in the potlatch.

From the point of view of the present study, Gunaakadeit is an important being not only because of his association with *tináa* and other treasures but because he represents a culture hero who brings good fortune to those who are pure, properly trained, and respectful of him.[56] While commoners and even very poor people could sometimes be so fortunate as to encounter him, chiefs and wealthy aristocrats were clearly the major beneficiaries of his generosity. Whereas Raven created the world and some of the basic elements of the social order, Gunaakadeit completed the latter by giving mankind attributes of aristocratic status and symbols of wealth.[57]

In the potlatch, coppers, like slaves, were either destroyed or given to the high-ranking guests. Coppers were thrown in the fire or the water, as was done with slaves who died a natural death or were sacrificed. The similarity between the ceremonial killing of slaves and breaking of coppers was further illustrated by the use of the same weapon, a pick or club, referred to sometimes as "slave-killer" and sometimes as "copper-breaker" (Vaughan and Holm 1982:63).[58] This drowning of *tináa* was an act of great generosity and a sign of special respect for the deceased himself, as well as the guests. Copper-drowning occurred in an important 1877 potlatch in Sitka, after the chief host rubbed, against the copper, the foreheads of twenty of his grandchildren being named and otherwise honored (Wells in Billman 1964:63).

Copper-drowning took place outside the potlatch as well, usually when the owner wanted to legitimize his claims to a certain territory or shame his opponent (e.g., Swanton 1909:63). Slaves were used interchangeably with *tináa* in these situations. For example, when a certain Angoon clan split in half, following some serious disagreement, one of the groups left the area, while the one that remained sacrificed and gave to the opposite moiety a large number of slaves, in order to solidify its position in the area. To mark the event, they also carved a picture of a *tináa* on the rocks near the shore which they claimed (de Laguna 1960:133–134). In similar situations, the blood of the sacrificial victims was used to make signs on the rocks located in the area the sacrificers claimed. Blood was seen as a permanent substance that would remain forever as evidence of the event.[59] Similarly, coppers sunk in a body of water claimed by their owner or carved on the rocks located in his territory were a perfect permanent marker of his claims.[60]

While no direct statements of this idea have been found in the Tlingit ethnography, it seems reasonable to assume that the drowning of a *tináa* was done to offer a valuable gift to the deceased and show the owner's grief.[61] Sinking a *tináa* and breaking it into pieces were seen as increasing its value. According to Oberg (1973:117), if a copper was broken and a piece was thrown into the sea, it increased in value equal to the part thrown away. Thus, if one half was thrown away, the copper was worth one and half times as much as it was originally. We do not know enough about the relationship between the fate of the *tináa* in the Tlingit potlatch and the increase of its value. In any case, a gift of copper required a return, and older copper that had been used in a large number of potlatches had higher value.[62] Among the Tlingit, coppers about to be drowned or broken could be requested as a gift by chief hosts as well as by a "brave" guest of low rank (see below; Olson 1933–1954, notebook 10:35–36).

In the final analysis, what did slaves and coppers have in common and what made them the aristocratic gifts par excellence? Both items were obtained through warfare and trade with non-Tlingit or encounters with powerful superhuman creatures of the outside. Warfare, trade with outsiders, and encounters with supernatural beings were activities controlled or at least supervised by the aristocracy and required purity, bravery, and wisdom. Both slaves and coppers were the personal property of the *aanyátx'i*, rather than of their entire matrilineal groups. Both were ambiguous kinds of wealth: slaves were treated as nonpersons, yet retained some degree of personhood, which made killing them a delicate matter; coppers and Chilkat blankets were treated as personal property yet they could cross the moiety line and represented crests. Like slaves, coppers were "alive" and hence were the quintessential wealth exchangeable for all other types of property.[63] In a way, by exchanging coppers and Chilkat blankets through the potlatch, the aristocracy was violating the rule against transferring crest-bearing property across clan and especially moiety lines.[64] The fact that the aristocracy could get away with this suggests that its power and influence were considerable (compare Chapter VI; see also Chapter X).[65]

Did the Potlatch Feasting and Gift-giving Have an Economic Function?

Having analyzed the rich symbolism of the objects distributed in the potlatch, I must comment on the economic interpretations of this ritual, which have been advanced since the time of Boas (compare Kan 1986:192). Prominent among them is the view that the potlatch was a "device for leveling off inequities in natural resources among the neighboring tribes and kinship groups" (see Suttles 1960, as summarized by Drucker and Heizer 1967:147). In my opinion, the Tlingit (and probably other Northwest Coast societies) had a number of simpler and less formal mechanisms for redistributing food resources, including exchanging gifts between affines and granting permission to non-members to share the resources of one's own matrilineal group in times of plenty (see Introduction).

Also disputing the resource redistribution interpretation is the fact that potlatches were not held when shortages were experienced but, on the contrary, when food supplies were large. Guests were invited on the basis of their affinal relations to the deceased and not their needs (compare Snyder 1975:151). In addition, while large amounts of food were, in fact, consumed and taken home by the potlatch guests, food was also wasted, at least, from the Western materialist viewpoint. Most of the potlatch gifts were not used for economic purposes but circulated back and forth between the two moieties. Even if gifts could occasionally be exchanged for food outside the potlatch domain, it was much more prestigious to keep them as the signs of their owner's participation in numerous potlatches (compare Oberg 1973:117).[66]

Equally erroneous is to view the Tlingit potlatch as a system used by the aristocracy to enrich itself. Terms like "credit," "loan," "bargaining," and others borrowed from Western economics which entered anthropology through Boas' discussion of the Kwakiutl potlatch—a discussion which was challenged by some other ethnographers of Boas' era (e.g., Curtis 1915:143)—do not do justice to the Tlingit potlatch. The whole idea of fixed rates of return for the gifts received from an affine, inside or outside the potlatch, contradicted the central cultural values of "honor and respect." As Shotridge (1928:361), himself a Tlingit aristocrat, explained,

> In those days the exchanging of important things was done in a respectful manner. A man of high character was never known to name or set a price upon his skill or labor, and it was according to his own sense of honor, too, that a man expressed his thanks.

De Laguna (1972:357), writing half a century later, expressed a similar idea, "In dealing with one's equals, one did not seek economic profit. Rather, one desired to prove one's worth by giving lavishly, in the hope that it would be recognized by an equivalent lavishness in return."

My own informants repeatedly stated that it was impossible to get rich by potlatching. Instead, if all the participants in the potlatch system acted in good faith, as they tended to do until westernization began to affect indigenous cultural values, the amount of wealth one spent on a potlatch eventually came back (Kan 1979–1987; see Olson 1967:59). Hence, temporary imbalances in interpersonal and intergroup relations caused by the donors' generosity were supposed to be balanced out, in the long run. Of course, in reality, this did not always happen, so that some persons and kinship groups gained status while others lost it. However, the desire to beat an opposite with one's generosity was constrained by the etiquette of love and respect towards one's living affines and dead matrikin.

As I have shown, the most intense competition occurred not between members of the two moieties but between lineage, clan, and moiety kin. It was they who tried to legitimize their claims to crests and, thus, raise their rank and status.[67] Once again, it was not a struggle over material wealth but over symbolic capital—reputation, prestige, and honor.

What the wealth expended by the hosts bought was an increase in their status and rank, as embodied in their crests. That is why, in order to gain value, the crests had to be clearly visible and closely connected with the body of the giver during the presentation of the gifts. Often the wealth was distributed from the crest itself, as if it, and not its living guardians, were the true donors. Thus in one potlatch I attended, the money collected for the distribution was first placed inside a headdress representing the hosts' chief crest and then given out (Kan 1979–1987).[68] The potlatch wealth also served as the measure of the value of the names given to the hosts; thus the wealth was distributed immediately following the name-giving ceremony.[69] All in all, whatever economic function the potlatch had was minor.

The potlatch's economic function, if any, was secondary and indirectly increased subsistence activities and trade which generated the necessary surplus food and items of value.[70] An additional, though relatively minor economic function, was the return of some of the wealth from the aristocrats to the commoners. Although each free person was supposed to make a contribution to the potlatch, the aristocracy carried a heavier burden, periodically channeling the surplus wealth they accumulated with the help of their matrikin into the potlatch system. This did not significantly alter the social hierarchy but did present the *aanyátx'i* as generous senior kin who took care of their less affluent relatives of lower rank (see Chapter X).

This redistributive nature of the potlatch, its secondary, economic function, was exemplified by the practice of allowing those on the very bottom of society to obtain wealth. Coppers, for example, could be claimed either by the leading guests or the poor ones. Thus, according to Olson (1933–1954, notebook 10:35–36), a poor guest could ask for a *tináa*, if all the other guests were "too shy" (?) to do so. He could also pick up a copper thrown by the host into the fire and make several small coppers out of it, called *tináa yátx'i*, "copper's children." He then put his own crest on them and claimed them as his personal property. Though the *tináa yátx'i* were fragments of the *tináa*, they were valued less than the original copper. Similarly, a poor person could receive a very generous gift, if he were able to give the correct answer to a difficult riddle offered by the hosts to the guests (Kan 1979–1987). Such practices obviously did not transform a commoner into an aristocrat but did increase his wealth and, more importantly, his dignity and status.[71]

Like other Northwest Coast peoples, the Tlingit valued and enjoyed handling and manipulating wealth rather than hoarding it (compare de Laguna 1972:357).[72] Wealth was given to others in order to send a variety of messages. The flaw of cultural ecological and materialist explanations of potlatching is their neglect of this multi-vocality of the food and gift items which served as a mode of communication. As Weiner (1976:213f) points out in her discussion of the Trobriand exchange, objects circulating between persons and kin groups

> cannot be detached from the human experience of *regeneration* and *immortality*. They are not alienated from the basic concerns of society, and therefore social relationships are not merely relations between impersonal things, in Marx's terms, but remain relations that reify the cyclicity of *life*, *death*, and *rebirth*. (italics mine)

Similarly, wealth and food distributed in the Tlingit potlatch carried messages about the immediate strategies, concerns, and emotions of their donors as well as such fundamental cultural values and principles as matrilineal continuity, immortality, respect for one's dead matrikin, and love for one's opposites. In that sense, artifacts served the same purpose as words; in fact, the two complemented each other, with gift giving requiring as much skill as oratory (compare Gewertz 1984:193).

The aristocracy's management of the exchange of both tangibles and intangibles clearly contributed to its special position in society. Its role in the potlatch was not only dominant but rather ambiguous as well. On the one hand, the aristocrats acted as senior clan members who helped their lower-ranking matrikin in accumulating wealth for distribution and in displaying their *shagóon* through costume, song, dance, and oratory; they also redistributed some of their surplus wealth among the lower-ranking members of the opposite moiety. On the other hand, they tried to create a separate system of exchange for themselves, in which such prestigious items of wealth as coppers and slaves circulated. However, by the end of the nineteenth century, they had not succeeded in completely separating the two types of exchange. The cooperation between aristocrats and commoners continued to be central to the potlatch, while the aristocratic gifts themselves remained a relatively small portion of the total wealth given out. Egalitarian values and structural principles continued to impede further social differentiation.

The Guests Resisting Domination

Despite all of this pressure placed on the guests, they were not the helpless victims of the hosts' manipulation. The guests entered the potlatch with their own expectations, and if those were not met, they had several means of protesting. Like the hosts, the guests could manipulate kinship sentiments to accomplish their political goals. For example, when the close paternal/affinal relatives of the chief hosts turned down the gifts they were entitled to (see Chapter VIII), their behavior, while presented as love and respect for the opposite moiety, was a clever status-raising maneuver. Because of its high cost, only those of the highest rank attempted it (McClellan 1954:84). An ambitious guest could also step forward and claim a valuable item which the guests were about to burn for the benefit of their own ancestors. This practice was called ya-s'aa, as in 'i óonayi xwaas'áa,' "I claim your rifle (which was going to be destroyed)" (Story and Naish 1973:47). Such a claim could be made during the funeral, when the deceased's personal possessions were about to be cremated. More often, however, this occurred during the potlatch, when food and gifts, especially such valuables as coppers and slaves, were asked for by some guest, who had to repay the donors at a later time. In addition, the guests relied on potent "medicine" (possibly a magical herb) to ensure that they would receive more gifts than the others and thus increase their status and prestige (de Laguna 1972:616–617; Kan 1979–1987).

A guest unhappy with the seat or the gift offered to him could express his displeasure by various rhetorical devices and his demands were usually understood and satisfied. A different seat or a larger gift plus an apology would be offered to diffuse the tension. If, however, the hosts failed to respond to his subtle hints, an angry guest might use a more direct approach. Thus Olson (1967:63) provides a following illustration of this:

> If a man is not satisfied with what he receives he may embarrass the host by rising and saying, "I have looked into your eyes on other occasions. Now why do you look over me instead of looking into my face?" (that is, "When I gave feasts I paid you enough. Why have you not paid me justly?"). The host then speaks to his clanmen and more goods are paid to the dissatisfied one.

Of course, a high-ranking guest had a much better chance of having his demands satisfied than a low-ranking person whose complaints might be ignored.

If all else failed, a disappointed guest could leave the potlatch. Such radical action would force the hosts to accede to his demands, since they would not want to jeopardized their alliance with this person and his matrilineal group.[73] At the conclusion of the potlatch, the guests expressed their feelings collectively. The happy guests showed their gratitude by entertaining their hosts with songs and dances. They might even stage a small feast of their own in which a portion of the food and gifts they had received was returned to the hosts. If the guests were not fully satisfied, their departure was hasty, but if they were satisfied they would stay in the hosts' village for some time (Wells in Billman 1964:63)

While it is impossible to establish how frequent such open disagreements between the two sides were, it appears that much of the intermoiety negotiation of rank and status was a subtle give and take, expressed through the metaphors of oratory and symbolic acts. The most common and effective method of appeasing the opposites, as well as one's own matrikin, was to invoke the memory of and sentiments about the dead.

Grief, Mourning, and the Use of the Dead in Rhetoric

Having looked at the material presented in this chapter, one might conclude that the potlatch began as a mourning ritual but quickly turned into the major arena of intra- and intermoiety competition and rivalry, with the rhetoric of "love and respect" for the dead and the living participants serving only to conceal or soften the harsh reality of politics. Several ethnographers have arrived at precisely that conclusion, casting their interpretations of the potlatch in predominantly political terms (e.g., Oberg 1973:125; Tollefson 1976:203–234). Equally erroneous, however, would be to accept as the whole story the native ideology of the potlatch, aptly characterized by de Laguna (1972:612) as "dignity, sympathy, high respect for all, with the exalted chief and the poor and lowly united in sorrow and honor for the ancestors."

My own approach has been to show how the political aspects of this ritual were intertwined with the religious ones, and how competition and cooperation, hierarchy and equality, attitudes towards the living and the dead were dialectically related to each other. The presence of the dead, seen as being among the addressees of the oratory and the recipients of the prestations, played a major role in the potlatch. For some of the hosts, it served as a motivation to be more cooperative with each other or more generous with the guests. For some of the guests, it was an encouragement to be more receptive to the hosts' actions and rhetoric. For other participants it was a force that restrained their overly ambitious conduct. Those who skillfully used the rhetoric of love and respect for the dead were able to portray themselves as the truly moral social selves and thus derive personal satisfaction from their role in the potlatch, while also raising their status and prestige.

The centrality of the dead and of the death-related beliefs and sentiments in the Tlingit culture explains why even those occasional potlatches that were not part of some person's mortuary cycle had to be presented as such in order to be legitimate. Thus a matrilineal group which decided to bolster its position in the social hierarchy by pot-latching and had the means to do so had to announce an urgent need to place the remains of its ancestors in new containers or repair the existing ones. The opposites whom this group had planned to invite to the potlatch would then be entrusted with the funerary tasks. The fact that the graves in question might have been in need of repair for many years would be conveniently overlooked (Kan 1979–1987).

Within the memorial potlatch itself, a host who contributed more wealth than one would expect, given his kinship ties with the deceased or his rank, would justify such action by invoking his grief or a special emotional closeness he had allegedly had with the person being memorialized. At the same time, serious conflicts between the hosts were often phrased in terms of their love and respect for the deceased, or the lack thereof. Thus, when the close matrikin of a certain deceased chief bypassed his brother and asked his more distant but wealthier relative to host the potlatch, the offended man went about the village loudly mourning the deceased and saying that the organizers of the memorial ritual would not be able to show his beloved brother proper respect (Kan 1979–1987; compare McClellan 1954:90).

When it came to the rivalry between the two groups of guests, the dead might also be invoked to restore peace. It was done by the hosts who had to step in if all the other methods of diffusing a tense situation failed. In a case like that, they would appeal to the memory of their own matrikin who were also the spouses, fathers, or children of the guests involved in a confrontation. They might also silently display their crests to remind the guests of all the dead that had used them in the past. The guests were supposed to become peaceable and "respect the emblem" (Wells in Billman 1964:105). Finally, the hosts might appeal to their opposites through oratory. Thus, Golovin (1983:105) reported a conflict, discussed above, between two groups of guests at a mid-nineteenth century potlatch in Sitka. There the hosts used all of these methods to calm the disputants down: they brought out the crest-bearing headgear of their famous chiefs killed some time previously, sang their clan songs, and in the name of their dead demanded that everyone put down their weapons.

The delicate aspects of intermoiety relations were also cast in and handled through the rhetoric of mourning and memorializing the dead. The riddles that the hosts addressed to the guests frequently referred to the deceased's biography and tested the opposites' familiarity with it. The most knowledgeable guest was then the one who demonstrated the greatest love and respect for the person being memorialized (Kan 1979–1987).[74] Similarly, when an informant of mine tried to refuse a gift that was too lavish for him to reciprocate, he was told that it was given because of the deceased's special love for him (Kan 1979–1987). The fact that the essence of each prestation was destined for the dead also made them very hard to refuse. Thus a traditionalist friend of mine, who does not smoke, feels compelled to accept cigarettes which are often distributed among the male guests in today's potlatches (Kan 1979–1987). Swanton (1908:442) reported that if a guest felt dissatisfied with what he had received and started to walk out, the host went in front of him "with a dead man's name" (i.e., mentioning the name of a dead relative), made him sit down, and doubled the amount of property given to him. A very interesting phrase used by some hosts to discourage a stubborn guest from turning down his gift was recorded by Olson (1967:66). By asking such a guest "Are you going to close the door to the land of the dead?" the host appeared to be saying that the refusal was depriving the deceased of his due share and was thus threatening to interrupt the flow of gifts between the two moieties as well as between the living and the dead.

The use of the dead in political rhetoric was clearly more prominent in the potlatch, where the mourners' grief was weaker, than in the funeral. Nevertheless, some sincerity was expected of the potlatch participants, as was the case in the previous stages of the mortuary cycle (see Chapters VI and VII). Thus a man whose wife nudged him frequently to deliver lengthy and ornate speeches of condolence at funerals, so as to be paid well, was seen as too grasping (Olson 1933–1954, notebook 4:57). Similarly, the reputation of a potlatch host suffered if his proclamations about his love for his deceased predecessor were known to be utterly false (Kan 1979–1987). The key notion of the entire Tlingit potlatch was moderation, a proper balance between reason and emotion, politics and religion, competition and coopera-tion.

part four

DEATH IN NORTHWESTERN
NORTH AMERICA AND BEYOND

chapter ten

TLINGIT MORTUARY COMPLEX,
A COMPARATIVE PERSPECTIVE

So far I have looked at the Tlingit mortuary complex from the inside, with only occasional comparisons with the neighboring Subarctic and Northwest Coast cultures. In this chapter I make these comparisons more detailed and systematic, with two goals in mind. On the one hand, a comparative perspective helps bring out the essential features of Tlingit culture and thus strengthens my interpretation of the main causes of the mortuary complex's prominence in it. On the other hand, it enables me to move from a specific case to a general question of correlation between elaborate mortuary rites (including double obsequies) and particular types of ideological/sociopolitical orders.

Several recent works attempt to examine death-related beliefs and rituals in a comparative perspective by assembling case studies from around the world (Huntington and Metcalf 1979; Humphreys and King 1981; Bloch and Parry 1982). One of their main concerns is not unlike mine: to establish the logic behind the variability between mortuary symbolism in different types of social systems. While any cross-cultural comparison of death-related beliefs and practices is a productive endeavor, I believe that it is more useful to begin with what Eggan (1975:196–197) calls a method of "controlled comparison," i.e., "the utilization of the comparative method on a smaller scale and with as much control over the frame of comparison as it is possible to secure."[1]

Comparison of the mortuary complex of the Tlingit with that of their likely ancestors, the Subarctic Athapaskans located west of the continental divide (see fig. 2), on the one hand, and of several major Northwest Coast cultures (see fig. 1), on the other, allows me to separate resemblances due to a common origin from those resulting from direct borrowing, or similarities in ecology, modes of subsistence, levels of sociopolitical complexity, and beliefs. An interesting phenomenon revealed by this comparison is that, despite significant differences in economy and sociopolitical organization, as well as cultural logic, nineteenth century Athapaskan eschatology and mortuary rites exhibited extensive similarity to those of the Tlingit, and to a lesser extent the other two northern Northwest Coast cultures, the Haida and the Tsimshian.[2] At the same time, despite such important shared sociocultural phenomena as the existence of ranking, the presence of corporate kinship groups owning tangible and intangible property, and lavish ritualized distribution of gifts by one such group to another, northern Northwest Coast death-related beliefs and practices differed significantly from the central and southern ones (Kwakiutl, Nootka, Bella Coola, and Salish).[3]

By tracing the origins of the Tlingit mortuary complex we can differentiate between its antecedent Proto-Athapaskan base and its Northwest Coast features developed after the Tlingit ancestors' arrival in southeastern Alaska. These differences give us clues for understanding the transformation that the mortuary complex of an egalitarian society might undergo when differentiation based on wealth and rank develops in it. Because of my concern with contrasting mortuary rituals of the egalitarian and ranked societies, much of this chapter focuses on the Athapaskan rather than the coastal groups. A detailed discussion of the latter would require a special study and is beyond the scope of the present work.

At the conclusion of this chapter, the findings of my "controlled comparison" are placed in a broader perspective by a brief examination of the societies of the Malayo-Polynesian world, where mortuary rites are also elaborate, include double obsequies, and play the central role in the sociocultural order. That order itself shows important resemblances with the Tlingit one, and those resemblances raise interesting questions for comparative ethnology.

Death in Western Subarctic Athapaskan Cultures

Reconstructing Athapaskan culture prior to the time it became significantly affected by the fur trade is not an easy task. Ethnographic data from that period are relatively scarce and unevenly distributed among different groups. With a few exceptions, systematic anthropological research did not begin in that part of the world until the first decade of the twentieth century. The fur trade resulted in an infusion of wealth into the interior and an increase of contact with both the Europeans and the coastal groups acting as middlemen. This increased contact affected both the social organization and the ceremonial life of the western Subarctic Athapaskans. Their mortuary rites and particularly the "feast of the dead" or memorial potlatch, began to evolve in the direction of the coastal one. While some of these changes were most likely caused by direct borrowing from the coast, many others were due to the gradual convergence of some important aspects of the two regions' cultures (see Van Stone 1974; de Laguna 1975).

Nevertheless, ethnographers have been able to arrange the existing information in chronological order (see Helm et. al. 1975), because the fur trade began to make a major impact on the Athapaskan social organization and world view, and specifically the mortuary complex, only in the second half or, even the end of, the nineteenth century and because this transformation was rather limited among some of the groups. Data from such interior groups as the Koyukon, Ingalik, Tanana, and Kutchin, who were either less affected by the fur trade or whose involvement in it took place later than that of other groups, can be used to reconstruct a hypothetical Proto-Athapaskan mortuary complex (compare Rosman and Rubel 1983).

Prominent in that complex was frequent communication between the living and the dead through dreams, visions, and other channels. The centrality of the dead in the life of the living was also expressed in and reinforced by a widespread belief in the reincarnation of the ancestors in their descendants (Jetté 1911; Loyens 1964; Slobodin 1970). Subarctic eschatologies and ethnopsychologies were complex, with many of their elements resembling those of the Tlingit. Thus, for example, the Proto-Athapaskan model of the person seems to have been based on the same opposition between the person's temporary and impure flesh, the person's immortal and pure noncorporeal attributes, and such intermediate entities as bones.[4]

Although the western Subarctic Athapaskans shared with the Tlingit a fear of pollution emanating from the corpse, they too displayed the deceased, dressed in the finest garments, for several days of the mourning ritual. Like the three northern Northwest Coast groups, most western Subarctic Athapaskans practiced cremation.[5] Even though other modes of disposal of the dead existed in the nineteenth century, cremation seems to have been the most widespread and, according to Subarctic ethnographers (e.g., Van Stone 1974:84–85), the *oldest* method.[6] Other Athapaskan uses of fire in the mortuary rites also resembled those of the Tlingit, including singeing the mourners' hair and interpreting the crackling of burning wood as voices of the dead. The various taboos imposed upon the Tlingit mourners also showed greater similarity to those of the western Subarctic Athapaskans than of the central and southern Northwest Coast societies.

Another key feature of the mortuary complex the Athapaskans shared with the Tlingit was the idea that members of a group other than that of the deceased had to perform the funerary services and act as the intermediaries between the departed and his or her own (matri)kin. The funeral workers were invariably remunerated in a memorial feast, which was the major ritual of most of the western Subarctic Athapaskans and resembled the Tlingit memorial potlatch in many of its basic features (McKennan 1959:138–139; Birket-Smith 1967; McClellan and Denniston 1981:384). In the late nineteenth-century it acquired the coastal label "potlatch" (see, e.g., Mauss 1967:41; McKennan 1959:134; Rosman and Rubel 1983:9–14). In the potlatch these funeral workers and their own kin acted as guests. At least among some of the Subarctic Athapaskans (Ingalik, Koyukon), the guests represented or incarnated the hosts' dead matrikin, so that the food and gifts given to them reached the hosts' dead relatives being memorialized (compare Chapter VIII).

The basic cycle of mortuary and memorial rites that I have outlined for the Tlingit was equally present among the western Subarctic Athapaskans, albeit on a much smaller scale. The Athapaskan memorial potlatch, the final ritual of this cycle, like its Tlingit counterpart, involved sending away the ghost and/or other noncorporeal attributes of the deceased (e.g., Guedon 1974:205–207). Among the Koyukon, the potlatch was explicitly aimed at hastening the reincarnation of the souls of the departed (Jetté 1911:100). It completed the mortuary cycle by marking and celebrating the deceased's final separation from the living as well as the mourners' release from the various taboos they were subjected to since their relative's death (Guedon 1974:205–207; Osgood 1936:125). It was also the main occasion to supply the needs of the deceased by sending him food, water and gifts and to show him "respect" (e.g., Osgood 1958:138). Whether these things were burned or given to the guests, their spiritual essence belonged to the dead (Osgood 1958:154; Loyens 1964; Kroul 1974).[7]

Despite all of these similarities,[8] significant differences in death-related beliefs and especially ritual practices between the two groups existed. Before exploring them in some detail and trying to explain them, I must briefly outline the western Subarctic Athapaskans' social organization of the pre- and early fur-trade era, and particularly those features that bear upon the mortuary complex.[9]

Western Subarctic Athapaskan Social Organization

Some of the fundamental features of the western Subarctic Athapaskans' social organization were typical for semi-nomadic hunters. The nuclear (McKennan 1959:116) or, more often, the extended family (McClellan and Denniston 1981) was the minimal domestic or co-residential unit. For much of the year, it also acted as the subsistence task force. The family links were often between adult siblings of the same or opposite sex, or between parents and their married children, or sometimes between hunting partners who were only distant classificatory kin. In the course of its existence, any nuclear family or any other segment of the domestic group might leave to join another household unit. As McClellan and Denniston (1981:384) put it, "the system was extremely flexible, and arrangements of many kinds were worked out in terms of general expedience and personal preference."

Because of this constant fission and fusion, the size of the local group at any particular time varied from a nuclear family to a number of related families/households, gathered for the fall caribou hunt or summer fishing. The cluster of related families/households, often labelled the "local band," was in some contexts designated by the area it habitually exploited and was thus held together by both kinship and territorial ties. Local bands tended to be exogamous. Among some of the groups or "tribes" (e.g., Tanana, Ingalik, and others on the Alaskan Plateau) several local bands within the same river drainage or foothill region were linked by ties of marriage and tradition, shared a regional dialect, and possessed some idiosyncrasies of culture (Hosley 1981). Such a unit has been termed a regional band (Helm 1965:375; Mc-

Kennan 1969:104–105). A regional band was largely endogamous, with its constituent local bands sharing one another's territorial resources on occasion and sometimes coming together as a unit for major cooperative endeavors (Hosley 1981:541).[10]

As one would expect of egalitarian or even incipiently stratified hunters and gatherers, western Subarctic leadership depended on hunting and/or shamanistic skills, wisdom, strong personality, and oratorical persuasiveness. Leadership and status were primarily achieved, and when a headman's personal powers declined, so did his authority, and his followers left to find a better provider elsewhere (Hosley 1981:541). Rosman and Rubel (1983:16) characterize this leadership system as a typical "big man" structure, in which the allegiance of followers is based upon gifts from the leader and prestige is not passed on to heirs. In the pre- and early fur trade eras, little wealth was accumulated by an individual and passed on to his heirs (see below). Consequently, no hereditary nobility existed, although descendants of big men did have somewhat higher status, based on greater spiritual power and knowledge, greater hunting success, and the slightly larger amount of property they owned. More unexpected for those anthropologists who think that hunting peoples tend to be bilaterally and patrilineally organized was the existence of named, exogamous, and usually non-localized matrilineal moieties and clans that crosscut local and regional band structure. Their origin has been a subject of intense debate, which will be mentioned here only very briefly.[11]

While Boas and some of the Boasians tried to locate the ancestors of the matrilineal societies of the northern Northwest Coast further south along the Pacific coast, the predominant view today, particularly among scholars familiar with both the coast and the interior, is that matrilineality and dual division antedate the split of the Proto-Athapaskans into the coastal and inland groups. First expressed by Murdock (1955:86–87), this view was later substantiated by McClellan (1964) and particularly de Laguna (1975) who seriously challenged, if not rejected, the notion that matrilineal clans and dualism were borrowed by the Athapaskans from the coast during the nineteenth century, along with the fur trade-generated wealth complex and group-owned crests. De Laguna demonstrated that even when the western Subarctic Athapaskan social organization appears to be tripartite, "a fundamental principle of duality underlies it" (1975:133; compare McKennan 1959:127).

On the basis of structural analysis of the social organization of a number of Western Athapaskan groups, Rosman and Rubel (1983) have recently arrived at a similar conclusion. They have postulated an "antecedent" social structure for northern Northwest Coast and interior Athapaskan groups west of the continental divide, which remained the "dominant" structure among the latter. This antecedent structure was characterized by "an underlying dual organization, of sides opposite to one another, which could take the form of moieties, exchanges of goods and services between these sides, particularly at funerals, and a preference for bilateral cross-cousin marriage" (Rosman and Rubel 1983:20). In their view, the social organization of the Tanaina, Upper Tanana, Kaska, and Kutchin resembled this prototype most closely.[12]

Surprisingly, none of the above-mentioned studies aimed at tracing the northern Northwest Coast culture to its Proto-Athapaskan base, focused on religious beliefs and rituals. In my view the similarities between the mortuary complexes of the Tlingit and the western Subarctic Athapaskans are strong and give further support to the common-origin hypothesis.[13]

Unilineal descent groups and dualism have left an important imprint on the mortuary complex of the western Subarctic Athapaskans. As among the northern Northwest Coast peoples, the clan's major function was the regulation of marriage and life-cycle rituals, avenging the injury or death of its members, and warfare (among some groups). Athapaskan clans, like their Tlingit counterparts, served as the primary units of identification for individuals. However, the former did not own a stock of material and symbolic property, including totemic crests and privileges associated with them. The identification between a matrilineal group and its animal (or sometimes other) symbol was weak (McKennan 1959:124; de Laguna 1975; Rosman and Rubel 1983).

In general, it appears that the place of the matrilineal group in the individual's social identity and especially daily life was somewhat less significant or clearly defined among the Athapaskans than among the peoples of the northern Northwest Coast. Thus, among the former, inheritance was not strictly in the matriline, so that a man's son, for example, could inherit some of his personal possessions. Due to greater mobility in the Subarctic, fission, fusion, and total disappearance of individual matrilineal groups were more frequent than on the Northwest Coast (McKennan 1959:127; de Laguna 1975).

One of the functions, if not *the* most important function, of the matrilineal clan was the mortuary one (e.g., Van Stone 1974:58). In fact, mortuary rites were among the few occasions on which large numbers of matrikin came together from more than one community and, thus, strengthened their solidarity. The taboo on handling the corpse of one's matrikin and the resulting practice of relying on members of some other group to do so were just as strong in the interior as they were on the coast. As in the northern Northwest Coast societies, the Athapaskan mourners were primarily the matrikin of the deceased, with strict and elaborate taboos imposed upon them which resemble those of the Tlingit. The existence of the unilineal descent groups also appears to have been directly related to the prevalence of beliefs in reincarnation in the western Subarctic and among the Tlingit, the Haida, and the Tsimshian.

Among the former, the polluting task of performing the mortuary services was usually taken up by the moiety other than that of the deceased. While moieties regulated marriage, moiety exogamy was violated more often than on the coast. Despite some fluidity of moieties,[14] it appears that in the western Subarctic Athapaskans' own conception of the world, the dual division of society was fundamental. Funeral workers, who eventually became the potlatch guests, were usually recruited from the same group as spouses. In fact, as de Laguna (1975:134–137) and Rosman and Rubel (1983) argue, a social system characterized by bilateral cross-cousin marriage has a potential for developing moieties. This seems to have been the case among the Subarctic Athapaskans, including groups located east of the continental divide which lacked matrilineality. Reciprocal relations established between affines, particularly services at life crises, with death being the most important one, if consistently carried out by cross relatives, would create that fundamental duality essential to a moiety system. Then as members of other families are included in memorial feasts and other social events, they would tend to be arranged into two parties, as hosts and guests, givers and receivers.

As I have shown in Chapter VIII, in the memorial potlatch of a number of western Subarctic Athapaskans as well as Eyak, the guests physically embodied the hosts' own dead matrikin and received gifts and food in their name. The idea that the deceased person being commemorated must be present at the memorial feast and that his presence could only be accomplished through the mediation of the "other" seems to constitute the core of the western Subarctic Athapaskan mortuary complex, with its echoes reverberating throughout the Tlingit potlatch.[15]

Athapaskan Versus Tlingit Mortuary Complexes

Having outlined the basic principles of social organization of the western Subarctic Athapaskans, we can now explain the major similarities as well as the differences between their mortuary complex and that of the Tlingit. The greatest resemblance appears to be in the eschatology and other death-related beliefs, which I have already outlined. The central role played by the dead in the life of their living descendants was undoubtedly an important aspect of the Proto-Athapaskan culture and its subsequent Subarctic and Northwest Coast offshoots. We could trace this phenomenon to northeastern Asia and the Pacific (compare Birket-Smith 1929:121; 1967), but would probably never find the ultimate answer to the question of *why* the mortuary complex was so central to the Proto-Athapaskan culture. We can, however, sort out and analyze specific resemblances.

To begin, the notion that the deceased had to be shown respect and honored as a member of a clan explains the lying-in-state ritual, present in all of these societies despite the fear of pollution emanating from the corpse. At the same time, this fear might explain the use of fire to dispose of the corpse. It is noteworthy, however, that the corpse and the ghost seemed to pose greater danger among the Athapaskans than the Tlingit. The former often destroyed or abandoned the dwelling where death occurred, disposed of much of the personal possessions of the deceased, and tabooed his name (McKennan 1959:130, 142, 147). As McKennan (1959:130) argued "originally inheritance had no place in Athapaskan society since what little property a man owned was destroyed upon his death." In the western Subarctic, persons performing funerary services had to undergo ritual purification and observe magical precautions to protect themselves from the danger of having been in contact with the deceased. Thus, for example, among the Peel River Kutchin, grave workers had to live apart from the rest of the people for about a month following the disposal of the body. This danger might explain the ritualized forced recruitment of grave workers by the close kin of the deceased in that society (Osgood 1936:145, 148–149).[16] The taboos imposed on the Kutchin funeral workers closely resembled those of the Tlingit mourners, with one important difference—the latter were the deceased's own matrikin rather than his opposites (Osgood 1936:145). Among the Tlingit themselves, I could find no evidence of the latter having to be purified and protected at the conclusion of the mortuary rites.[17]

The simplest, materialist explanation of the Athapaskan practice of destroying the deceased's dwelling and personal property and its absence among the Tlingit is the fact that the latter owned a great deal more than the former, including large winter houses, as opposed to much less permanent dwellings.[18] However, the greater danger posed by the corpse and everything associated with it among the Athapaskans requires further discussion. In my view, the Tlingit notion that the deceased—especially an aristocrat—owned and was associated with the various pure and immortal attributes of his matrilineal group's *shagóon* made the polluting flesh and the ghost less prominent in his entire social persona than among the Athapaskans whose own ancestors had a lot less to pass on to their descendants.[19] Similarly, the Tlingit did not taboo the deceased's name, since it too was part of his clan's *shagóon*.

The same difference in cultural logic might explain why among the Athapaskans the dead appeared more dangerous to the living than among the Tlingit. During the potlatch itself, the Athapaskan chief mourner/potlatch sponsor, whose conduct resembled that of the girl undergoing her first puberty confinement (see McKennan 1959:137–138),[20] was subjected to much stricter taboos than his Tlingit counterpart. These taboos were aimed at protecting him and ensuring his good fortune.

It is in the memorial potlatch that we find the major differences between the western Subarctic Athapaskans and the Tlingit. As I have said earlier, in its essential characteristic as the final rite of the mortuary cycle, the potlatch of the interior was quite similar to that of the northern Northwest Coast. However, the scale of the latter was much greater than that of the interior one. Although the Athapaskan memorial potlatch, like its Tlingit counterpart, marked the end of the mortuary cycle, it rarely involved double obsequies. Only some of the interior groups, like the Carrier, provided a new container for the cremated remains at the end of a year-long mourning period. Mortuary poles or gravehouses seem to have been a coastal influence, which took hold in the interior during the fur trade era, and even then were erected mainly by the wealthy. Greater fear of touching human remains, combined with nomadism and a much more modest material culture, was one of the main causes of the absence among the Athapaskans of this important feature of the coastal mortuary complex.

While the existing data is inconsistent, incomplete, and unevenly distributed among the different groups, it does appear that, prior to the infusion of wealth due to the fur trade, the western Subarctic Athapaskan potlatch was a simple feast accompanied by a modest distribution of gifts among those guests who had earlier performed funerary services. Because the interior groups saw the deceased's personal property as more polluted than the coastal ones, some of them burned most of that property along with the body, particularly if the deceased was poor (Osgood 1958:276). In the same societies, the remaining items were given to the guests at the potlatch.[21] Among other groups of the area, some of the deceased's possessions were passed on as mementos to his close kin who were often his matrilineal relatives. While we lack data to establish definitely whether destruction was an earlier form of disposal of the deceased's property than distribution, it appears that, in those Athapaskan societies where greater wealth could be accumulated by individuals and, certainly, among the Tlingit and other northern coastal groups, the emphasis on matrilineal inheritance rather than destruction of property was much stronger.

In my view, in this simplest Proto-Athapaskan version of the potlatch, much of which survived into the twentieth century among such groups as the Koyukon, most of the goods distributed were the personal property of the deceased (Loyens 1964; Kroul 1974).[22] To that property, his close kin, who acted as hosts, added some wealth of their own. Of course, they also supplied the food for the feast. In most Athapaskan potlatches, a single person would provide much of the food and wealth for distribution. A greater role played by the chief host in the Athapaskan potlatch, in comparison to the Tlingit one, clearly reflected the weaker ties among the matrikin and a greater emphasis on self-reliance and personal autonomy in Subarctic societies. Thus, while the Tlingit chief host always asked his matrikin for property contributions and other forms of assistance, his Upper Tanana counterpart was said to be "ashamed" to do so (McKennan 1959:135).

Among the Ingalik and, I believe, most other western Subarctic Athapaskans, a memorial potlatch was usually given by a single sponsor for one deceased. Other individuals could join him to commemorate the same deceased or sometimes their own close kin, but they had to do it "not collectively but in aggregate. In other words, each part of the procedure is duplicated by each potlatch giver" (Osgood 1958:138; compare McKennan 1959:132 on the Upper Tanana). In the nomadic and semi-nomadic societies of the western Subarctic, fewer clan relatives were able to assemble and cooperate in a potlatch for their departed matrilineal relative than on the Northwest Coast. The more rigid principles of unity and solidarity of clan members on the coast prevented the deceased's spouses and paternal kin from acting as the chief sponsors of his potlatch,[23] a practice not uncommon in the western Subarctic (Osgood 1936:126; 1937:149–159; McKennan 1959:132; Loyens 1964:136). This relative weakness of clan ties combined with a greater role played by the nuclear family, as a residential and productive unit, in Athapaskan societies, as compared to the northern Northwest Coast ones, explains why the chief host in the interior often received more financial and practical support from his immediate family than from his clan (e.g., McKennan 1959:134–135).

For the same reasons, the prestige derived from the potlatch by the chief host(s) was shared with his matrikin to a much greater extent on the coast than in the interior (e.g., McKennan 1959:132).[24] Even when the potlatch was given in memory of a clan head, his successor did not have to strain his resources and demand significant contributions from his matrikin in order to impress the guests, because relatively little power and prestige could be derived from that office in the pre-fur trade Athapaskan societies and among their Proto-Athapaskan predecessors.

Just as the host group was smaller in the Athapaskan potlatch than in the Tlingit one, so was the number of guests. In the earliest and the simplest Proto-Athapaskan potlatch, the guests consisted of the funeral workers plus a few of their kin. The former received the bulk of the gifts, while the latter were mainly feasted. Even when gifts were distributed among all of the guests, differences between them were not accentuated as much as in the Tlingit potlatch.[25]

Competition between the hosts and the guests, so central in the coastal potlatch, seems to have been relatively weak in the interior.[26] Of course, the recipients of the gifts had to reciprocate at some point by inviting their former hosts to perform funerary services and then remunerating them. As on the coast, this reciprocity served as the key link between the two moieties or other groups that exchanged ritual services connected with life crises.

While acting as the living representatives of their own clans, and sometimes villages and bands, the leading guests (former funeral workers) in the Subarctic potlatch incarnated the hosts' own dead matrikin being memorialized.[27] The dead took part in the Tlingit potlatch as well, their presence made possible by the opposite moiety. However, the Athapaskans tended to make it much more tangible and consequently more dangerous, with greater precautions having to be made to protect the living, especially children, during the festivities (e.g., Carlo 1978:61–69). While the Athapaskans used mainly the bodies of the potlatch guests to bring the hosts' ancestors into the ritual domain, the Tlingit relied much more on inherited names, crests, sacred regalia, songs, and oratory to accomplish that (see Chapter VIII). The use of these sacred attributes of clan history and identity (*shagóon*) increased the number of ancestors attending the Tlingit memorial potlatch. It appears that among the interior Athapaskans, where clans owned only the rudiments of such sacred property, the dead were not remembered as far back as on the coast and were consequently present in the memorial potlatch in smaller numbers.

Of course, such comparisons are difficult to make, since little published data on Athapaskan potlatch oratory, songs, and other performative genres exist. Nevertheless, the existing information does suggest that the memorial feast in the interior was focused much more on the recently deceased being commemorated than on his clan ancestors. Thus, for example, the oratory here referred more to the recently deceased; while the mourning songs were more often composed for the occasion. Whereas on the coast, the oratory was focused more on the ancestors, and the mourning songs were more likely to be inherited from them (e.g., Osgood 1936:126; Loyens 1964:135).

A greater emphasis by the coastal groups on the ancestral heritage, as well as the key role played by the aristocracy in their ceremonial life, explains the greater formalization of the ritual procedures that characterized the Northwest Coast potlatch, in comparison to the Athapaskan one. As Osgood pointed out in his description of the Kutchin potlatch, "speeches, songs, games and eating occur without special order and regularity" (1936:127).[28] Of course, even in the interior, the chief hosts, clan leaders, and elders did play a greater role than the rest of the participants, but compared to the Tlingit, this differentiation was minimal. Among the Athapaskans, the absence of a hereditary status group meant that much of the ritual expertise and knowledge was distributed more equally among the population and could be demonstrated by many of the potlatch participants.

Transformation of the Proto-Athapaskan Mortuary Complex

I have presented an argument that the mortuary complex described here was typical of the western Subarctic Athapaskans, prior to their intense involvement in the fur trade, and represented the Proto-Athapaskan base out of which the Tlingit death-related beliefs and practices, as we know them for the eighteenth and the nineteenth centuries, had developed. What we must establish now are those key ecological, economic, sociopolitical, and ideological factors that contributed to the transformation of this prototypical mortuary complex into its northern Northwest Coast, and particularly Tlingit, version.

My model of the evolution of the Tlingit mortuary complex from a prototypical Athapaskan base bears some resemblance to the one proposed by Rosman and Rubel (1983; 1986), except that to their emphasis on ecology, subsistence, and social structure I add religion (i.e., mortuary/ancestral complex) as a major factor. I agree with them that the difference in the resource base between the northern Northwest Coast and the interior Athapaskan societies was a key variable in this transformation. Greater abundance and variety of subsistence resources on the coast allowed the population to increase, both in size of community and density of population. Seasonal migration in response to resource variability still occurred, but permanent village settlements on the coast became larger than their interior counterparts. Ownership of subsistence resources became clearly defined and controlled by matrilineal groups, whose heads supervised the exploitation of those resources. While matrilineal descent remained the basis for social units, the social organization became more complex, with clans split into lineages and sublineages. Lineage membership did fluctuate, but there was much less movement between groups on the coast than in the interior, and residential groups (villages and tribes) became more fixed in their composition (compare Rosman and Rubel 1983:22).

Greater accumulation of food and goods allowed for their redistribution within and between matrilineal groups, which was now supervised by the heads of those groups. As Rosman and Rubel (1983:22) point out, "with this increase in wealth and goods, leadership positions among the Athapaskans which had been of the 'big man' type, become fixed and hereditary." An important change also occurred in the way labor was controlled. According to these authors,

> In the "big man" political structure of Athapaskan groups, followers must be attracted and continually held onto by the leader's gift-giving and success in the hunt. At the death of the leader the group disperses. The matrilineage, which is the resource exploitation group among the northern Northwest Coast societies, has continuity over time and a more or less stable membership; it does not collapse upon the death of the chief. This permits more systematic exploitation of the larger resource base and is in contrast to the fluid band organization of the Athapaskans. (Rosman and Rubel 1983:23; compare McKennan 1959:133)

The shift towards sedentariness, which allowed the matrilineal groups on the coast to lay claims to subsistence areas, stimulated the development of crests and other group-owned prerogatives that symbolized and legitimized those claims. Their validation was accomplished by the distribution of wealth to members of other groups, made possible by the greater abundance of resources. Leaders of matrilineal groups acquired more personal property which they could pass on to their direct descendants, along with their position in the group and the prestige associated with it. Through this process, hereditary aristocracy and rank developed. As I have shown in Chapter IV, the aristocracy's supervision of subsistence resources was linked to and legitimized by their control over their matrilineal groups' *shagóon*.

The consequences for the mortuary complex of these changes in the sociopolitical order were quite significant. As the role of inherited personal property and, more importantly, collective (tangible and intangible) property increased dramatically, so did the role of the dead and the centrality of the mortuary rites in the sociocultural order. Clan ancestors became not only the owners of but the symbols of the sacred heritage that made the living clan members what they were. The dead became less threatening, the importance of their idiosyncratic characteristics diminishing and that of their immortal attributes (names, regalia, and similar items) increasing. The scale of the mortuary rites also increased dramatically, including the number of participants, the amount of wealth involved, and the duration and formalization of the funeral and the potlatch. The mortuary rites, and especially the potlatch, became more prestige-oriented. The aristocracy began to use them, as well as other life cycle rites, to strengthen its dominant role in society and increase its status.

Succession developed from being a fairly insignificant aspect of the Proto-Athapaskan potlatch, into a rather important one in its coastal version. In fact, Rosman and Rubel (1971; 1983:22–23) use succession as the main explanation for the prominence of the *mortuary* potlatch, rather than any other kind, among the northern Northwest Coast groups. To some extent they are correct in pointing out that "the mortuary feasts of the Athapaskans become the true mortuary potlatches of the northern Northwest Coast, at which the claim of the new chief to the position is validated by the acceptance of goods on the part of other chiefs, who come as guests." We must remember, however, that the aristocrats conducted potlatches in cooperation with and on behalf of their lower-ranking matrikin, whose own prestige was increased through those rites as well. Hence I agree with Rosman and Rubel (1983:22–23) that the northern Northwest Coast memorial potlatch was "tied to the institutionalization of the position of chiefly leadership, not present among the Athapaskans," but would add that it was not limited to leadership succession.

What Rosman and Rubel overlook is a religious system that placed the dead at its center and gave them a crucial role in the sociocultural order. As I have shown, among the Tlingit, the concepts of the matriclan's immortality, on the one hand, and of the unity and solidarity of its members, on the other, were interrelated and discouraged the aristocracy from completely separating itself from its lower-ranking kin. We could say that the ancestral complex impeded the development of classes, even though individual actors did use their love and respect for the dead to legitimize their claims to specific prerogatives and, thus, enhance their status and prestige. I am suggesting that the development of the Tlingit culture on the coast did not involve a radical break with its Proto-Athapaskan base. Since attitudes towards the ancestors were among the main forces that kept the Tlingit clan mates unified, despite their differences in status and rank, the original egalitarianism was never completely replaced by a hierarchical social order.

As among the Athapaskans, the clan linked to that of the deceased through marriage performed mortuary service and at the potlatch received goods in return. However, the amount of wealth exchanged between moieties and the network of affinal ties linking a matrilineal group in one moiety to several groups in the other expanded significantly. Once again, the dead served as a social adhesive, solidifying ties between moieties, because violating intermoiety exchange meant jeopardizing the proper relationships between them and the living.

Even a cursory look at the anthropological interpretations of the fur trade's impact on the western Subarctic Athapaskan culture and society reveals a process not unlike the one that I propose for the development of the coastal Tlingit culture. A good illustration of this is presented in McClellan's (1975:489–490) work on the Tagish and the Tutchone. As she points out, the fur trade brought increased contact with coastal societies and the Europeans, generating greater wealth. This enabled the system to become more complex, so that the wealth was used to enhance the prestige of individuals to the point where a rank system of titles emerged. Because of their position in the pre-fur trade Athapaskan society, the "old time chiefs" were the most likely to become trading partners with coastal Tlingit or with individual white traders on the coast and were the most likely to accumulate wealth. As the possibility of having a lot of wealth, including exotic foreign trade items, grew greater, so did the chiefs' chances for giving elaborate potlatches patterned on the coastal model. Memorial feasts for the dead and other life crises became occasions for the distribution to members of the opposite moiety of truly impressive quantities of trade goods, in addition to the more traditional tanned hides, furs, and food (compare Rosman and Rubel 1983:21).

Where the profits from the fur trade had made stratified rank possible, potlatching also became a means to enhance or maintain rank and to assume or reaffirm lineage prerogatives (McClellan and Denniston 1981:385). Some Athapaskan groups even transformed indigenous rudimentary crests and other collective sacred possessions into a system more akin to the coastal one. Others, who had not had crests previously and/or were in closer contact with the coast, borrowed them from the Tlingit, Tsimshian, and other coastal groups (compare de Laguna and McClellan 1981). A few groups, such as the Upper Tanana, never developed full-fledged crests but did add some prerogatives that clan members shared.[29]

The intensification of trade and the infusion of wealth into the Subarctic could not, however, completely transform Athapaskan culture and society, including the mortuary complex. Many of the features of the pre-fur trade sociopolitical organization and religion, linked to a relative scarcity and uneven distribution of resources and the resulting nomadism, remained in place until the twentieth century when more radical changes were brought about by the interference of missionaries, schools, the state, and capitalist development of the North. Thus, in the

Athapaskan memorial potlatch, as compared to its coastal counterpart, the role of the chief sponsor/host remained greater while cooperation between matrikin was weaker.

Anthropologists disagree in their evaluation of the extent to which the fur trade had transformed the Athapaskan mortuary complex and, especially, the potlatch. These differences of interpretation parallel my own disagreement with those scholars who see the nineteenth century Tlingit potlatch as exclusively or predominantly a ritual of status and prestige aggrandizement and, for that reason, the differences are worth mentioning here. McKennan (1959:134–139), who conducted research among the Upper Tanana in the early 1930s, is the major proponent of the position that the indigenous view of the potlatch as a "festival for the dead" hardly gives the true picture of the importance of this institution in Upper Tanana as well as other Subarctic societies, particularly those where it became more formalized (e.g., the Tahltan and the Carrier). In McKennan's view, whatever its original purpose, the Upper Tanana potlatch had become, by the end of the nineteenth century, primarily the means by which an individual achieved prestige.[30] Some of the data he presents confirms this view, for example, the use of a distant relative's death by an ambitious man as an excuse for sponsoring a lavish potlatch, a practice not uncommon among the Tlingit (compare Van Stone 1974:55–66).[31]

Nevertheless, McKennan's denial of the mortuary dimension of the potlatch is particularly surprising, since his own Upper Tanana data suggest that the ritual was more than just a method of attaining prestige. Thus, he mentions that the family of the bereaved and, particularly, its headman organized a potlatch to "forget their sorrow." After the potlatch, the chief host was seen as "being spiritually a new man" and was, hence, the subject of a variety of taboos, similar to those imposed on persons undergoing other rites of passage. Other ethnographers (e.g., Osgood 1936; 1958; Loyens 1964; Kroul 1974; Guedon 1974) indicate that overcoming grief,[32] showing respect to one's affines, and a number of other rationales for potlatching existed. In my view, they paint a more nuanced picture of the Athapaskan potlatch than McKennan and Van Stone. Thus, while these two scholars would probably argue that prestige was the only, or at least the main criterion for selecting a particular affine to perform funeral services and then act as an honored guest, Osgood (1958:138) points out that, among the Ingalik, this selection was based on affection and a variety of other "little human factors" (compare Chapters VI and VII).

Prestige aggrandizement was undoubtedly present in all of the western Subarctic potlatches, but it was not their only function, and individual groups obviously varied in the extent to which prestige was important for them.[33] If, as I have demonstrated, eschatology and other key aspects of the Proto-Athapaskan mortuary complex had survived among the Tlingit, they certainly could not have totally disappeared in the interior.

To test my interpretation of the factors contributing to the centrality of the mortuary rites in the sociocultural order of the Tlingit and other northern Northwest Coast peoples, I compare them briefly with those of the central and southern societies of this culture area: Kwakiutl, Nootka, Bella Coola, and Salish. These groups, while sharing the Tlingit emphasis on the accumulation and distribution of wealth, rank, and hereditary privileges, lacked unilineal descent groups and moieties, as well as a religious system in which the living and the dead maintained close reciprocal relationships to the extent they did among the Tlingit. Based on these similarities and differences between the sociocultural systems of the northern Northwest Coast peoples and those of the rest of that culture area, we can expect that the mortuary complexes of the two regions would also show some major resemblances as well as dissimilarities. The main questions I would like to address are whether the mortuary complex was equally important among the northern Northwest Coast groups and their coastal neighbors to the south, and if not, why was there a difference.

Northern Versus Central and Southern Northwest Coast Mortuary Complexes

Of course, even a cursory survey of Northwest Coast death-related beliefs and rituals could not be incorporated into a single chapter. Existing data on the coastal mortuary complex is richer than on the Athapaskan one but, once again, that data is uneven and unequally distributed among different groups. For example, despite an enormous amount of information on the Kwakiutl, little is known about their ethnopsychology, eschatology, or mortuary rites. Despite these difficulties, I believe that by briefly addressing this issue, I can further strengthen my argument about the factors that contributed to the role played by death in Tlingit culture and provide additional components for the model of the mortuary complex in ranked societies.

Having examined a number of area ethnographies as well as Drucker's (1950) "culture element distribution" list and Birket-Smith's (1967) brief comparative study of the "potlatch" in the Pacific, I have concluded that the dead did play a significant role in the cultural systems of the Northwest Coast, but that the role of the dead has been underestimated (compare Kan 1986:194).[34] Examples of practices reminiscent of the Tlingit ones include sending food and property to the dead through the fire, participation of the ancestral spirits in pot-latches and other ceremonies, keeping some of the ancestors' remains as relics which could bring good fortune, and some form of double obsequies—most commonly, erection of memorial posts and other grave structures. While different Northwest Coast groups potlatched on different occasions, all of them had the mortuary potlatch, which Birket-Smith (1967:35–36) referred to as a "fundamental trait" (compare Drucker 1950:231).

The rhetorical use of the dead and of the death-related emotions in the central and southern Northwest Coast potlatches is also strongly reminiscent of the Tlingit one. Among the Tsimshian, gifts distributed among the guests were called "things with which to wipe the tears" (Garfield 1939:250). Similarly, the Nootka referred to the property dis-tributed by the deceased's heir among the guests at a feast held a few days after the funeral as a show of how "heartbroken" he was and said that it was "carried away under the arm to accompany the dead" (Drucker 1951:148–149). The Bella Coola called the potlatch gifts the "tears" of the chief mourner (McIlwraith 1948, vol. I:471), while the Coast Salish described the property contributed by his relatives as "a staff to support him in his grief" (Barnett 1955:229).

Despite these important similarities, the dead and the mortuary rites did not play as central a role in most of the southern and central Northwest Coast cultures as they did among the Tlingit, the Haida, and the Tsimshian. Thus, beliefs in reincarnation were not very com-mon outside the northern Northwest Coast area and communication between the realms of the living and the dead was not as intense in the central and southern areas. The fear of the corpse and the ghost seems to have been stronger among those groups that lacked moieties and, thus, could not rely on their opposites to handle the polluting at-tributes of the deceased. Few groups outside the northern coastal area displayed the corpse dressed in ceremonial regalia for several days of mourning. Instead, many of them, particularly the Nootka and the Salish, removed it from the house as soon as possible (Drucker

1950:216–218; 1951:147). Central and southern Northwest Coast groups tabooed the name of the deceased, and destroyed or gave away to non-kin most of the deceased's personal property (Drucker 1950:230; Stern 1934:36–37; Collins 1974:232). The Nootka were the extremists in this respect: when a high-ranking person or chief died, some hereditary privileges, such as songs and dances were discarded or at least "put away," for several years, along with the deceased's name, until a special potlatch was held and these restrictions were lifted (Drucker 1951:148). Having no opposite moiety to dispose of the corpse, these societies relied on kin, friends, or ritual experts possessing special powers that prevented them from being harmed by pollution. All of these corpse handlers had to be purified after they had fulfilled their duty (Drucker 1951:218; Elmendorf 1960:449–450).

While the memorial potlatch did mark the end of a liminal period for the mourners and the deceased and usually coincided with the erection of a monument, rare among these central and southern coastal groups was the northern practice of actually replacing the container for the remains.[35] This fact suggests that, in the memorial potlatch, the body of the deceased was not the center of attention, as it was in the north. Among the central and southern groups, the presence of the ancestors in the potlatch was ensured by their descendants' use of inherited names, crests, regalia, and other prerogatives. However, little evidence could be found of a presence as tangible as we saw among the Tlingit.[36]

Finally, among most of the central and southern coastal groups, death was only one of many occasions for having a potlatch. Unlike the Tlingit, they frequently potlatched to celebrate birth, first naming, a girl's puberty rite, and marriage. Rosman and Rubel (1971; 1986:562–563) relate this directly to the cognatic social structure of these societies, which they describe as follows:

> corporate descent groups with overlapping membership are present, i.e., several groups may claim the same individual as a member and one person may belong to several groups; an individual may reside with any of the groups to which he belongs, but with only one group at a time; a wife continues to belong to her natal group after marriage but usually lives with her husband and his group; there is no marriage rule.[37]

Unlike the Tlingit, who gave ceremonial names/titles to children as part of the mortuary potlatch, cognatic societies often held separate potlatches to celebrate naming. In the latter case, the giving of names held by one kin group to a child at a potlatch was a reaffirmation of that child's membership in the kin group as well as a demonstration of a future claim over that child. This was a consequence of an overlapping kin group membership resulting from cognatic descent. Since kin-group membership was not determined by a unilineal descent rule, membership was negotiable, and "potlatching was a dynamic mechanism for laying claims to individuals" (Rosman and Ruvel 1986:562–563). Similarly, in these cognatic societies, marriage required potlatching since there was no fixed preferential rule of marriage. Thus, marriage served as a way of claiming children. This was in contrast to the northern Northwest Coast societies, where there was a relatively fixed marriage rule and marriage was usually not an occasion for potlatching.[38]

Rosman and Rubel also see different rules of succession that existed in the north and on the rest of the coast as major factors contributing to the greater or lesser importance of potlatching at death. Thus, among the Kwakiutl and Nootka, chiefly name and position were passed on during the chief's lifetime to an heir. Since chiefly heirs were determined by primogeniture and since the title was passed before the chief died, there was no competition for succession as occurred among the matrilineal societies in the north. While the importance of the rule of succession in shaping the potlatch cannot be denied, I believe that Rosman and Rubel overstate it. As I have shown, among the Tlingit, the incumbent's identity was determined prior to the potlatch, while in the course of the mortuary ritual it was only validated. More importantly, I argue that among central and southern coastal groups, death was not the major occasion for potlatching. In their religious system the dead were not central as they were in the Tlingit world view. The Tlingit had to potlatch at death not only because succession was at stake—after all, not all of the dead were heads of matrilineal groups—but because the ideology of love and respect for the ancestors was so prominent.

In connection with this argument, one might ask whether the central and southern Northwest Coast potlatches completely lacked this commemorative dimension. In other words, were the mortuary potlatches among the Bella Coola, Nootka, Kwakiutl, and Coast Salish only about prestige and status aggrandizement, as some scholars have argued, or did the dead play some of the same roles in them as those that I have described for the Tlingit?

Like a few of the Athapaskan ethnographers cited above, several scholars who studied the coastal groups saw references to ancestors, frequent in all of the Northwest Coast potlatches, simply as rhetoric used by the living to enhance their own status and legitimize their claims to inherited prerogatives. Snyder's discussion of such use of the dead among the Skagit (a Coast Salish group) exemplifies this position:

> When descendants distinguished themselves, worthy ancestors were celebrated in memory. In Skagit society many a great name was made long after the death of a holder, who had been, by comparison, a nobody in life. But Skagit did not live to die or die to live. Memorial services and recitations of genealogies honoring the dead were not expressions of ancestor worship. On the contrary, Skagit lived very much in the present, and to honor ancestors was manifestly to honor oneself and the living. The illustrious ancestor was frequently a fiction made up or capitalized upon by some aspiring descendant. (1964:195–196)

Other ethnographers of the Coast Salish (e.g., Olson 1936:113; Elmendorf 1960:456) lend further support to this view by describing how the wealthy used the secondary treatment of the dead, involving the redressing and reburial of the remains, as an excuse for lavish potlatching.

Such practices were quite similar to those of the Tlingit; but did they necessarily negate other attitudes towards and relationships with the ancestors? Already twenty-five years ago Wike (1952:102) suggested that the dead constituted a "religious" tradition within the Northwest Coast ceremonial life, which gave more "spiritual depth to Northwest Coast status striving, inheritance, and the potlatch" and "some rather needed supports for Northwest Coast hereditary chieftainships." More recently, Amoss (1978:12), who studied the Nooksack, another Coast Salish group, spoke about the importance of the connection between the potlatch and duties to the dead, and interprets it as "a kind of supernatural support for the periodic intertribal redistribution of wealth."

Finally, McIlwraith's (1948, vol. I:459–460) detailed ethnography of the Bella Coola provides a more balanced view of the potlatch, similar to the one I have proposed for the Tlingit. According to him, the Bella Coola made a clear distinction between the memorial potlatch, given as soon as possible after the death of its sponsor's close and beloved relative, and the ordinary potlatch, which could be given at any time. The former was seen as being motivated by the sponsor's desire to commemorate the deceased and to console himself and his immediate family. The latter was given by a chief desirous of increasing his prestige. Despite the fact that the two rituals were quite similar and both involved the appearance of a dancer impersonating the deceased person being commemorated, they were perceived as being quite distinct.

It appears, even from these scattered data, that attitudes towards the ancestors did extend beyond pragmatism, especially in the memorial potlatch. The role of the dead in most of the ceremonial systems of the central and southern groups was not as significant as in the north, and especially among the Tlingit, but it was important nevertheless. It is also possible, as some scholars indicate, that their role declined by the end of the nineteenth century, with the increased interpersonal and intergroup competition and commercialization of the potlatch. Wike (1952:103) made such a suggestion for all of southern and central Northwest Coast societies, while Drucker and Heizer (1967:153) applied it to the Kwakiutl. Thus, McIlwraith (1948, vol. I:242–243) hypothesized that the central feature of the Bella Coola potlatch, the return of a dead ancestor, might have been "an old feature, decayed in other tribes through the ever-increasing economic aspects of the potlatch, which are of less import in Bella Coola." Finally, Piddocke (1965:256–257) made an intriguing suggestion that the destruction of property so frequent in the late nineteenth century Kwakiutl potlatch might have developed out of an earlier tradition of making offerings to the dead in the funeral context, "with the idea of honoring the dead perhaps providing the semantic link between the two contexts, and the new wealth consequent upon contact providing the means."[39] Is it then possible, I would ask, that the decline of this ideology of venerating the dead among the late nineteenth century Kwakiutl was, at least partially, responsible for an increase of competitive potlatching, whereas its survival among the Tlingit, as well as, some of the other coastal groups, constrained rivalry and emphasized cooperation and harmony?

In other words, I suggest that the nineteenth century Northwest Coast societies varied according to the relative strength of hierarchy versus equality, and competition versus cooperation. Among the Tlingit these forces seem to have been in a state of balance, whereas in Kwakiutl society hierarchy and competition were greater than equality and cooperation. Of course, the development, among the Tlingit, of a somewhat separate cycle of exchange, in which prestigious types of wealth circulated among aristocrats, seems to indicate that the transformation of the potlatch proposed for the Kwakiutl was beginning to occur in their society as well. At this point, however, it is difficult to speculate on the subsequent development of this process, since it was cut short by the more dramatic changes in Tlingit culture and society that took place around the turn of the century.

Having examined the Tlingit mortuary complex in a comparative perspective, I can now outline the main factors that contributed to its centrality in the larger sociocultural order. I begin with a summary of those features that the Tlingit way of death inherited from the egalitarian Proto-Athapaskans, followed by those that it shared with the stratified coastal societies, and end by reiterating the unique Tlingit configuration of mortuary rites.

1. The Athapaskan Base of the Tlingit Mortuary Complex

Sociopolitical organization is egalitarian, decentralized, and fluid, typical of nomadic hunters and gatherers, except for matrilineal descent and moiety dualism. Ethnopsychology differentiates between the impure and temporary flesh, the pure and eternal spiritual entities, and the intermediate bones. One of the deceased's spirits is reincarnated in his (usually matrilineal) descendant. The dead communicate frequently with the living and play a prominent role in their life, bringing their (primarily matrilineal) descendants good fortune, especially in hunting and other subsistence activities, in return for food and gifts, as well as remembrance. If ignored, the dead harm the living. The dead are honored and memorialized mainly as members of unilineal descent groups. The two moieties are linked perpetually in a cycle of reciprocity/exchange of spouses and ritual services, the mortuary ones being the most important ones. The opposite moiety mediates between the living and the dead members of the matrilineal group, and is remunerated for its funerary services at the "the feast of the dead"/memorial potlatch, which concludes the cycle of mortuary rites initiated at the funeral and is sponsored by the (primarily, though not exclusively, matrilineal) descendants of the deceased. The potlatch periodically brings together the living and the dead.

2. Northwest Coast Society and Mortuary Complex

A surplus-producing economy generates wealth exchanged between corporate descent groups, particularly affines. Centralized political leadership is absent, and each individual society or ethnic group is an amalgamation of economically and politically autonomous corporate groups sharing territory and resources. Social organization is characterized by descent groups, with each group being conceived of as the owner of a store of names/titles, some of them held by individuals and others vacant. Descent groups claim other prerogatives inherited from their ancestors. The ancestors are associated with the unchanging sacred past which serves as the guide and the foundation for the present social order. The claims made by the living to resources, status, and social identity are based, in large part, on the ties they can demonstrate with the deceased members of their descent group.

To validate these claims and to bestow names and other prerogatives on individuals, wealth must be distributed to some other group (often consisting of affines) acting as a witness. The distribution takes place in the context of feasts (potlatches) linked to life crises. Death is one of them, with the mortuary rites of the head of the descent group involving a formal presentation of an heir.[40] Mortuary rites include double obsequies or at least the construction of a memorial to the deceased, which serve as an occasion for potlatching. The potlatch carried out between corporate groups serves both to create communication between them via the exchange of property and the witnessing of claims to status, and to establish and maintain boundaries between these groups by defining the frame of group membership.

Society is ranked, with aristocrats acting as the guardians of ancestral resources, moral values, and esoteric knowledge, including expertise on conducting potlatches. Their own ancestors are of higher rank than those of the commoners. Aristocrats claim a special relationship with the ancestors and the ancestral heritage, but they have to share it and the prestige based on it with the rest of their descent group members. Controlled by those of the higher rank, the potlatch becomes highly formalized and serves as the main arena in which the aristocracy's special status is demonstrated, enhanced, and legitimized. At the same time, the prestige of every member of the host group is enhanced as well. Status is based on a combination of ascription and achievement. Competition is limited by inherited status and rules of propriety. Cooperation tends to be emphasized to a different degree in different societies.

3. The Tlingit Version of the Northwest Coast Society and Mortuary Complex

The basic characteristics of the sociopolitical order are the same as those presented in item two (above), with several important distinctive features derived from the Proto-Athapaskan ancestors: corporate groups are based on matrilineal rather than bilateral descent; unity and cooperation among matrikin and their veneration of the ancestors serve as a check on the development of rigid social hierarchy and inequality; pervasive dualism structures marriage as well as all of the ritual services involved in life crises, mortuary ones being the major ones among them;[41] the dead play a more prominent role in the sociocultural order than in the rest of the Northwest Coast societies; mortuary rites are the most important and elaborate of all, culminating in double obsequies and the memorial potlatch; they not only restore the social order but, to a large extent, constitute it.[42]

Beyond Northwestern North America

After completing this comparative analysis of the Tlingit and other northwestern North American mortuary complexes, I began perusing anthropological literature in search of other cases where the mortuary rites had a similar structure and played a similar role in the sociocultural order. Although that survey was far from thorough, I did make some interesting discoveries. As it turned out, one region where mortuary rites tend to be elaborate, include double obsequies, and play the central role in the sociocultural order, and where most of the recent anthropological studies of death have been conducted, includes Indonesia, Melanesia, New Guinea, and Madagascar. A large portion of its inhabitants speak Austronesian languages.

Societies that attracted my special attention were those that had at least some of the following characteristics: a native theory of procreation linked to the model of the person as consisting of various elements (bones, flesh, blood, and so forth) contributed by different types of kin; a theory of descent and filiation linked to this ethnopsychology; mortuary rites in which these (pure and impure) attributes of the person are redistributed and recycled; erection of imposing mortuary and memorial structures as part of the double obsequies; unilineal descent groups which own tangible and intangible property, including sacred valuables inherited from the ancestors; concern with genealogies; moieties exchanging spouses and ritual services related to life crises and particularly death; eschatology in which the ancestors have a cosmological significance, represent the sacred order, and play an important role in the life of the living members of their descent group; accumulation of wealth which is distributed to enhance the donors' status and prestige; ranking and the presence of hereditary leaders who control the knowledge of their descent group's sacred traditions and use mortuary rites for status aggrandizement; succession linked to mortuary rites.

It is not surprising that Hertz's own seminal work, which focused on double obsequies and laid the foundation for the anthropological study of death, was based on a survey of mostly Indonesian ethnographies. The direct heirs of that tradition are Huntington and Metcalf (1979; Metcalf 1982), who tested Hertz's model on several Indonesian societies, especially the Berawan of Borneo. Elsewhere in Indonesia, Traube (1980) and several other scholars (e.g., Forman 1980) have examined the cosmological and sociological roles played by the dead in the cultures of Timor. In Madagascar detailed ethnographies of the mortuary complex include Kottak (1980), Bloch (1971), and Huntington (1973), with the latter two authors, in different ways, developing Hertz's model. In Melanesia, two recent works make death-related beliefs and practices the focus of their analysis: Weiner's (1976; 1980) study of the mortuary transactions in the Trobriands and Keesing's (1982) book on the living and the dead in Kwaio religion. Finally, Rosman and Rubel (1970; 1978; 1981) have published several comparative works on New Guinea and Melanesia, focusing on the same issues of social organization, ranking, leadership, exchange, and dualism that they also deal with in their research on Athapaskan and northern Northwest Coast societies.

North Americanists have long been intrigued by similarities between Northwest Coast and Pacific cultures. Common origin and subsequent circumpacific diffusion of cultural traits have been postulated to explain them (e.g., Kroeber 1923; Drucker 1963; Birket-Smith 1967).[43] My own goal here is not to engage in speculation but to suggest that the parallels I have mentioned could also be seen as resulting from a similarity in the level of social and political complexity and religious ideology. On both sides of the Pacific, we are dealing with societies ranging from incipiently stratified to ranked, whose leaders vary from "big man" to "chieftains." In many of these societies, wealth is accumulated and distributed to enhance status and prestige.[44] It would be interesting to try to correlate these different types of sociopolitical organization with particular kinds of mortuary complexes. We have more comparative studies of social and political organization on the western side of the Pacific, Sahlins' (1963) typology of political types in Melanesia and Polynesia being one well-known example (compare Allen 1984). On the American side, fewer works of this kind exist, and only Rosman and Rubel (1970; 1971; 1981) have been concerned with comparing societies in northwestern North America and Oceania.[45]

What these comparative studies lack, in my opinion, is an equal attention to sociopolitical and religious systems, a kind of focus on all of the relevant aspects of culture and society that I have tried to demonstrate in the present work. I believe we need a better understanding of the cosmological and sociopolitical roles of the ancestors in each culture, as well as a better grasp of the intricacies of the mortuary rites themselves, before we can engage in systematic comparison and construction of typologies, evolutionary and otherwise. I believe that my own comprehensive analysis of the Tlingit mortuary complex, contextualized within the larger sociocultural order, as well as my comparison of northern Northwest Coast and Athapaskan death-related beliefs and practices provide data and ideas for this kind of a comparative study of death.

TLINGIT MORTUARY COMPLEX AND THE ANTHROPOLOGY OF DEATH

Our long journey through the nineteenth century Tlingit mortuary rites is over. It has demonstrated that traditional aspects of North American Indian cultures are still a rich field for anthropological research and that the best way to undertake that research is to combine archival data and reanalysis of the existing accounts with fieldwork. The latter, if possible, must include interviewing as well as participant observation, with the stress on the participant. Of course one must pay careful attention to historical change, so as not to mistake innovation for tradition and vice versa. Nevertheless, in many cases, particularly when one's focus is on the nineteenth century, there is ample historical and ethnographic data to combine synchronic and diachronic analysis, and to link the past with the present. The existing ethnographic corpus on the Northwest Coast and other areas, much of it bequeathed to us by the Boasians, is substantial enough to be (re)analyzed, utilizing an array of new methods (linguistic, symbolic, structuralist, and others) and theories. In addition, controlled comparison of data from neighboring groups could fill some of the gaps in the ethnographic record of the culture one is trying to reconstruct.

As an anthropological study of death, the present work clearly shows that the Hertzian model remains a very useful framework for ordering data on the mortuary ritual. This model is remarkably revealing of what is happening in the funeral and the potlatch and their articulated institutions and ideologies. By interpreting the potlatch first and foremost as double obsequies, i.e., as part of the mortuary ritual sequence, I have been able to explain how the ritual involved the individual's progress through life and death, the interaction of the living and the dead as collectivities, and the significance of the dead in legitimizing the social order of the living. I have also suggested that the Hertzian model would work very well in the study of western Subarctic Athapaskan and Northwest Coast death-related rituals, especially the final "feast of the dead"/memorial potlatch.

Another great French anthropologist whose ideas inspired and are supported by this work is, of course, Marcel Mauss. I have shown that the Tlingit mortuary rites, and especially the potlatch, definitely were Mauss' "total social phenomenon" or what he called "that fleeting moment when the society and its members take emotional stock of themselves and their situation as regards others" (1967:77–78). As Mauss correctly saw it, Northwest Coast potlatches could only be fully understood as both "politics" and "religion" and, as I have demonstrated, it is the interarticulation of these two dimensions that contributed to the centrality of the mortuary/ancestral complex in the nineteenth century Tlingit sociocultural order.

In this ranked society, the dead—or more precisely the sacred heritage (*shagóon*) that their matrilineal descendants received from them in the form of tangible and intangible property—were the most valuable political resource that had to be periodically regenerated and claims to which had to be legitimized in a public setting. So much of the social identity, power, and prestige of the living depended on this ancestral heritage, that social reproduction had to take place in the context of the mortuary rites where the symbolic manifestations of *shagóon* were transferred from the dead to their matrilineal descendants. Thus in Tlingit society, with its powerful and all-encompassing ancestral ideology, the social order was not simply reconstituted in the mortuary rites, as Hertz himself and his functionalist followers suggested, but was, to a large extent, created there (compare Bloch 1982;

Bloch and Parry 1982).[1] The relative ranking of individuals and matrilineal groups depended heavily on their performance in the last potlatch which they hosted. Of course, their success or failure in daily life and in warfare, trade, and marriage alliances affected their status and prestige as well, but it was in the potlatch that their accomplishments could be translated into legitimate claims to a particular position in the social hierarchy. This explains why relationships of inequality and competition were more pronounced in the potlatch than in daily life.

The social hierarchy itself was based on an unequal access to subsistence resources and wealth as well as symbolic capital which legitimized this access. The existence of this hierarchy and the value placed on the enhancement of individual and collective rank and status stimulated competition, both within and between matrilineal groups. The larger this disputed material and symbolic capital was, the more elaborate the mortuary rites had to be. The difference in scale between the Tlingit and the Athapaskan mortuary rites supports this argument, since their ancestral ideologies were rather similar but the resources at stake were much greater among the Tlingit than among the Athapaskans.

Thus in their mortuary rites the Tlingit transformed death from a threat to the social order into the major opportunity for strengthening and enhancing it. In a system like this, I suggest, one can expect to find an elaborate ritual of secondary treatment of the dead. To make the deceased into a valuable cultural resource, the ritual must separate his perishable and polluting attributes from the immortal and pure ones. The funeral begins this process, but usually some time is needed for all the elements constituting his total social persona to be separated from each other, for the perishable and impure ones to be discarded, and for the immortal ones to be channelled back into the social order of the living. As Bloch (1982:223–224) suggests, whenever the sociopolitical order and its authority structure are grounded in a larger ideal and unchanging ancestral order, the funeral rituals have to overcome in one way or another the individuality of a particular corpse. Consequently, in such societies, there will always be a double aspect to funerals. In Bloch's words, "One side will focus on pollution and on sorrow, something which in the end has to be removed and another side will always assert the continuity of something else, a reassertion of the vanquishing and victorious order where authority has its legitimate place" (1982:223–224).

Since in societies like Bloch's Merina of Madagascar or the Tlingit, positions of power and authority are conceptualized as being inherited directly from the ancestors, persons with stronger and more legitimate ties to the ancestral order, would occupy them. As Bloch puts it,

> In such a system, where power is represented as traditional authority, power-holders are legitimized insofar as they appear, not as the makers of their own superiority, but as caretakers of a well-organized world. It is not as individuals that people have legitimate positions in society but because of their positions in the eternal order which they temporarily incarnate. (1982:223)

As those who guarded and controlled their matrilineal relatives' *shagóon*, the aristocrats used the ancestral/mortuary complex as an ideology legitimizing their dominant role in society. While linked to their supervision of production and especially the distribution of resources, this domination was perceived as being based on their esoteric knowledge and ritual expertise. Because they controlled much of *shagóon*, the *aanyátx'i* appeared to be the ancestors' mouthpieces (compare Bloch 1974; 1975). Thus, their coercion of their lower-ranking matrikin was exercised not through brute force but mainly through "symbolic violence," i.e., oratory and other forms of ritual/symbolic action (compare Bourdieu 1977). The hierarchical nature of this society was linked to and reinforced by the formalized language and ritual, so prominent in Tlingit life.

The use of the formalized language of oratory and song as well as the non-verbal forms of ritual action (dancing, feasting, and gift-giving) allowed the aristocracy to euphemize its political strategies and actions and present them as a show of love and respect for the dead and their living matrikin and opposites. This was also true of other Northwest Coast potlatches, including that of the Haida, characterized by Boelscher as follows:

> Words and deeds are presented in the only form in which they are socially and culturally recognizable: that of gifts, kin obligation, honor, respect and mutual support. It is only underneath the overtly ritualized acts, and outside the feast-hall, that the arbitrary and strategic nature of words and acts rendered in the guise of reciprocity spell out strategic political acts. While they are officially

rendered in the language of legitimacy and persuasion, they translate, in the context of the social relationships they involve, into a subtle kind of coercion. (1985:168–169)

Despite this cultural emphasis on "imitating the ancestors," i.e., faithfully repeating the exact versions of the origin myths, condolence speeches, and mourning songs and displaying the ancestral crests, to be used as a political resource *shagóon* had to be subtly modified and manipulated. Contrary to Bloch's (1975:57) view of formalized language as "impoverished," i.e., incapable of expressing the speaker's own thoughts and feelings because in it "many of the options at all levels are abandoned so that choice of form, of style, of words and syntax, is less than in ordinary language," I have argued that the potlatch participants, particularly the ritual experts, had plenty of opportunities to insert their own message in the most "traditional" speeches and even songs.[2] In addition, a potlatch participant had the option of creating a new song, speech, or joke rather than repeating those used by his ancestors. In other words, within the constraints of tradition there was considerable room for subtle innovation.

To act as a political instrument, formalized language had to be convincing, which meant that it had to be eloquent.[3] As two Tlingit authors stated in a discussion of the potlatch, "The timelessness of clan relations, history, and crests becomes . . . apparent, and forces that were the ancestors are felt—this is especially true when master orators are in charge" (Littlefield and Littlefield 1980:1). Finally, we should remember that the potlatch oratory required a response. Bloch is correct when he says that it is difficult to argue with a speech or a song, especially when it is presented as the "voice of the ancestors." In the Tlingit case, however, the audience had to somehow acknowledge its acceptance of the speaker's statement. While the addressees rarely contradicted a potlatch speech, they were expected to indicate their approval by interrupting it with frequent *aaa* and *awe*, "that's right, yes," or *gunalchéesh*, "thank you." In their own speeches and songs given in return, the former addressees could also subtly express their reaction to what they had heard. Because they were multivocal symbols, crests and other tangible and intangible representations of *shagóon* could be manipulated to send a variety of messages, from the speaker's status-aggrandizing aspirations to his feelings about and attitudes towards the deceased or his audience.

It would be a mistake, however, to see the potlatch rhetoric of love and respect for the dead and the living participants as only a mask hiding the brute facts of power, inequality, and competition. I have shown that the ancestral/mortuary complex was much more than a form of "false consciousness"—an ideology legitimizing the aristocracy's dominance over the rest of the population.

Thus competition between individual hosts and their respective matrilineal groups was balanced by their cooperation, with the hosts being obligated to present a unified front vis-à-vis their opposites. The need to have competition as a dynamic force in the potlatch was acknowledged, but a concerted effort was made to contain it, so as to prevent it from destroying the social fabric. In fact, the potlatch structured social relationships in such a way as to show that competition and cooperation, and hierarchy and equality could coexist in a dialectical relationship. Thus, each matrilineal group was internally ranked, with each member expected to strive for higher status, and by doing so, to enhance the status of his or her entire group. At the same time, each lineage and clan was unified vis-à-vis other groups in its own and the opposite moiety, as well as in relation to its ancestors, who were collectively mourned and honored. Similarly, while the intermoiety competition was symbolically dramatized and even exaggerated to emphasize intramoiety solidarity, it was presented as subordinate to the values of love and respect between opposites, the latter, in turn, underscored by the ritualized rivalry between the two guest parties. Of course, the potlatch itself gave the hosts the upper hand, but their superiority over the guests was expected to last only until the next potlatch, when the two moieties traded places.

As the participants emerged from the ritual, they were supposed to leave their conflicts, disputes, and jealousies behind. The agreement they reached about the current distribution of power and prestige in their social universe was a fragile one, and it lasted only until their next potlatch. Nevertheless, some sense of order was imposed on the flow of social life, and this imposition was quite an accomplishment in a decentralized society of competing individuals and groups.

Thus the ideology of matrilineal solidarity (itself grounded in the ancestral complex) and moiety reciprocity was an idiom and mechanism of both ranking and competition, on the one hand, and equivalence and cooperation, on the other. It prevented individuals from totally subordinating the interests of their kin to their own self-aggrandizement and kept the aristocracy from forming a separate class.

The fact that the negotiation of rank and status took place not through litigation or warfare but in a *ritual* context was of great significance. It meant that the *sacred* was a major limitation on individual self-maximization and on hierarchical tendencies as well as a source of motivation for abiding by the rules of generosity and cooperation. For a participant to openly disagree with others or, worst of all, to walk out, was not only to insult them and thus jeopardize his position in society but, more importantly, to offend and harm the ancestors, highly revered superhuman beings believed to be present and taking a lively interest in the mortuary rituals.

Beliefs about the dead and their sanctity were central to the Tlingit cosmology and ethnopsychology and constituted what Rappaport calls the "ultimate sacred postulates" of this culture. In his words, "These understandings, the significations of which are not material and are beyond the reach of logical refutation, are neither verifiable nor falsifiable, but are nevertheless taken to be unquestionable" (1979:117). As the ultimate sacred postulates, beliefs about the dead stood at the apex of the conceptual structure embodied in the mortuary complex, and were more sacred, enduring, invariant, and authoritative than its other, contingent and instrumental components. In the native ideology, all the other elements of the ritual system of the potlatch were based on and secondary to these death-related beliefs and practices.

The significance of the religious motivation for potlatching is supported by the native exegesis. Even those individuals who used the dead as a rhetoric to euphemize their more mundane goals believed that the ancestors benefited from the distribution of food and gifts to members of the opposite moiety. When asked why memorial potlatches have to continue to be held, even in this modern age when fewer and fewer participants fully understand their meaning, traditionalist Tlingit informants often start by saying that it is bad luck not to do so. A common view among them is that more deaths would occur in a family that fails to honor its deceased member with a potlatch. Others say such behavior results in illness, poverty, and other misfortunes. At the same time, mortuary rituals properly carried out bring their hosts good fortune/blessing (*laxeitl*), while mistakes one makes during the rites of the mortuary cycle are not simply an embarrassment and a threat to one's status, but could be a source of bad luck (Kan 1979–1987).

Mortuary rituals, especially the potlatch, were the most appropriate context in which the living could interact with the dead, more sacred and more beneficial to the ancestors than dreaming, feeding the spirits through the fire and other less formal, more privatized modes of interaction. That is why a Tlingit who saw his deceased relative in a dream, which was usually interpreted as a sign of the spirit's hunger, preferred to satisfy its wishes through a potlatch-type feast rather than by simply putting some food in the fire. Of course, by potlatching the sponsor also increased his status, but the concern about and the veneration of the deceased were clearly important motivating forces behind his action.

It was precisely the role of the dead as the ultimate sacred postulates that made references to them such a persuasive form of rhetoric. How could a guest refuse his gift, if by doing so he would deprive his hosts' ancestor of its share? What I am suggesting is that the beliefs about the sanctity of the dead were a powerful force that kept the participants from breaking out of the ritual framework, encouraging them to be more cooperative and avoid conflict.

In analyzing the various functions of the mortuary ritual in any society, we should not lose track of its special nature, which distinguishes it from all other types of rituals. Funerary rites are more often past- and ancestors-oriented and hence more likely to be imbued with awesome sacredness. Rules of the mortuary complex are less likely to be broken than many others and often constitute a more conservative aspect of a sociocultural system. No matter how important their various sociopolitical functions are, mortuary rites must deal with fundamental cognitive and emotional predicaments confronting humankind.

As human beings everywhere, the Tlingit were faced with the problem of the inevitability of death. They too had to try to salvage some element or attribute of their deceased loved ones and thus deny the finality of human life. Their world view, particularly beliefs in reincarnation and the survival of other noncorporeal entities of the dead, gave them some powerful tools for creating a sense of symbolic immortality. The concept of *shagóon*, which enabled all the dead members of a matrilineal group to survive eternally through its collective symbolic representations, was equally powerful. The mortuary rites themselves, and especially the memorial potlatch, put this death-denying ideology into practice, bringing the living and the dead closer together than in any other context. In contrast to the funeral, which was unplanned and tragic, the potlatch was an attempt to transform death from an unpredictable rupture in the flow of social life into a planned, seasonal, and largely life-affirming event punctuating social time.

To accomplish this transformation the Tlingit mortuary rites had to affect the mourners' emotional state, helping the mourners overcome or, at least, assuage their grief. An impression I get from the accounts of nineteenth century funerals and potlatches, as well as my own observations, is of their effectiveness. To begin with, the structure of the mortuary cycle itself seems to reflect an indigenous theory of catharsis as well as some universal psychological manifestations of mourning. Thus, during the funeral, the mourners were first thrust into a state of social death, their physical suffering magnifying and reiterating their emotional pain. Having been put through this ordeal, they were then gradually released from their unfortunate condition, with the private and the more idiosyncratic expressions of mourning increasingly replaced by the more public and ritualized ones. The potlatch itself began with a cathartic reliving of the grief that had dominated the funeral, followed by its dramatic expulsion from the mourners' bodies and the ritual domain itself, and then by the various performances that emphasized life, vitality, and social reproduction.

While some of the major sad songs performed in the potlatch were the same as those used in the funeral, their function was different. Immediately following death, the mourners' grief was so strong that it probably overwhelmed them when they sang these songs or listened to speeches of condolence. In the potlatch, however, they were able to distance themselves somewhat from their loss, so that catharsis could be more readily achieved.[4]

The existence of an elaborate final memorial ritual, occurring at least one year after death, must have played an important role in helping the mourners deal with their grief. As Rosenblatt et al. (1976:90) concludes on the basis of a broad cross-cultural survey of mortuary rituals, final ceremonies put a time limit on the bereavement period. By having a well-defined and substantial time during which mourning norms allow or coerce expressions of grief, feelings may be vented, and the process of working through can occur. The resolution may well be facilitated by anticipation of a final ceremony. Where a final ceremony is to occur, the bereaved person goes through the mourning period knowing that there will be a point at which the expressions of feelings are expected to end. Consequently, during the time leading up to the final ceremony, the bereaved is likely to be going through psychological preparation for the postmourning period. At the final ceremony, he becomes publicly committed to finish with mourning.

The sequence and interaction between the performative genres of the potlatch emphasized its key theme—the transition from sadness to joy, from the hosts' being the   passive recipients of help and condolence to being the active givers of songs, speeches, spiritual power, food, and gifts. Attention to this sequential dimension of the entire cycle of mortuary rites and of the potlatch itself, as well as concentration upon the ritual as *performance*, is essential for understanding how it could affect the participants' emotional experience. Using Kapferer's (1979a:157) terminology, we could say that the Tlingit mortuary ritual performance was both representative and transformative. It was representative in the sense that it provided definitions of reality as understood by the mourners, a reality in which death reigned supreme. By the end of the funeral and especially in the memorial potlatch itself, their image of reality began to be replaced by one in which death could be overcome by the immortality and recycling of the deceased's spiritual entities and in which grief was diminished by the kind words of their opposites, cast in the role of loving and empathetic fathers.

The transformation of the mourners' definitions of reality was facilitated by their interaction with other potlatch participants whose emotions were not dominated by grief. The latter could experience other feelings stimulated by this exciting cultural celebration, such as pleasure or joy. With their help, the chief mourners were able to change their own perspective, at least to a certain extent, and construct a new social reality (compare Danforth 1982:139–149; see also Kapferer 1979b).

To understand the transformation of the mourners' emotional experience one must also pay attention to the specific performative genres used to express grief and offer condolence. In the Tlingit case, these were songs and dances, as well as ritualized oratory and other verbal genres. Music and dance, with their special time structure and internal coherence, have a potential for eliciting and expressing appropriate emotion, by "rendering as copresent and mutually consistent those dimensions of experience that might appear as distinct, opposed, even contradictory, from the rational perspective of the everyday world"

(Kapferer 1986:198–199). As I have shown, it was when the Tlingit had their ancestors' sacred regalia put on them by their loving paternal/affinal kin and then "imitated" those ancestors by singing and dancing, that they came closest to experiencing the immortality of the matrilineal group and the reciprocity between moieties—the two fundamental principles of their sociocultural system.

This ability of dance to move its performers and audience is, in large part, based on the involvement of the body. As Kapferer (1979a:159) suggests, "dance links the body as the center for, and the expressive medium of, individually felt emotion into the symbol system of gesture, converting individual expression as sign into symbol recognized and realized by others." The Tlingit seem to have been well aware of the importance of the bodily experiences in profoundly affecting the participants' emotions. Wearing ancestral regalia directly on one's skin, having valuables rubbed on the forehead, and engaging in other ritual acts involving the body helped transform unarticulated inner feelings into culturally sanctioned public emotions, and transform abstract cultural values into personally held beliefs and feelings. Hence such statements as "we are the crests of our ancestors, we are the life of our ancestors" are not only expressions of the ancestral ideology but of deeply felt emotion.

Of course, these speculations about the transformation the mourners' emotions and experience underwent in the mortuary rites are only tentative, since little information is available on how the mourners actually felt at the conclusion of the memorial potlatch. Yet those few references to this subject that could be located in the nineteenth century sources, combined with my own observations, suggest that cultural expectations and individual experience often matched. Thus, contemporary Tlingit often comment on a radical change in their emotions, once the funeral cycle has been completed. Some speak about a kind of psychological and physical rebirth, as well as a sense of peace with oneself (Kan 1979–1987).

This sense of well-being seems to come not only from having worked through one's grief with the help of the performative genres I have discussed but from other sources having to do with one's duties as a potlatch host rather than a mourner. Pride in being able to sponsor an impressive feast and distribute a large quantity of gifts, or a sense of satisfaction in having fulfilled one's duty and upheld the reputation of one's own name and clan, undoubtedly softened the pain of losing a loved one.[5]

Of course one should not be so naive as to expect the mortuary ritual to have had a positive effect on the feelings of each mourner. For some, the grief was too intense, so that none of the speeches of condolence or mourning songs could assuage it. For others, sadness was mixed with anger or other ambivalent feelings, and for them the ritual did not offer any solution. And for somebody else, the ritualized mourning could have been simply a burden forcing him to express emotions he did not really have.

Along the same lines, I would argue that the image of the social/cosmic order constructed in the Tlingit mortuary rites was only an ideal. Even within the ritual context itself and certainly outside of it, individual actors continued to see themselves and the world in somewhat different terms that those prescribed by the ancestral/mortuary complex. Despite the ritual's insistence on a single (hegemonic) vision of reality, some room remained for deviation from and disagreement with it. Thus, some of the mourners continued to grieve during and even after the memorial potlatch. For several generations, the deceased might remain in their memory as an unique individual and not just as a depersonalized ancestor or actor playing a role. He might even come back to confront them in their dreams, challenging the notion that all of the attributes of his social persona had already been recycled. Thus even this society, with its cyclical world view and the emphasis on the immutability of the ancestral order, could not completely overcome human individuality and linear time.[6] Perhaps, in the Tlingit case, we could speak of two models of time: a dominant one which was long-term and cyclical, and a subordinate one which was short-term and linear.[7]

Similarly, the potlatch did not completely eliminate ambiguity and conflict from interpersonal and intergroup relations. Some participants never accepted the outcome of these rituals, challenged them in private, and tried to undo them in the subsequent potlatches. While many of the actors did reach an agreement on the current distribution of power and prestige in their social universe, some new conflicts and ill feelings were generated, since the etiquette of rank could be used to shame an enemy, or an inadvertent slight could be interpreted as an intentional insult. Despite all the rhetoric of unity and solidarity of matrikin, the aristocracy maintained its own exchange system, in which high-status wealth items circulated. For some of the actors, these rites were not about death and mourning but about status-aggrandizement. For others, the potlatch's victory over death appeared rather unconvincing.

All of this should not surprise us. Ritual is not simply an event of social reconciliation which solves all problems and overcomes all contradictions. As Knauft (1985:272) has recently pointed out,

> In its active capacity, ritual transforms problems and creates new problematics through the very solution it offers. The ritual as such does not "work" conclusively or unambiguously in a functional or structural-functionalist sense. Rather, ritual works in the transitive and open-ended sense of "working upon" individual experience in ways that are creative and problematic as well as normatively legitimized.

The mortuary rites of the Tlingit could never completely overcome the specific contradictions of their society—hierarchy versus equivalence and competition versus cooperation—or bridge the universal opposition between death and life. Nevertheless I would argue that the mortuary complex and particularly the potlatch were the best solution the nineteenth century Tlingit seemed to have for maintaining the cognitive and the social orders. In this society that lacked any centralized authority and territorial/political organization beyond the matrilineage, the main alternative to this solution was war. The Tlingit did engage in war, but only to a point. Fighting with wealth and oratory prevailed over fighting with weapons.

Much of the power and effectiveness of the potlatch came from its strong aesthetic appeal. It dealt with the fundamental political, religious, and emotional issues through the medium of eloquent words and beautiful material objects created with maximum skill and perfected from one potlatch to the next. The pleasure and fun of participating in this ritual made it the most exciting and meaningful collective activity of the Tlingit people.

The Potlatch Lives

The strength, effectiveness, and stability of the mortuary ritual system has been attested by its ability to survive the changes brought about by the initial European contact and the more dramatic upheavals of the American era. This observation is not meant to suggest that the Tlingit mortuary complex and the larger sociocultural order were static. On the contrary, some modifications in the funeral and the potlatch, such as an increase in their scale, undoubtedly took place even before the European presence began to have an effect. There was also a potential within the culture and the mortuary rites themselves for a more radical transformation. Thus, I would hypothesize that if the fur trade era had not been cut short and the American political domination had not been imposed on the Tlingit, further social differentiation could have taken place, with the aristocracy closing its ranks even further, increasing its control over trade, warfare, and potlatching, and thus accumulating more wealth, especially such high-status items as slaves, coppers, and European goods. If such changes were to take place, they would have been channeled through and manifested in the potlatch and other rites of the mortuary cycle and would have undermined the ideology of matrilineal solidarity and equivalence.

Some scholars thought that all this had already happened by the mid- to late-nineteenth century. My own analysis indicates that this was not the case and that the potlatch had not become "an end in itself," as Oberg (1973:120–121) suggested. In the twentieth century, as wealth and prestige became increasingly available from sources outside the native society, as ties between matrikin began to weaken, and as the aristocracy's dominant role in social life started to diminish, one would have expected a parallel decline of the traditional mortuary rites. This was, in fact, what the missionaries predicted, as they fought to replace the indigenous funeral and memorial rites with Christian ones. Because of their direct pressure and due to major economic, sociopolitical, and ideological changes in the Tlingit world, the role of the matrilineal group in the mortuary ritual diminished and many aspects of the Christian way of death replaced traditional ones or were syncretized with them (Kan 1985; 1987).

Nevertheless, such basic elements of the nineteenth-century mortuary complex as the reliance on the opposite moiety to perform funerary services and its subsequent remuneration in the potlatch have survived, at least among the more conservative people. The sociopolitical significance of the potlatch has obviously diminished, while the importance of its commemorative dimension has increased. In a way, the potlatch has come full circle: it started out as a simple mortuary feast among the Proto-Athapaskan ancestors of the Tlingit, went through a period of being a total social phenomenon (with a particularly strong political emphasis), and has now, once again, become more of a memorial rite than an arena for waging major political battles.

The amazing survival of the memorial potlatch, despite decades of Euro-American harassment and criticism and the challenges the potlatch had to confront as the Tlingit world became increasingly different from what it had been in the nineteenth century, affirms, in my view, its cultural import and its intellectual and emotional centrality in the Tlingit experience, past and present. Even though the dead today dwell in the Christian Heaven and the living can pray to God to show mercy to their souls, many Tlingit still express their grief through the ancestral songs and find comfort in the condolence speeches of their opposites. The beauty of the Christian rites, which they are fond of, cannot replace the emotional and aesthetic appeal of the traditional ceremonialism, just as the status one gains by holding a well-paying job or being a leader in native and nonnative civic organizations cannot completely outshine the prestige one acquires by sponsoring a major potlatch and assuming the role of a lineage or clan head.

In the modern potlatch, which is the last stage in a cycle of mortuary rites that include a Christian funeral and, for many, a memorial feast borrowed from the Orthodox Church and syncretized with indigenous elements (Kan 1985; 1987), the Tlingit present an idealized image of their society and cosmos for themselves and some of the sympathetic non-Tlingit affines, friends, and allies whom they have chosen to invite. Today, however, this idealized image is much further removed from the reality of their daily life than it was one hundred years ago. This image is a model of the world in which pedigree still plays a central role, matrilineal kin still work together, and affines are still recruited from the opposite moiety, where the native language is spoken by everybody and where the Tlingit people still control their own destiny. In other words, the potlatch continues to link the past with the present, but has acquired an additional quality as a key symbol of a partially lost ancestral world of order and control (Kan 1989).

Consequently, keeping this ritual alive is essential not only because it still orders some aspects of the social universe and brings emotional comfort and satisfaction, but because it ensures the survival of at least some of the ancestral heritage which distinguishes the Tlingit in a positive way from members of the larger society in which they live. This idea could hardly be expressed any better than they way it was done by an elderly lineage chief who spoke at a potlatch I attended in 1980:

> If we did not perform the potlatch, we would have lost our Tlingit culture (*kusteeyí*, also 'way of life') a long time ago. This is what is holding up our Tlingit culture: the money that we bring out and the ceremonies that we conduct. Our past is sacred and there is no price tag on it. That is why we make such an effort to earn this money and then give it to our in-laws who help us in times of sorrow. This is what is keeping our Tlingit culture alive. Many things stem from our Tlingit culture and our [potlatch] ceremonies. Love for each other stems from it. Respect for each other stems for it. That is why it is so close to our hearts. (Kan 1979–1987)

Echoes of this elder's words can be heard in a poem written by a young man who no longer speaks Tlingit but has become involved in potlatching through his active participation in a traditional dance group for youngsters. In it he speaks about the old Tlingit and the universal human quest for symbolic immortality:

> As a man stands on earth
> he has only two reasons
> for being here:
> living and dying.
> And whatever comes between
> is just a form of being remembered.
>   (Dauenhauer and Dauenhauer 1981:75a;
> Kan 1979–1987)

NOTES

Introduction

1.   Knowledge of Russian and familiarity with Orthodoxy gave me an advantage in that project.

2.   It was not really a balanced exchange, since most of the knowledge came from the Tlingit; my efforts to reciprocate consisted mainly of translating, for those of my friends who were interested, Russian Orthodox documents that I had found in archives. Since none of the Tlingit, with one or two exceptions, can read Russian, it was a useful service; some of my translations were subsequently published in *Neek*, newsletter of the Sitka Community Association (the tribal government of the native people of the Sitka area) and in *Raven's Bones* (Hope 1982), a book published by the Association.

3.   The term "mortuary complex," used throughout this work, refers to the entire cycle of mortuary rituals, from the funeral to the potlatch. The "ancestral complex" is a broader term which includes all of the beliefs and ritual practices related to the dead. I prefer it to "ancestor cult" or "ancestor worship," since the Tlingit, as I will explain, never worshipped the dead, at least not in the manner of the peoples of Africa and East Asia.

4.   For an eloquent statement about the significance of the past in the life of the Tlingit, see de Laguna (1972:7).

5.   This is not to imply that the Tlingit currently in their fifties and sixties will not be able to preside over potlatches and other traditional activities, when

they themselves become the elders. In fact, some of them, including several of my best friends and informants, are fluent speakers of Tlingit and very knowledgeable about traditional issues. Nevertheless, with the passing of the present elders, who grew up in the early 1900s–1910s, much of the more esoteric knowledge and ritual expertise will be gone and the number of fluent speakers of the language will be significantly reduced (Dauenhauer and Dauenhauer 1987:x–xi; Kan 1989).

6.   Of course, all of these works, and particularly those of de Laguna and McClellan contain many insightful observations on the interarticulation of social organization, religion, and other aspects of Tlingit culture and society. For a strong defense of the classic monograph format, see de Laguna (1972:6).

7.   McClellan's (1954) article on the potlatch is the main exception. Some of her ideas inspired the present work.

8.   Thus Olson (1967:111), otherwise a sensitive ethnographer, made the following erroneous statement:

> Much of Tlingit ceremonialism centers on memorial festivals for the dead. In fact nearly all potlatches and feasts are given for or in the name of deceased kin of the clan. But religious factors overtly enter into Tlingit ceremonialism to only slight degree. This is in sharp contrast to, say, the Pueblo tribes or the native Australians. Instead, Tlingit ceremonies focus mainly on the social system; on maintaining and strengthening the status of family, household, and clan. They bear little relation to the supernatural world. *Their linkage with the memories of the dead and spirits of the deceased is only nominal.* (italics mine)

9.   See Kan (1986) for a more detailed critique of Rosman's and Rubel's work on the Tlingit; the ethnographic inaccuracy of their portrayal of other northern Northwest Coast societies is discussed by Adams and Kasakoff (1973); Vaughan (1975; 1984); and Boelscher (1982); see also Lévi-Strauss (1976:191–193; 1986). The value of the more recent comparative work of these two authors on Athapaskan, Northwest Coast, and Melanesian societies (Rosman and Rubel 1978; 1981; 1983; 1986) is discussed in Chapter X.

10.   For a review of these works, see Irwin (1977); Adams (1981); Boelscher (1982); and Kan (1986).

11.   I also use structural analysis to establish the underlying principles of Tlingit cosmology, ethnopsychology, and other ideational systems, as well as of oratory, songs, and other types of ritual performance.

12.   Compare Metcalf's (1982) approach to the mortuary rite of the Berawan of Borneo.

13.   As Ortner (1981:361) points out, the analysis of "egalitarian" systems entails identifying the hidden constraints on prestige-oriented action, while the analysis of hierarchies entails locating the hidden possibilities for such action (compare Myers 1986).

14. As Huntington and Metcalf (1979:98) point out in their discussion of Van Gennep's tripartite scheme of the rites of passage,

> In following this theoretical approach, it is necessary not merely to apply an old formula to new rituals, but in a sense to create anew the rites de passage in a dynamic relationship among the logic of the schema (transitions need beginnings and ends), biological facts (corpses rot), and culturally specific symbolizations.

15. Goldman (1975) does try to incorporate the dead into his analysis of Kwakiutl religion, which he sees as the foundation and the essence of Kwakiutl politics. The latter, however, is only peripheral to his study.

16. The only existing cross-cultural study of grief and mourning (Rosenblatt et al. 1976), despite methodological problems typical for a large-scale literature survey, did establish a series of universals and near-universals (e.g., crying) in human response to the death of a significant other.

17. Only in McIlwraith's (1948, vol. I) account of the Bella Coola memorial potlatch could I find references to the ritual's impact on the mourners' emotion. Thus, for example, his discussion of condolence speeches delivered at the Bella Coola funeral mentions that they "clearly helped the mourners to bear up under their grief" (McIlwraith, vol. I:447–448) This fact was emphasized by several informants and in addition the ethnographer himself was able to observe it on several occasions.

18. In referring to this biological substrate, Gerber (1985:123) uses the term "basic affect," which she defines as "an inborn psychophysiological program, which is activated by cultural evaluations of external situations, defined and modified by cultural concepts, and expressed in culturally appropriate behaviors." Others have suggested that in the ritual context psychobiological sensations become culturally constituted emotions, once they are defined and shared with other actors (Karp 1977). For the most comprehensive recent survey of these issues see Lutz and White (1986).

19. Of course, as Gerber (1985:122) points out, this innate psychobiological patterning is always culturally defined and is probably never directly experienced.

20. Despite a bad reputation that psychological testing has acquired in the eyes of many cultural anthropologists, some recent studies (e.g., Poole 1982) demonstrate that a careful use of testing that tries to minimize its (Western) cultural bias can be a good supplement to participant observation, interviewing, and other non-psychological methods.

21. Of course, this is a delicate task where direct interviewing might be particular callous in relation to the mourner and harmful for one's research. In my own experience, the mourners would often volunteer comments about their emotions, once they had decided that the ethnographer is sensitive and has empathy for them.

22. R. Rosaldo (1984:187) has been the most outspoken critic of this approach, arguing that "the work of grieving, probably universally, occurs both within obligatory ritual acts and in more everyday settings where people find themselves alone or with close kin."

23. To give an example from a recent potlatch of the two brothers that co-sponsored it, one was clearly preoccupied with his own and his family's status while the other was so deep in his sorrow that his actions, including emptying his bank account completely to cover the costs of the ritual, appeared to be motivated more by his grief than any other emotional, religious or political factors. The generosity of both men was appreciated, although the latter received more public and private sympathy and gained additional moral capital. At the same time, a distant relative of theirs, who tried to justify a role in the potlatch that was out of proportion with his rank and degree of relatedness to the deceased, was treated with some suspicion and was criticized in the discussions following the event (Kan 1979–1987).

24. It would be very interesting and important to document and analyze the more specific changes of the fur trade era, but that is not possible on the basis of the published accounts by European traders only. Rather, it would require an extensive analysis of the unpublished records of the Russian-American Company and the Hudson's Bay Company. For an early attempt to assess the fur trade's impact on the cultures of the entire Northwest Coast, see Wike's (1951) doctoral dissertation, based mainly on published and some archival materials.

25. At present, all of the early archaeological site data comes from the off-shore islands. Investigations are needed on the mainland to determine the time of the earliest occupations and the type of subsistence pattern. The information on area prehistory presented here comes from a symposium,"Man and Land in Southeastern Alaska: Current Research Perspectives," held in 1987 as part of the 14th Annual Conference of the Alaska Anthropological Association (*Newsletter of the Alaska Anthropological Association*, vol. 12, no. 1:7).

26. The current Tlingit population is roughly estimated to be over 15,000, including persons residing outside Southeast Alaska.

27. The most detailed analysis of Tlingit subsistence and economy is found in Oberg (1973); see also de Laguna (1972). For an interesting recent discussion of traditional food, written by Tlingit themselves, see Jacobs and Jacobs (1982).

28. De Laguna (1983:82) lists these local groups as follows: *Southern Tlingit*: Tongass, Sanya, Stikine, Henya, Klawak, Kuyu, Kake; *Northern Tlingit*: Sumdum, Taku, Angoon, Auk, Sitka, Chilkat, Chilkoot, Hoonah; *Gulf Coast*: Dry Bay, Yakutat, Controller Bay. She also mentions two *Inland Tlingit* bands (Atlin and Teslin), established by some coastal Tlingit who had migrated, in search of furs, into the Yukon Territory/British Columbia border area in the post-contact era. They retained strong cultural ties with the coast, reinforced by continued trading and intermarriage. In this study I use Inland Tlingit ethnography

reported by McClellan (1975) in a major recent publication (see also McClellan 1981).

29. This following sketch of aboriginal Tlingit sociopolitical organization relies heavily on de Laguna's (1952; 1972; 1983) work.

30. One clan, the Neix.ádi, married into both moieties, this intermarriage was probably due to the clan's foreign origin (de Laguna 1983:73).

31. De Laguna (1983:8) argues that by treating clan heads and other native leaders as autocratic "chiefs" of entire communities, the Europeans and Americans strengthened chiefly power and authority. Consequently, it was in areas where Russian, British, and American influence was the strongest, that chieftainship became most highly developed. I must point out, however, that despite this, chiefs still had rather little influence outside their own clans.

32. Discussion of these changes (presented in Drucker 1958:7–16; de Laguna 1972 passim; Tollefson 1976:235–321; Hinckley 1982; Kan 1985; 1987) is beyond the scope of this work.

chapter one

1. This composite picture of the nineteenth century Tlingit funeral and potlatch is based on the following sources listed in chronological order: Veniaminov ([1840] 1984:419–424); Markov (1849:37–38); Holmberg ([1855–1863] 1985:23–24); Cracroft ([1870] 1981:28); Anonymous (1877); Krause ([1885] 1956:155–166); Donskoi (1893:856–857); Gould (1895); Kamenskii ([1906] 1985:77–79); Swanton (1908:429–431, 434–443); Shotridge (1917:106–109); Emmons (1920–1945, ch. VI; Shukoff's Account: 4–8); McClellan (1954); Teichmann (1963 [1925]:234–243); Billman (1964); Olson (1967:58–69); de Laguna (1972:531–539, 609–651); Kan (1979–1987; 1986).

2. Compare Willard's description of an infant's funeral she witnessed in 1882, while serving as a Presbyterian missionary among the northern Tlingit of Chilkat:

> The small face was painted with vermilion, the head turbaned with a bright handkerchief, and every article of good clothing he possessed, together with what I had given him, was on him now; and, besides, they had made mittens and tied them on his hands. In a little bag hung about his neck were charms for his safety and a paper containing a quantity of red powder for use on the way. The body was placed in a sitting posture, with the knees drawn up against the breast and held in place by a bandage. Then over and around all were beautiful white woolen blankets enough to make any mother's heart comfortable. (1884:251)

3. For the most detailed eyewitness accounts of cremation, see Anonymous (1877:374); Emmons (1920–1945, Ch. VI:19–22); Gould (1895); Keithahn (1955). The only photograph of cremation known to me, was taken by Emmons in

Sitka and is located in the Anthropological Archives of the American Museum of Natural History.

4.   The only uncremated remains discovered by the Europeans were probably those of shamans (see Chapter V).

5.   Such structures were seen and described by La Perouse in 1786 and Beresford in 1787 (quoted in de Laguna 1972:539–540).

6.   According to native traditions recorded by Emmons (1920–1945, ch. VI:22) and Olson (1933–1954, notebook 1:48; 1967:45–46), the mortuary and memorial poles came to the Tlingit from the Haida (see also Barbeau 1950:5–13). In fact, a freestanding totem pole was not typical the Tlingit, with the exception of the southern groups which bordered on and were more influenced by the Haida and the Tsimshian. Unlike their southern neighbors, the Tlingit preferred to carve their crests on the corner posts and the screen located inside the house (Shotridge and Shotridge 1913:94; Jonaitis 1986:17–18).

7.   Most of the sources describe the memorial potlatch as a single ceremony. However, several of Olson's (1967:60–63) informants insisted that the death of any free person, and especially an aristocrat, called for four "crying" and four "joy" feasts. The fourth crying feast and all of the joy feasts they described resemble the memorial potlatch outlined here. The four joy feasts seem to be a single potlatch consisting of four consecutive feasts. Since the number eight represented wholeness and completeness and was the favorite ritual number, I suspect that these eight feasts represent an ideal, rather than a typical case.

chapter two

1.   For a recent discussion of these analytic issues and their ethnographic illustration, see Comaroff (1985).

2.   In the Tlingit language, body parts, like kinship terms, are used only with possessive pronouns (see Chapter III).

3.   (A)daa is a locative noun, often used as a suffix, meaning circumference, outer side of a round object, place around something, etc. (see Boas 1917).

4.   See Drucker (1950:222; 283–286) for a discussion of the importance of this notion in all of the Northwest Coast cultures.

5.   Although the Yakutat Tlingit cremated salmon bones, instead of returning them to the water, the rationale for this act was the same—to allow the spirit of a dead fish to be reincarnated in the body of another one (de Laguna 1972:824).

6.   An Inland Tlingit shaman, who allegedly visited heaven during a trance, reported being told by the "assistant to God" that in the past, to restore a cremated person back to life, all of his bones had to be gathered and put together (McClellan 1975:558).

7. The joints of the body figured just as prominently in Tlingit art as the skeleton. The artist sometimes omitted the representation of the skeleton per se and simply indicated the point at which one bone met another by means of a face, eye, or ovoid (compare de Laguna 1972:761–762; Jonaitis 1986:131).

8. Thus, the various magical practices that the body of an adolescent girl was subjected to in her puberty confinement fell into periods of eight days, usually with reference to the eight bones, and were said to strengthen or complete them (de Laguna 1954:175).

9. The shaman wore a variety of necklaces made of dangling bone rods, which made a noise when he danced. He also wore the bones of those creatures whose power he wished to appropriate (e.g., de Laguna 1972:689). Animal bones were also used in fortune-telling (de Laguna 1972:807–808).

10. Story and Naish (1973:301) list the following verbs derived from the same stem *saa*: *ya-saa* (tr) "to name, to call by name"; *di-saa* (in), "to breathe"; *x'a-ya-saa*, "to call on spirits" (from *x̱'é*, "mouth").

11. Compare Swanton (1908:460): "The soul of a living person was called *ḵaa toowú* or *wáa sá ituwatee* ('what feels'), because when a person's feeling is gone he is dead."

12. The exact location of the (*ḵaa*) *toowú* is not clear, although it is possible that it occupied the entire space within the body. Some obscure references to the intestines and the liver as the seat of emotion, and the head as the location of thoughts were also made in the past, but can no longer be retrieved (compare de Laguna 1972:176). Although a distinction was drawn between thinking and feeling, both seem to have originated from the same undifferentiated source.

13. Orthodox missionaries used this term to express the Christian notion of "spirit," particularly the "Holy Spirit," which they translated as *L ulitoogu Ḵaa Yakgwahéiyagu* (literally, "Spirit of a Pure/Clean Person;" Donskoi 1895). More recently, Protestant missionary linguists also glossed it as "spirit" (Story and Naish 1963:77).

14. Russian missionary Veniaminov, who compiled a small Tlingit-Russian dictionary and made the first attempt to translate Christian prayers from the Church Slavonic into Tlingit, glossed it as "soul" (Russian *dusha*; 1846:50); a similar gloss was offered by Story and Naish (1963:77).

15. This association between the face of the person and one of his noncorporeal attributes is also suggested by the taboo on running in front of the deceased, imposed on the children, and the reluctance of the adults to pass by the front of the house where a body lay in state (Kan 1979–1987).

16. In addition, each human being was believed to have a guardian spirit, called (*ḵaa*) *kinaayéigi*, "person's spirit above," from *yéik*, "shaman's tutelary spirit" located outside the body, above the head. It acted as a protector as well as a moral force, monitoring the person's adherence to the norms of proper behavior. If the latter were violated, the *kinaayéigi* abandoned the person, ex-

posing him to misfortune, illness, or death. Every human being lost his *kinaayéigi* at the time of death. Despite an obvious resemblance between this notion and the Christian concept of the guardian angel, there are reasons to believe that it was indigenous, since the early Russian missionary as well as the secular late nineteenth-century American accounts mention it (e.g., Veniaminov 1984:397; Kamenskii 1985:72; Emmons quoted in de Laguna 1972:813). In more recent times, this spirit has been identified either with the guardian angel (among the Orthodox) or the Christian God himself (among the Protestants; Kan 1979–1987).

17. Emmons refers to the two scratching stones or amulets he obtained in Yakutat as *tes-sate*, which could be derived from *té*, "stone" and *s'aatí*, "master" (quoted in de Laguna 1972:666–667). Additional terms for such objects, reported by de Laguna (1972:666–667) are *daaxás'aa*, "body-scratcher" and *ḵaa x'adaatteiyí*, "around someone's mouth stone." According to some sources (e.g., Krause 1956:102), many Tlingit wore a small stone around their neck as an amulet, which was probably used as a scratcher.

18. Similar to other living beings (animals, plants, and some phenomena that we would call natural), rocks had spirits within them, called *té ḵwáani*, "stone people," compare *x̱áat kwáani*, "salmon people."

19. In addition to being "heavier" than the bodies of young people, those of the old were probably seen as "drier," especially after the men had ceased their sexual activity and the women had passed the menopause. However, the frailty of the body that came in the old age was expressed by a euphemistic term *di-naaḵw*, "to rot," as in *ax sáni de yaa ndanáḵw*, "my paternal uncle is already really old" (Story and Naish 1973:176).

20. Compare Boas (1916:447) on the centrality of shame in Tsimshian culture.

21. Drucker (1950:205) reported that the infant's face was shaped but gives no details of this procedure.

22. Even a disfigured corpse was considered an embarrassment to the deceased himself and his matrikin. Thus, Teichmann (1963:215–216) reported visiting a Tlingit house in 1868 where the body of a hunter who had suffered a fatal accident was lying in state. The entire body was covered with a blanket and the European visitors were not allowed to uncover it to see the mutilated corpse. Angry victors sometimes mutilated their slain enemies' bodies.

23. Babies, even the unborn ones, seemed to have a mind or will of their own. Thus, the cravings of the pregnant woman were thought to be the will of the unborn child. If these cravings were not satisfied, the baby might become ill, or it migth decide it did not want to be born and die before birth. Of course, since each newborn was believed to possess a reincarnated soul of a matrilineal ancestor, it is not surprising that infants were seen as persons, albeit not fully socialized (compare de Laguna 1965:5). This explains why, if a pregnant woman died, the fetus was buried separately (Emmons 1920–1945, ch. VI:25).

24. According to de Laguna (1965:15), this instruction began when the child could talk, while Olson's (1956:678) informant said that instruction happened as soon as the child "came to himself."

25. The concept of "power" (*latseen*) seems to have been central to the Tlingit culture, although we lack sufficient information to substantiate this. According to McClellan (1975:70), the same concept, whether consciously formulated or not, "lies at the heart" of the Inland Tlingit and other southern Yukon cultures.

26. Aristocratic families could "wash away" their children's blemishes by giving away property (see Chapter IV).

27. A good illustration of this is the self-control and self-denial that the adolescent girl was supposed to practice while in her puberty confinement. During the ceremony of her "coming out," these qualities were tested, when somebody in the audience yelled "fire!" A well-trained girl was supposed to ignore the warning and proceed with the ritual (Knapp and Childe 1896:56).

28. The importance of the face in Tlingit ethnopsychology is illustrated by a wide use of human and animal faces to depict the entire creature. Faces of animals or just their eyes were also used to depict the indwelling anthropomorphic souls or a special power attributed to a certain body part, e.g., small faces inside the ears of a bear represented this animal's unique hearing ability (compare de Laguna 1972:761–763; Jonaitis 1986:131–132).

29. The painting of clan crests on the face is discussed in Chapter IV.

30. Swanton (1908:437) mentions that a certain type of labret, the long one, was given to the woman by a man who was in love with her.

31. Compare the Tsimshian practice of ridiculing a woman who had no ear perforations as being "without ears" (Garfield 1939:194).

32. The shaman's main source of power was a bundle containing a tongue of a land otter or another animal he had killed during his first power and vision quest (Jones 1914:164; Jonaitis 1978:66).

33. According to Oberg (1973:45), at betrothal an aristocratic woman sometimes cut her hair and presented it to her groom's family as a precious gift. It was later displayed at the wedding ceremony and finally became an emblem (possibly a minor crest) of the husband's clan. One such emblem is now located in the University Museum of the University of Pennsylvania (see Shotridge 1929).

34. According to my most reliable informant, a special ceremony, similar to the pubescent girl's coming out party following her confinement, was held when the boy's hair was tied in this fashion for the first time. It was a sign of his maturity, since for a young man warfare was the most glorious activity. This is an interesting piece of information, especially since so little is known about the male puberty rites among the Tlingit (Kan 1979–1987). Garfield (1939:196–197) reports a similar observance among the Tsimshian.

35. Among the Inland Tlingit, the shaman frequently slept with his patient's clothing, which was a symbolic substitute for him (McClellan 1975:547).

36. Many Tlingit men, and especially aristocrats, had special boxes for their amulets, magical substances and other objects utilized to ensure and increase the owner's luck and power (see Chapter IV).

37. The parallel between the "eight long bones" of the body and the posts of the house is clearly expressed in the following information obtained by Swanton (1908:437), "When he was about to undertake any task, a man who had eight house posts in his house had to fast eight days, one for each post." The homology between the human body, the house, and other containers, including the universe as a whole, is discussed in more detail in my own earlier work (Kan 1978) as well as in Peter Stone's (1971) unpublished manuscript. Compare MacDonald (1981) on a general Northwest Coast human body/house/cosmos homology and his own (1983) application of this model to the Haida material. In addition, several recent symbolic analyses of the role of boxes and other containers in Kwakiutl and Tsimshian culture have suggested ideas similar to those presented here (see Walens 1981; Seguin 1984; 1985). Thus Seguin (1984:113) points out that the Tsimshian saw humans as container images. One of the terms for the chief's speaker was galdmalgyax, a "box of speeches." She also claims that the emphasis on containers in Tsimshian images, metaphors, and even the set of locative proclitics which include terms suggestive of the house as one of the central metaphors in the system support her interpretation (Seguin:115).

38. Neighboring coastal tribes whose material culture, social organization, and ethos resembled those of the Tlingit were seen as morally superior to the Interior Athapaskans, Eskimos, and others who did not share those characteristics.

chapter three

1. See de Laguna (1960:17–18) for an insightful discussion of the effect of the clan on the Tlingit sense of history and geography, and their interrelationship.

2. In general, moiety relatives were also supposed to be treated that way, but their unity and solidarity was seen as being weaker than those between clan mates.

3. There are accounts of aristocratic women committing suicide rather than having to witness such cowardly behavior on the part of their sons or brothers (Kan 1979–1987).

4. In addition, the Tlingit tend to be reluctant to discuss their beliefs about procreation. Such beliefs often form the core of indigenous ethnopsychologies (e.g., Huntington and Metcalf 1979:98–101; Poole 1985:193–194, 200–201).

5.   The closeness of the ego's ties with both the maternal and the paternal relatives is also illustrated by the absence of the possessive suffix at the end of *every* kinship term, e.g., *aχ káak,* "my maternal uncle"; *aχ éesh,* "my father"; *aχ shát,* "my wife." Like body parts, which were also used without the possessive suffix, relatives were seen as one's inalienable possessions. This also explains why kinship terms had to be used with a possessive pronoun.

6.   The addressee, expected to be flattered by this comment, was supposed to respond by saying, "From among you, I look the same," and by giving the speaker a small gift to indicate being pleased by this reminder of his or her paternal ancestry (Olson 1967:15–16).

7.   The reference to a carving suggests that the father contributed to the child's "outside."

8.   Although the person's maternal ancestry was clearly this term's primary connotation, in its broader sense, *shagóon* could also refer to the paternal one. In some contexts, it could also mean the ancestry, origin, and destiny of the entire Tlingit nation, although this particular usage has become more common only in this century, as the Tlingit began forging a stronger sense of ethnic identity.

9.   Twentieth century Tlingit use *shagóon* to refer to "God," "God's Law," or the "Law(s) of Nature" (de Laguna 1972:813–814; Kan 1979–1987). The first use of this concept to refer to the Christian God is found in Veniaminov's (1846) Tlingit language dictionary.

10.   Compare Goldman's (1975:62–63) discussion of the Kwakiutl crests.

11.   The ownership of crests was so essential that the Tlingit extended clan kinship on the basis of crest correspondence to the neighboring groups (e.g., Haida, Tsimshian, and similar tribes) and even to Europeans. Thus, for example, members of the Eagle Clan adopted the U.S. Navy as their relatives, because of the American Eagle depicted on their uniforms (de Laguna 1972:450).

12.   Thus the Kaagwaantaan, famous for their bellicosity, displayed a special "angry scowl" in public, to bear out their reputation and were also reputed to have high foreheads and to accentuate this feature by plucking some of the hair at the margin of the scalp (Olson 1956:687).

13.   The discussion of names is based primarily on the work of de Laguna (1972:781–790) as well as Veniaminov (1984:415–416), Emmons (1920–1945 passim), Oberg (1973:46–47), Olson (1933–1954 passim) and Kan (1979–1987).

14.   On the other hand, more than one ancestral spirit could be reincarnated in the same person (see Chapter V).

15.   For example, when a white man I knew was adopted into the lineage of his close friend, she gave him a "big name" of her recently deceased brother. Another one of her brother's "big names" had been bestowed upon his own son's young son earlier. While the child was believed to be the reincarnation of the deceased, the adopted non-Tlingit was not. However, his sister explained

that one of the reasons she had given him the name was that both he and the deceased were interested in learning. She also stated that, having spent a lot of time with her, following the death of her brother, her new friend was, in a way, replacing the deceased (Kan 1979–1987).

16.   Compare Goldman (1975:26–45; 56–62) on Kwakiutl and Halpin (1984b) and Seguin (1985:114–115) on Tsimshian names. Despite the similarity between the Tlingit view and use of names/titles and that of other Northwest Coast societies, one fundamental difference existed. When valuable names outnumbered their potential legitimate holders, the Tsimshian and the Haida would sometimes try to solve the problem by adopting members of the opposite moiety, usually close paternal relatives (Seguin 1985:76–87; Halpin 1984b; Boelscher 1985; Stearns 1984). The Tlingit, however, would never violate the fundamental rule of matrilineal descent and moiety exogamy (see Chapter X).

17.   The birth name was the one most closely tied to its owner's body and idiosyncratic persona. Thus, Emmons (1920–1945, Ch. VI:5) reports that, like bodily secretions and clothing, one's birth name was concealed from strangers for fear of its owner being bewitched.

18.   The Tsimshian say that "names make you heavy" (Halpin 1984b:59) and that they are "put on" and sometimes "taken off" a person (Seguin 1984:114).

19.   Among the Tsimshian, Seguin (1984:114–115) argues, "personness is grounded in names, rather than vice versa—the two names held by an individual are two separate social persons."

20.   For more information on the origin and meaning of names, see de Laguna (1972:788–790).

21.   The only type of name that alluded to the paternal side of the individual's social identity was the teknonymous one given to a male. It consisted of the child's name plus the word éesh, "father." As de Laguna (1972:784) points out, normally or, perhaps, originally teknonymous names were like nicknames derived from the name of the oldest or the favorite child. However, there was a tendency to pass these names through the maternal line, especially if the child became a famous or high-ranking person. However, in order to have a right to acquire such a name, a man had to marry into the same lineage or clan as its previous owners had done. For example, if a man of the lineage X wished to have the name "father of Y" and if that name belonged to the lineage Z, he had to marry a woman of that lineage. Thus, teknonymy strengthened the preference for marrying into the same matrilineal group as one's own matrilineal ancestors had done in the past.

22.   Recently Dauenhauer and Dauenhauer (1987:28–29) offered an interpretation of shagóon that differs somewhat from de Laguna's and mine. They suggest that shagóon referred primarily to the human ancestors of the matrilineal group, whereas another term, shuká, encompassed the human ancestors (shagóon), their totemic crests, and the material representations of those crests

(*at.óow*). In addition, in their view, *shagóon* referred mainly to the past, while *shuká* was both past and future.

23. Sex-related jealousy was often a real cause of strife, rather than just its rationalization.

24. An example of such an unresolved conflict was a bitter dispute between two clans of the Raven moiety residing in Sitka, both of which claimed the frog as their crest. One of the two was the original founder of the community, while the other began settling there in the nineteenth century. The conflict reached its climax in the early 1900s, when the latter, having become equal to the former in wealth and numbers, began openly displaying the disputed crest and using it in potlatches. Only the interference of American authorities prevented the resulting violence from escalating into warfare (see de Laguna 1972:288–291; Hinckley 1982:248–249; Kamenskii 1985:117–22).

25. Thus, for example, Olson (1967:38) reported that the first chief to see a sailing vessel put it on his totem pole, so that in time the object would become his clan's crest.

26. Thus, if a certain warrior turned out to be a coward, the head of his clan would forbid the use of his name by any member of the clan or, at least, the males and from that time on, it either died or became a female name (Kan 1979–1987).

27. This was a fairly slow process, since it took several generations to significantly alter a name's status. The highest ranking names, given to lineage and clan heads and their immediate matrikin, tended to remain on the top of the scale for many generations.

chapter four

1. The moiety affiliation of the person addressed as "my grandparent" could be established from the context of the conversation.

2. Tlingit kinship terminology makes a distinction between a man's older and younger brother, and a woman's older and younger sister, but does not indicate the relative age of the two siblings of the opposite sex.

3. The woman too had some authority over her own and her sisters' children, but the mother-child relationship was seen as more indulgent than that between the man and his maternal nephews and nieces.

4. Compare similar views on the limited power and authority of the Tlingit lineage and clan heads expressed by Litke ([1835] 1948:73) and Golovin ([1862] 1979:28).

5. As one of my own informants put it, "a person of high rank in his own village may not amount to much in another one" (Kan 1979–1987).

6. Compare Drucker (1939:141) and Fried (1967:120).

7.   Giddens (1971:166–167) also points out that, "Stratification by status is not, for Weber, simply a 'complication' of class hierarchies: on the contrary, status groups, as differentiated from classes, are of vital significance in numerous phases of historical development. . . . Both class and status group membership may be a basis of social power."

8.   Goldman's (1970) classification of Polynesian societies divides them into "traditional," and "stratified." The former are the least complex in terms of organization of the rank system, and the latter are the most complex; in addition, the societies located between the two types are labelled "open" (compare Ortner 1981:403). The Tlingit system of rank is closer to that of the "traditional" Polynesian societies. Compare Goldman's (1975:1) discussion of the similarity between the "primitive aristocracies" of Polynesia and the Kwakiutl.

9.   Compare Boelscher's recent assertion that "the 'symbolic life' of the Northwest Coast Indians—myth, ritual, art, religion, totemic representations—has received much ethnographic and analytic attention, but has usually been studied and presented as dissociated from the dynamics of sociopolitical life" (1985:3). She goes on to argue that only if we take into the account the modes and properties of symbolic communication can we grasp the nature of the political process in Northwest Coast societies.

10.   According to Garfield (1939:194), among the Tsimshian,

> "Children of high ranking or wealthy parents were involved in the complexity of the potlatch system from birth. . . . Among the early public events given for children were the perforation ceremonies. These were: the perforation of the lobe and helix of the ear for the wearing of ear ornaments for both boys and girls; the perforation of the lower lip for girls and of the septum of the nose for boys.

Compare also Murdock's (1936) discussion of the Haida perforation ceremonies.

11.   For the most detailed account of this ceremony, see Olson (1933–1954, notebook 1:15–16). It appears that the father's involvement in this ritual was couched in the idiom of the "love and respect" he had for his wife and children. In fact, his wife might have been seen as the official sponsor, although he contributed the larger share of the wealth. Thus the principle of paying the opposite moiety for its ritual services was maintained, although, in reality, much of the property distributed came from the guests' own maternal relative.

12.   Veniaminov (1984:424) says that in the 1830s there were no Tlingit in Sitka with the full complement of ear perforations, and only a few with two or three of them.

13.   After the arrival of the Europeans, the Tlingit aristocracy quickly identified the clothing of the newcomers' leaders as more valuable and began wearing it. According to Litke (1948:59), who visited Sitka in the late 1820s, the Tlingit chiefs wore the Russian military uniforms of the latest style and were

determined to have their wives wear the Russian women's clothing. Khleb-nikov (1976:30) supported this information but also mentioned that European attire was worn only on those occasions when the Tlingit aristocrats interacted with the Russian civil and military authorities.

14. According to Olson (1933–1954, notebook 9:1), among the southern Tlingit of the Klawock area, aristocratic children not only had their hands tattooed but the ankles and the chest as well. This suggests the marking of the "four long bones" plus the center of the body and parallels the ritual marking of the newly constructed house's corners and fireplace, mentioned earlier.

15. *Tléil li-took*, literally means "not rancid, not too potent [to taste bad]" (Story and Naish 1973:48; 56). The missionaries combined it with the term for "spirit" to translate "Holy Spirit" into Tlingit as *L ulitoogu Ḵaa yakgwahéiyagu*.

16. Compare Swanton's description of a box with a specially potent "wealth medicine" owned by chief Katlian of Sitka (1908:448).

17. This identification of the aristocracy with physical and moral strength (*latseen*) is reiterated further by the term *x'alitseen*, "it is expensive, valuable, or precious" (Story and Naish 1973:297).

18. Compare this notion with an Inland Tlingit belief that, to the shaman, the body of a patient with a minor illness appeared transparent, while that of a seriously ill one looked opaque (Emmons 1920–1945, chapter XI:26).

19. The treatment of a dead aristocrat's skull resembled that of a slain bear, the most powerful and anthropomorphic of all the animals (Drucker 1950:287–288).

20. The cultural logic of preserving the heads of slain warriors is discussed in the next chapter.

21. The *aanyátx'i* were expected to be more knowledgeable and eloquent, but to ensure that their performance met these high standards, each chief had an advisor, who stood behind him during a potlatch ready to help if the chief was at a loss for words (de Laguna 1972:466).

22. Boelscher (1985:96) reports that this was also the case among the Haida.

23. Compare the special relationship between a Cree head of a hunting group and the animals inhabiting its territory (Tanner 1979).

24. Despite the importance of the aristocracy's role in warfare, a war party could not function without a shaman who predicted the outcome of battles and strengthened the warriors with his superhuman power.

25. For more details on this topic, see de Laguna (1972:461–469).

26. Compare an emphasis on modesty and the discouragement of bragging in the Haida theory of aristocratic conduct (Boelscher 1985:147–152).

27. As, for example, in the statement, *Lingítx haa sateeyí, sh yáa ayatoodinéi*, "we respect ourselves as Tlingit."

28. Boelscher (1985:134–135) explains it as follows:

> The emphasis on respect implies that not only genealogical position and the formal distribution of property are necessary concomitants of rank validation, but the public evaluation of a person's social position depends also on his/her social conduct, which in turn requires knowledge of what is expected. Being respected, then, is tied to a network of social and ritual obligation. . . . Respect for self gained by showing respect for others has a moral dimension in that it circumscribes the moral conduct expected of a high-born person. Respect is gained through ritual observance in social intercourse and in intercourse with nature, through being generous, not insulting to others, refraining from excess and gluttony, [and] choosing the proper words for proper occasions.

Compare Blackman (1982:141): "'Respect for self' represents a traditional behavioral ideal in Haida culture. The concept embodies proper speech, proper etiquette, proper behavior, respectability, and self-assurance."

29. A man would seek a prospective son-in-law who combined high rank with hard work; the rough skin on his hands was evidence of the latter (Swanton 1908:429; Kan 1979–1987).

30. In Shotridge's account of the procedures involved in the marriage of *aanyátx'i* (based, probably, on his own experience), the groom's bride-service is performed by his male matrikin (1929:137).

31. Lazy persons were clearly looked down upon; however, in stories and myths, orphans and others who had low status because of their birth were treated sympathetically. Katishan, Swanton's chief informant, even said that "years ago it always happened that the poor people to whom others were unkind brought luck to the village" (1909:192). However, such view might have been somewhat atypical, since Katishan's thinking was definitely affected by Christianity. At the same time, early Russian sources mention the support given to the orphans and the destitute by the aristocracy (e.g., Litke 1948:75).

32. Compare Boelscher (1985:115) on similar ideas in Haida culture.

33. Compare Colson's (1953:202–205) description of the Makah views of rank distinctions in their pre- and early-contact society. While they admitted that the classes of commoners and aristocrats existed, Colson found little agreement on the criteria by which individuals were assigned to one or the other. This weakening, in many of the post-contact Northwest Coast societies, of generally accepted standards of what constituted a valid claim to high status might have also been caused by the rise, in the second half of the nineteenth century, of wealthy commoners to the top of the hierarchy. With the weakening of the indigenous forms of social control, Colson's twentieth-century informants can now exaggerate their own status, without the fear of censure, especially when they talk to a non-native, including an anthropologist (Kan 1979–1987).

34. Unlike other scholars of the Tsimshian, Adams sees the rights to resources as the main criteria for assigning an individual to one of these classes. Thus,

chiefs, princes, and nobles lived on their own land. Commoners lived on the land belonging to other Gitksan, and slaves were aliens who had no rights to land at all (1973:38). This emphasis on land ownership and use might be partially the result of the Gitksan intensive involvement in fur trapping and hunting.

35. Halpin (1973:43) indicates that the Coast Tsimshian chiefs were characterized as being "strong," "heavy," and "solid like a rock." They "took pity" on the commoners, which meant that they fed and protected them. In return, the latter had to "respect" the chiefs. Both Halpin (1973:43) and Seguin (1985:6) emphasize that beliefs about superhuman power and the spirits of the ancestors were, in the native view, the foundation of aristocratic status and prestige, and that the main duties of the chief were religious in nature. Another recent work points out that, among the Haida, rank was "tied to a wider system of symbolic classification, associating aspects of food, space, clothing, ritual pollution, and the ethic of industry with attributes of superiority or inferiority" (Boelscher 1985:135). This work also shows that no sharp distinction was made between the chief's power and control over his junior kin and his possession of magical (superhuman) power obtained by observing rules of ritual purity (Boelscher:120–125). Finally, the symbolic analyses of the Kwakiutl religion and world view undertaken by Goldman (1975) and Walens (1981) show the centrality of ideas about superhuman power, and other fundamental "religious" concepts and categories in the Kwakiutl view of the aristocracy. All of these authors agree that the aristocrat was the ideal person, whose behavior was to be emulated by the rest of the people. In Halpin's (1973:11) words "to be a high-ranking Tsimshian man was to be a Tsimshian in the fullest sense the culture afforded." It should be pointed out, however, that among all of the Tsimshian and most other Northwest Coast tribes, chiefs and aristocrats played the leading role in the ceremonies involving the demonstration of superhuman power by members of secret societies; while the Haida and especially the Tlingit were only beginning to acquire the dances and songs associated with these ceremonies, when the impact of westernization (particularly missionization) put an end to them.

36. Goldman's overstating the distinction between the aristocracy and the rest of the population results, to a large extent, from his exclusive concern with the native religious ideology and his neglect of social action. See Reid's (1977) critique of the idea that Kwakiutl commoners had no access to the type of superhuman forces and powers that the aristocracy controlled. See also Walens (1977; 1979) and Suttles (1979).

chapter five

1. The fact that these spirits were usually those of his paternal/affinal kin suggests that they were playing the same role vis-à-vis the deceased as his living opposites who provided the funerary services and offered comfort to the mourners.

2.   Jones (1914:19) reported having seen men with their burial clothes on, two or three days before they died. Upon their relatives' request, Emmons photographed several men like that, shortly before they expired (Archives, Anthropology Department, American Museum of Natural History).

3.   The focus on the breath's departure as a sure sign of death is illustrated by the expression "he stopped breathing," used as a euphemism for dying (Story and Naish 1973:68).

4.   While De Laguna (1972:765) agrees that ḵáawu here stands for "person," she says that her informants did not recognize s'igee as being related to s'uugí, "bone." However, even if my own informants offered only a folk etymology, the fact that they did make this connection is very suggestive.

5.   The Inland Tlingit believed that death put the ghost into a temporary state of shock or paralysis, which made it feel the need to take somebody along (McClellan 1975:371).

6.   The fear of pollution emanating from the corpse was illustrated dramatically by an incident that occurred during a funeral in Sitka in the late 1860s or early 1870s. While the body was being taken out through the smokehole, it fell into the fireplace, causing great fear and confusion. "All the coals and ashes upon which the body had fallen were then hastily scraped up with pieces of bark. . . carried out and thrown into the sea, for the fear they might bring down unheard of evils upon the heads of the living inmates of the house" (Anonymous 1877:372–374). The accident was interpreted as the ghost's refusal to exit through the smokehole; so, the body was then removed through the door.

7.   The latter was reserved primarily for the dead shaman (see below). In the post-contact era, windows were also used.

8.   In the Tlingit mythology, the dog appeared as an anthropomorphic creature which originally had the ability to speak as a human being but later lost it because of its foolish behavior. The dog was the only domestic animal treated with ambivalence. On the one hand, it was the hunter's useful helper and protector of the village from witches and other evil creatures, but on the other hand, when a dog behaved too much like a human being (e.g., walked on its hind legs or made sounds resembling human speech) it had to be killed.

    For a symbolic analysis of the attitudes towards and the treatment of the dog in Northwest Coast cultures, see Amoss (1984).

9.   According to some accounts, before the corpse was placed on the pyre, it was turned around four times "in the direction followed by the sun" to ensure quick reincarnation (Kan 1979–1987).

10.   In an earlier study of Tlingit cosmology and eschatology, de Laguna (1954:181) reported that to exceed the ordinary span of life was to "go around shaan geeyí and return to the place one had started from. To die prematurely was to "go only half-way round."

11. This text incorporates a brief summary of the main features of the Tlingit view of reincarnation. For a more detailed discussion, see de Laguna (1954; 1972:776–781) and Stevenson (1966).

12. Emmons claimed that some spirits were new and did not come from a deceased ancestor. He also reported that no reason was given why some spirits reincarnated while others did not (1920–1945, Chapter VI:25). Other sources (e.g., de Laguna 1972:776) indicate that every baby possessed a spirit of its deceased matrilineal relative, but the identity of that person was not always known. Occasionally a person was believed to be the reincarnation of two ancestors.

13. The corpse's hand could also be placed on the woman's bare breast, while she made a silent wish, or a string could be tied to connect the feet of the corpse to her waist (McClellan 1975:349).

14. For a period between two and eight years after birth (depending on a particular source of information) the child also remained linked to the mother, which was symbolized by the umbilical cord worn around the child's neck. At the time when the child was said to be "old enough to learn," the cord was ceremonially disposed of (Kan 1979–1987).

15. Compare the discussion of the *wet/dry* opposition in Chapter II.

16. Jones (1914:119) reported that,

> According to the belief of the natives, burning the dead assured the spirit of the deceased a warm and comfortable place in the spirit land. As natives are seldom uncomfortable from heat in this life, but often suffer from cold, they dread the cold far more than they do the heat. Hence a seat near the fire is the seat of honor and pleasure. In the future life their concern is to avoid the cold and to procure a seat near the fire. If burned, the spirits of the dead would detect it, and seeing that the dead has been used to the fire, give him a seat where he may be comfortable.

17. The square or rectangular shape of the fireplace resembled that of the house itself. Both of them had four corners that were specially marked in various ritual contexts, for example, when the corners of the house were "fed" with oil during its dedication or when the food for the dead was placed at each of the fireplace's corners. When slaves were sacrificed at the dedication of a newly constructed house, their bodies were buried underneath the four corner posts as well as the fireplace in the center, clearly marking the most important areas in the house (Kan 1978).

18. Dried fish and meat were particularly important during the fall and winter, when they were not only one of the main types of daily food but were served in large quantities to the guests at the potlatch.

19. According to Krause (1956:106), "The fire in the middle of the house is kept up all day, but in the houses of poor people it is very small."

20. For example, it was customary for a woman whose daughter married without her consent to put out the fire and sit in the ashes (Swanton 1909:133).

21. Some myths mention "the spirit of the fire" which waited upon the spirits in the "village of the dead."

22. Shamans made good weather by lighting fires on the beach and burned the clothing of a missing person to establish his whereabouts (de Laguna 1972:806–808).

23. Compare a Bella Coola belief that the barrier between ghosts and humans was little more than a wall of smoke, just too dense for ordinary eyes to penetrate (McIlwraith 1948, vol.I:500).

24. Among the Inland Tlingit, in the 1950s, bits of charcoal were still tied as amulets on children who had lost a parent and were thus in danger of being carried away by the ghost (McClellan 1975:373).

25. Thus, when they passed a shaman's grave (usually while travelling in a canoe), the Tlingit threw some tobacco in the water.

26. While the smoking of tobacco appears to be a post-contact practice, it seems to have fitted well into the indigenous symbolic scheme. In addition, eighteenth-century European visitors reported that the Tlingit grew a tobacco-like plant, which they roasted, mixed with lime (probably from shells), and sucked or chewed (Krause 1956:108–109; de Laguna 1972:410–411). The indigenous origin of tobacco is suggested by an episode from the cycle of creation myths in which Raven teaches the Tlingit how to plant and chew tobacco (Swanton 1909:89). Krause (1956:108–109) reported that the Tlingit chewed pitch and the root of lupine, which, like tobacco, induces a form of intoxication. It would be interesting to find out whether this effect of tobacco was related to the fact that the living smoked with and for the dead.

27. The data on the Tlingit cosmology are rather limited and often inconsistent. These contradictions must have resulted from gaps in ethnography, regional and temporal variations, internal inconsistency of the native cosmology itself, and the influence of Christianity. De Laguna (1972:792) is probably correct in her suggestion that the Tlingit did not have a developed cosmological scheme. Rather, there were "various uncoordinated sets of notions" that were presented in myths. Even within a single story one encountered "the inconsistent or illogical as well as the inexplicable." Nevertheless, myths, rituals, and the occasional statements made by informants reveal many basic indigenous concepts about the world. The structure of that universe was also implicit in the social action of daily life. I might add that the need for consistency and internal logic in a cosmology is our own cultural, and especially scientific, bias, not shared by many non-Western peoples (compare Brunton 1980 and Keesing 1982:184, 243).

28. At the same time, many things in the land of the dead were the opposite of those of the world of the living. Thus, when the deceased shouted for help to cross the river separating him from the s'igeekáawu aaní, nobody responded, but

when he got tired and began yawning, the spirits on the other side heard him and sent a boat to take him across.

29. The idea of punishment in the afterworld for the transgressions committed in this one was foreign to the Tlingit (Khlebnikov 1976:27). Such concepts as the "Dog Heaven" for sinners seem to be the product of Christianization (Swanton 1909:81; de Laguna 1972:771).

30. This expression comes from Metcalf's (1982:235) discussion of the Berawan eschatology.

31. Such a Platonic view of the world was not uncommon among American Indians. For example, among the Navajo, according to Haile,

> "all natural phenomena, including human beings, are believed to have outer forms, that can be seen, and inner forms (be'gisti'n, 'one who lies within it' or 'the inner form of it'). The inner form is believed to exist independently of its outer shell and to control the latter." (quoted in Kaplan and Johnson 1964:205)

32. One of the names given to Raven or to his uncle was "Raven at the Head of Nass," Nass being one of the main rivers in the region.

33. Compare the women's association with the house ("center") with that of the aristocracy ("children of the village"). See Chapter VIII for more information on the image of woman and Chapter IV for the discussion of the latter. Of course, in real life women were more mobile than in this ideal scheme. For instance, they travelled with their husbands to trade and attend feasts. In addition, while descent was matrilineal, residence was generally virilocal.

34. Compare Jonaitis (1986:13); see also Boelscher's (1985:5–57) and MacDonald's (1983:6–7) discussion of the structural principles and oppositions ordering the Haida view of the world.

35. It is interesting that in order to make a drowning man into a land otter person, a kóoshdaa ka̲a had to capture him before his spirit left him (Olson, 1933–1954, notebook 10:37). This suggests that the body without the spirit could not be transformed into another form, even a nonhuman one. On the other hand, if the body of a drowned person was later recovered and cremated, his spirit could still reach the s'igeeka̲awu aaní (Emmons 1920–1945, chapter VI:28).

36. Given the reputed power of the land otter person, it is no wonder that the shaman's major source of power came from the tongue of a land otter that he killed during his initial quest (compare Jonaitis 1978).

37. It appears that some of these symptoms are those caused by hypothermia, the most common victims of which are people lost in the forest and exposed to rain and cold temperatures.

38. An important aspect of the shaman's funeral was the rites aimed at inducing his main spirit to enter the body of another person, who would assume the role of the deceased. Thus, in the course of the funeral, the paraphernalia of the

deceased were lowered into the house through the smokehole (Krause 1956:201-202). For the most detailed descriptions of a shaman's funeral, see Veniaminov (1984:404–405); Krause (1956:201–202); Emmons (1920–1945, ch. XI:31–32). According to one account (Emmons, n.d., notebook 7), the shaman's body could even be removed through the door, which suggests that it was seen as so pure that this act did not threaten the living inhabitants of the house.

39. The etymology of this term is not clear; its literal translation is "the lord of *keewa.aa*" (Leer, personal communication, 1984–1985), but no information on this being has been obtained.

40. The living did offer them some food and clothing but placed those on the roof of the house instead of the fire (Jones 1914:234).

41. Emmons (n.d., notebook 7) mentions briefly that "the poor burn [the dead] at once, but the rich may keep the body in [a] gravehouse and one year after burn and have [a] feast." Except for a brief reference in a book by Knapp and Childe (1896:148), which is not entirely reliable, no other source confirms this practice. According to the latter authors, "Of late years, it has become the custom to put the body of a chief in a casket, after it can no longer be displayed, and allow it to remain in the house, in state, for a year or even longer, the rest of the family moving out and finding other quarters." We do know, however, that among the Kaigani Haida, the Tlingit neighbors to the south, the famous chief Skowl of Kasaan was displayed in such a manner (Niblack 1890:plate LXVII). If some of the Tlingit groups did, in fact, observe this custom, it would simply strengthen my argument about the greater purity of the body of a high-ranking person. Compare also a similar custom among the Tsimshian, where often bodies of shamans and chiefs were not cremated but placed in grave houses on a rocky point removed from the village, or where the grave box was placed in a cave (Garfield 1939:241).

42. This concept was present in other Northwest Coast cultures (e.g., Swanton 1908:38); see also a paper by Wilson Duff, as well as a collection of papers dedicated to his memory (Abbott 1981), both of which bear the title "The World Is As Sharp As A Knife."

43. An important concern for the Tlingit was that their death would be avenged. In fact, if the murderer or his relative was not killed, the victim was not able to enter the warriors' heaven. A powerless person unable to punish his enemy or obtain retribution for insults would often commit suicide, in order to force his own kin to carry out the punishment (Krause 1956:155).

44. Thus when a person was killed by an inanimate object (e.g., a climbing board which wrapped around his neck and choked him) or an animal (e.g., a bear), the instrument or the agent of death was killed and kept as a trophy. Thus, among the Inland Tlingit, a tree branch that killed a man might be kept in his family's cache (McClellan 1975:396).

45. Despite the generally positive image that the ancestors had in the eyes of the living, a certain ambivalence towards them seems to have existed. It is

suggested by the fact that the dead were believed to celebrate the arrival of new spirits in s'igeekáawu aaní and to wish for more deaths, since those would result in more memorial feasts—their main source of sustenance (e.g., Knapp and Childe 1896:159). At the same time, however, in several myths and stories, the dead help their close matrilineal relatives who die prematurely to return to the world of the living, before their bodies are cremated (Kan 1979–1987).

46. Thus, the origin of witchcraft itself was attributed to the act of a man who wished to punish his unfaithful wife; to acquire the evil power he drank water from a human skull (Emmons 1920–1945, ch. XI:22; *North Star*, vol. 5, no. 7, June 1892). The violation of the proper relationship between the living and the dead was only one of the crimes committed by witches. Others included incest and efforts to kill their own close matrikin. The latter was accomplished by placing a fingernail or a hair of the victim inside human remains or a dog's carcass. The witch was the epitome of evil because he (or, more rarely, she) violated all of the fundamental laws of Tlingit society—moiety exogamy, matrilineal solidarity, and the proper relations between the living and the dead.

chapter six

1. There seems to be some inconsistency here. If the spiritual components of the deceased were supposed to be released by cremation, how could the mourners' singing during the wake assist the spirit in its journey?

2. Some accounts indicate that most of the face, except for the eyes and the forehead, was covered with a kerchief or part of the blanket and was uncovered only during the nightly ritualized cries, just as the carved corner posts of the house were (see below). However, even if part of the face was covered, some of the crest designs would still be visible.

3. Even though the information on the regalia that adorned those dead who were not aristocrats is scanty, it appears that some type of crest-bearing garment and headdress was placed on or near every deceased, regardless of rank.

4. Thus, for example, the Yakutat Tlingit, who ordered their *naaxein*s from Chilkat Tlingit, could not identify the creatures represented and trusted the maker to depict the animal of the person ordering the blanket (de Laguna 1972:441).

5. This practice has not been mentioned by my predecessors, with the exception of a brief note in Olson (1967:52), but has been clearly established on the basis of informants testimony, contemporary practice, and photographs of the lying-in-state ceremony taken around the turn of the century (Kan 1979–1987).

6. Goldman (1975:54) offers the following apt statement on the view of slaves in Kwakiutl culture:

> Slaves . . . were a full-fledged caste. Captive aliens, they had no kinship con-
> nections with their new homes, and no genuine ties any longer with their
> original tribes and villages. As persons violently torn loose from their roots,
> *slaves existed in a state equivalent to being dead.* Being on the margins of death
> they were by Kwakiutl standards the proper sacrificial victims for cannibalistic
> feasts. . . . Slaves were totally undifferentiated except by gender. *The slave had
> become a fully generalized symbol of human life comparable to the animal.* If the slave
> had been reduced to being the counterpart of, say, the seal he had the higher
> ritual value as being human. (italics mine)

7.   While I do not intend to engage in a lengthy discussion of the nature of Northwest Coast slavery, I must point out that several recent works on the subject (Donald 1983; Ferguson 1984) tend to exaggerate the degree of the slaves' importance in the economy. The findings of the only existing Russian census, imperfect as they are, indicate that slaves constituted about 10 percent of the total Tlingit population (Tikhmenev 1978:428). This figure is supported by other Russian and American sources (e.g., Olson 1967:53–55). While slave labor made a certain contribution to the economy, the idea of keeping slaves for what they could produce rather than as a sign or wealth, military success, and high status seems to have been absent (see Chapter IV; compare also Khlebnikov 1976:32; Garfield 1939:271; de Laguna 1972:472). The complicated subject of slavery obviously requires further study.

8.   If a dying *aanyádi* declared that he wished his slaves to be set free rather than killed at his funeral, his wish was carried out (Emmons 1920–1945, ch. VI:16). Responding to Russian and, later on, American pressure, the Tlingit gradually replaced the killing of slaves with their manumission.

9.   A potlatch had to be held in order to eliminate ("wash away") the disgrace of slavery. The gifts distributed to the guests were supposed to "shut their mouths," that is, prevent them from making references to the person's embarrassing past. Despite this, the disgrace was never totally wiped out.

10.   Schwatka (1885:72) reports that favorite slaves chosen to be killed at a potlatch were usually given an opportunity to escape and could return after the ceremony, without fear of being punished.

11.   Compare the following Bella Coola observance described by McIlwraith (1948, vol. I:186):

> Before the corpse of a chief is removed from the house where he has died, a
> speaker always announces the number of potlatches he has given and the total
> value of goods distributed in them. *These gifts in a vague way are felt to make easy
> the deceased's path in the next world as they have done in the present.* (italics mine)

12.   Another term for a mourning song was ḵaa *eetisheeyt*, literally, "song in place of a person" (Kan 1979–1987).

13.   I have modified Swanton's translation to bring it closer to the original.

14. The reference to the clan's drum in the second stanza not only amplifies the tragedy by comparing the death of a clan member with the loss of its important crest object, but alludes to the announcement of death by the sound of the drum.

15. The use of the box drum throughout the entire wake, as well as the mourners' periodic pounding on the floor with long staffs during the performance of the crying songs, substantiates Needham's thesis about an association of percussion with transition (see Huntington and Metcalf 1979:46–53).

16. In contrast to this, according to some sources the mourners did not even cut their hair when a child died (de Laguna 1972:536).

17. A protagonist of one of the stories recorded by Olson (1967:50) says, "When a village is lonesome and quiet, then soon an *aanyádi* will die."

18. Similarly, the Bella Coola felt that no ordinary explanation was sufficient to account for the death of a great chief. No matter what the actual case might have been, it was always said that the supernatural Carpenters, who in the beginning of time had created mankind, came down and "seized" or "called back" the deceased, thinking he was too good for this world (McIlwraith 1948, vol. I:435).

19. When the Tlingit painted their face black for protection against sunlight or mosquitoes, they used melted pitch or spruce gum, but for mourning, charcoal and grease were always used. The black color was also associated with anger, hence warriors and other persons preparing for a dangerous undertaking covered their faces with charcoal. Frequently referred to as "the color of death," it was juxtaposed to red, the color of life (Olson 1967:71).

20. According to some accounts, the mourners' hair was not cut but singed. This was done twice: immediately after a relative's death and, again at the conclusion of the funeral, during cremation, when the grieving matrikin of the deceased allegedly put their heads in the pyre (Veniaminov 1984:420).

21. Thus, for example, bad weather might be attributed to the pubescent girl's violation of some rule of her confinement.

22. Compare Keesing's (1982:143–167) discussion of the Kwaio mortuary rites.

23. The woman's hair was considered more precious than the man's (see Chapter II). Every Tlingit woman hoped to retain her black hair—one of the main manifestations of her beauty and youth—until late in life.

24. According to one of my own informants, a similar ritual was performed by men who killed a bear—they lifted their hands towards the sun and said a wish for good fortune (Kan 1979–1987).

25. Even though one must be careful in using contemporary data for understanding the nineteenth-century grieving, since today spontaneous expression of sorrow is more common and more tolerated, I would agree with de

Laguna's (1972:533) comment that, "To judge by modern custom, the expressions of grief were very violent."

26. It is worth pointing out that the other major context in which violent behavior was expected and tolerated was warfare, which, like the funeral, was related to death. In case of war, however, the dominant emotion was anger rather than grief.

27. Compare similar Kwakiutl practice described by Curtis (1915, vol X:99) and Drucker (1963:148). According to the latter, this act was called "sending someone with the dead chief" and "making other people mourn also."

28. For the same reason too much crying over a relative who went away for a long time was discouraged (de Laguna 1972:533).

29. Grief was sometimes personified as "the spirit of sadness," that could enter the body of the mourner and cause illness or even death (Kan 1979–1987).

30. Harrison (1925:78–80), in his account of the Haida funeral, reports a similar alternation between wailing (performed primarily by women who cried, "Alas, my beloved") and the ritualized wake in which speeches of consolation were delivered by the opposites and the virtues of the deceased were extolled by them as well as the mourners.

31. Harrison (1925:114) reports that during the Haida wake, periods of wailing were followed by periods of long silence, when a voice asked questions and all seemed to await a reply. Harrison's interpretation was "There is little doubt that on these occasions the Haida actually believed that they were conversing with the dead, and were consoled accordingly."

32. Compare this song with several Haida mourning songs recorded by Swanton (1912:56–60), for example:

> What medicine shall I use (in my affliction)?
> What medicine shall I use?
> I have nothing to comfort me.
> Your dear face (I long for).
>
> It becomes too much dear (repeated four times)
> (i.e., my grief is too great to bear).
>
> If I could see the trail (of the dead), I would enter upon it.
> Elder brother, (I want to see) your whole body.

33. According to Katishan, Swanton's (1908:437) informant, the most valuable among these songs were those allegedly composed during the Great Flood and referring to the people lost in that great mythical disaster. The special value of such songs could be explained by the fact that they were created at the crucial moment of the formation of the Tlingit clans.

34. For additional discussion of the history and poetics of Tlingit songs, see de Laguna (1972:566–577) and Dauenhauer (1975:143–185).

35. For example, on the first day of a funeral witnessed by Shotridge (1917:106), "the women began by fasting, meanwhile the men held a council, laying out plans, rehearsing speeches and songs for the occasion."

36. A chief's staff was usually appropriately called aankÃ¡awu, "chief's" wootsaagayÃ. See Kamenskii (1985:35–38) for the discussion of these objects and a detailed account of the history of one of them.

37. According to some accounts (e.g., Krause 1956:156) and a drawing from the 1840s by a Russian observer (see fig. 5), some women mourners held their own staves but did not strike the floor.

38. As it was explained to me (Kan 1979–1987), the man is supposed to put all his feelings into the movement of the staff.

39. In cases of serious illness, the preparation and administration of remedies was entrusted, whenever possible, to the patient's relatives in the opposite moiety, who were paid for their services (de Laguna 1972:657).

40. This expression was explained to me as "something precious surrounding me, like a glass bowl" (Kan 1979–1987).

41. The fact that witches engaged in sexual relations with members of their own moiety and with their own dead matrikin further illustrates the notion of a link between the exchange of spouses and of ritual services between the moieties.

42. Another reason why fathers could not physically punish their children was the rule forbidding any insult or injury to opposite moiety members.

43. In addition to kinship terms, special forms of address aimed at honoring and flattering the mourners were used. Some of them have already been mentioned; others included sh yÃ¡a awudaneix'Ã, "you people of honor," and aanyÃ¡tx'i sÃ¡ani, "children of aristocracy."

44. I have slightly modified and corrected Swanton's translation to bring it closer to the original, which he also provided.

45. Among the Kutchin, an interior Athapaskan group, the widow was supposed to remain near her husband's body for a year to protect it from animals and other dangers. Only after the corpse had properly decayed and had been cremated, was she released from mourning and allowed to remarry (Hardisty 1872:320). The easternmost Carrier, another Athapaskan group, apparently required widows to carry the bones of their deceased husbands on their backs during the mourning period, hence the name "Carrier" (Tobey 1981:428).

46. The more conservative, older widows still follow the basic mourning rules, which allowed me to obtain some new information on the subject (Kan 1979–1987), supplementing the data collected by Emmons (1920–1945, passim), Olson (1933–1954, passim), de Laguna (1972:537–538), and others.

47. Among the Athapaskans, the widow and the widower were also treated differently. For example, among the Carrier, the widower was exempt from the

ill-treatment often suffered by the widow in the hands of her dead husband's kin (Jenness 1943:535).

48. According to McClellan (1975:375–376), among the Tagish, this belt also represented the life of the widow's future husband, which her conduct was aimed at prolonging.

49. A similar distribution was sponsored by the widower, although usually there was less property to be distributed.

50. Thus, according to one eyewitness account (Barnett 1891:178), about thirty to forty feet from the fire a hole had been dug in the ground and partially covered with brush, and in that hole the widow was attended by several women who combed her hair and changed her clothes, actions which they explained would cleanse her and make her eligible for matrimony again.

51. A similar practice existed among many of the interior Athapaskans, including the Koyukon, who also added a special ceremony of the widow's surrender to their feast of the dead, a ritual resembling the Tlingit memorial potlatch. According to Jetté (1911:717), a widow who was still marriageable had to present herself to the public, entirely naked, indicating that she no longer reserved her body as the exclusive property of her dead husband and was willing to remarry.

52. Among the Carrier, the widow was expected to embrace her husband's burning body until she could no longer stand the smoke and flames. If her husband's kinsmen were displeased with her performance as a wife, they had the right to push her repeatedly into the fire (Jenness 1943:535).

53. Among the Kwakiutl, the similarity between the pubescent girl's and the widow's rite of passage was expressed even more strongly, since the latter had to dwell in a separate hut in the woods, reminiscent of the one used by the former (Curtis 1915:58–59).

54. Of course, the male puberty is not marked by such an important physiological change as the onset of menstruation. Among the Tlingit, the boy's puberty was marked by a celebration of his first major kill. Unfortunately, it disappeared much earlier than the female puberty rite and hence we know little about it.

55. Nevertheless, Emmons (1920–1945, Shukoff's Account:18) says that, if the widower married into another matrilineal group, his wife's female matrikin "tried to make trouble for him and his new wife."

56. The role of matrilineal descent and virilocal residence as the key factors responsible for the much more extensive mourning observances of the Tlingit widow, compared to those of the widower, is further supported by the evidence that in such bilateral societies as the Bella Coola and the Salish widow's and widower's mourning observances were similar (e.g., McIlwraith 1948, vol. I:456; Barnett 1955:225–226).

57. Thus, Swanton (1908:424) was told in Sitka, in the early 1900s, that an initial gift of $3.00 brought $5.00 back, while my own informants indicated that the difference between the two gifts could be much greater. For example, an expensive rifle could be asked in return for a $5.00 _ḵeenás_ (Kan 1979–1987).

58. This could also be a way of compensating him for the bridewealth which was larger than the return gift from the bride's matrikin.

59. The use of such a belt by the wife was common throughout the Subarctic and the Northwest Coast.

60. Compare this notion with the idea, discussed in Chapter II, that the woman's "inside" exerted weaker control over her conduct than the man's.

61. Thus, according to Russian sources (e.g., Tikhmenev 1978:154), some of the Tlingit women who had married Russian men and settled in Novo-Arkhangel'sk warned their spouses about their relatives' plans to attack the fort.

62. Despite this similarity, however, the woman's status was higher among the Tlingit than among their Athapaskan relatives in the interior, because the latter lacked much of the Northwest Coast emphasis on passing down the collective heritage through the unilineal descent group, while the former were not as dependent on hunting for their survival and hence were somewhat less preoccupied with the danger of the menstrual blood (compare Chapter X).

63. It is interesting that despite the crucial role of the woman in linking the two moieties, an active verbal form was used to refer to the man's marrying a woman, and a passive one to speak about the woman's marrying a man (de Laguna 1972:490).

64. The ambiguity of the woman's role in culture and society has been noted by other Northwest Coast ethnographers, e.g., Snyder (1964:254–263), who worked among the Skagit, and Blackman (1982), who has studied the Haida.

65. According to de Laguna (1972:494), on some occasions by preference and on others in default of a man, a sister-in-law acted as a _naa káani_.

66. As one elder recently explained, a _naa káani_ stood between the two warring sides and nobody could touch him because of "respect" for him (Peck 1975:42).

67. Compare Huntington's discussion of the mortuary rites of the Bara of Madagascar which, like the Tlingit ones, include a secondary treatment of the remains:

> One can view the whole funeral sequence as a simple rite of passage, seeing the original burial as a rite of separation, the gathering as a period of liminality, and the reburial as the ceremony of reintegration. It is a question of how wide a perspective one takes. There are transitions within transitions. (Huntington and Metcalf 1979:118)

Chapter 7

1.   I do have some interesting data on how these backstage negotiations are conducted today but must use this data with caution because of the major sociocultural changes that have taken place in the last one hundred years.

2.   Compare Boelscher's (1985) discussion of the Haida concept of conducting the potlatch and other ceremonies "in the right way" but without "overdoing it."

3.   At the same time, a more recent account of the Tlingit funeral, also written by a native ethnographer, presents a somewhat different view from Shotridge's, "The disposition of the bodies of those not so high in rank as chiefs, and of common people other than slaves, are similar to that of chiefs, only not so imposing and expensive. But no matter how poor a family, they strain every point to give their dead an expensive funeral" (Peratrovich 1959:72).

4.   Contrary to what Rosman and Rubel (1971:37), quoting de Laguna (1952:6), suggest, the potlatch was not "the arena where potential heirs compete for coveted honors and where the victor triumphs over his rivals." As we shall see later on, there was some competition in the funeral and a lot more of it in the potlatch, but not over the title/position of the incumbent. I must point out that de Laguna herself has recently retracted her earlier statement (personal communication, 1986). Compare Stearns' (1984: 201–202) discussion of the Haida potlatch:

> Much of the competitive behavior described in ethnographic accounts refers to efforts of junior men to improve their status by potlatching. This status rivalry should not be confused with competition for highest office, in which . . . public opinion imposes strict limits.

5.   In fact, it was said that if the enemies saw that the young man was willing to die to save his maternal uncle's life, they might be moved by this loyalty and decide that both the uncle and the nephew deserved "respect." Consequently, they might settle for indemnity paid in wealth instead of blood (Kan 1979–1987).

6.   He was called "the husband intended for" (de Laguna 1972:526–527). If the young man decided to marry while his mother's brother was still alive, the ideal spouse was the man's daughter. Regardless of the bride's identity, the groom's maternal uncle had to help him amass the wealth needed to pay the bride-price.

7.   Conflicts between houses of the same clan often centered around crests and other ceremonial privileges. Since the head of the senior house acted as the guardian of the main crests of his entire clan, he had considerable leverage over the other houses and their leaders who had to obtain his permission to use those regalia in their own potlatches and other ceremonies. In daily life, individual houses were rather independent from the authority of the senior

house's leader. It was in warfare, mortuary rituals, and other ceremonies that the individual houses were not free in their actions but had to coordinate them with the leader of the senior house. If the clan head decided that a certain junior house was aspiring too high, he could refuse to lend its leader a high-ranking crest, the use of which could enhance his and his lineage's status and rank (see Chapter IX).

8.   A male Tlingit used different terms for his older and his younger brothers.

9.   McClellan (1961) discovered the existence of this practice among the Inland Tlingit, who described this avoidance as "shyness," which involved not looking each other straight in the face and communicating through a third person.

10.   The major sources for the Raven myth include Veniaminov (1984:386–396), Kamenskii (1985:57–65), Swanton (1909:3–21; 80–154), and de Laguna (1972:839–873). See also Stone (1971) and Meletinskii (1973; 1979).

11.   In one of his attempts to kill his nephew, he covers the world with water.

12.   According to Tollefson (1976:86), the house chief's successor inherited about one half of his personal property.

13.   The process of selecting a new clan head was a bit more complicated, and sources disagree on the exact procedure. Thus, according to Olson (1967:5), each house had a chief, usually the eldest of a group of brothers, who were heirs of the last chief. One such house chief was regarded as being of higher rank than the other house chiefs of his clan and was considered the clan head. There was no special title for this office, but everyone knew which chief it was. In theory, the clan chieftaincy resided in the same house through the generations; in practice it shifted from house to house, according to prestige based on potlatching, wealth, success in warfare, and so on. The position was not strictly hereditary. Oberg's view on this subject is somewhat different:

> While there are differences of rank between the houses, these differences do not seem to override the importance of generation. Thus the *aan ḵáawu*-ship [chiefship] of the G̲aanaxtedí clan has in the past 30 years, passed successively from the Whale house to the Raven house and then the Frog house. At present there are two brothers in the Frog house belonging to the older generation, and after the *aan ḵáawu*-ship has passed through the hands of both of these men it will go to the Raven house where the oldest nephew now resides. (1973:42)

I think that Olson's view is more accurate. The senior house is often recognized as the original one, generation after generation. At the same time, potlatches and other factors, like demography, could lead to the loss of this status and its acquisition by another house.

14.   In her discussion of succession among the Haida, Stearns (1984:193–194) speaks about "an automatic rule of hereditary succession," while Garfield (1939:178–179) states that among the Coast Tsimshian, the most likely successor was "the eldest man most closely related to the deceased."

15.   The Tsimshian said that a prospective chief was "pushed up" by distributions of property on his behalf at feasts (Seguin 1985:6).

16.   So important was the rule of marrying one's predecessor's widow that in the twentieth century, when the whites began enforcing monogamy, Tlingit men chosen to replace their deceased maternal uncles and older brothers divorced their own wives to be able to fulfill their duty.

17.   Among the Tsimshian, this direct link between the spirit of the deceased and his successor was dramatically expressed in the following manner: "While the body lay in the house the successor was brought forward and made 'to look on the face of his brother,' thus acquiring his predecessor's power and making known his readiness to assume the position" (Garfield 1939:240). Garfield (1939.:247) also reported that, "in the older days, the successor was supposed to lie down upon the body of the deceased to receive his power." This latter practice is similar to one of the ways in which power was transferred from the deceased shaman to his successor, among the Tlingit.

18.   Similar rhetorical use of grief characterized the mortuary rites of other Northwest Coast peoples. For example, in a 1930s feast which took place right after the funeral of a Tsimshian chief, towels distributed to the opposite moiety members were referred as "things with which to wipe the tears" (Garfield 1939:250).

19.   Of course, it was not the crest itself but only its temporary incarnation that was destroyed. The new object carried the same name as its predecessor but had a higher value.

20.   I do not know whether this story was a creation of a single man or is part of a shared body of oral traditions. In either case, it makes sense in terms of the Tlingit culture, and its point is quite clear.

21.   On the other hand, the moral character of the deceased was not supposed to be reflected too much in the behavior of the mourners. Even a witch who had confessed and destroyed the substances that caused his victim harm was mourned, especially if he were of high rank and possessed valuable names and other attributes of his matrilineal group's shagóon. An especially evil and notorious witch might be killed. In such case, there was no funeral and his name was no longer used.

Chapter 8

1.   Ideally, every person's mortuary cycle was supposed to end in a potlatch, but I suspect that the bodies of those on the very bottom of society were never "finished." Unfortunately almost no data on the subject exists.

2.   Compare the role of the Berawan secondary obsequies, called nulang, as described by Metcalf (1982).

3.   The widower's sadness was especially strong, since he had been overwhelmed by grief and seemed to resist letting go of his wife's memory.

4.   The use of the secondary treatment of a single deceased to celebrate and commemorate all of his ancestors makes the Tlingit memorial potlatch quite similar to the Berawan *nulang* characterized by Metcalf (1982:155) as follows:

> In ideological terms, the *nulang* celebrates the termination of a final and unpleasant phase in the soul's career. Now it has completed the dreary metamorphosis to pure spirit and is consequently acceptable to the land of the dead. So the festival is also a celebration of the reunion of the deceased with his or her ancestors. Furthermore, because the dead individual is, as it were, a messenger travelling from the community of the living to the greater community of the dead, it becomes also a festival of the ancestors. They are conceived of as being present *en masse* throughout the event and more especially at certain moments in the death songs, and it is their presence, the fusion for a brief period of the living and the dead, that gives *nulang* its supremely sacred character.

5.   In recent times, when fewer people remember the names of their ancestors, the hosts would call on any knowledgeable elder present for help; when the Tlingit name cannot be recalled, English names are allowed to be used (Kan 1979–1987).

6.   Some sources suggest that every dead member of the hosts' matrilineal group participated in and benefitted from the potlatch.

7.   To make it more accurate, I have modified the English translation published in the 1984 edition of Veniaminov's book.

8.   Goldman (1975:245) found evidence of the same idea in Boas' Kwakiutl ethnography. According to him, the verb *yaxwede*, "to give away property" is related to such terms as *yaq*, "to lie dead, dead body, to distribute" and *yaqawe*, "to be beaten, to lie dead."

9.   In an account of the potlatch recorded by Swanton (1909:353), the phrase *has du x̱'éix̱ at wuduwatee* is rendered as "they [hosts] gave them [guests] food" but is also literally translated as "their mouths things they put into."

10. Since those pieces were subsequently made into shirts and dresses, the notion of "dressing" the guests makes sense (see below).

11. Among the Tlingit, who placed more emphasis on the clan ownership of names, this practice of temporarily granting members of the opposite moiety the use of one's own names would have been unthinkable.

12. Recently, a major potlatch was delayed for one year because of the chief mourner's claim that his grief was still too fresh; his feelings were respected despite the fact that the rest of the mourning lineage was ready for the ceremony (Kan 1979–1987).

13. According to some of my informants, they also "chanted the grief," that is, performed a chant to remove the hosts' grief. However, in potlatches I attended, this was not performed (Kan 1979–1987).

14. Many of these names contained only an allusion to an event that transpired during the potlatch, so that only knowledgeable persons were able to interpret them. For example, the name "Stands Beside It" might be bestowed on a host in reference to a slave who stood beside a *tinaa*, before both of them were given to the guests.

15.   As de Laguna (1972:609) explained:

> Without a potlatch for the dead, to whom the house is in effect dedicated, the builder is simply an owner, not a house chief (*hít s'aatí*). The house is only a shelter, not a monument to the forefathers of the lineage, and has no right to a name. The builder lacks status, and the house its personality.

16.   In the potlatches I attended, the financial help given to the hosts by their affinal/paternal kin was quite substantial. An individual host might receive money from up to two dozen guests, amounting to 30 percent, if not more, of his total contribution. It is difficult to say at this point whether this practice became more prevalent in this century or was simply overlooked by previous ethnographers.

17.   Compare similar practice among the Tsimshian (Halpin 1973:640).

18.   The first detailed discussion of a Northwest Coast oral tradition appeared in Dauenhauer's (1975:185–204) unpublished dissertation. It addressed two Tlingit oral genres—condolence oratory and songs—and attempted to relate them to the social structure and ceremonialism. While my knowledge of the Tlingit language in no way matches that of Dauenhauer, my own work goes further in trying to situate the oral genres within the context of the mortuary ritual and relate them to the larger sociocultural order. I owe a great deal to my friends Richard and Nora Dauenhauer for sharing their knowledge of this subject with me and I am pleased that we are in agreement on some of the major principles of Tlingit oratory. Aside from this work, two recent studies also address Northwest Coast ceremonial oratory—Seguin (1985) on the Tsimshian and Boelscher (1985) on the Haida.

19.   My own sample of potlatch condolence speeches is much larger than my sample of those given at funerals, since the former have not been affected by Christianity as much as the latter. Earlier recordings also emphasize the potlatch rather than the funeral oratory (Swanton 1909:372–389; Dauenhauer 1975:184–205).

20.   This utmost significance of balance in all aspects of intermoiety relations, particularly in relation to death, was clearly expressed by one of my older and most reliable informants who explained:

> One of the best things about the Tlingit culture was how the two sides comforted each other. Our people always relied on the opposite side when they needed comfort and help. Thus, they always kept the balance: if your side was in sorrow, the opposite one brought you back to normal life; when they lost a

relative, it was your side's turn to help. See, it was always that balance! (Kan 1983:55)

21. It is not accidental that metaphors of the condolence oratory were also used in the peace ritual, aimed at restoring proper balance between the two warring parties belonging (ideally) to the two moieties (Swanton 1909:164–165). Hence the transition from death and sorrow to life and joy was homologous to the one from war to peace (compare Chapter IX).

22. Compare Haida potlatch joking, similarly aimed at cheering up the mourners (Boelscher 1985:163).

23. For example, if clans A and B of the moiety X, habitually intermarried with clan C of the moiety Y, then many members of clans A and B would belong to the category of "children of clan C."

24. One of the chief hosts of a 1979 potlatch I attended used his clan crest, a certain type of salmon, to poke fun at himself, his matrikin, and the dominant non-native society. He said that, although the Department of Fish and Game had closed the salmon fishing season, there were plenty of "fat and juicy" salmon in the room. Being overweight, he obviously meant that he was one of them (Kan 1979–1987).

25. "Love songs" is also the most common term, that I encountered among the English-speaking Tlingit, for this genre.

26. The structure of the love songs is quite uniform. They usually consist of two stanzas. The first line is a statement, a question, or an opening image; next the addressees are named by their fathers' clan name; and then the opening image is further developed and finally resolved. Each song is performed twice and is often accompanied by refrains or burden syllables (see Dauenhauer 1975:152).

27. Compare the more explicit sexual imagery and much less restrained behavior in the so called "hot dance," which was part of the mortuary potlatch of the distant relatives of the Tlingit, the Ingalik (Osgood 1958:143–146).

28. Rosman and Rubel (1971:179) acknowledge that the various categories of things distributed in the potlatch have different "symbolic meaning," but do not pursue this subject, concentrating instead on the relationship between the potlatch and the social structure.

29. Compare my approach to Weiner's analysis of ceremonial exchange in the Trobriands (1976). See also Forman's recent essay on mortuary and marriage exchanges among the Makassae of East Timor. As he puts it, "important advances in the study of social process can be made by examining both the material and nonmaterial or ideological content of exchanges as they affect the quality and extent of social relationships in particular sociocultural contexts" (1980:152).

30. Compare the modern Gitksan practice of referring to money distributed in the potlatch as "blankets," "pillows," and "cloaks" (Adams 1973:67).

31. Compare the way in which one Inland Tlingit family distributed gifts among the guests invited to the party marking its adolescent female member's coming out of her puberty confinement. According to McClellan (1975:391), she had to dance into the house swathed in yards of calico, which was cut off for distribution while she continued to dance.

32. Nowadays money is used in that fashion.

33. Another discovery made by Mauss was that in the potlatches and feasts of many of the peoples of the Northwest Coast, Alaska, and Eastern Siberia "gifts to men are also gifts to gods" (1967:12). What he meant was that potlatches in these societies involved not only the living but the spirits of the dead which took part in the transactions. He emphasized that this aspect of the potlatch was particularly evident in Eskimo, Tlingit, and one of the two Haida potlatches and referred to their living participants as "masked incarnations" of the spirits of the dead whose names they carried. The participation of the dead in the gift exchange explained, in his view, the destruction of property in the Northwest Coast and Northeast Asian potlatches—it was done not simply to show power and wealth, but to offer a sacrifice to the spirits, who were the donor's namesakes and allies (Mauss 1967:13–14; see p. 102, for the discussion of the role of the dead in the Tlingit potlatch).

Chapter 9

1. At the same time, Olson's (1933–1954, Notebook 4:51) statement that the "richest man might give either first, last or in between" suggests that those on the top of the hierarchy could violate this rule.

2. Despite the difference in the roles played by commoners and aristocrats in the potlatch, their relationship was not strongly antagonistic. Although the deceased's heir and other high-ranking members of the host group made the largest contributions of wealth, they could not carry out a potlatch without the help of their lower-ranking matrikin. The latter, on the other hand, were interested in having their leaders increase their personal rank and prestige, since that reflected favorably upon their entire matrilineal group.

3. This issue is discussed in Chapter III. The original object is usually more valuable than its more recent duplicate.

4. Despite the fact that a clan's status and rank were supposed to be based mainly on its history and current performance in potlatching, military successes allowed larger and more aggressive clans to compete with groups that might be older and whose ancestors had sponsored more potlatches. As one of Swanton's (1908:415) informants put it, "Some families [lineages, clans] were too poor to have an emblem, and on the other hand it is said of some of the great ones . . . that they were so rich that they could use anything."

5.   In more recent times, with the decline of many of the clans and the shortage of ritual experts, representatives of more than one clan usually take part in the potlatch. Although a single clan still plays the role of the chief host, the degree of the other clans' participation has increased. If the latter disagree with a particular claim made by the hosts, they either ignore it or make a veiled statement expressing their own viewpoint. In case of extreme displeasure, they might walk out of the potlatch, although such a walkout happens rarely, since this is considered a very serious insult to the hosts. More likely, if these clans suspected that claims with which they disagree were going to be made in an upcoming potlatch, they would not attend at all (Kan 1979–1987).

6.   As some of the more devout Christian families began in the 1900s to rely on their churches for mortuary services and ignore their opposites, the latter would sometimes send them a bill for what they saw as their legitimate right (Kan 1979–1987).

7.   The nonlocal guests arrived with their own spouses who, being members of the same moiety as the hosts, provided them with some assistance.

8.   In fact, even if the guests happened to come on foot, as they sometimes did in the Yakutat area, they were furnished with canoes for their ceremonial arrival at their hosts' village the next day (de Laguna 1972:611).

9.   Hunting and warfare were seen as similar activities, both demanding bravery from men, producing wealth, and increasing individual and group status. I must thank William Merrill (1987, personal communication) for pointing out the allusion to hunting in this episode. According to some accounts (e.g., de Laguna 1972:620), the leaders of the two parties also engaged in a verbal duel, trading difficult riddles, which only a person knowledgeable about the two groups' history could answer (see below).

10.   Compare the following episode in an account of a war, recorded by Swanton (1909:78): the departing warriors push down their canoe on skids made of the bodies of the two women they had captured from their enemies on a previous expedition.

11.   The sun, as we have seen earlier, was associated with life, peace, wealth, high rank, and other good things.

12.   The dances themselves rarely had anything to do with warfare.

13.   According to Swanton's (1909:117–118) informant Katishan, Raven was the first one to greet his guests with a bow and arrows.

14.   This form of rhetoric was probably also a reflection of the notion that the world of the dead was the reversal of that of the living (see Chapter V).

15.   In addition, as I have explained in Chapter III, to injure one's clan and even moiety mate was unthinkable, since it contradicted the fundamental principle of matrilineal unity and solidarity.

16. The ambiguity of intermoiety relations is further illustrated by a story recorded by de Laguna (1972:770), in which the spirit of a man who was about to die violently visited Kiwaa, the abode of the slain persons. While the spirits of his own dead matrikin tried to cover the entrance to this realm (perceived as an opening or a "mouth" in the clouds), his dead opposites tried to prevent them. Their action could be interpreted in two ways. On the one hand, similar to the inhabitants of the ordinary village of the dead, they wanted to have more of their paternal/affinal relatives in their domain. On the other hand, this desire to be with their beloved opposites meant that they wanted them to be killed.

17. An insulted group would often capture the offenders' crest and hold it as ransom until restitution was offered to them.

18. Warriors fought wearing helmets depicting their crests and died uttering the cry of their crest animal. The crest headdresses themselves are believed to have originated from these helmets.

19. The importance of the connection between warfare and marriage alliance is illustrated by the use of war symbolism in the Tsimshian aristocratic marriage ritual, described by Boas (1916:531). In a Haida account of a war between the Haida and the Tsimshian, peace is solidified by an exchange of women (Swanton 1905:395).

20. This idea is nicely illustrated by the myth about a man who invited bears to his potlatch and thus made friends with them. Its teller commented that in the old days "when they gave a feast, no matter if a person were their enemy, they would invite him and become friends" (Swanton 1909:222).

21. For accounts of the wars and feuds of that era, see Olson (1967:69–81).

22. While I agree with Ferguson (1983:133) that potlatching was a means of transforming hostile relations into peaceful and cooperative ones, I believe he overstates the significance of war in Northwest Coast social life, in arguing that "war made redistributive exchange [i.e., potlatching] between neighboring groups necessary."

23. According to de Laguna (1972:485–488), who discusses *naa yátx'i* joking in more detail, in Yakutat, men could not joke with women or juniors with seniors; in Sitka and other central communities there was greater freedom but one still had to be careful not to offend someone whose rank and power were superior.

24. The erroneous nature of this interpretation is discussed in Lévi-Strauss (1976:191–194) and Kan (1986:192–193; 208); see also Lévi-Strauss (1986).

25. Even the example provided by Swanton, which serves as the basis of Rosman and Rubel's argument, does not fit their model of the marriage system. In the potlatch he described, the hosts were the Chilkat Gaanax.ádi and the guests, the Kaagwaantaan of Chilkat and Sitka. While the data provided by Durlach (1928:173–177) supports Rosman and Rubel's, information given by

several Chilkat informants indicates that the Chilkat Gaanax.ádi intermarried with a number of other local and nonlocal clans (Kan 1979–1987).

26. Compare the oratorical contests in the Upper Tanana potlatch, which informants likened to fights (Guedon 1974:223–224).

27. Similar to "love songs," riddles were used during the negotiations between the two clans of the opposite moieties, prior to the performance of the peace ceremony. The negotiators did not openly state their demands and intentions but used "riddle talk," which the other side had to guess (Peck 1975:44). Thus, fighting with weapons was replaced by a verbal duel.

28. In the recent potlatches, the dancers of *yéik utee* were those hosts who had just been given new names; the dancing thus validated their new identity and the increase in their status (Kan 1979–1987).

29. Swanton's (1908:436) informants spoke about *yéik utee* songs being performed in the potlatch, which means that their use in this context goes back to at least the late nineteenth century if not earlier.

30. This preoccupation with balance and reciprocity was made very clear in a 1980 banquet I attended. Organized by the regional Native corporation for the Tlingit elders, it included a performance by local teenagers who had been attending Indian Education classes. Among the songs and dances they performed to entertain the elders, were several *yéik utee* songs. While being happy about the youngsters' knowledge of and the desire to carry on the heritage, the elders were uneasy about leaving the *yéik utee* performance unanswered. Although most of them were not prepared to perform their own songs and dances of this type, the elders did rise one after another to respond to them by mentioning their own *yéik utee* songs and dances. As one elder put it in his speech made in English, which I recorded:

> It's too heavy, too heavy for us . . . how they come out . . . Indian doctor [shaman's] song . . . . We can't just walk out of here and forget about it. They [the young performers] ask the Indian doctor to bless us, so we would have power. In return with our songs we are holding hands with them; . . . in order that . . . the Indian doctor songs would not hurt anybody. And I hope that all of you are blessed [by this]. (Kan 1979–1987)

Most of the speeches delivered at that banquet have been published, along with an English translation, by Dauenhauer and Dauenhauer (1981).

31. Compare Walens' (1981:80) characterization of the Kwakiutl potlatch food-givers (i.e., hosts) as superior to the food-receivers (i.e., guests).

32. This view originates, to a large extent, from Boas' erroneous interpretation of the Kwakiutl potlatch.

33. We can speculate that the food vomited into the fire went directly to the hosts' own matrilineal ancestors. Compare Walens (1981:16–17) on the symbolism of vomiting in Kwakiutl culture.

34. For accounts of specific eating contests see Olson (1967:67–68).

35. A remnant of these eating contests is a current practice of distributing dishes full of berries and fruits among selected guests who, with the help of their close kin sitting with them, try to finish the food as fast as they can. This competition is accompanied by a great deal of laughter and joking (Kan 1979–1987; compare Worl 1984).

36. This practice of taking food home from the feast is so pervasive that it is done today even at small-scale lunches, church socials, and any other gatherings where food is served (Kan 1979–1987).

37. Only a few references to the destruction of property performed outside the potlatch context in order to shame a rival could be found in the Tlingit ethnographic materials. Thus, for example, Jones (1914:95–96), who is not always reliable, described a quarrel between two women, in which one of the opponents scattered silver dollars among the people watching the argument in order to "shut up" her rival.

38. But see Swanton (1905:162) on the reference to the Haida potlatch gift-giving as "fighting an inferior."

39. Unlike the southern Northwest Coast societies, the Tlingit did not have "named" seats or positions based on rank; instead the assignment of guests to specific seats was done at each potlatch (compare Olson 1967:64).

40. It also seems that aristocratic informants tended to emphasize the disparity between what they and the rest of the guests received.

41. In today's potlatches, men and women receive an equal amount of money and gifts, some of which differ in nature (e.g., socks and ties versus cosmetics and scarfs) but are comparable in value.

42. Thus, it seems unlikely that in a nineteenth-century potlatch, the chief host would give half of the total accumulated wealth to four of his siblings-in-law, as was done in one of the potlatches I participated in (Kan 1979–1987).

43. My own findings are also corroborated by those of Guedon (1974:216–217) on the modern Upper Tanana memorial potlatch. She found that the rank and prestige of the recipient were the major factors; but others were also taken into consideration: his needs, the amount of discomfort involved in the trip from his village to the hosts', the personal esteem in which he was held by the host or the person for whom the potlatch is given, and his participation in the potlatch itself (e.g., whether he sang or not, and if so, how good he was). Finally, if he showed that he shared the hosts' grief or did something special to relieve it, he was given a special gift.

44. Compare Boas (1916:541) and Garfield (1939:274) on a Tsimshian custom of killing slaves and destroying canoes and coppers as a show of disregard for wealth.

45. I have found only one reference—and not a very reliable one at that—to competitive slave-killing engaged in outside the potlatch context by two rival chiefs, reminiscent of the Kwakiutl potlatch rivalry. An American captain who reported this did not witness the incident himself but claimed to have been told about it by the Chief Manager of the Russian-American Company in Sitka, which the captain briefly visited in 1837 (Belcher 1843:104–105).

46. Another example of this drama is the following account by one of Emmons' (1920–1945, Shukoff's Account:8) main informants who described how a slave might be asked to take out the "slave-killer" club and then put it back. If he put it back "nicely," he was set free.

47. Garfield's (1939:193) claim that only major potlatches involved the use of slaves supports Olson's argument.

48. "Coppers" have been a subject of several studies, which I am drawing upon, including Keithahn (1964), MacDonald (1981), and Lévi-Strauss (1982). The most recent and authoritative is an essay by de Widerspach-Thor (1981).

49. Lisianskii (1814:150) reported that the coppers he saw in Sitka in the early 1800s were worth 20 to 30 sea otter skins, themselves an expensive commodity due to the European demand. Swanton's informant interviewed in 1904 placed their value at four to six slaves (1908:437), while Olson (1967:67) said they were worth three to five slaves.

50. George Hunt (quoted in de Widerspach-Thor 1981:158), Boas chief inform-ant among the Kwakiutl, described the test of a copper's authenticity which involved its hardness, smell, and taste.

51. Compare the Tsimshian custom of distributing among the potlatch guests shreds of moose skin used to wrap around the grave box of the deceased being honored; they were also called "bones of the [deceased] chief" (Garfield 1939:238).

52. Compare a Bella Coola notion that the copper thrown onto the ground where a masked representation of the deceased had just trodden was supposed to give him "stability" (McIlwraith 1948, vol. I:222).

53. Kwakiutl, Bella Coola and Haida often placed several wooden repre-sentations of coppers on the grave of aristocrats, presumably to indicate how much wealth they owned and/or in how much of an esteem their kin held them (see de Widerspach-Thor 1981:168, fig. 15; McIlwraith 1948, vol. I:plate 22; Niblack 1890:plate III).

54. Veniaminov (1984:426–427) reported that the first smith among the Tlingit was "a halfman" (Russian *zhenomuzh*, bisexual, or transvestite) named Shukas-kaa who lived among the Chilkat. He does not mention what metal he worked with but I presume it was copper which the Chilkat people obtained from the Athapaskans.

55. Swanton (1909:165–173) recorded two myths of the origin of this creature. Most of the Northwest Coast mythologies feature underwater monsters similar

to Gunaakadeit, e.g., the Haida Gonakada (Qonoqada), the Kwakiutl Komokwa (Qomogwa) and Sisiutl (see Goldman 1975 passim; Lévi-Strauss 1982 passim). In fact among the names of the Kwakiutl Qomogwa are "Copper Maker" and "Wealthy" (Boas 1935:68; 128).

56. In his detailed analysis of Northwest Coast myths about monsters and monster masks, Lévi-Strauss (1982) argues that creatures like Gunaakadeit were also the guardians of mankind's proper observance of the exogamy rules; compare MacDonald (1981).

57. Space limitations do not permit me to discuss fully another mythical master of wealth, Tl'aniaxeedakw, a female counterpart of Gunaakadeit. She is also an aquatic creature but her domains are the inland freshwater lakes and the beach. She carries copper shields on her back and has copper fingernails. She also carries a child on her back whose crying can be heard by man. The lucky one who hears this sound must follow a prescribed ritual of purification and then try to snatch the baby away from the woman. She may give the attacker a *tinaa* in return for the baby or may scratch him with her nails. The scabs resulting from this eventually turn into copper (see Swanton 1909:173–175; 292–293; 365–368; see also Kamenskii 1985:68–70; de Laguna 1972:884–885). Lévi-Strauss (1982) analyses both the coastal and the interior (Athapaskan) versions of this myth in detail (see also McClellan 1963).

58. See Boas (1897:522) for a Kwakiutl example of an explicit comparison of slaves' heads and coppers.

59. In 1979–1980 I was shown what was believed to be such markings.

60. Peter Metcalf (personal communication, 1987) has suggested that the coppers thrown in the water "flow" like the blood of the sacrificed slaves.

61. Compare a similar Kwakiutl notion reported by Drucker and Heizer (1967:131): in a nineteenth century potlatch sponsored by their informant's mother, she ordered a copper sunk and insisted that this was done to show her grief for her deceased father and not as a rival gesture to anyone, as was the case in a subsequent potlatch in which her uncle came forward to "challenge her heritage."

62   This concept was not as highly developed among the Tlingit as among the Kwakiutl among whom the value of the copper increased rapidly as it changed hands in the potlatch system (compare Drucker 1951:232–233; Oberg 1973:117–118).

63. Compare the Haida term for the copper, *tau* [possibly *taow*], "property above all else" (Keithahn 1964:77); in one of the Tlingit myths it is referred to as "an everlasting living thing" (Swanton 1909:262).

64. There is some evidence that, as a crest-bearing object, a *tináa* could be displayed rather than disposed of in the potlatch, with the value of all the property spent by its owners added to its original worth (Keithahn 1964:75). Of course, coppers were not as valuable as other regalia representing crests.

65. In his detailed discussion of the symbolism of coppers in Kwakiutl culture, where the symbolism seems to have been richer than among the Tlingit (compare Oberg 1973:123), Goldman (1975) arrives at a somewhat similar conclusion. He establishes an association of coppers with the sun, salmon, fire, and blood. Furthermore, he outlines a hierarchy of objects that served as the potlatch gifts; in this hierarchy, animal skins and food are on the bottom, slaves in between, and coppers on the very top, incorporating all the three cosmic realms of earth, sky, and sea (Goldman 1975:126–127). Goldman describes the Kwakiutl copper as an "energetic commodity" moving constantly between tribes through marital and potlatch exchanges, and endlessly being converted into animal skins. In his words, it is a "mobile and generative symbol, reaching out like the chiefs themselves to encompass multi-associative meanings" (Goldman 1975:83). Finally, for Goldman, it is an "overloaded and hence elusive symbol," which synthesizes all the other forms and realms of life (Goldman 1975:157–158; compare Walens 1981:148–149). Similarly, de Widerspach-Thor (1981:172) characterizes the Northwest Coast copper in general as a "metaphor of energy" and a "container and a catalyst of energy held in each individual, each chief, each tribe."

66. McIlwraith's (1948, vol. I:260–261) discussion of Bella Coola coppers expresses a similar idea. In his words,

> It is almost impossible to define coppers in the nomenclature of economic theory. They are not mere articles of barter, since they have no practical use outside the ceremonies of chiefs. Nor are they standardized units of trade or currency, since each differs not only from all other coppers, but also at different periods. In a sense they serve as tokens of what has been expended. . . . It [copper] grows more valuable at every transmission in accordance with the goods expended, so that it serves as a visible and tangible memorandum of the chief-like generosity of its owner.

67. Of course, crests represented ownership of specific food-producing areas, hence, intramoiety competition over crests must have played some role in competition over fishing grounds, berry-picking areas, and so forth. This is, in fact, what Seguin (1985:14) has recently suggested for the Coast Tsimshian. We do have some evidence that this occurred among the Tlingit as well. However, it is my impression that more often ownership of resources was disputed and changed through warfare rather than potlatching, with the stronger clans simply seizing crests, property and land from the weaker members of their own moiety. Some of these changes in the distribution of tangible and intangible property have never been acknowledged by the losers (Kan 1979–1987). This subject requires further investigation.

68. Compare the following statement by Oberg (1973:125):

> A clan is worth the amount of wealth given at its last potlatch added to its former prestige value. The measure of clan value, the medium through which it is expressed, is its crest. The value of the crest is the value of the clan, and the potlatch is the mechanism through which the crest is given value.

69.   At least this is when the distribution occurs in the modern potlatch. While I do not know exactly how it was performed in the nineteenth century, I suspect that the modern practice is not a recent innovation.

70.   The potlatch also encouraged warfare as a mechanism of obtaining slaves, luxury items, and even food.

71.   The idea that the potlatch helped redistribute wealth and prevented the aristocracy from monopolizing it was suggested by Osgood (1937:135) in his ethnography of the Tanaina Athapaskans.

72.   Compare Townsend (1980:140–141) on the importance of owning and manipulating exotic wealth items obtained through trade and raiding for the maintenance of aristocratic status, in the societies of the Pacific Rim (i.e., Northwest Coast, Athapaskan, Eskimo, and Aleut).

73.   Some guests had added leverage with the hosts, if the latter failed to be generous. Thus the widow could threaten not to move out of her dead husband's house, if his matrikin failed to "pay her off" well.

74.   Compare an Eyak custom of giving special gifts to the potlatch guest who could sing the dead person's song most accurately (Birket-Smith and de Laguna 1938:172).

Chapter 10

1.   Compare Huntington and Metcalf's (1979:81–92) comparative analysis of the mortuary rites of various related Indonesian groups.

2.   Despite significant similarities between the mortuary complexes of the Tlingit, Haida, and Tsimshian, particularly in contrast to the rest of the coastal societies, death-related beliefs and rites of the Tlingit stand somewhat apart and show greater resemblance to those of the western Subarctic Athapaskans. The Athapaskan's cultural and linguistic ties with the Tlingit are clearer than the Haida's with the Tlingit (see Levine 1979). The origin of the Tsimshian, whose language belongs to the Penutian stock, different from either the Tlingit or the Haida, is still an unresolved question, although a recent work (Ives n.d.) identifies the Carrier, a western Athapaskan group, as one of their potential ancestors. While I make references to the three northern coastal groups in this chapter, my primary focus is on the Tlingit.

3.   The comparison presented here is also useful because it confirms a hypothesis of the origin of the Tlingit in the interior of Alaska, Yukon Territory and northern British Columbia, a hypothesis based upon comparative studies of Athapaskan and Northwest Coast social organization, analyses of linguistic data, and, to some extent, archaeology.

4.   Unfortunately, only some of the area ethnographers were concerned with or managed to obtain information on eschatology and ethnopsychology; the

most prominent among such works are Jetté (1911); Osgood (1958; 1959); Mc-Clellan (1975).

5.   MacLeod (1925:127) was the first to point this out and indicate that crema-tion in northwestern North America correlated well with matrilineality.

6.   In fact, Birket-Smith (1929:121) and McKennan (1959:149) suggest that cremation could be part of a "basic culture stratum of the North Pacific Area," including Alaska, northern Northwest Coast and northeast Asia.

7.   Other more specific similarities between the Tlingit and the Athapaskan potlatches, such as the use of sad mourning songs as well as lively ones (the latter resembling the Tlingit "love songs"), condolence oratory, certain styles of dancing, eating contests, and others could also be attributed to the groups' common origin, although subsequent borrowing or both cannot be ruled out (see e.g., Loyens 1964:135).

8.   I should mention that the Tlingit and the western Subarctic Athapaskan mortuary/ancestral complexes, including the presence of the dead incarnated by the guests at the memorial feast, show major similarities with that of the western and southwestern Alaskan Eskimo (Lantis 1947; Birket-Smith 1967:23–26; Sonne 1978). This might ultimately be attributed to the common origin of the Proto-Eskimo and Proto-Athapaskan groups (see Dumond 1987). In addi-tion, the Northwest Coast practice of redistributing wealth through the pot-latch was shared by the ranked societies of the Pacific Rim, which included Aleuts, Tanaina, Koniags, Chugach, Ahtna, and Eyak (Townsend 1980) (see figure 3).

9.   This reconstruction is based on my own survey of Athapaskan eth-nographies, studies by de Laguna (1975) and Rosman and Rubel (1983), as well as the "Subarctic" volume of the new *Handbook of North American Indians* (Stur-tevant 1981) the most recent collective statement on the subject by leading area specialists (see especially McClellan and Denniston 1981; Hosley 1981).

10.   Beyond the "local" or the "regional" band were the groups whom the whites had given the overall "tribal" (or "ethnic group") names used in the ethnographic literature. With the exception of some groups who allegedly had a sense of "nationhood" (e.g., the Kutchin as described by McKennan 1965), most of the Subarctic "tribes" shared only a recognized commonality of linked dialects, customs, and contiguous territory (McClellan and Denniston 1981:384).

11.   For the most detailed summary of this debate see de Laguna (1975); see also Van Stone (1974).

12.   The model of Rosman and Rubel is further supported by an earlier reconstruction of the Proto-Athapaskan kinship system by Dyen and Aberle (1974). The two authors used the methodology of historical linguistics and examined synchronic distributions of kinship terminology of the Eyak-Athapaskan language family. Their reconstructed prototype is matrilineal and matrilocal, located possibly in the interior of Alaska. Current linguistic re-

search, while disputing the existence of Sapir's Na-Dene genetic group, which supposedly included Tlingit, Haida, and Subarctic Athapaskan languages, indicates that some similarity between Tlingit and Athapaskan-Eyak languages does exist, at least in phonology and grammatical structure (Krauss and Golla 1981). Krauss and Golla hypothesize that the Tlingit language might be a "hybrid" between Athapaskan-Eyak and an unrelated stock and that the homeland of the Proto-Athapaskan was in eastern interior Alaska, the upper drainage of the Yukon River, and northern British Columbia, or some part of that area—the same region suggested by Rosman and Rubel (1983) and Dyen and Aberle (1974) as the homeland of the Proto-Athapaskans. The possibility of the coastal peoples' ancestors arriving from the interior (around 5000 B.P.) has also been suggested by some recent archaeological work (e.g., Fladmark 1975; Ives 1985; n.d.; Rosman and Rubel 1986:570–571).

13.   Scholars interested in this question of origin might also examine other domains of Tlingit and Athapaskan religions, for example beliefs and rituals surrounding the onset of puberty and menstruation in general. In addition, Tlingit beliefs about and practices related to animals seem more similar to the Athapaskan than to the central and southern Northwest Coast ones.

14.   De Laguna (1975) helps explain this fluidity by arguing that in the interior, clans rather than moieties were more fundamental to the social system. As she points out, in any given region, clans become aligned into moieties because of the consistency with which their members contract unions. But the clans themselves, as bodies of kinsmen, remain fundamental to the social system. At any given time, in any given place, for any given married couple and their kin, the dual arrangement of opposites is established. But the moiety system remains fluid, because it is in essence a way of arranging individuals, and is not a fundamental supergroup that is subdivided into clans. De Laguna (1975) makes a similar argument for the northern Northwest Coast, hypothesizing that clans preceded moieties among the Tlingit, which is plausible from an historical viewpoint. However, to me moieties seem much more stable and uniformly distributed geographically among the Tlingit than in the western Subarctic. In addition, the Tlingit themselves view the moieties as the most fundamental unit of the sociocultural order. In fact, McClellan (cited in de Laguna 1952:2) had suggested earlier that, for the Tlingit, there may be no question of either clan or moiety priority. The present moiety-clan system may have developed as a unit, or may represent the fusion of two different traditions, which would have occurred prior to the emergence of the Tlingit as a recognizable group. This entire question requires further research. For the discussion of moieties among all three of the northern Northwest Coast peoples, see Dunn (1984).

15.   While in many of the Athapaskan groups the alignment of mourners/hosts and funerary workers/guests was based on clans and moieties, in some of them (e.g., Kutchin and Ingalik) the role of the other was played by residents of another community, or occasionally marginal persons, such as the old and the poor (Slobodin 1962:34; Osgood 1956:152; 1958:138). Nevertheless, even among the Kutchin, "it was felt that matrilineal sib [clan]

membership was the historically proper basis for alignment" (Slobodin 1962:34).

16. According to Osgood (1936:148–149), the deceased's closest kin went to the house of the man chosen to do the funerary work and called him to come out. The latter rushed out and attempted to escape without having the gifts thrust into his hands. If he was unsuccessful, which was usually the case, he had to fulfill his obligation as a grave worker (compare the Ahtna mortuary rites, as described by de Laguna and McClellan 1981:659).

17. Even if this practice had existed some time in the nineteenth century, it must have been a rather insignificant aspect of the mortuary complex, since neither my predecessors nor contemporary informants report it.

18. Osgood (1958:276) pointed out that the Ingalik "dispose of their property easily and in the case of the deceased, one might say eagerly."

19. Compare the Athapaskan notion that the dead brought their descendants success in hunting versus the Tlingit view that they simply bestowed sacred prerogatives on them and, hence enabling the living to increase their status and prestige.

20. This ritual period lasted for one hundred days following the potlatch and failure to observe its rules resulted in bad luck in hunting and the subsequent inability to accumulate property for any future potlatches (McKennan 1959:137–138). Compare my own discussion of liminality in the Tlingit rites of passage (Chapter VI).

21. Among the Koyukon, the funeral workers received the deceased's best possessions at his potlatch (Gate 1911:716). Nothing of that property could be used by his close kin (Kroul 1974:43).

22. Kroul (1974:43) reports that the modern Koyukon still believe that the spirit of the deceased cannot truly rest until his goods have been disposed of.

23. As I have shown in Chapter VIII, they could contribute significantly to the wealth distributed in the potlatch but did so "in the name" or on behalf of their deceased's matrikin, that is, their own paternal relatives and spouses.

24. Among such groups as the Ahtna and the Tanaina, whose social organization was closer to the coastal model, greater cooperation existed between the chief host and his matrikin (de Laguna and McClellan 1981:659; Townsend 1981:632).

25. Animal skins and furs, as well as exotic items obtained through intertribal trade were the main of gifts distributed in the pre-fur trade memorial feasts.

26. Data on this competition is limited; even less is known about the rivalry among the guests. We do know about eating contests and other play-like rivalry among them, but the general tone of their interaction appears less competitive than in the coastal potlatch.

27. This representation of the dead by the guests was most clearly expressed in the Koyukon and the Ingalik potlatches, but was, in my opinion, present to a greater or lesser degree in all of the western Subarctic potlatches.

28. My own Tlingit informants, who had taken part in Athapaskan potlatches, invariably commented on the "lack of order and formality" in them (Kan 1979–1987).

29. See the discussion of such societies—the Eyak, the Tahltan, and the Carrier—in Rosman and Rubel (1983:9–14). A classic work on this subject, which deals with the borrowing of crest privileges by the Alkatcho Carrier from the Bella Coola, is Goldman (1941).

30. McKennan (1959:138) also saw the Tlingit potlatch as being primarily a method of attaining prestige, a view that my study challenges as limited.

31. In his survey study of the northern Athapaskans, Van Stone (1974:55–66) reiterates McKennan's view, arguing that the "religious elements" in the potlatch were of "minimal significance" and discussing the potlatch in the chapter on "social institutions."

32. Kroul (1974:42), among others, mentions that mortuary rites were accompanied by a great display of grief, in a society where (as among the Tlingit) there is otherwise little public display of emotion.

33. Consequently, in some indigenous models of this ritual, competition and struggle for status were downplayed more than in others. Thus, McKennan's Upper Tanana were probably more emphatic in their discussion of prestige in the potlatch, while the Koyukon, whose potlatch remained closer to the pre-fur trade model, insisted on its relative insignificance (Kroul 1974:39; 44). The fact that other Koyukon ethnographers (e,.g., Jetté 1911:139; Sullivan quoted in Loyens 1964:137) found aggrandizement rather important indicates the danger of reducing such a complex phenomenon as the potlatch to a single function.

34. One of the initial inspirations for my survey was a significant but rarely cited paper by Wike (1952), in which she argued that the role of the dead in the cultures of the Northwest Coast was more important than had been thought previously and cited a number of examples to support her claim. Drucker, who had written extensively on the Kwakiutl, Nootka, and other area cultures, acknowledged this fact for the first time in his last major work—a monograph on the Kwakiutl potlatch, written together with Heizer (1967:130–132).

35. Some of the Central Nootka groups performed a kind of a secondary treatment when they removed the skull of a chief from his grave box at the time of the potlatch marking the lifting of the taboo on his name and on other ceremonial prerogatives (Drucker 1951:149).

36. The Bella Coola were an important exception: in their funeral, an effigy imitating the corpse was carried out of the house through the smokehole by a wooden representation of the crest, into which the deceased was believed to be eventually transformed; during his memorial potlatch the deceased reap-

peared, impersonated by a dancer dressed in the costume representing the same crest. Bella Coola mortuary rites are well documented and require a detailed analysis in order to explain their greater elaborateness than was typical of the central and southern Northwest Coast (see McIlwraith 1948, vol. I:182–244; 431–512).

37. Of course some restrictions on the identity of a proper spouse existed, including prohibition on marrying one's first cousin, village endogamy, and so forth. What Rosman and Rubel mean is that in the north cross-cousin marriage defined the ego's potential spouses much more clearly.

38. I must point out that Rosman and Rubel overestimate the rigidity of marriage rules among the northern groups and fail to distinguish clearly between rules and practice (compare Boelscher 1982). Marriages in the northern Northwest Coast area did involve some feasting and property exchange, but these were rather modest in comparison to mortuary potlatches.

39. Compare also the works of Goldman (1975) and Walens (1981) which treat the dead as important actors in Kwakiutl ceremonial life.

40. Compare Drucker and Heizer (1967:154), whose own scheme of the development of the Northwest Coast potlatch bears some resemblance to mine, although it is less comprehensive.

41. The fact that among the Tlingit and western Subarctic Athapaskans reciprocity between the living and the dead appears to be linked to that between the two moieties was first noted by McClellan (1954:83), who offered the following plausible hypothesis:

> The need to join the real and the spirit worlds at death, may, indeed, have helped to lay the pattern for the moiety structuring of other ceremonials, and perhaps reaches back in Tlingit history. For the notion of having to feed people from outside one's own group at a death feast is widespread among other northern peoples. However, this in turn may be an aspect of an even more fundamental pattern of having to validate any important social action in the presence of an out-group or "opposite" witness.

McClellan (1954:83) also made an interesting suggestion that the idea of having to feed one's "opposites" in order to supply one's own matrilineal ancestors with food might be related to the "reversal theme characteristic of the spirit world" (compare Chapter V).

42. Some of the factors contributing to the shape of the Northwest Coast potlatch that I have outlined here are mentioned in Birket-Smith's (1967:38) comparative study of "potlatches and feasts of merit" in western North America, Southeast Asia and Oceania. In his words,

> In order to make potlatch possible, wealth must be combined with a system of rank such as we find among the Northwest Coast tribes with their hereditary privileges that can be claimed only if the owner has proved his rights before a

number of witnesses. *Potlatch is therefore here of fundamental importance to the whole social organization, and just because the prerogatives are hereditary, the claim is naturally connected with the feast of the dead.* [italics mine]

43. Some of these arguments seem reasonable, while others are rather far-fetched. It is feasible that a common cultural base may underlie and explain similarities between the mortuary complexes of northwestern North America, Western Siberia, East and Southeast Asia, and Oceania, particularly in the domain of eschatology and cosmology. To document this we need more solid evidence from linguistics and archaeology as well as more systematic research in comparative ethnology.

44. As Rosman and Rubel (1981:248) point out, one very significant difference between the American and Oceanian societies in question is the mode of production; the former are based primarily on hunting, fishing, and gathering, the latter, on horticulture. From this they suggest that relations of production may be more significant than the mode of production.

45. Mauss (1967) and several other French ethnologists and sociologists of his era spoke about ceremonial exchanges in Melanesia reminiscent of the Northwest Coast potlatch (see Birket-Smith 1967:78).

Conclusion

1. The type of mortuary analysis I am advocating resembles, in some respects, the so-called "reproductive perspective," developed by Weiner (1976; 1980) on the basis of her research on Trobriand exchange. Emerging, like my own study, out of the work on a society where mortuary transactions are critical, her model attempts to link the living and the dead, the social and the cosmic transactions, "politics" and "religion." Weiner shows that in the Trobriands, exchange is a process that holds a system of power relationships in balance. She examines power within a broad framework that incorporates both cosmic and social ordering of time and space, rather than the more traditional narrow focus on power in its political phases only. Any society, she argues, must reproduce and regenerate certain elements of value in order for it to continue. In hierarchical societies, like the Trobriand and the Tlingit ones, "these elements of value include human beings, social relations, cosmological phenomena such as ancestors, and resources such as land, material objects, names, and body decorations" (1980:71). Unlike the present study, however, Weiner's work, whose scope is broader than the mortuary transactions per se, does not present a detailed symbolic analysis of death-related beliefs and practices.

2. For a comprehensive critique of Bloch's view of formalized language, see Paine (1981) and Brenneis and Myers (1984).

3. On the Tlingit view of rhetorical skills and the criteria for evaluating oratory, see Dauenhauer (1975).

4.   This argument is influenced by Scheff's (1977) theory of catharsis through the distancing of emotion in ritual.

5.   As McIlwraith points out in his discussion of the Bella Coola memorial potlatch, not only does it comfort a man and assuage his sorrow to know that he has shown fitting respect to the dead, there is also a gain in social prestige, so that "he is pleased and gratified to such an extent that his grief is dulled" (1948, vol. I:474).

6.   This possibility is not considered in Bloch's (1982) notion of the "denial of individuality and duration" in the double obsequies.

7.   Compare the distinction made by de Laguna's (1960:21, 129) informants between the more remote "myth time" and the more recent "historical time."

GLOSSARY

aan ḵáawu   chief, headman, rich person, aristocrat
aanyádi   same as above (pl. *aanyátxʼt*)
at.óow   crest, regalia
(ḵaa) daakeidí   mortuary pole, grave house, coffin, grave
daganḵú   land of the dead
guneitkanaayí   opposite moiety
hít   house
hít sʼaatí   master of the house, lineage head
jinaháa   bad luck, unknown future
ḵáa   human being, man
ḵaa naawú   corpse, dead person
(aẖ) ḵáani   (my) in-law
ḵéenás   a form of gift-giving between affines
keewaḵáawu   celestial realm of the dead
(ḵaa) kinaayéigi   person's spirit above, guardian spirit
kóoshdaa ḵáa   land otter person
ḵu.éexʼ   party, potlatch
ḵwáan   local group, tribe
latseen   strength, power
laẖeitl   good luck, blessing
ligaas   it is taboo, bad luck, contrary to moral law

lingít   Tlingit, person

naa   clan

naaxein   Chilkat blanket

nichkakáawu   bastard, outcast

(kaa) s'aagí   (human) bone

s'aatí   master

shagóon   ancestry, ancestors, heritage, destiny

shakee.át   ceremonial wooden headdress with sea-lion whiskers and
     ermine skins

shuká   same as *shagóon*

s'áaxw   ceremonial headdress

s'eik   smoke

s'igeekáawu   ghost

s'igeekáawu aaní   land of the dead

tináa   copper shield

(kaa) toowú   mind and soul

wootsaagáa   ceremonial staff

x'aséikw   breath, life (force)

(kaa) yahaayí   soul, spirit

(kaa) yakgwahéiyagu   soul, spirit

yéik   shaman's spirit (helper)

yéik utee   shaman's spirit song(s)

REFERENCES CITED

Individual Works

Abbott, Donald N., ed.
    1981   *The World Is as Sharp as a Knife: An Anthology in Honor of Wilson Duff.* Victoria: The British Columbia Provincial Museum.

Adams, John W.
    1973   *The Gitksan Potlatch: Population Flux, Resource Ownership and Reciprocity.* Toronto: Holt, Rinehart, and Winston.

    1981   Recent Ethnology of the Northwest Coast. *Annual Review of Anthropology* 10:361–392.

Adams, John W., and Alice B. Kasakoff
    1973   Review of *Feasting with Mine Enemy* by Rosman and Rubel. *American Anthropologist* 75:415–417.

Allen, Michael
    1984   Elders, Chiefs, and Big Men: Authority Legitimation and Political Evolution in Melanesia. *American Ethnologist* 11(1):20–41.

Amoss, Pamela T.
    1978   *Coast Salish Spirit Dancing: The Survival of an Ancestral Religion.* Seattle: University of Washington Press.

    1984   A Little More than Kin, and Less than Kind: The Ambiguous Northwest Coast Dog. In *The Tsimshian and Their Neighbors on the*

North Pacific Coast edited by J. Miller and C. M. Eastman, 292–305. Seattle: University of Washington Press.

Anonymous
1877   Cremation among the Sitka Indians. *American Naturalist* 11:372–374.

Barbeau, Marius C.
1950   *Totem Poles.* Anthropological Series 30. 2 vols. National Museum of Canada Bulletin 119. Ottawa.

Barnett, George
1891   Cremation at Sitka. *The North Star* 4(9):178.

Barnett, Homer G.
1938   The Nature of the Potlatch. *American Anthropologist* 40:349–357.

1955   *The Coast Salish of British Columbia.* Studies in Anthropology Monograph 4. Eugene, Oregon: University of Oregon Press.

Bateson, Gregory
1936   *Naven.* Cambridge: Cambridge University Press.

Belcher, Capt. Sir Edward
1843   *Narrative of a Voyage Round the World, Performed in Her Majesty's Ship Sulphur, during the years 1836–1842. . . .* 2 vols. London: no publisher.

Benedict, Ruth
1934   *Patterns of Culture.* New York: Houghton Mifflin.

Berger, Peter
1969   *The Sacred Canopy: Elements of a Sociological Theory of Religion.* Garden City, New York: Doubleday and Company, Inc.

Billman, Esther
n.d.   Untitled Paper on the Father-Child Bond in the Tlingit Kinship System. Billman Collection, Archives, Stratton Memorial Library, Sheldon Jackson College, Sitka, Alaska.

1964   A Potlatch Feast in Sitka, Alaska. *Anthropological Papers of the University of Alaska* 14(2):55–64.

Birket-Smith, Kaj
1929   The Caribou Eskimos: Material and Social Life and Their Cultural Position. *Report of the Fifth Thule Expedition 1921–1924,* Vol. 5, pt. 1. Copenhagen.

1967   Studies in Circumpacific Culture Relations, I. Potlatch and Feasts of Merit. *Det Kongelige Danske Videnskabernes Selskab. Historisk-filosofiske Meddelelser* 42, 3.

Birket-Smith, Kaj, and Frederica de Laguna
  1938   *The Eyak Indians of the Copper River Delta, Alaska.* Copenhagen: Levin and Munksgaard.

Blacking, J., ed.
  1977   *The Anthropology of the Body.* London: Academic Press.

Blackman, Margaret B.
  1982   *During My Time: Florence Edenshaw Davidson, a Haida Woman.* Seattle: University of Washington Press.

Bloch, Maurice
  1971   *Placing the Dead: Tombs, Ancestral Villages, and Kinship Organization in Madagascar.* London: Seminar Press.

  1974   Symbols, Song, Dance and Features of Articulation. Is Religion an Extreme Form of Traditional Authority? *European Journal of Sociology* 15:55–81.

  1975   Introduction. *Political Language and Oratory in Traditional Society,* edited by M. Bloch, 1–28. New York: Academic Press.

  1982   Death, Women and Power. In *Death and the Regeneration of Life,* edited by M. Bloch and J. Parry, 211–230. Cambridge: Cambridge University Press.

Bloch, Maurice, and Jonathan Parry, eds.
  1982   *Death and the Regeneration of Life..* Cambridge: Cambridge University Press.

Blomkvist, E. E.
  1951   Risunki I. G. Voznesenskogo [Voznesenskii's Drawings]. *Sbornik Muzeia Antropologii i Etnografii,* 13:270–300.

Boas, Franz
  1895   *Indianische Sagen von der Nord-Pazifischen Kuste Amerikas.* Berlin: A. Asher.

  1897   The Social Organization and the Secret Societies of the Kwakiutl Indians. In *Report of the U.S. National Museum for 1895,* 311–738. Washington, D.C.: U.S. Government Printing Office.

  1916   Tsimshian Mythology. *Thirty-first Annual Report of the Bureau of American Ethnology.* Washington, D.C.: U.S. Government Printing Office.

  1917   Grammatical Notes on the Language of the Tlingit Indians. *The University Museum Anthropological Publications,* Vol. 8, no. 1. Philadelphia: University of Pennsylvania.

  1935   *Kwakiutl Tales.* New Series. Columbia University Contributions to Anthropology 26(1). New York.

1966   *Kwakiutl Ethnography*. Chicago: University of Chicago Press.

Boelscher, Marianne
1982   The Potlatch in Anthropological Literature: A Re-evaluation of Certain Ethnographic Data and Theoretical Approaches. *Abhandlungen der Volkerkundlichen Arbeitsgemeinschaft*, heft 34. Nortorf, West Germany.

1985   The Curtain Within: The Management of Social and Symbolic Classification among the Masset Haida. Ph.D. diss., Anthropology, Simon Fraser University, Burnaby, British Columbia.

Bourdieu, Pierre
1977   *Outline of a Theory of Practice*. Translated by R. Nice. Cambridge: Cambridge University Press.

Brenneis, Donald L., and Fred R. Myers, eds.
1984   *Dangerous Words: Language and Politics in the Pacific*. New York: New York University Press.

Brunton, Ron
1980   Misconstrued Order in Melanesian Religion. *Man* (n.s.) 15(1):112–128.

Carlo, Poldine
1978   *Nulato: An Indian Life on the Yukon*. Fairbanks: no publisher.

Chase, Walter G.
1893   Notes from Alaska. *Journal of American Folklore* 6:51–53.

Codere, Helen
1950   *Fighting with Property: A Study of Kwakiutl Potlatching and Warfare, 1792–1930*. Monographs of the American Ethnological Society, Vol. 18. New York: J.J. Augustin.

1961   Kwakiutl. In *Perspectives in American Indian Culture Change*, edited by E. H. Spicer, 431–516. Chicago: University of Chicago Press.

1967   Kwakiutl Society: Rank without Class. *Indians of the North Pacific Coast*, edited by R. McFeat, 147–158. Seattle: University of Washington Press.

Collins, June M.
1974   *Valley of the Spirits: The Upper Skagit Indians of Western Washington*. Seattle: University of Washington Press.

Colson, Elizabeth
1953   *The Makah Indians*. Manchester: Manchester University Press.

Comaroff, Jean
1985   *Body of Power, Spirit of Resistance: The Culture and History of a
        South African People.* Chicago: University of Chicago Press.

Cracroft, Sophia
1981   *Lady Franklin Visits Sitka, Alaska, 1870: The Journal of Sophia
        Cracroft, Sir John Franklin's Niece,* edited by R. N. DeArmond.
        Anchorage, Alaska: Alaska Historical Society.

Curtis, Edward S.
1915   *The North American Indian,* Vol. 10. Cambridge, Massachusetts:
        The University Press.

Danforth, Loring M.
1982   *The Death Rituals of Rural Greece.* Princeton, New Jersey: Prin-
        ceton University Press.

Dauenhauer, Nora M., and Richard Dauenhauer
1976   *Beginning Tlingit.* Anchorage, Alaska: Tlingit Readers, Inc.

1981   *Because We Cherish You . . . . Sealaska Elders Speak to the Future.*
        Juneau, Alaska: Sealaska Heritage Foundation Press.

1987   *Ha Shuka, Our Ancestors: Tlingit Oral Narratives.* Seattle: Univer-
        sity of Washington Press. Juneau: Sealaska Heritage Foundation.

Dauenhauer, Richard
1975   Text and Context in Tlingit Oral Tradition. Ph.D. diss., Compara-
        tive Literature, University of Wisconsin, Madison.

Davis, Henry
1976   *English-Tlingit Dictionary. Nouns.* Sitka, Alaska: Sheldon Jackson
        College.

Donald, Leland
1983   Was Nuu-chah-nulth-aht (Nootka) Society Based on Slave
        Labor? In *The Development of Political Organization in Native
        North America.* 1979 Proceedings of The American Ethnological
        Society, edited by E. Tooker, 108–119. Washington, D.C.:
        American Ethnological Society.

Donskoi, Valdimir
1893   Sitkha i koloshi [Sitka and the Tlingit]. *Tserkovnye Vedomosti*
        22:822–828; 23:856–862.

1895   *Molitvy na koloshenskom narechii* [Prayers in the Tlingit Lan-
        guage]. Sitka, Alaska: no publisher.

Douglas, Mary
1966   *Purity and Danger: An Analysis of Concepts of Pollution and Taboo.*
        Washington: Frederick Praeger.

1973   *Natural Symbols: Explorations in Cosmology.* New York: Vintage Books.

Douglas, William A.
1969   *Death in Murelaga: Funerary Ritual in a Spanish Basque Village.* Seattle: University of Washington Press.

Drucker, Philip
1939   Rank, Wealth, and Kinship in Northwest Coast Society. *American Anthropologist* 41:55–64.

1950   Culture Element Distributions XXVI: Northwest Coast. *University of California Anthropological Records* 9(3):157–294.

1951   *The Northern and Central Nootkan Tribes.* Bureau of American Ethnology Bulletin 144. Washington: U.S. Government Printing Office.

1958   *The Native Brotherhoods: Modern Intertribal Organizations on the Northwest Coast.* Bureau of American Ethnology Bulletin 168. Washington, D. C.: U. S. Government Printing Office.

1963   *Indians of the Northwest Coast.* Garden City, New York: The Natural History Press.

1965   *Cultures of the North Pacific Coast.* Scranton, Pennsylvania: Chandler Publishing Company.

Drucker, Philip, and Robert F. Heizer
1967   *To Make My Name Good: A Reexamination of Southern Kwakiutl Potlatch.* Berkeley: University of California Press.

Duff, Wilson
1981   The World Is as Sharp as a Knife: Meaning in Northern Northwest Coast Art. In *The World Is as Sharp as a Knife: An Anthology in Honor of Wilson Duff,* edited by D. N. Abbott, 209–224. Victoria: The British Columbia Provincial Museum.

Dumond, Don E.
1987   A Reexamination of Eskimo-Aleut Prehistory. *American Anthropologist* 89(1): 32–56.

Dumont, Louis
1970   *Homo Hierarchicus: The Caste System and Its Implications,* translated by Mark Sainsbury. Chicago: University of Chicago Press.

Dunn, John A.
1984   International Matri-moieties: The North Maritime Province of the North Pacific Coast. In *The Tsimshian. Images of the Past: Views for the Present,* edited by M. Seguin, 99–109. Vancouver: University of British Columbia Press.

Durlach, Theresa M.
1928   The Relationship System of the Tlingit, Haida, and Tsimshian. *American Ethnological Society Publications* 11:1–177.

Dyen, Isidore, and David F. Aberle
1974   *Lexical Reconstruction: The Case of the Proto-Athapaskan Kinship System.* New York: Cambridge University Press.

Eggan, Fred
1975   *Essays in Social Anthropology and Ethnology.* Chicago: Department of Anthropology, The University of Chicago.

Elmendorf, William W.
1960   *The Structure of Twana Culture.* Washington State University Research Studies 28.

Emmons, George T.
1907   The Chilkat Blanket. *Memoirs of the American Museum of Natural History* 3:329–401.

1908   Copper Neck-rings of Southern Alaska. *American Anthropologist* 10:644–659.

1916   The Whale House of the Chilkat. *Anthropological Papers of the American Museum of Natural History* 19:1–33.

1920–45 Unpublished Manuscript on Tlingit Ethnography. Archives, American Museum of Natural History, New York.

n.d.   Notes on the Tlingit. Provincial Archives, Victoria, British Columbia.

Ferguson, Brian R.
1983   Warfare and Redistributive Exchange on the Northwest Coast." In *The Development of Political Organization in Native North America,* edited by E. Tooker. *1979 Proceedings of The American Ethnological Society,* 133–147. Washington, D.C.: American Ethnological Society.

1984   A Reexamination of the Causes of Northwest Coast Warfare. In *Warfare, Culture, and Environment,* edited by B. R. Ferguson, 267–328. Orlando, Florida: Academic Press.

Fladmark, Knut R.
1975   *A Paleoecological Model of Northwest Coast Prehistory.* Mercury Series, Archaeological Survey of Canada Paper 43. Ottawa, Canada: National Museum of Man.

Forman, Shepard
1980   Descent, Alliance, and Exchange Ideology among the Makassae of East Timor. In *The Flow of Life: Essays on Eastern Indonesia,*

edited by J. J. Fox, 152–177. Cambridge, Massachusetts: Harvard University Press.

Fried, Morton H.
1967   *The Evolution of Political Society: An Essay in Political Anthropology.* New York: Random House.

Garfield, Viola E.
1939   Tsimshian Clan and Society. *University of Washington Publications in Anthropology* 7(3):167–340.

Garfield, Viola E., and Linn A. Forrest
1961   *The Wolf and the Raven: Totem Poles of Southeastern Alaska.* Seattle: University of Washington Press.

Geertz, Hildred
1959   The Vocabulary of Emotion: A Study of Javanese Socialization Processes. *Psychiatry* 22:225–237.

Gerber, Eleanor R.
1985   Rage and Obligation: Samoan Emotions in Conflict. In *Person, Self, and Experience: Exploring Pacific Ethnopsychologies,* edited by G. M. White and J. Kirkpatrick, 121–167. Berkeley: University of California Press.

Gewertz, Deborah
1984   Of Symbolic Anchors and Sago Soup: The Rhetoric of Exchange among the Chambri of Papua New Guinea. In *Dangerous Words: Language and Politics in the Pacific,* edited by D. L. Brenneis and F. R. Myers, 192–213. New York: New York University Press.

Giddens, Anthony
1971   *Capitalism and Modern Social Theory.* Cambridge: Cambridge University Press.

Glazer, Myron
1972   *The Research Adventure: Promise and Problem of Fieldwork.* New York: Random House.

Goldman, Irving
1941   The Alkatcho Carrier: Historical Background of Crest Prerogatives. *American Anthropologist* 43:396–418.

1970   *Ancient Polynesian Society.* Chicago: University of Chicago Press.

1975   *The Mouth of Heaven: An Introduction to Kwakiutl Religious Thought.* New York: John Wiley & Sons.

Golovin, Pavel N.
1979   *The End of Russian America. Captain P. N. Golovin's Last Report, 1862,* translated, introduced, and annotated by B. Dmytryshyn

and E. A. P. Crownhart-Vaughan. Portland: Oregon Historical Society.

1983   *Civil and Savage Encounters: The Worldly Travel Letters of an Imperial Russian Navy Officer, 1860–1861,* translated and annotated by B. Dmytryshyn and E. A. P. Crownhart-Vaughan. Portland: Western Imprints, The Press of the Oregon Historical Society.

Goody, Jack
1962   *Death, Property and the Ancestors.* London: Tavistock Publications.

Gould, R. R.
1895   Cremating an Alaskan Chief. *Home Mission Monthly* 9 (5): 108–109.

Guedon, Marie-Francoise
1974   *People of Tetlin, Why Are You Singing?* Mercury Series Paper 9. Ottawa, Canada: National Museum of Man, Ethnology Division.

Gunther, Erna
1972   *Indian Life on the Northwest Coast of North America as Seen by the Early Explorers and Fur Traders During the Last Decades of the Eighteenth Century.* Chicago: University of Chicago Press.

Haeberlin, Hermann, and Erna Gunther
1930   The Indians of Puget Sound. *University of Washington Publications in Anthropology* 4(1):1–84.

Hallowell, A. Irving
1955   *Culture and Experience.* Philadelphia: University of Pennsylvania Press.

Halpin, Marjorie Myers
1973   The Tsimshian Crest System: A Study Based on Museum Specimens and the Marius Barbeau and William Beynon Field Notes. Ph.D. diss., Anthropology. University of British Columbia, Vancouver.

1984a   The Structure of Tsimshian Totemism. In *The Tsimshian and Their Neighbors on the North Pacific Coast,* edited by J. Miller and C. M. Eastman, 16–35. Seattle: University of Washington Press.

1984b   Feast Names at Hartley Bay. In *The Tsimshian. Images of the Past: Views for the Present,* edited by M. Sequin, 57–64. Vancouver: University of British Columbia Press.

Hardisty, William L.
1872   The Loucheaux Indians. In the *Annual Report of the Smithsonian Institution for the Year 1866,* 311–320. Washington: Smithsonian Institution.

Harrison, Charles
   1925   *Ancient Warriors of the North Pacific.* London: H. F. & G. Witherby.

Helm, June
   1965   Bilaterality in the Socio-territorial Organization of the Arctic
           Drainage Dene. *Ethnology* 4(4): 361–385.

Helm, June et al.
   1975   The Contact History of the Subarctic Athapascans: An Overview.
           In Vol. 1 of *Proceedings: Northern Athapascan Conference 1971*, Mer-
           cury Series, Ethnology Service Paper 27, edited by A. M. Clark,
           302–349. Ottawa, Canada: National Museum of Man.

Hertz, Robert
   1960   *Death and the Right Hand*, translated by C. and R. Needham. New
           York: Free Press.

Hinckley, Ted C.
   1982   *Alaskan John G. Brady, Missionary, Businessman, Judge, and Gover-
           nor, 1878–1918.* Columbus: Ohio State University Press.

Holm, Bill
   1983   *Box of Daylight: Northwest Coast Indian Art.* Seattle: Seattle Art
           Museum and University of Washington Press.

Holmberg, Heinrich J.
   1985   *Holmberg's Ethnographic Sketches*, translated by F. Jaensch. The
           Rasmuson Library Historical Translation Series, Vol. I. Fair-
           banks: University of Alaska Press.

Hope, Andrew, III, ed.
   1982   *Raven's Bones.* Sitka, Alaska: Sitka Community Association.

Hosley, Edward H.
   1981   Environment and Culture in the Alaska Plateau. In *Handbook of
           North American Indians.* Vol. 6, *Subarctic*, edited by William C.
           Sturtevant, 533—545. Washington: Smithsonian Institution.

Hultkrantz, Ake
   1953   *Concepts of the Soul among North American Indians.* Monograph
           Series, Publication No. 1. Stockholm: The Ethnographical
           Museum of Sweden

   1979   *The Religions of the American Indians.* Berkeley: University of
           California Press.

Humphreys, S. C.
   1981   Death and Time. In *Mortality and Immortality: The Anthropology
           and Archaeology of Death*, edited by S. C. Humphreys and H.
           King, 261–283. London: Academic Press.

Humphreys, S. C., and Helen King, eds.
1981   *Mortality and Immortality: The Anthropology and Archaeology of Death.* London: Academic Press.

Huntington, Richard, and Peter Metcalf
1979   *Celebrations of Death: The Anthropology of Mortuary Ritual.* Cambridge: Cambridge University Press.

Irwin, Terry T.
1977   The Northwest Coast Potlatch Since Boas, 1897–1972. *Anthropology* 1(1):65–77.

Ives, John W.
n.d.   The Tsimshian Are Carrier. *Ethnicity and Culture.* Proceedings of the 18th Annual Chacmool Conference, edited by R. Auger et al. Calgary: Archaeological Association, University of Calgary, forthcoming.

1985   Northern Athapascan Social and Economic Variability. Ph.D. diss., Anthropology, University of Michigan, Ann Arbor, Michigan.

Jacobs, Mark, Jr., and Mark Jacobs, Sr.
1982   Southeast Alaska Native Foods. In *Raven's Bones,* edited by A. Hope, III, 112–130. Sitka, Alaska: Sitka Community Association.

Jenness, Diamond
1943   *The Carrier Indians of the Bulkley River: Their Social and Religious Life.* Anthropological Papers 25, Bureau of American Ethnology Bulletin 133.

Jetté, Jules
1911   On the Superstitions of the Ten'a Indians (Middle Part of the Yukon Valley, Alaska). *Anthropos* 8:95–108, 241–259, 602–615, 699–723.

Johnson, Andrew P.
n.d.   *Kaax'achgook.* College, Alaska: Tlingit Readers, Inc. and Alaska Native Language Center.

Jonaitis, Aldona
1978   Land Otters and Shamans: Some Interpretations of Tlingit Charms. *American Indian Art Magazine* 4(1):62–66.

1986   *Art of the Northern Tlingit.* Seattle: University of Washington Press.

Jones, Livingston F.
1914   *A Study of the Thlingets of Alaska.* New York: Fleming H. Revell Co.

Kamenskii, Anatolii
  1985   *Tlingit Indians of Alaska,* translated, introduced, and supple-
          mented by S. Kan. Vol. 2, The Rasmuson Library Historical
          Translation Series. Fairbanks: University of Alaska Press.

Kan, Sergei
  1978   The Winter House in the Tlingit Universe. Master's thesis,
          Anthropology, University of Chicago, Chicago.

  1979–87 Ethnographic Notes from 15 Months of Fieldwork among the
          Tlingit Indians of Southeastern Alaska. Unpublished manuscript
          in author's possession.

  1983   Words That Heal the Soul: Analysis of the Tlingit Potlatch
          Oratory. *Arctic Anthropology* 20(2):47–59.

  1985   Russian Orthodox Brotherhoods among the Tlingit: Missionary
          Goals and Native Response. *Ethnohistory* 32(3):196–223.

  1986   The Nineteenth-Century Tlingit Potlatch: A New Perspective.
          American Ethnologist 13(2):191–212.

  1987   Memory Eternal: Russian Orthodoxy and the Tlingit Mortuary
          Complex. *Arctic Anthropology* 24(1):32–55.

  1989   Cohorts, Generations, and Their Culture: The Tlingit Potlatch in
          the 1980s. *Anthropos* 84 (4–6) (forthcoming).

  n.d.   Potlatch Songs Outside the Potlatch. Unpublished manuscript in
          author's possession.

Kapferer, Bruce
  1979a   Emotion and Feeling in Sinhalese Healing Rites. *Social Analysis*
          1:153–176.

  1979b   Mind, Self and Other in Demonic Illness: The Negation and
          Reconstruction of Self. *American Ethnologist* 6: 110–133.

  1983   *A Celebration of Demons: Exorcism and the Aesthetics of Healing in
          Sri Lanka.* Bloomington, Indiana: Indiana University Press.

  1986   Performance and the Structuring of Meaning and Experience. In
          The Anthropology of Experience, edited by V. W. Turner, and E. M.
          Bruner, 188–203. Urbana: University of Illinois Press.

Kaplan, Bert, and Dale Johnson
  1964   The Social Meaning of Navaho Psychopathology. In *Magic, Faith,
          and Healing,* edited by A. Kiev, 203–229. New York: The Free
          Press.

Karp, Ivan
  1977   Reply to "The Distancing of Emotion in Ritual" by Thomas J.
          Scheff. *Current Anthropology* 18(3):496.

Keesing, Roger M.
1982   *Kwaio Religion: The Living and the Dead in a Solomon Island Society.*
New York: Columbia University Press.

Keithahn, Edward L.
1954   Human Hair as a Decorative Feature in Tlingit Ceremonial
Paraphernalia. *Anthropological Papers of the University of Alaska*
3(1):17–20.

1955   The Cremation of Chief Kowee. *The Alaska Sportsman* 3:18–19.

1963   Burial Customs of the Tlingits. *The Alaska Sportsman* 29(4):18–19,
33–36.

1964   Origin of the "Chief's Copper" or "Tinneh." *Anthropological
Papers of the University of Alaska* 12(2): 59–78.

Khlebnikov, Kyrill [Kiril] T.
1976   *Colonial Russian America: Kyrill T. Khlebnikov's Reports, 1817–1832,*
translated, introduced, and annotated by B. Dmytryshyn and
E. A. P. Crownhart-Vaughan. Portland: Oregon Historical Society.

1985   *Russkaia Amerika v "Zapiskakh" Kirila Khlebnikova. Novo-
Arkhangel'sk* [Russian America in Kiril Khlebnikov's "Notes."
New-Archangel.] Moscow: Nauka.

Klein, Laura F.
1987   Demystifying the Opposition: The Hudson's Bay Company and
the Tlingits in Alaska. *Arctic Anthropology* 24(1):101–114.

Knapp, Frances, and Rheta Louise Childe
1896   *The Thlinkets of Southeastern Alaska.* Chicago: Stone & Kimball.

Knauft, Bruce M.
1985   *Good Company and Violence: Sorcery and Social Action in a Lowland
New Guinea Society.* Berkeley: University of California Press.

Kobrinsky, Vernon
1975   Dynamics of the Fort Rupert Class Struggle: Fighting with
Property Vertically Revisited. In *Papers in Honor of Harry Haw-
thorn.* Bellingham, Washington: Western Washington State College Press.

Kottak, Conrad P.
1980   *The Past in the Present: History, Ecology and Cultural Variation in
Highland Madagascar.* Ann Arbor, Michigan: University of
Michigan Press.

Krause, Aurel
1956   *The Tlingit Indians,* translated by Erna Gunther. Seattle: University of Washington Press.

Krauss, Michael E., and Victor K. Golla
    1981   Northern Athapascan Languages. In *Handbook of North American Indians*, Vol. 6, *Subarctic*, edited by W. C. Sturtevant, 67–85. Washington: Smithsonian Institution.

Kroeber, Alfred L.
    1923   American Culture and the Northwest Coast. *American Anthropologist* 25: 1–20.

Kroul, Mary V.
    1974   Definitional Domains of the Koyukon Athapascan Potlatch. *Arctic Anthropology* 11(suppl.): 39–47.

de Laguna, Frederica
    1952   Some Dynamic Forces in Tlingit Society. *Southwestern Journal of Anthropology* 8(1):1–12.

    1954   Tlingit Ideas about the Individual. *Southwestern Journal of Anthropology* 10(2):172–191.

    1960   *The Story of a Tlingit Community: A Problem in the Relationship between Archaeological, Ethnological and Historical Methods.* Bureau of American Ethnology Bulletin 172. Washington: U.S. Government Printing Office.

    1965   Childhood among the Yakutat Tlingit. In *Context and Meaning in Cultural Anthropology*, edited by M. E. Spiro, 3–23. New York: Free Press.

    1972   *Under Mount Saint Elias: The History and Culture of the Yakutat Tlingit.* Smithsonian Contributions to Anthropology 7. 3 Pts. Washington: Smithsonian Institution Press.

    1975   Matrilineal Kin Groups in Northwestern North America. In Vol. 1, *Proceedings: Northern Athapascan Conference, 1971.* Mercury Series, Ethnology Service Paper 27, edited by A. M. Clark, 17–145. Ottawa, Canada: National Museum of Man.

    1983   Aboriginal Tlingit Sociopolitical Organization. In *The Development of Political Organization in Native North America* 1979 Proceedings of The American Ethnological Society, edited by E. Tooker, 71–85. Washington, D.C.: American Ethnological Society.

de Laguna, Frederica, and Catherine McClellan
    1981   Ahtna. In *Handbook of North American Indians*, Vol. 6, *Subarctic*, edited by W. C. Sturtevant, 641–663. Washington: Smithsonian Institution.

Langsdorff, Georg H. von
    1814   *Voyages and Travels in Various Parts of the World, during the Years 1803, 1804, 1805, 1806, and 1807.* Part 2. London: n. p.

Lantis, Margaret
    1947   *Alaskan Eskimo Ceremonialism.* Monographs of the American Eth-
            nological Society 11. Seattle: University of Washington Press.

Leach, Edmund R.
    1958   Magical Hair. *Journal of the Royal Anthropological Institute,* 88:147–
            164.

Levine, Robert D.
    1979   Haida and Na-Dene: A New Look at the Evidence. *International
            Journal of American Linguistics* 45(2):157–170.

Lévi-Strauss, Claude
    1943   Guerre et commerce chez les Indiens de l'Amerique du Sud.
            Renaissance 1:122–139.

    1976   *Structural Anthropology.* 2 vols. New York: Basic Books, Inc.

    1982   *The Way of the Masks.* Seattle: University of Washington Press.

    1986   Comment on "The Nineteenth-century Tlingit Potlatch: A New
            Perspective" by S. Kan. *American Ethnologist* 13:804.

Levy, Robert I.
    1984   Emotion, Knowing, and Culture. In *Culture Theory: Essays on
            Mind, Self, and Emotion,* edited by R. A. Shweder, and R. A. Le-
            Vine,, 214–237. Cambridge: Cambridge University Press.

Lifton, Robert Jay
    1983   *The Broken Connection: on Death and the Continuity of Life.* New
            York: Basic Books.

Lisianskii, Urey [Iurii] F.
    1814   *A Voyage Around the World.* London: John Booth Publisher.

    1947   *Puteshestvie vokrug sveta na korable* Neva *v 1803–1806 godakh* [A
            Voyage Around the World on Board the Ship *Neva* in 1803–
            1806]. Moscow: Gosudarstvennoe Izdatel'stvo Geograficheskoi
            Literatury [State Publishing House for Geographical Literature].

Litke, Fedor P.
    1948   *Puteshestvie vokrug Sveta na Voennom Shliupe* Seniavin, *1826–1829.*
            [A Voyage Around the World on Board the Military Ship
            Seniavin, 1826–1829]. Moscow: Gosudarstvennoe Izdatel'stvo
            Geograficheskoi Literatury [State Publishing House for
            Geographical Literature].

Littlefield, Christine, and Gregory Littlefield
    1980   Dedication of a Tlingit Crest. *Neek,* 1(2):1–2.

Loyens, William J.
    1964   The Koyukon Feast of the Dead. *Arctic Anthropology* 2(2): 133–148.

Lutz, Catherine
    1985   Ethnopsychology Compared to What? Explaining Behavior and Consciousness among the Ifaluk. In *Person, Self, and Experience: Exploring Pacific Ethnopsychologies,* edited by G. M. White and J. Kirkpatrick, 35–79. Berkeley: University of California Press.

Lutz, Catherine, and Geoffrey M. White
    1986   The Anthropology of Emotions. *Annual Review of Anthropology* 15:405–436.

McClellan, Catherine
    1954   The Interrelation of Social Structure with Northern Tlingit Ceremonialism. *Southwestern Journal of Anthropology* 10:75–96.

    1961   Avoidance between Siblings of the Same Sex in Northwestern North America. *Southwestern Journal of Anthropology* 17:103–123.

    1963   Wealth Woman and Frogs among the Tagish Indians. *Anthropos* 58(1–2): 121–128.

    1964   Culture Contacts in the Early Historic Period in Northwestern North America. *Arctic Anthropology* 2(2):3–15.

    1975   *My Old People Say: An Ethnographic Survey of Southern Yukon Territory.* 2 vols. Ottawa, Canada: National Museum of Man, Publications in Ethnology.

McClellan, Catherine M., and Glenda Denniston
    1981   Environment and Culture in the Cordillera. In *Handbook of North American Indians,* vol. 6, *Subarctic,* edited by W. C. Sturtevant, 372–386. Washington: Smithsonian Institution.

MacDonald, George F.
    1981   Cosmic Equations in Northwest Coast Indian Art. In *The World Is as Sharp as a Knife: An Anthology in Honor of Wilson Duff,* edited by D. N. Abbott, 225–238. Victoria: The British Columbia Provincial Museum.

    1983   *Haida Monumental Art: Villages of the Queen Charlotte Islands.* Vancouver: University of British Columbia Press.

    1984   Painted Houses and Woven Blankets: Symbols of Wealth in Tsimshian Art and Myth. In *The Tsimshian and Their Neighbors on the North Pacific Coast,* edited by J. Miller and C. M. Eastman, 109–136. Seattle: University of Washington Press.

McFadyen, Annette Clark
    1970   Koyukon Athabascan Ceremonialism. In *Western Canadian Journal of Anthropology* 2(1), 80-88. A special issue on Athapaskan Studies edited by Regna Darnell.

McIlwraith, Thomas F.
    1948   *The Bella Coola Indians*. 2 vols. Toronto: University of Toronto Press.

McKennan, Robert A.
    1959   *The Upper Tanana Indians*. Yale University Publications in Anthropology 55. New Haven, Connecticut.

    1965   *The Chandalar Kutchin*. Arctic Institute of North America Technical Paper 17. Montreal.

    1969   Athapascan Groupings and Social Organization in Central Alaska. In *Anthropological Series 84, National Museum of Canada Bulletin 228*, 93–115. Ottawa.

MacLeod, William C.
    1925   Certain Mortuary Aspects of Northwest Coast Culture. *American Anthropologist* 27:122–148.

Markov, A.
    1849   *Russkie na vostochnom okeane* [Russians on the Pacific]. Moscow: Moscow University.

Mauss, Marcel
    1938   Une Categorie de l'esprit humain: la notion de personne, celle de "moi." *Journal of the Royal Anthropological Institute* 68:263–362.

    1967   *The Gift*, translated by I. Cunnison. New York: Norton and Co.

    1973   Techniques of the Body, translated by B. Brewster. *Economy and Society* 2(1):70–88.

Meletinskii, Eleazar M.
    1973   Typological Analysis of the Palaeo-Asiatic Raven Myth. *Acta Ethnographica*, [Budapest] 22(1–2):107–155.

    1979   *Paleoaziatskii mifologicheskii epos: tsikl vorona* [Palaeo-Asiatic Mythology: Raven Cycle]. Moscow: Nauka.

Metcalf, Peter
    1982   *A Borneo Journey into Death: Berawan Eschatology from Its Rituals*. Philadelphia: University of Pennsylvania Press.

Miller, Polly and Leon Gordon Miller
    1967   *Lost Heritage of Alaska*. New York: Bonanza Books.

Murdock, George P.
    1936   *Rank and Potlatch Among the Haida.* Yale University Publications in Anthropology 13. New Haven, Connecticut.

    1955   North American Social Organization. *Davidson Journal of Anthropology* 1(2): 85–95.

Myers, Fred
    1979   Emotions and the Self: A Theory of Personhood and Political Order among Pintupi Aborigines. *Ethos* 7:343–370.

    1986   *Pintupi Country, Pintupi Self: Sentiment, Place, and Politics among Western Desert Aborigines.* Washington: Smithsonian Institution Press.

Needham, Rodney, ed.
    1973   *Right and Left: Essays on Dual Symbolic Classification.* Chicago: University of Chicago Press.

Newsletter of the Alaska Anthropological Association
    1987   *Newsletter of the Alaska Anthropological Association* 12(1):7.

Niblack, Albert P.
    1890   The Coast Indians of Southern Alaska and Northern British Columbia. In *Annual Report of the United States National Museum for 1887–1888,* 225–386. Washington: U.S. Government Printing Office.

Oberg, Kalervo
    1934   Crime and Punishment in Tlingit Society. *American Anthropologist* 36:145–156.

    1937   The Social Economy of the Tlingit Indians. Ph.D. diss., Anthropology. University of Chicago, Chicago.

    1973   *The Social Economy of the Tlingit Indians.* Seattle: University of Washington Press.

Obeyesekere, Gananath
    1981   *Medusa's Hair: An Essay on Personal Symbols and Religious Experience.* Chicago: University of Chicago Press.

Olson, Ronald L.
    1933–54 Unpublished Fieldnotes on the Tlingit of Southeastern Alaska. Archives, Bancroft Library, University of California, Berkeley.

    1936   The Quinault Indians. *University of Washington Publications in Anthropology,* 6(1):1–194.

    1956   Channeling of Character in Tlingit Society. In *Personal Character and Cultural Milieu,* 3rd rev. ed., edited by D. G. Haring, 675–687. Syracuse: Syracuse University Press.

1967   *Social Structure and Social Life of the Tlingit Indians in Alaska.* University of California Anthropological Records 26. Berkeley, California.

Ortner, Sherry B.
1978   *Sherpas Through Their Rituals.* London: Cambridge University Press.

1981   Gender and Sexuality in Hierarchical Societies: The Case of Polynesia and Some Comparative Implications. In *Sexual Meanings: The Cultural Construction of Gender and Sexuality,* edited by S. B. Ortner, and H. Whitehead, 359–409. Cambridge: Cambridge University Press.

1984   Theory in Anthropology Since the Sixties. *Comparative Studies in Society and History* 26:126–166.

Ortner, Sherry B., and Harriet Whitehead
1981   Introduction: Accounting for Sexual Meanings. In *Sexual Meanings: The Cultural Construction of Gender and Sexuality,* edited by S.B. Ortner and H. Whitehead, 1–27. Cambridge: Cambridge University Press.

Osgood, Cornelius
1936   *Contributions to the Ethnography of the Kutchin.* Yale University Publications in Anthropology 14. New Haven, Connecticut.

1937   *The Ethnography of the Tanaina.* Yale University Publications in Anthropology 16. New Haven, Connecticut.

Osgood, Cornelius
1958   *Ingalik Social Culture.* Yale University Publications in Anthropology 53. New Haven, Connecticut.

1959   *Ingalik Mental Culture.* Yale University Publications in Anthropology 56. New Haven, Connecticut.

Paine, Robert, ed.
1981   *Politically Speaking: Cross-Cultural Studies in Rhetoric.* Philadelphia: Institute for the Study of Human Issues.

Palgi, Phylis, and Henry Abramovitch
1984   Death: A Cross-Cultural Perspective. *Annual Review of Anthropology* 13:385–417.

Peck, Cyrus E., Sr.
1975   *The Tides People.* Juneau, Alaska: Indian Studies Program.

Peratrovich, Robert J., Jr.
1959   Social and Economic Structure of the Henya Indians. M.A. thesis, Anthropology. University of Alaska, Fairbanks, Alaska.

Piddocke, Stuart
  1965   The Potlatch System of the Southern Kwakiutl: A New Perspective. *Southwestern Journal of Anthropology* 21:244–264.

Poole, Fitz J. P.
  1982   The Ritual Forging of Identity: Aspects of Person and Self in Bimin-Kuskusmin Male Initiation. In *Rituals of Manhood: Male Initiation in Papua New Guinea,* edited by G. H. Herdt, 99–154. Berkeley: University of California Press.

  1985   Coming into Social Being: Cultural Images of Infants in Bimin-Kuskusmin Folk Psychology. In *Person, Self, and Experience: Exploring Pacific Ethnopsychologies,* edited by G. M. White and J. Kirkpatrick, 183–242. Berkeley: University of California Press.

Rappaport, Roy A.
  1979   *Ecology, Meaning, and Religion.* Berkeley, California: North Atlantic Books.

Ray, Verne F.
  1955   Review of *Franz Boas: The Science of Man in the Making,* by Melville J. Herskovits. *American Anthropologist* 57:139–140.

Reid, Susan
  1977   Review of *The Mouth of Heaven: An Introduction to Kwakiutl Religious Thought,* by Irving Goldman. *Canadian Review of Sociology and Anthropology* 14:448.

Richards, Audrey I.
  1956   *Chisungu.* London: Faber and Faber.

Ringel, Gail
  1979   The Kwakiutl Potlatch: History, Economics, and Symbols. *Ethnohistory* 26(4):347–362.

Rosaldo, Michelle Z.
  1984   Toward an Anthropology of Self and Feeling. In *Culture Theory: Essays on Mind, Self, and Emotion,* edited by R. A. Shweder, and R. A. LeVine, 137–157. Cambridge: Cambridge University Press.

Rosaldo, Renato I.
  1984   Grief and a Headhunter's Rage: on the Cultural Force of Emotions. In *Text, Play, and Story: The Construction and Reconstruction of Self and Society,* 1983 Proceedings of the American Ethnological Society, edited by S. Plattner, and E. M. Bruner, 178–195. Washington, D.C.: The American Ethnological Society.

Rosenblatt, Paul C.
  1976   *Grief and Mourning in Cross-cultural Perspective.* Human Relations Area Files Press.

Rosman, Abraham, and Paula G. Rubel
   1971   *Feasting with Mine Enemy: Rank and Exchange among Northwest
          Coast Societies.* New York: Columbia University Press.

   1978   *Your Own Pigs You May Not Eat: A Comparative Study of New
          Guinea Societies.* Chicago: The University of Chicago Press.

   1981   Structure, Transformation and Evolution: A Comparison of the
          Northwest Coast-Athapascan and Island Melanesian Cases. In
          *The Future of Structuralism. Papers of the IUAES-Intercongress,
          1981,* 229–251. Amsterdam: Edition-Herodot.

   1983   The Evolution of Exchange Structures and Ranking: Some
          Northwest Coast and Athapascan Examples. *Journal of
          Anthropological Research* 39(1):1–25.

   1986   The Evolution of Central Northwest Coast Societies. *Journal of
          Anthropological Research* 42(4):567–572.

Ruyle, Eugene E.
   1973   Slavery, Surplus, and Stratification on the Northwest Coast: the
          Ethnoenergetics of an Incipient Stratification System. *Current
          Anthropology* 14(5):603–631.

Sackett, John
   1987   Stickdance: Koyukon Athapascan Feast for the Dead. *Alaska Na-
          tive Magazine* 5(5): 8–12.

Sahlins, Marshall
   1963   Poor Man, Rich Man, Big Man, Chief: Political Types in
          Melanesia and Polynesia. *Comparative Studies in Society and His-
          tory* 5:285–303.

   1968   *Tribesmen.* Englewood Cliffs, New Jersey: Prentice-Hall, Inc.

Samuel, Cheryl
   1982   *The Chilkat Dancing Blanket.* Seattle: Pacific Search Press.

Sapir, David J., and Christopher J. Crocker, eds.
   1977   *The Social Use of Metaphor: Essays on the Anthropology of Rhetoric.*
          Philadelphia: University of Pennsylvania Press.

Scheff, Thomas J.
   1977   The Distancing of Emotion in Ritual. *Current Anthropology*
          18(3):483–505.

Schieffelin, Edward L.
   1976   *The Sorrow of the Lonely and the Burning of the Dancers.* New York:
          St. Martin's Press.

Schwatka, Frederick
   1885   *Report of a Military Reconnaissance Made in Alaska in 1883.*
          Washington: U.S. Government Printing Office.

Seguin, Margaret
    1984   Lest There Be No Salmon: Symbols in Traditional Tsimshian Pot-latch. In *The Tsimshian. Images of the Past: Views for the Present*, edited by M. Seguin, 99–109. Vancouver: University of British Columbia Press.

    1985   *Interpretive Contexts for Traditional and Current Tsimshian Feasts.* Mercury Series, Canadian Ethnology Service Paper 98. Ottawa, Canada. National Museum of Man.

Sheets, A. M.
    1909   A Historical Sketch. *The Thlinget* 1(9):1–3.

Shotridge, Louis
    n.d.   Unpublished Notes on Tlingit Ethnography (1915–1926). Archives, Alaska State Historical Library, Juneau, Alaska.

    1917   My Northland Revisited. *The Museum Journal* 8:105–115.

    1920   Ghost of Courageous Adventurer. *The Museum Journal* 11:11–26.

    1922   Land Otter-Man. *The Museum Journal* 13:55–59.

    1928   The Emblems of the Tlingit Culture. *The Museum Journal* 19:350–377.

    1929   The Bride of Tongass: A Study of the Tlingit Marriage Ceremony. *The Museum Journal* 20:131–156.

Shotridge, Louis, and Florence Shotridge
    1913   Chilkat Houses. *The Museum Journal* 4:81–98.

Slobodin, Richard
    1962   *Band Organization of the Peel River Kutchin.* Anthropological Series 55, National Museum of Canada Bulletin 179. Ottawa, Canada.

    1970   Kutchin Concepts of Reincarnation. *Western Canadian Journal of Anthropology* 2(1):69–79. A special issue on Athabascan Studies edited by Regna Darnell.

Smith, Marian W.
    1940   *The Puyallup-Nisqually.* Columbia University Contributions to Anthropology 43. New York.

Snyder, Sally
    1964   Skagit Society and Its Existential Basis: An Ethnofolkloristic Reconstruction. Ph.D. diss., Anthropology, University of Washington, Seattle.

    1975   Quest for the Sacred in Northern Puget Sound: An Interpretation of Potlatch. *Ethnology* 14:149–161.

Sonne, Birgitte
    1978   Ritual Bonds between the Living and the Dead in Yukon Eskimo Society. *Temenos* 14:127–183.

Stanley, Samuel L.
    1958   Historical Changes in Tlingit Social Structure. Ph.D. diss., Anthropology, University of Chicago, Chicago.

Stearns, Mary Lee
    1984   Succession to Chiefship in Haida Society. In *The Tsimshian and Their Neighbors on the North Pacific Coast,* edited by J. Miller and C. M. Eastman, 190–219. Seattle: University of Washington Press.

Stern, Bernhard J.
    1934   *The Lumni Indians of Northwestern Washington.* Columbia University Contributions to Anthropology 17. New York.

Stevenson, Ian
    1966   *Twenty Cases Suggestive of Reincarnation,* Vol. 26 of *Proceedings of the American Society for Psychical Research.* New York.

Stone, Peter
    1971   Reciprocity: The Gift of a Trickster. Unpublished Manuscript.

Story, Gillian L., and Constance M. Naish
    1963   *English-Tlingit Dictionary. Nouns.* Fairbanks, Alaska: Summer Institute of Linguistics.

    1973   *Tlingit Verb Dictionary.* College, Alaska: Alaska Native Language Center.

Stromberg, Peter G.
    1986   *Symbols of Community: The Cultural System of a Swedish Church.* Tucson, Arizona: University of Arizona Press.

Sturtevant, William C., ed.,
    1981   *Handbook of North American Indians,* Vol. 6, *Subarctic.* Washington: Smithsonian Institution.

Suttles, Wayne P.
    1960   Variation in Habitat and Culture on the Northwest Coast. In *Akten des 34 Internationalen Amerkanistenkongresses, Wein, 1960,* 522–537. Vienna: International Congress of Americanists.

    1967   Private Knowledge, Morality, and Social Class among the Coast Salish. In *Indians of the North Pacific Coast,* edited by T. McFeat, 166–179. Seattle: University of Washington Press.

    1979   *The Mouth of Heaven* and the Kwakiutl Tongue: A Comment on Walens and Goldman. *American Anthropologist* 81:96–98.

Swanton, John R.
 1905   *Haida Texts and Myths. Skidegate Dialect.* Bureau of American Ethnology Bulletin 29. Washington: U.S. Government Printing Office.

 1908   Social Conditions, Beliefs, and Linguistic Relationship of the Tlingit Indians. In *Twenty-Sixth Annual Report of the Bureau of American Ethnology for the Years 1904–1905,* 391–512. Washington: U.S. Government Printing Office.

 1909   *Tlingit Myths and Texts.* Bureau of American Ethnology Bulletin 39. Washington: U.S. Government Printing Office.

 1912   Haida Songs. In *Publications of the American Ethnological Society,* Vol. 3:1–63. Leyden: Brill.

Tanner, Adrian
 1979   *Bringing Home Animals: Religious Ideology and Mode of Production of the Mistassini Cree Hunters.* New York: St. Martin's Press.

Teichmann, Emil
 1963   *A Journey to Alaska in the Year 1868: Being a Diary of the Late Emil Teichmann.* New York: Argosy-Antiquarian Ltd.

Teit, James A.
 1956   Field Notes on the Tahltan and Kaska Indians, 1912–1915. *Anthropologica* 40–171.

Tikhmenev, Petr A.
 1978   *A History of the Russian-American Company,* translated and edited by R. A. Pierce and A. S. Donnelly. Seattle: University of Washington Press.

To the Totem Shore
 1986   *To the Totem Shore: The Spanish Presence on the Northwest Coast.* Madrid: Ediciones El Viso.

Tobey, Margaret L.
 1981   Carrier. In *Handbook of North American Indians,* Vol. 6, *Subarctic,* edited by W. C. Sturtevant, 413–432. Washington: Smithsonian Institution.

Tollefson, Kenneth D.
 1976   The Cultural Foundation of Political Revitalization among the Tlingit. Ph.D. diss., Anthropology. University of Washington, Seattle.

Townsend, Joan B.
 1980   Ranked Societies of the Alaskan Pacific Rim. *Occasional Papers of the National Museum of Ethnology. Seri Ethnological Studies* (Osaka, Japan) 4: 123–156.

1981 Tanaina. In *Handbook of North American Indians,* Vol. 6, *Subarctic,* edited by William C. Sturtevant, 623–640. Washington: Smithsonian Institution.

Traube, Elizabeth G.
1980 Affines and the Dead: Mambai Rituals of Alliance. *Bijdragen tot de Taal-, Land- en Volkenkunde* 136:90–115.

Trefzger, Hardy
1963 *My Fifty Years of Hunting, Fishing, Prospecting, Guiding, Trading and Trapping in Alaska.* New York: Exposition Press.

Turner, Terence S.
1980 The Social Skin. In *Not Work Alone,* edited by J. Cherfas and R. Lewin, 112–139. Beverly Hills, California: Sage Publications.

Turner, Victor W.
1967 *The Forest of Symbols.* Ithaca, New York: Cornell University Press

Tyjberg, Tove
1977 Potlatch and Trade among the Tlingit Indians of the American Northwest Coast. *Temenos* 13:189–204.

Van Gennep, Arnold
1960 *Rites of Passage,* translated by M. Vizedom and G. Caffee. Chicago: University of Chicago Press.

VanStone, James W.
1974 *Athapascan Adaptations: Hunters and Fishermen of the Subarctic Forests.* Chicago: Aldine.

Vaughan, Daniel J.
1975 Haida Potlatch and Society: Testing a Structural Analysis. Paper presented at the Northwest Coast Studies Conference, Simon Frazer University, Burnaby, British Columbia.

1984 Tsimshian Potlatch and Society: Examining a Structural Analysis. In *The Tsimshian and Their Neighbors on the North Pacific Coast,* edited by J. Miller and C. M. Eastman, 58–68. Seattle: University of Washington Press.

Vaughan, Thomas, and Bill Holm, eds.
1982 *Soft Gold: The Fur Trade and Cultural Exchange on the Northwest Coast of America.* Portland: Oregon Historical Society.

Vayda, A. P.
1961 A Re-examination of Northwest Coast Economic Systems. *Transactions of the New York Academy of Sciences* 23:618–624.

Velten, H.
1939 Two Southern Tlingit Tales. *International Journal of American Linguistics* 10(2–3):65–74.

Veniaminov, Ivan
    1846   *Zamechaniia o koloshenskom i kadiakskom iazykakh* [Notes on the
            Tlingit and the Kodiak Languages]. St. Petersburg: Imperial
            Academy of Sciences.

    1984   *Notes on the Islands of the Unalashka District*, translated by L. T.
            Black and R. H. Geoghegan. Kingston, Ontario: The Limestone
            Press and The University of Alaska Press.

Walens, Stanley
    1977   Review of *The Mouth of Heaven: An Introduction to Kwakiutl
            Religious Thought*, by Irving Goldman. *American Anthropologist*
            79(1):149.

    1979   In the Teeth of the Evidence: A Rejoinder to Suttles. *American
            Anthropologist*, 81:98–99.

    1981   *Feasting with Cannibals: An Essay on Kwakiutl Cosmology*. Prin-
            ceton, New Jersey: Princeton University Press.

Wallis, W. D.
    1918   Ethical Aspects of Tlingit Culture. *American Journal of Psychology*
            29:66–80.

Waterman, Thomas
    1923   Some Conundrums of Northwest Coast Art. *American
            Anthropologist* 25:435–451.

Weber, Max
    1958   Class, Status, Party. In *From Max Weber*, edited by H. H. Gerth
            and C. W. Mills, 180–195. New York: Oxford University Press.

    1964   *The Theory of Social and Economic Organization*. New York: The
            Free Press.

Weiner, Annette B.
    1976   *Women of Value, Men of Renown: New Perspectives in Trobriand Ex-
            change*. Austin, Texas: University of Texas Press.

    1980   Reproduction: A Replacement for Reciprocity. *American Eth-
            nologist* 7:71–85.

Wells, William
    n.d.   Unpublished Papers. Billman Collection, Stratton Memorial
            Library Archives, Sheldon Jackson College, Sitka, Alaska.

White, Geoffrey M., and John Kirkpatrick, eds.
    1985   *Person, Self, and Experience: Exploring Pacific Ethnopsychologies*.
            Berkeley: University of California Press.

de Widerspach-Thor, Martine
1981   The Equation of Copper. In *The World Is as Sharp as a Knife: An Anthology in Honor of Wilson Duff*, edited by D. A. Abbott, 157–174. Victoria: The British Columbia Provincial Museum.

Wike, Joyce A.
1951   The Effect of the Maritime Fur Trade on Northwest Coast Indian Society. Unpublished Ph.D. diss., Anthropology, Columbia University, New York.

1952   The Role of the Dead in the Northwest Coast Culture. In Vol. 3 of *Indian Tribes of Aboriginal America: Selected Papers of the 29th International Congress of Americanists*, edited by S. Tax, 97–103. Chicago: University of Chicago Press.

Wilbur, Bertrand K.
n.d.   JAM [Just About Me]: Medical Missionary to Sitka, Alaska, 1894–1901. Unpublished Manuscript, Archives, Sitka Historical Society, Sitka, Alaska.

Willard, Eugene S.
1884   *Life in Alaska. Letters of Mrs. Eugene S. Willard.* Philadelphia: Presbyterian Board of Publication.

Wood, C. E. S.
1882   Among the Thlinkets in Alaska. *The Century Magazine* 24(3):323–339.

Worl, Rosita
1984   Spiritual Food for the Dead: Tlingit Potlatch Bowls. *Alaska Native News* (May/June):43.

Periodicals

The Alaska Herald, 1892–1894.
The Alaska Searchlight, 1895–1896.
The Alaska Times, 1869–1871.
The Alaskan, 1885–1907.
The Assembly Herald, 1908–1914.
Home Mission Monthly, 1915–1923.
Neek, 1979–1984.
North Star, 1889–1898.
Russian Orthodox American Messenger, 1896–1939.
Thlinget, 1908–1912.
Verstovian, 1914–1972.

Manuscript Collections

Alaska [Russian Orthodox] Church Collection. Manuscript Division, Library of Congress. Washington, D. C.

Archives of the Diocese of Alaska, Orthodox Church in America. Records of the Sitka and Other Southeastern Alaska Parishes. Sitka, Alaska.

Archives of St. Nicholas Russian Orthodox Church. Records of the Juneau, Hoonah, and Killisnoo/Angoon Parishes. Juneau, Alaska.

Archives, Stratton Memorial Library, Sheldon Jackson College. Andrews Collection and Billman Collection. Sitka, Alaska.

INDEX